P9-CMN-689

COMPARATIVE RELIGIOUS ETHICS

For John H. McCombe

COMPARATIVE RELIGIOUS ETHICS

A NARRATIVE APPROACH

Darrell J. Fasching and Dell deChant
University of South Florida

BLACKWELL
Publishers

Copyright © Darrell J. Fasching and Dell deChant 2001

The right of Darrell J. Fasching and Dell deChant to be identified as authors of
this work has been asserted in accordance with the Copyright, Designs and Patents
Act 1988.

First published 2001

2 4 6 8 10 9 7 5 3 1

Blackwell Publishers Ltd
108 Cowley Road
Oxford OX4 1JF
UK

Blackwell Publishers Inc.
350 Main Street
Malden, Massachusetts 02148
USA

British Library Cataloguing in Publication Data

A CIP catalogue record for this book is available from the British Library.

Library of Congress Cataloging-in-Publication Data

Fasching, Darrell J., 1944–
 Comparative religious ethics : a narrative approach / by Darrell J. Fasching
and Dell deChant.
  p.   cm.
 Includes bibliographical references and index.
 ISBN 0–631–20124–6 (alk. paper) — ISBN 0–631–20125–4 (pbk. : alk. paper)
 1. Religious ethics—Comparative studies.   I. deChant, Dell.   II. Title.
BJ1188 .F35 2001
291.5—dc21

00–009181

Typeset in 10½ on 13 pt Galliard
by Ace Filmsetting Ltd, Frome, Somerset
Printed in Great Britain by T.J. International, Padstow, Cornwall
This book is printed on acid-free paper.

CONTENTS

PREFACE

This book is dedicated to the Reverend Dr. John H. McCombe, retired Dean of Hendricks Chapel at Syracuse University, a world traveler and living example of one who has spent a lifetime practicing "the way of all the earth." I owe him a great debt for both friendship and inspiration. The methodological foundations for a narrative approach to comparative religious ethics were laid in my previous book, *The Ethical Challenge of Auschwitz and Hiroshima: Apocalypse or Utopia* (State University of New York Press, 1993). I owe a special debt to two scholars whose work inspired this approach, Stanley Hauerwas and John Dunne. Without their work on narrative, religion, and ethics I cannot imagine this book ever coming into existence. I also owe a great debt to my former student and now teaching colleague and co-author, Dell deChant. Without his help it would have taken another year to complete this project. Both Dell and I wish to express our appreciation to Margo Smith for her editorial work on the manuscript, and to Jim Anderson and Paul Laughlin for reading earlier versions. Their advice greatly improved this text. It would probably have been even better had we followed more of it.

Darrell J. Fasching
University of South Florida, Tampa

ACKNOWLEDGMENTS

The authors and publisher gratefully acknowledge permission to reproduce copyright material.

The New Jerusalem Bible, excerpt, copyright © 1985 by Darton, Longman & Todd, Ltd., and Doubleday, a division of Random House Inc. Reprinted by permission.

Scripture quotations are from the *New Revised Standard Version Bible*, Catholic Edition, copyright 1989 and 1993 by the Division of Christian Education of the National Council of Churches of Christ in the USA. Use by permission. All rights reserved.

Thich Nhat Hanh, reprinted from *Call Me By My True Names: The Collected Poems of Thich Nhat Hanh*, with permission of Parallax Press, Berkeley, California.

Malcolm X, from *The Autobiography of Malcolm X* by Malcolm X with the assistance of Alex Haley. Copyright © 1964 by Malcolm X and Alex Haley. Copyright © 1965 by Alex Haley and Betty Shabazz. Reprinted by permission of Random House Inc. and Hutchinson and Co., London.

John Henrik Clarke (ed.) *Malcolm X: The Man and His Times* (Collier Books, New York, 1969).

PART I
POST/MODERN STORIES OF WAR AND PEACE

INTRODUCTION: STORYTELLING AND COMPARATIVE RELIGIOUS ETHICS

In April of 1968, Martin Luther King, Jr., often referred to as "the American Gandhi," went to Memphis to help black workers settle a garbage strike. At the time, this Baptist minister from the black church tradition was looking forward to spending the approaching Passover with Rabbi Abraham Joshua Heschel. Heschel, who had marched with him in a civil rights protest at Selma, Alabama three years earlier, had become a close friend and supporter. Unfortunately, King was not able to keep this engagement. Like Gandhi before him, on April 4, 1968, Martin Luther King, Jr., a man of non-violence, was violently assassinated. Another of King's friends, the Buddhist monk and anti-Vietnam war activist, Thich Nhat Hanh, whom King had nominated for the Nobel Peace Prize, received the news of his death while at an interreligious conference in New York City. Only the previous spring, King had officially come out against the Vietnam War, partly at the urging of Thich Nhat Hanh and Abraham Joshua Heschel. This occurred under the auspices of Clergy and Laymen Concerned about Vietnam, founded by Heschel, John Bennett, and Richard Neuhaus. Now, the man who had called for an end to hatred, violence and war was dead. But the spiritual and ethical vision he shared with his friends, across religions and cultures, was not. It is alive and well.

Our task in this book is to understand how a Christian minister, a Jewish rabbi, and a Buddhist monk, all inspired by a Hindu "Mahatma" (Great Soul), Mohandas K. Gandhi, were able to share a common ethical vision of non-violence while maintaining their respective religious identities. We shall do so while taking into account important questions concerning this ethic raised by the Muslim Malcolm X, and the feminist voices of Rosemary Ruether (Christian) and Joanna Macy (Buddhist). Out of the dialogue among them we believe an important spiritual and ethical path for a new millennium is emerging. It is what

John Dunne (1972) calls "the way of all the earth" – a biblical phrase that could also be translated as "the way of all flesh," or "the way of all mortal beings."

We live in a developing global civilization made up of many religions and cultures interconnected by the mass media, international transportation, international corporations, and the internet. No longer can any person, country, or religion be an island: we are more and more interdependent. The twentieth century began with great hopes that science and technology would usher in a secular age of rationality, peace, and progress. Instead, it ushered in an age of apocalyptic nightmares – an age of nationalism, racism, and global conflict leading to two world wars and an estimated 100 million deaths. Science and technology, it seems, were better at creating instruments of mass destruction, like the gas chambers of Auschwitz and the atomic bombs dropped on Hiroshima and Nagasaki, than the instruments of peace. The question that hangs over our heads is whether this new century (indeed, the new millennium) will bring more of the same, or whether diverse religions and cultures will find ways to build bridges to an era of peace. It remains an open question whether the religions of the world will be part of the problem or part of the solution.

In addressing this question we are, moreover, faced with the serious challenge of cultural and ethical relativism. Are religions and cultures so different from one another that all their interactions inevitably result in conflict and misunderstanding? Are they so different from each other that no ethical consensus can be reached? The study of ethics must be more than an "objective" survey of abstract theories taught in a noncommittal fashion. It ought to convey the wisdom one generation has to pass on to the next. To leave the next generation with no wisdom in an age as dangerous as ours is to create a cynical generation that believes there are no standards, and so one view of life is thought to be as good as another. The wisdom that has come to birth in our time, we are convinced, is that which has emerged in response to the atrocities of World War II, the indignities of racism, sexism, and colonialism everywhere, and the violation of our environment by modern scientific/technological civilization. What the dangers of our time call for is an interreligious and international strategy for turning around our science and technology, protecting the human dignity of all peoples, and restoring the ecology of our mother earth. The study of comparative religious ethics has an important role to play in addressing these issues.

The answers we seek, however, lie not so much in theories as in the life stories of extraordinary people who have wrestled with questions of justice, nonviolence, and ecological well-being in an age of racism, sexism, religious prejudice, nationalism, colonialism, and nuclear war. Our story picks out a thread from the human drama of history that begins with the Russian novelist Tolstoy (1828–1910), who in turn influenced Gandhi (1869–1948), who in turn influenced a generation that includes Martin Luther King, Jr. (1929–68), Abraham Joshua Heschel (1907–72), Thich Nhat Hanh (1926–), and Malcolm X (1925–65). King, a Southern Baptist, drew on Gandhi's Hinduism to launch the civil rights movement and protest the Vietnam War. Heschel, a Hasidic Jew, marched with King and was himself a leader in the protest against the Vietnam War. King nominated the Buddhist Thich Nhat Hanh for the Nobel Peace Prize for his non-violent struggles against the Vietnam War. And of course, Malcolm X argued with King about the merits of non-violence even as he moved closer to King after his conversion to mainstream Islam.

Out of these lives (and the lives of others we cannot explore here), we believe, has emerged an interreligious and international ethic of human dignity, human rights, and human liberation. These individual lives of tireless struggle for human dignity and human rights, their common involvement in issues of justice, war, and peace, and their involvement in each other's lives and religions, we contend, demonstrate that not only can a shared ethic emerge, but it is emerging among people of different religions and cultures. There is a Jewish tradition that says that God always sees to it that there are thirty-six righteous people hidden in the world for whose sake God spares the world, despite rampant evil. This book is not so much about ethical theories as it is about such people – individuals whose holiness has changed, and continues to change, the world. It is about them and about the religious stories and spiritual practices that sustain them.

There are many ways to study religious ethics comparatively. One approach would be to study moralities empirically through comparative ethnography – an *anthropological*, purely descriptive, study of moral practices in different communities, which would contrast similarities and differences. A related approach would require making an *historical* study of the changes in moral practices that have evolved in different religions and cultures. Or we could take a *philosophical* approach. This could be descriptive, comparing ethical theories across cultures, or else prescriptive, attempting to theoretically formulate a universal ethic of what we ought to do, and advocating that it be shared by all religions and cultures. All are important, and we will, in some modest degree, draw on most of them. However, our main approach will take us in a different direction.

Our approach will be through *comparative storytelling* and *comparative spirituality* in response to some of the defining events of the twentieth century – the struggle against colonialism, racism, and sexism and the human capacity to inflict mass death revealed at Auschwitz and Hiroshima. We will not be looking to the philosophers and legal experts for guidance but to the stories of heroes and saints, both ancient and modern; those whose heroism and holiness have shaped and continue to shape each tradition. So we will look to stories of ancient figures like Gilgamesh, Socrates, Moses, Muhammad, Jesus, Arjuna, and Siddhartha (the Buddha), and also to contemporary figures like Abraham Joshua Heschel, Malcolm X, Martin Luther King, Jr., Mahatma Gandhi, and Thich Nhat Hanh. And we shall seek to recover the missing voices of women through the lives of Rosemary Ruether and Joanna Macy.

There are several assumptions and historical factors that shape this approach. First, the primary way in which ethical insights occur and are communicated within religious traditions is through story and ritual rather than through theory.

Our narrative approach to ethics is founded on the assumption that our under-standing of good and evil is primarily shaped by the kind of story we think we are in and the role we see ourselves playing in that story. While every religious tradition tends to develop experts on settling complex ethical issues, that kind of ethics is necessarily the activity of a religious and intellectual elite. Their activities do not reflect the way morality functions for the typical believer. Philosophical and legal expertise do play an important role in every tradition, but not the most important role. It is misleading to try to understand the role of religion in morality by putting the emphasis on experts. For most religious traditions, philosophical and/or legal reason, unaided by story and ritual, is incapable of leading to an understanding of what is good and what we ought to do. The primary and most pervasive ways religious traditions shape ethical behavior are through storytelling and spiritual practices. Storytelling shapes the ethical imagination of its members, especially through stories of heroes and saints. Spirituality shapes the character of its members through ritual activities such as worship, prayer, meditation, fasting, and so on, aimed at bringing about a transformation in individual and communal identity and action. These aspects of religious ethics will be our central focus, for the deciding factor in religious ethics is not good arguments (although they are important) but spiritual trans-formation.

Second, living in a global civilization after Auschwitz and Hiroshima, we live in an interconnected world where people are often deeply shaped not only by the stories of their own traditions but also by those of others – for example, Gandhi's ethical views were shaped not only by his own Hinduism but by Tolstoy's writings on Jesus' Sermon on the Mount, and King's ethical views were deeply shaped by Gandhi's insights into the Hindu scripture the *Bhagavad Gita*. Gandhi did not become a Christian and King did not become a Hindu, but in each case their own religious identity was deeply influenced by the other. Martin Luther King, Jr. was a different kind of Christian because of Gandhi and Gandhi was a different kind of Hindu because of Tolstoy. Gandhi and King provide us with a model for engaging in comparative religious ethics as a genu-ine quest to discover wisdom not only in one's own tradition but in that of others. In this book, you are invited to engage in such a quest.

Third, while different religious traditions do sometimes offer unique per-spectives on common problems, more often than not the dividing line between people on ethical issues is not between people of different religions but between people within the same religious tradition. A corollary of this is that there is no one Buddhist, Christian, Hindu, Jewish, or Islamic position on ethical issues, and that very often people of different religions find themselves allied with each other against others in their own tradition – this is certainly the case today with abortion, for example. Our goal, then, is not to ask what is the Buddhist or Christian position on this or that (a misleading question) but rather, how might the stories of Buddhism, Hinduism, Judaism, Christianity, Islam, and others shape our ethical imagination when dealing with a particular problem, and how might the spiritual practices of each help to transform us into better human beings? In this book we will explore the life stories of Gandhi, King, and other contemporary figures, in order to understand how story and spirituality can inspire lives committed to social justice and the alleviation of suffering in our technologically oriented global civilization.

Our task will be to pass over through sympathetic imagination into the stories of diverse religions and religious figures, see the world and the problems we face through these stories and their lives, therefore returning to our starting point with new ethical insight. We shall seek to do what Martin Luther King, Jr. did when he passed over into Gandhi's Hinduism and the story of the *Bhagavad Gita*, only to come back to his own Christian Baptist heritage with new insight into the Sermon on the Mount, and how it could be used to deal with racism non-violently. In this process of seeing the world through the stories of others, we shall pay attention to certain narrative themes that have deeply influenced more than one religion and culture. We shall explore, for instance, the oldest of all epics, the story of Gilgamesh, as a model for two of the most pervasive themes of religious narrative: (1) wrestling with the stranger and (2) the quest for an answer to the problems of old age, sickness, and death. Out of these two themes a number of key issues for narrative ethics after Auschwitz and Hiroshima will be explored, especially those of obedience vs. audacity in relation to authority, hostility vs. hospitality in relation to the stranger, and violence vs. non-violence as a strategy for achieving social justice. We will find these to be organizing themes for many, but not all, of the stories we will encounter in our journey through the world's religions.

This book is an example of the very narrative themes we shall discover and explore. That is, our task is the common human task of wrestling with the stranger as we engage in a quest to find answers to the problems of old age, sickness, and death – answers that enable us to relate to the stranger with justice and compassion. We shall strive to understand how others see life and death and how their stories either encourage or discourage hospitality to the stranger. We shall strive to come to understand the meaning of good and evil through the stories of strangers from other religions and cultures, as well as our own (wherever we find ourselves beginning). And we shall look for convergences and divergences that might be used to construct a common cross-cultural ethic that could encourage peace and justice among religions and cultures in the third millennium.

Finally, our approach will be contemporary, applied, and normative. We shall be reflecting on the ethical challenges presented by science, technology, and human diversity in the contemporary world. And we shall be seeking a normative interreligious and cross-cultural ethic that will help us decide what we ought to do about the challenges we face. In this sense, we do not pretend to have written a neutral text. Instead we seek to persuade you of the importance of "the way of all the earth" and the ethic of interdependence and audacity we see emerging from the spirituality of passing over and coming back exemplified in the lives of Gandhi, King, and others (including their feminist critics) for a post/modern world. Yet we hope to do this not by dictating to you but by challenging you to make your own journey and arrive at your own insights.

In the introductory chapter, we will examine what we mean by terms such as "religion," "ethics," and "morality," and how these terms are related to storytelling as a mode of ethical reflection. In chapter 2 we shall turn to the stories of Auschwitz and Hiroshima that have shaped the religious and ethical imagination of human beings on a global scale in the twentieth century. And we shall trace the emergence of a cross-cultural and interreligious ethic of human dignity, human rights, and human liberation articulated through the lives of Tolstoy, Gandhi, King, and others in the nineteenth and twentieth centuries.

In Part II (chapters 3 through 8) we will engage in a historical survey that will allow us to pass over into some of the key stories and practices (myths and rituals) of the great world religions that are available to shape and inspire our ethical imaginations. In successive chapters we will look at five of the world's great religious traditions from three narrative perspectives. We shall look at the classical cosmic story (or stories) that have shaped the worldview of each religious tradition. We will also study a formative narrative, a key story that has deeply shaped each tradition, such as the life of the Buddha or the life of Jesus. And then we examine the life story of a twentieth-century individual who has brought these ancient stories alive in new and ethically transformative ways through his/her own actions. In each case we shall be looking at the life story of someone, like Gandhi or King, whose commitments to justice and compassion have not only made them models of the ethical life but whose lives have typically had a transformative influence on how that tradition interprets the requirements of an ethical life in the world we live in today. Finally, beginning with chapter 4, each chapter will end with "comparative reflections," which will suggest some of the key ethical issues that emerge from comparing these lives. In our comparative reflections we will be taking sides on some of these issues. We do so not to dictate the conclusions you must come to, but to point out to you important areas of creative tension among the social activists we are studying, and invite you to the debate. Consequently, each chapter will end with some possible questions for further discussion.

In Part III, we shall, in chapter 9, consider the missing voices of women in the world's religions and how the inclusion of their voices may alter comparative religious ethics by introducing themes of interdependence and ecology. For the ancient history of the world's religions is dominated by male heroes and saints, and these religions seem to downplay the role of women in the religious and ethical life. The contemporary inclusion of women's voices is having a transformative impact on virtually all religious traditions. Finally, in the concluding chapter, we will review our journey and suggest that it is possible to see in contemporary ecofeminism a reconciling bridge between Eastern and Western ethical traditions. Drawing on the lives we have studied – of the men and women who have passed over into other religions and cultures and come back with new insight into their own – we shall suggest the contours of the global ethic we see emerging in our time. Our hope is that the journey we are taking, and the strangers we wrestle with along the way, will help us to discover what they discovered, namely, "the way of all the earth" – an ecological ethic of human dignity and human liberation appropriate for an emerging global civilization.

REFERENCE

Dunne, John. 1972. *The Way of All the Earth.* Notre Dame, IN: University of Notre Dame Press.

I

RELIGION, ETHICS, AND STORYTELLING

Human religiousness is defined by two opposing types of experience that tend to shape the way stories are told and interpreted. Moreover, our understanding of good and evil is defined by the kind of story we think we are in and the role we see ourselves playing in that story. The terms "the sacred" and "the holy," which have typically been used interchangeably, are proposed here as names for these opposing types of experience. The sacred defines those who share a common identity as "human" and sees all others as profane and less (or less than) human. The sacred generates a morality expressed in narratives of mistrust and hostility toward the stranger. The holy, by contrast, generates an ethic which calls into question every sacred morality in order to transform it in the name of justice and compassion, especially toward the stranger. The task of an ethic of the holy is not to replace the morality of a society, but to transform it by breaking down the divisions between the sacred and profane, through narratives of hospitality to the stranger, which affirm the human dignity of precisely those who do not share my identity and my stories.

Religion: The Sacred and the Holy

Human destiny and the sacred

Life, it has been said, is just a bowl full of stories. As far back as we can see into the misty recesses of time and the human adventure, human beings have been not only storytellers but story dwellers. Their stories coursed through their veins and sinews and came to expression in song and dance. To this very day human beings see and understand the world through the lenses of their stories. And for most of human history the primary stories that have inspired the human imagination and human behavior have been the great religious stories. To understand the nature of religion, the types of religious story, and their relation to ethics is our goal in this chapter.

Let's suppose that we could somehow transport ourselves back to first-century Rome. Why are we interested in that time and place? Because our word "religion" was invented by the Romans, therefore understanding what they meant by it should help us understand our topic. So imagine yourself now walking down a street in Rome in the first century. Indeed, let us suppose that you are a reporter writing a newspaper article on Roman religious behavior. You approach a small group of Romans on a street corner and you ask them: "What religion are you?" They look at you a bit oddly, as if you are speaking a foreign language (which of course you are – Latin). They understand the individual words you used, but the phrasing is awkward. People don't normally use the words the way you are using them. Some give you blank stares while others just look puzzled. Frustrated, you try rephrasing your question and ask: "Are you religious?" Suddenly their faces light up, they smile, and one of them says, "Of course, isn't everyone?"

In first-century Rome, with very few exceptions, people didn't belong to a religion as a distinct and exclusive community. Rather, being religious was the same as being part of one's culture. Our first-century respondents would probably continue their answer to your question something like this: "Am I religious? Of course I am. Isn't everyone? It's simply a matter of common sense. I respect all those powers of nature that govern my destiny. Therefore I worship all the gods and goddesses. It would be stupid not to. If I am going to war I want the god of war on my side. It would be suicide to engage in battle with him as my enemy. So I perform the correct ritual sacrifices before going into battle. And if I am intent on pursuing an attractive marriage partner, I certainly want the goddess of love on my side. And needless to say, if I am planting my crops I certainly want the goddess of fertility and the gods of the wind and rain on my side. I am not a complete idiot. Anything else would be stupid."

What does this tell us? For the ancient Romans, and nearly all other human beings in all places and all times throughout history, religion has been about what people hold sacred. To say that something is sacred is to say that it matters more than anything else. And what typically matters most to people is their destiny – avoiding suffering and death and living meaningful and secure lives. Their response is embodied in a way of life meant to address these issues. Everywhere in the world what people seem to hold most sacred is their way of life and the powers they believe make such a life possible.

Although there are other possibilities, the word "religion" is most likely derived from the Latin *religare*, which means "to tie or bind." It expresses our sense of being "tied and bound" by relations of obligation to whatever powers we believe govern our destiny and secure our way of life – whether these powers be natural or supernatural, personal or impersonal, one or many. For ancient peoples everywhere, the powers they believed governed their destiny were the forces of nature. Why? Because the forces of nature were experienced as that awesome, overwhelming collection of powers that surround human beings, providing them with life and all the good things in it (such as food, clothing, and shelter) on the one hand, and on the other hand, these same powers could turn on human beings and destroy them quite capriciously, through earthquakes, storms, and floods. The forces of nature, therefore, evoked in human beings the ambivalent feelings of fascination and dread. Rudolf Otto, the great nineteenth-century pioneer of comparative religions, argued that the presence of these two ambivalent emotions is a sure sign that you are in the presence of the sacred. They are a defining mark of religious experience across cultures. They are the emotions that are elicited by the uncanny experience of being in the presence of that power or those powers which one believes have the ability to determine one's destiny – whether one lives or dies, and beyond that, how well one lives.

Myth and ritual

We can say then, that whatever powers people believe govern their destiny will elicit a religious response. That is, it will inspire them "to tie or bind" themselves to these powers in relations of ritual obligation – a way of life that assures that these powers will be on their side. How do we know what our obligations to these powers are? Throughout history this knowledge has been communicated through myth and ritual. Our word "myth" comes from the Greek *mythos*, which means "story." Myth, we could say, is a symbolic story about the origins and destiny of human beings and their world, which relates them to whatever powers they believe ultimately govern their destiny and explains to them what these powers expect of them. Ritual is the symbolic enactment of these stories whereby they are passed on from one generation to the next.

Myth and ritual are typically tied to the major festivals or holy days of a religious tradition, so that by celebrating a cycle of festivals spread throughout the year one comes to dwell in the stories that tell you who you are, where you came from, and where you are going. For example, Passover is one of the most important holy days in Judaism. At Passover, Jewish families gather for a meal at which the story of the Exodus, the liberation of the Jews from slavery in Egypt, is retold. As the story is retold, certain foods are eaten to remind the participants of what happened. The Passover Seder is not a literal reenactment of the Exodus, but a symbolic one. Nevertheless, this symbolic reenactment is experienced as having the power to make one an actual participant in the original event of the Exodus. The distance between past and present is felt to dissolve, and the events of the Exodus are felt to be "happening to me now."

Through participation in the Passover Seder, Jews experience who they are – a chosen people, called by the God of all creation to live justly and be a light (that is, example) to the nations, preparing for the messianic day when death will be overcome, justice will reign, and the heavens and the earth will be made new. In this way each Jew knows that his or her life is not trivial. On the contrary, each life has cosmic significance, helping to bring about the fulfillment of all things. In this way, the myth and ritual perform a religious function – that is, they "tie or bind" the life of the individual into a great cosmic drama that gives life meaning and purpose, which is expressed in the Jewish way of life (*halacha*). Our example focused on Judaism, but what we said is true of the myths and rituals of all religions.

The sacred and the holy: the dialectical tension between morality and ethics

If the great nineteenth-century historian of religions, Rudolf Otto, focused on the psychological aspects of religious experience (especially fascination and dread), one of the greatest historians of religion in the twentieth century, Mircea Eliade, showed that the experience of the sacred is always accompanied by a sense of sacred space articulated in myths and rituals about the origin of the sacred order of the cosmos. In his comparative studies of primal (tribal) and archaic (early urban) societies, Eliade noted that invariably their stories and rituals of creation functioned to explain how divine beings and/or sacred ancestors overcame the forces of chaos and created a sacred cosmic and social order within which humans could safely dwell. These myths and rituals divided the world into two realms, the sacred and the profane – the sacred order of the cosmos in which one's people live and the profane realm of chaos that lurks beyond the boundaries of one's world and constantly threatens its sacred order.

Anthropologists tell us that the inhabitants of such sacred worlds tend to have names for themselves which mean "the human beings," while the identity of others remains a puzzle. All who live in their sacred order are human, but the identity of all others (those who live on the other side of the mountain, for example) is open to question, for the stranger comes from the realm of chaos – their ritual patterns are different, and these differences threaten the life-sustaining stability of their sacred order.

Eliade showed that around the world, ancient preliterate or tribal societies imagined themselves to be living at the center of the cosmos (the "navel" of the universe, as it is frequently called in such societies). In such societies, to enter certain sacred places was to stand at the center of the world, the very place where, at the beginning of time, the gods and ancestors brought things into being. Thus, to stand in such a sacred place was to draw close to the awesome power or powers that determine life, death, and human destiny. In such societies ritual and ethics are the same thing – the "right" way is the "rite" way – the way of ritual. The answer to the question "Why do we do things the way we do?" is "Because in the beginning the gods and the ancestors did it this way, thus showing us the right (rite) way to be human." Therefore, for every activity in such a society – whether laying out a new village, building a hut or a canoe, or recognizing the transformation of a child into an adult – there is a ritual accompanied by a myth or story about how the sacred powers and ancestors established this practice in the beginning.

In such a world, society is not an arbitrarily created human order but a part of the divinely created cosmic order. Society reflects the sacred order of the cosmos in miniature – it is the cosmos writ small. In such societies, "Is" equals "Ought." The way things are done (as established by sacred powers and ancestors) is the way they ought to be done. The Latin root (*mos, mores*) from which we get our word "morality" means the "customs" of the people. In such societies the customs or mores are sacred and unchangeable: they are beyond question. To violate them is sacrilegious.

Morality is an inherent dimension of the sacred order of society. In large part, what gives a society social stability is the sense that its way of life is sacred and unchangeable. Moreover, every society seems to be ordered by some sense of the sacred, so that even modern societies that do not explicitly appeal to established religious stories tend to exhibit a sacred morality. Sometimes, in order to recognize the presence of religion, we have to begin with the sense of sacred order expressed in a society's customs, even if, at first glance, the stories told to justify these customs seem quite non-religious or "secular." In this sense, there is a religious dimension to every morality, no matter how secular it appears.

To say that something is sacred is to say it is what matters most. For most Americans, to observe someone burning the American flag would be deeply offensive. An attack on the flag is an attack on what is sacred. It is experienced as an attack on their way of life and the lives of those lost protecting the American way of life. To desecrate a cross would be equally offensive to most Christians. They would view it as impugning the saving power of Jesus Christ and the Christian way of life. Both of these are examples of things held to be sacred, even though, on the face of it, one is "purely political" and the other is more obviously "religious" in the eyes of most. Things become even more complicated when we realize that different embodiments of a sense of the sacred can coalesce. Thus, for example, for many citizens America is sacred because they view it as a "Christian nation." But the two need not be mixed, for even Americans who do not think of themselves as "religious" are still likely to hold the American way of life as sacred, and therefore worthy of both living for and dying for. So we see that religion is about more than "the gods" – it is about whatever people hold sacred, especially their way of life. For them what is truly sacred is the highest good – that which provides them with meaning even in the face of suffering and death, so that they are willing to die for it and even to kill for it. Consequently, going to war to protect one's people's way of life is typically understood to be a sacred duty.

Everything we have said up to this point suggests that religion, morality, and society are different faces of a single reality – a society's way of life expressed in sacred customs. Indeed, for one of the great founders of sociology, Emile Durkheim, religion is to be understood as a human response to the overwhelming (and therefore sacred) power of society upon which we depend for our existence. Without being fully conscious of the reason for their actions, he would say, tribal peoples revere their sacred ancestors, or totems (both human and non-human), as symbols of the sacred order of their society. For Durkheim, the singular purpose of religious myth is to sacralize society so that its customs can be considered sacred and bring social stability to human life.

Yet another of the great founders of sociology, Max Weber, argued that this is not the only social function of religion. Weber argued that while religion functioned much of the time to sanction the "routine order" of society (sacred customs), as Durkheim claimed, still sometimes religion manifested the dramatic power to desacralize and disenchant society, and in so doing bring about dramatic social change. It does this by calling into question the supposed sacredness of the old order. Indeed, the same religious tradition can at different times do both. Sometimes religion sacralizes society and sometimes it secularizes it. Thus, Weber argued that Roman Catholic Christianity functioned to sacralize the social order of the Middle Ages, while Protestant Christianity functioned to secularize that social order, contributing to the emergence of the modern secular society. (Of course, once it is established, there is nothing to prevent a secular order from becoming a new sacred order.) Sometimes, says Weber, "charismatic" figures emerge in the history of religion, like Martin Luther, who began the Protestant Reformation in Christianity, who serve to destabilize and transform society.

A similar view was put forward by the French sociologist Jacques Ellul, in the last half of the twentieth century. Following Weber's perspective, he argued that in the ancient world people believed that they depended on the forces of nature for their existence and therefore treated these forces as sacred powers (as gods and goddesses) that governed the sacred order of society. Then ancient Judaism came along and began to desacralize the world, insisting that God (the creator of the universe) alone is holy. The prophets of Israel (like Jeremiah in the sixth century BCE) insisted that this God demanded a life of holiness which called into question the sacred order of society in the name of justice for the widow, the orphan and the stranger (those neglected by the sacred order of society). Ellul proposed, therefore, that we need to understand that the requirements of sacred morality are different from those of an ethic of the holy.

In a parallel fashion, we argue (as we shall see in chapter 5) that the Buddha (who lived in India at about the same time as Jeremiah lived in ancient Israel) called into question the sacred order of the caste system and welcomed lower castes and outcastes into his holy community (the *sangha*), as equal with persons from all higher castes. Some three centuries later, in ancient Greece, Socrates repeated this pattern in his "invention" of ethics as a category in Western philosophy. The Greek roots of our term "ethics" (*ethos, ethike*), like its Latin parallel (*mos, mores*), "morality," once meant the "customs" of the people – the sacred customs. However, after Socrates, ethics came to mean "the questioning of the sacred customs" by asking: Is what people call "good" really the good? As we shall see (in chapter 3), this is a dangerous question. Socrates was put on trial and executed for "impiety towards the gods" and "corrupting the youth" because he dared to question the sacred way of life of Athenian society. Yet Socrates' goal was not to demean the Athenian way of life but to raise it to a higher level.

The paradox of Socrates' criticism of the sacred morality of Athenian society was that it was rooted in religious experience – an alternative form of religious experience. Socrates insisted that he was neither irreligious nor an atheist. On the contrary, he said he was commanded to doubt and to question by his own "daimon," or god, who sent him as a "gadfly" to the citizens of Athens, to teach them to lead virtuous lives and seek justice. As we shall see in chapter 3, Socrates insisted that a good society can never be one which is just the "cosmos writ small" (mirroring its sacred order). It must also be the "human writ large" – where the measure of the human is an "Unseen Measure" – the Good.

The life and death of Socrates illustrate the tension between the sacred and the holy. Every society needs the stability provided by a sense of sacred order. But sometimes order is achieved in society at the expense of virtues such as justice. No society can be a good society that sacrifices justice for human beings in the name of sacred order. Morality need not simply be a mirror of sacred order. It can be transformed to meet the demands of the holy. If you want to transform a society you need to transform its morality – its customs or patterns of life. The goal of an ethic shaped by the experience of the holy is not to destroy the morality of a society but to criticize and transform it, raising it to a new level, one that includes justice for even the least of its members. A society's customs, its morality, need to reflect *both* a sense of order *and* of justice. Socrates opposed "the way things are" (Is = Ought) with an understanding of the Good that transcends the sacred order of things and calls it into question (Is vs. Ought). His death in protest of unjust laws while respecting the need for law, as we shall see, became a model of civil disobedience for both Eastern and Western exemplars of the ethical life, like Gandhi and King. It was both an act of respect for morality (the laws) and at the same time an ethical call to transform that morality in the name of justice. These three (Jeremiah, the Buddha, and Socrates) offer us examples of a form of religious life that gives rise to "ethics," as the questioning of sacred morality in the name of what we shall call "the holy" as opposed to "the sacred" – a holy reality (God, Emptiness, the Unseen Measure) that, in all three cases, can neither be seen nor imaged.

Why do we wish to separate sacred moralities from various ethics of holiness? After all, "sacred" and "holy," as well as "morality" and "ethics," are terms that generally have been used interchangeably (as synonyms) rather than as we are proposing (following the suggestion of Jacques Ellul), as opposites or antonyms. We do so to clarify the ambiguity surrounding the influence of religion on human behavior. How is it that most Christians in Nazi Germany, either actively or passively, supported Hitler's attempted annihilation of the Jews, while some felt their faith required them to oppose Hitler and rescue Jews? Or how is it that, in the Southern United States in the middle of the twentieth century, both the proponents of segregation and the opponents of segregation (in the civil rights movement led by King) could each think of themselves as following the Christian way of life? The proponents of segregation interpreted the Christian story in such a way as to divide the world into sacred and profane spaces. Only whites were permitted full access to the sacred order of society: blacks were profane and permitted only in certain controlled areas (separate schools, separate bathrooms, separate entrances to buildings, and so on). The opponents of segregation interpreted the Christian story in exactly the opposite direction, as one that demanded the desacralization of sacred order in the name of all that is holy so as to bring about equality and justice. The histories of religions and cultures are rife with such examples.

The distinction between the sacred and the holy is meant to express the idea that religious experiences are not all the same – "the sacred" and "the holy" name two categories of types of experience (in each category the experiences are not necessarily all the same, either, but can be grouped together because they have similar functional impacts on society) that shape the narrative imagination in opposing directions, so that the very same tradition and the very same stories can be interpreted very differently, encouraging opposing patterns of behavior. By separating the uses of "sacred" and "holy" (and in a parallel manner, "morality" and "ethics") in this way we are saying that the collection of social behaviors that are generally labeled "religious" are not all religious in the same way. So we are arguing that it is very helpful to give separate meanings to terms that have been used interchangeably in order to help us see and understand these differences.

Figure 1.1, Characteristics of the Sacred and the Holy, outlines some of the key features of these opposing patterns of religious ways of life. In a sacred society all who are alike (for example, share a common ethnic identity) are the same – sacred and human. All strangers – that is, all who are different – are profane and less (or less than) human. The experience of the sacred sacralizes the finite order of the society, seeing a society's way of life as an expression of the sacred cosmic order of things. And what is sacred is held to be beyond question. The way things are in this sacred order is the way they ought to be (Is = Ought). A very different form of religious experience gives rise to the holy community. For the experience of the holy generates a human response to the sacred, which calls it into question by insisting that ultimate truth and reality are radically different than this world and its sacred powers and sacred orders. Consequently, the holy encourages doubt and questioning. The way things are is not the way they ought to be, and so the way things are must be called into question by the way things ought to be (Is vs. Ought).

The experience of the holy desacralizes and calls into question the sacredness of a way of life in three distinct ways – what Paul Tillich calls the mystical, prophetic, and secular-rational criticisms of the sacramental (Tillich's term for what we are calling "the sacred"). There is a type of mysticism that criticizes the sacred metaphysically or ontologically, declaring that the holy is radically differ-

Sacred Society	*Holy Community*
Center (ideal of identity) within itself	Center outside of itself in the stranger
Sameness = measure of the human	Difference = measure of the human
Hostility to the stranger	Hospitality to the stranger
Sacred is opposed to profane	Holy and secular are complementary
Sacralization of the finite cosmos/society, expressed in a sacred way of life	Desacralization or secularization of the finite in the name of the infinite – only the holy is holy: the world is not profane but secular
Cosmos writ small (sacred order)	Human writ large (dignity and justice)
Answers are absolute: answers imprison us in the finite	Questioning and doubt as measure of faith: we always have more questions than answers, and this keeps us open to the infinite
God/the holy in the image of self/in-group	Created in the image of a God/the Holy without image
Honor (morality defined by social status)	Dignity (ethics of equality and interdependence)
Hierarchical	Equality and interdependence
Morality	Ethics
Is = Ought The way things are is the way they ought to be	Is vs. Ought The way things ought to be calls into question the way things are
This-worldly	Other-worldly

"The sacred" and "the holy" name two tendencies at war in every person and in every community. The experience of the sacred encourages us to divide the world into sacred and profane, such that we see ourselves as human and all strangers as profane and less (or less than) human. The experience of the holy encourages us to break down that division and discover the humanity of the stranger. The first creates sacred societies, the second holy communities. The first tends to ethnocentricity; the second is anti-ethnocentric. A sacred society sees the Ultimate (God, or Brahman, or however the Ultimate is named) in its own image and rejects all others (strangers) as less than human. A holy community, by contrast, sees all persons as created in the image of a holy that is without image (God, or Emptiness, or however named) and believes that to welcome the stranger or the outcast is to welcome the holy. The task of an ethic of the holy is not to eliminate the morality of a society, but to transform it by breaking down the divisions between the sacred and profane through narratives of hospitality to the stranger, which affirm the human dignity of precisely those who do not share one's identity and one's stories.

Figure 1.1   Characteristics of the Sacred and the Holy

ent or "wholly other" than this world and therefore cannot be identified with any finite thing. This occurs, for instance, when Buddhists declare the highest spiritual realization, *nirvana*, to be beyond description and to be therefore best described in negative terms, as emptiness, nothingness, and no-self. The prophetic criticizes the ethical danger of identifying the finite (one's particular way of life) as ultimate in being and value, for to do that is to reduce what "Ought" to be to what "Is." Such an identification leads to treating one's sacred way of life as beyond all criticism.

The power of the sacred lies, in great part, in its ability to surround itself with a sense of "taboo" that forbids all doubt and questioning, seeing such criticism as a sacrilege. Yet the experience of the holy seems to have the capacity to evoke the audacity to doubt and question precisely what is "beyond question." Indeed, as Paul Tillich has argued, both mystical and prophetic criticism function this way. Moreover, by desacralizing the sacred, they also prepare the way for the secular-ethical critique of the irrationality of the sacred. This is the kind of critique the Greek philosopher Socrates engaged in when he asked if what people called the "good" or "virtue" really was good or virtuous or just. The seeming secularity of Socrates' rational critique, we have suggested, is really rooted in an alternative kind of religious experience that demands doubt and questioning (we will explore this in more detail in chapter 3). This kind of critique calls into question the demonic irrationality that allows religions and cultures to teach hatred and prejudice toward others (strangers) and call it good because doing so preserves what is sacred, or because "God commands it."

These three critical expressions of the holy oppose the way things are with the way things ought to be. They call the sacredness of a particular way of life into question on the basis of an experience of openness to an infinite that can neither be named nor measured because it is beyond all measures a finite mind can apply to it. In each case a sacred way of life is called into question as not doing justice to the infinite mystery of being human. In each case, an experience of an infinite or "wholly other" dimension which was beyond measure and imagination was thought to provide a true measure of the human, calling for a transformed way of life. Each of these is a precursor for what today we call human dignity. Like the holy, human dignity can neither be named or imaged. We cannot say what it is, only what it is not. It does not reside in our race, in our gender or even our religion. Human dignity, we say, is what we have in common despite differences in race, gender, social class, and religion. Our dignity ought to be respected in spite of our differences, and so we criticize the way our differences are sacralized so as to make some seem worthy of respect while others are not.

While a sacred society is founded on a shared set of answers that belong to the finite world of "the way things are," a holy community is founded on experiences of openness to the infinite. The experience of the infinite is not an experience "of" some "thing" but of a "lack" or "absence" that opens us up to seeing and acting on new possibilities. This type of experience is expressed in our capacity for doubt. To be seized by doubt, we are suggesting, is to be seized by the holy, that is, by the infinite. Indeed, doubt is probably the most common human experience of the infinite. While doubt tends to negate and undermine the way things are, it is not a purely negative force. For the experience of doubt separates us from the world as it is in order to make it possible to imagine infinite possibilities for the world as it *might be* and/or *ought to be*. To the degree that we are willing to make a leap of faith and learn to trust our doubts, and follow the trail of questions they generate, we become open to the possible rather than remain a prisoner of the actual. We ask, "Why must things remain the way they are?" or "Why couldn't things be different?" Once we experience doubt and its questions we are, like Socrates, freed from the tyranny of the finite, the tyranny of "the way things are."

While the center of a sacred society is within its boundaries and measured by all who share the same identity, in a holy community the center is to be found, paradoxically, outside its boundaries, in the stranger who is wholly other. For strangers and outcasts are those whose identity does not fit within the sacred order of things and consequently cannot be named or measured in its categories. A holy community is typically a subculture which functions as a "counterculture," an alternative community within a sacred society whose way of life calls that society's sacred order into question. In the traditional caste system of ancient Hindu society, for example, there was a sacred hierarchy of selves, from the highest *Brahmin* priest to the lowly *Shudra*, and beyond that sacred circle were the outcasts. However, in the Buddhist sangha (holy community), all, even outcasts, were welcomed as equal because all selves were seen as equal in their "emptiness" (*sunyata*). The interdependence and equality of all within the sangha was a consequence of the indefinability of the self. Since all selves were empty, no self could be more valuable than another. The experience of the holy desacralizes all societal hierarchies and sets in motion the development of an ethic of hospitality to the stranger.

Unlike the sacred and the profane, the holy and the secular are not opposites but complementaries. The world is experienced as secular, for it is not the holy (the infinite), which is always wholly other (immeasurable and indefinable) than the finite world. The stranger's "differentness" is a reminder of this wholly-otherness.

The distinction we are making between the sacred and the holy is typological. That is, it is a model to be used to help us sort out human experiences and behaviors. If taken too literally, however, it may become a stereotype. Although we have chosen vivid examples from certain religious traditions to illustrate our distinctions, the difference between the sacred and the holy is not a difference to be found between religions, as if some were pure models of one and some pure models of the other. Rather, the sacred and the holy should be seen as opposing tendencies, or ways of experiencing life, to be found in all persons and all communities (whether they appear to be religious or not). Every actual culture and religion (indeed, every person's identity) is likely to embody tendencies of both models – the sacred and the holy – in a complex and sometimes self-contradictory way of life. Thus, for instance, to cite the Buddhist sangha as an example of a holy community does not mean that it has not also functioned much of the time as a sacred society. Likewise for Christianity or any other tradition.

The Awakening of Ethical Consciousness: The Power of Religious Stories, East and West

The story of David and Nathan

Having suggested that the experience of the sacred expresses itself in stories that encourage an ethnocentric morality while experiences of the holy call such stories into question in such a way as to recognize the humanity of the stranger, we are in a position to better understand the role that storytelling plays in awakening ethical consciousness. While morality in the pre-modern world was governed by a sense of sacred cosmic order, the social sciences, which emerged in the nineteenth century, compared the differences in belief about cosmic order and morality across religions and cultures and concluded that all cultural/moral orders are relative. Such comparisons gave rise to cultural and ethical relativism, because the differences among cultures made it clear that each culture was not a mirror of a universal and unchangeable sacred cosmic order but the product of human imagination and interpretation. As a result, beginning with the Enlightenment philosophers, especially Immanuel Kant, Western philosophy sought to ground ethics not in cosmic order but in reason – reasoning about the correct application of rules and principles.

Modern philosophical forms of ethics have sought to achieve the "ethical point of view" by adhering to "rational objectivity." The ethical point of view that everyone must strive to achieve is interpreted as the point of view that "any disinterested observer" could supply. This "observer" is thought to be objective because he or she has no stake in the outcome of the ethical decision that has to be made in a given situation, and therefore is not biased for or against any individual involved. This disinterested observer is imagined to proceed as an objective outsider who can apply rationally derived universal rules or norms to a specific case. These rules are thought, by those influenced by Kant, to be "deontological" – a matter of rationally derived duties or obligations (i.e., some things are right or wrong no matter what the consequences of our actions) – and by others in the Utilitarian tradition, such as J. S. Mill, to be consequentialist in nature (i.e., right and wrong are determined by the good and bad consequences of our actions as measured by the sum total of pleasure or pain they produce).

However, while rules and principles can be useful summaries of some of our best ethical insights, they are no substitute for genuine ethical insight itself. In fact, apart from genuine ethical insights, which are derived from achieving an ethical point of view, rules and principles will likely seem to be arbitrary and capricious. When it comes to communicating what genuine ethical consciousness is, however, it is much easier to tell a story than to explain it abstractly. In fact, without the story, the abstract explanation will itself seem unconvincing. Since the view of ethics defined in terms of the "disinterested observer" who applies rules and principles arose in the West, we begin our consideration of a narrative approach to comparative religious ethics with a story found in the Torah of Judaism. We turn to the story of David and Nathan – a story about a story that illustrates the way in which narrative can enable us to achieve an ethical point of view. It has been told and retold through countless generations. It is about David, the greatest King of ancient Israel (c.1000 BCE).

> It happened toward evening when David . . . was strolling on the palace roof, that he saw . . . a woman bathing; the woman was very beautiful. David made inquiries about this woman and was told . . . "that is Bathsheba, . . . the wife of Uriah the Hittite." Then David sent messengers. . . . She came to him, and he slept with her. . . . The woman conceived and sent word to David, "I am with child." . . . [David then called Uriah home from the battlefield and tried to persuade him to sleep with his wife, but he refused all such pleasure while his comrades were still on the field of battle.]
>   Next morning David wrote a letter to Joab and sent it by Uriah. In the letter he wrote, "Station Uriah in the thick of the fight and then fall back behind him so that he may be struck down and die". . . . And Uriah the Hittite was killed. . . . When Uriah's wife heard that her husband Uriah was dead, she mourned for her husband. When the period of mourning was over, David sent to have her brought to his house; she became his wife and bore him a son. But what David had done displeased Yahweh [God]. . . .
>   [So Yahweh, the God of Israel, sent the Prophet, Nathan, to tell David a story.] He came to him and said: In the same town were two men, one rich, the other poor. The rich man had flocks and herds in great abundance; the poor man had nothing but a ewe lamb, one only, a small one he had bought. This he fed, and it grew up with him and his children, eating his bread, drinking from his cup, sleeping on his breast; it was like a daughter to him. When there came a traveler to stay, the rich man refused to take one of his own flock . . . to provide for the wayfarer . . . Instead he took the poor man's lamb and prepared it for his guest.
>   David's anger flared up against the man. "As Yahweh lives," he said to Nathan, "the man who did this deserves to die! He must make fourfold restitution for the lamb, for doing such a thing and showing no compassion." Then Nathan said to David, "You are the man." (*New Jerusalem Bible* 1966: 2 Samuel 11: 1–12: 7)

The logic of this story carries us beyond the typical approach of "modern" philosophical forms of ethics that have sought to achieve the "ethical point of view" by adhering to "rational objectivity." It is doubtful that such abstract

modes of reflection are really able to function effectively in the actual complexities of our everyday life. One could imagine the great philosopher,
Immanuel Kant, for example, advising David: "always act so as to be able to
universalize your action without contradiction." (That is: "Don't do it if you
are not willing to accept the consequences of letting everyone else do it as
well.")

A narrative ethic differs from a rationalistic ethic of principles and reasons by
insisting that it is not enough to know the good in order to do it. We seldom
feel ourselves compelled to act on the basis of a logical conclusion. In ethics
reason must follow, not precede, emotion. Not just any emotion, of course,
but emotions of empathy that lead one to identify with the one who will be
affected by our actions. In fact, what separates religious ethics from purely
philosophical ethics is the notion that our ordinary state of consciousness is
distorted and disoriented by deeply (unconscious) selfish emotions. Therefore,
until the self has undergone a profound spiritual transformation of personality,
it is not capable of seeing, understanding, and reasoning correctly. Thus, unlike philosophical ethics, religious ethics usually entails engagement in rituals
and spiritual practices in combination with powerful orienting stories (cosmic
stories, stories of saints and heroes) intended to bring about such a reorienting
transformation through which the individual, like David, comes to identify
with the pain and suffering of the other. Such transformations have typically
been called experiences of "conversion" in Western religions and experiences
of "enlightenment" in Eastern religions. Stories play an important role in such
reorientations precisely because, unlike reasons alone, stories are often able to
reach down and touch the deepest unconscious levels of someone's personality, releasing emotions, insights, and actions that reason alone could never
touch.

In the story of David and Nathan, for instance, while the story does create
a moment of philosophical disinterestedness or detachment, that is only the
first step. It does not allow David to remain in that state of mind. Because it
is a "story" – either fictive or at least about someone else – it disarms David.
It does place David in the situation of the disinterested observer who sees
immediately that an injustice has been done and needs to be redressed. But
then, in a second step, the story quickly moves David emotionally from disinterestedness to empathy. That is, it creates in him a sense of identification
with the victim that outrages him and compels him to act. Only then is David
prepared to reason objectively about what is good and what is evil and unwit-
tingly stand in judgment of himself. For Nathan's abrupt turning of the story
into an allegory for David's own situation forces David to confront his own
actions. The story has managed to capture the complexities of his own particular situation and offers him no place to hide. Ethical insight is about our
relationships to other human beings and about the obligation we experience
when another person's life makes a claim on our own. Genuine ethical insight
occurs when we see and judge our own actions through the eyes of the one

who will be affected by our actions. This is what Nathan's story enables David to do.

In coming to his realization, David is not the victim of authoritarian values and rules imposed by others. No one (not the religious community, nor the state, nor even God) tells David he has broken a rule or violated a principle. And yet there is nothing subjective or arbitrary about David's final ethical judgment. He is unable to excuse his own actions with the libertarian claim that he has a right to make his own rules, deciding for himself what is right and what is wrong. He tried that and failed. He failed because the story seduced him into identifying with the victim of his actions, which enabled him to see the injustice of his actions by enabling him to empathically identify with the victim's experience of injustice – of being wrongfully violated. The ethical point of view induced in David by Nathan's story transcends both authoritarianism and libertarianism and leads David to condemn himself in spite of himself. When David identifies with the victim, he realizes that what he has violated is not a rule or a principle but another person like himself. He recognizes the humanity of the stranger and the claim that humanity makes on his own conscience.

The story acts on David emotionally, but not irrationally. Rather, reason coincides with emotional identification with the victim. A proposal made by one of the leading contemporary philosophers of ethics, John Rawls, can help us understand why this is true. The story is our own but it is inspired by Rawls's theory of "the veil of ignorance" (Rawls 1971).

The parable of the veil of ignorance

Once upon a time, there was a community in which everyone argued and fought with each other all the time. Many persons in this community simply looked after their own interests and did not care what happened to others. They said that everyone had a right to choose their own values as long as they didn't interfere with the rights of others. A small group of concerned citizens, fearful that this would lead to chaos, got so angry that they wanted to take over and force everybody to live by a set of rules they would devise under threat of severe punishment. What was clear was that everybody, on all sides, felt they knew best what was right and what was wrong, although, of course, they violently disagreed on actual cases. The disagreements were so heated that everyone recognized that something needed to be done if they were to save their community from violence. So they all agreed to consult the wisest and oldest person in the city, a person whom everyone admired and respected. They asked: "Are justice and goodness merely subjective [i.e., in the eyes of the beholder only] or is there some way we can understand what a just society really is?" And the wise one responded by saying: "If you want to know what justice is, each of you must imagine that you have been granted the opportunity to remake the world in any way you see fit. There are only two restrictions on your freedom. First, that you yourself must live in the world you create. Second, that you will not be able to determine or know in advance what position you will occupy in this world you create. The society you imagine under these conditions will be as just as it is humanly possible for a society to be."

This contemporary parable helps us to understand the logic of David's emotions. For David arrives at his ethical insight behind what Rawls calls a "veil of ignorance," which leads David to unknowingly stand in judgment of himself. Unlike most philosophers, Rawls defines the ethical point of view, not as that of the disinterested observer but rather as that point of view a person would be forced to assume if he or she were to imagine and plan a society behind a "veil of ignorance" – without knowing what particular role he or she would be asked to play in that society. Rawls's theory forces one to identify, not with everyone equally (the "disinterested observer"), but rather with the alien, the stranger, and the outcast – since you can never be sure that you will not be placed in their position. Or, to put it in the terms of modern liberation theologies and philosophies, justice requires a "preferential option" for the poor and the oppressed. While the logic of this position is obvious, its conclusion is controversial, for it seems to imply that justice is biased rather than impartial. We think this objection is mistaken insofar as it misses the paradox that identification with the least privileged in society really ensures that all – not just some – will receive fair treatment. The controversy concerning this view of justice is one that we will have occasion to review from diverse religious perspectives throughout this book.

None of us, of course, is ever likely to be in the position to create a whole society. And yet our parable of the "veil of ignorance" is not without real-life applications. In the "real world" it is narrative that has the power to create the required *veil of ignorance*. It is precisely the aesthetic distance of the narrative, its disarming quality as a *story*, which puts David behind this "veil," seducing David into identifying with the one most vulnerable to injustice in this particular situation. Then, when the veil is lifted, as Nathan draws the analogy, David stands condemned by his own judgment.

The power of Nathan's story, however, cannot be understood in isolation. Nathan and David are not isolated individuals but members of a community with a tradition. Nathan is able to tell this story and David is able to arrive at the judgment he does because both of them have been formed by a shared tradition of stories which we will call "the myth of history" (which began with Judaism and was embraced and added to by Christianity and Islam): stories of origin and destiny, of creation and exodus, of exile and return, of promise and fulfillment, and of prophetic demands for justice, mercy, and hospitality to the stranger. Indeed, in the biblical tradition, the command to welcome the stranger occurs more often than any other command (some thirty-six times) in the Torah (holy scripture) of Judaism. In fact, this narrative tradition insists that to welcome the stranger is to welcome God, God's Messiah or at the very least a messenger (angel) of God.

The important test for any ethic is how to treat the stranger who will be affected by our actions. We are all willing to treat well those with whom we identify – those like ourselves. The test of justice is whether we are willing to recognize the humanity of the stranger, treating equally well those who are different. Not all stories are ethical. Many reflect a sacred order that denies the humanity of the stranger. Ethnocentrism is the most common bias of every culture. Ethnocentrism is just one of many forms of "centrism" (religious bias, racism, sexism, and so on), which focus on one's self and one's group identity without due consideration for the well-being of others. An ethical story is one that runs counter to this bias, a story that encourages us to welcome and protect the stranger and the outcast – those most likely to be the victims of our own egocentric, ethnocentric, and even religiocentric, actions.

Every religious community is an ongoing tradition that nests stories within stories. The story of David and Nathan belongs to such a great narrative tradition – the myth of history (originating in the Middle East – it is found in the Torah of Judaism, which was later adopted by Christianity), which sees both individual lives and the life of the whole cosmos as an unfolding story that has a beginning and an end – the world was created and the world will come to an end in a final judgment and final fulfillment.

There are other stories, belonging to other traditions, which, in their own way, also exemplify the narrative power of the veil of ignorance. For example, the narrative tradition of the myth of liberation that originated in India. This tradition is shared by Hinduism and Buddhism and sees both individual lives and the cosmos as a whole as going through endless cycles of death and rebirth. According to the myths of liberation, each of us has lived many lives before, and will probably live many future lives. In each of these lives or "incarnations" our task is to learn certain ethical lessons that we failed to learn in our past lives, until we finally achieve total selflessness in some future incarnation and are liberated from the "wheel of death and rebirth" into a final state of bliss or transcendence beyond all rebirths. In this great cosmic story, it is thought that every human being has been one or more animals in previous births and then, gradually, through unselfish acts, earned the right to be reborn a human being – one step closer to final liberation. However, it is also thought that if one lives a particularly selfish life, one can find oneself moving backward into an incarnation as an animal again. Thus, for Hindus and Buddhists, the story of the cosmos as a wheel of death and rebirth functions as a kind of veil of ignorance. It is a story that encourages you to identify with the pain and the suffering of even the least creature in the universe, for you never know when you might be reborn as such a creature.

The doe, the hunter, and the great stag: a Buddhist parable of reincarnation

According to the Jataka tales (which recount the past lives of Siddhartha Gautama), the Buddha, in one of his early reincarnations, was a great stag, the leader of a herd of deer who lived in the forest. This tale is retold in Rafe Martin's *The Hungry Tigress* (1990: 108–9, 207–8). The stag and a doe, his wife, shared a great love and respect for each other, and the whole herd lived peacefully – at least, until the day a human hunter showed up and set a snare in which the stag became entangled and fell injured. The herd fled in fear but his wife remained, refusing to abandon him. She encouraged him to try to get up, but he was not able. The stag urged her to flee but she would not. Soon the hunter appeared on the scene. Although terrified, the doe held her ground, as the hunter, spear in hand, confronted them both and expressed his surprise and good fortune to find two deer when the snare could hold only one. The doe approached the hunter bravely and offered herself in exchange for the life of the stag. The hunter was amazed. He looked from the doe to the helpless stag and back again. His face softened. He stabbed his spear point down into the earth. "Lady," he said, "your words have touched my heart, I have never released a single creature from my snares before. But this day, you and your mate shall go free. I am a hunter. It is true. But I'm also a man. And here I exercise my choice and say you both shall live."

With this statement the hunter knelt down and released the stag from his snare. As the stag rose painfully, he spoke to the hunter: "Friend, virtue is a priceless jewel and, man or beast, it remains our only refuge in times of danger. You have done a noble deed this day. Let me repay you." And the stag dug his antlers into the dirt and revealed a "priceless gem." Use it to support your family, the stag commanded, so that from this day forward "you shall never need to kill again."

This tale is one that reveals great courage and compassion on the part of all the major figures – the hunter, the stag, and the doe. Any one of them could have been the Buddha in a past incarnation, and indeed every one of them, the Buddhist tradition would say, was on his or her way to becoming a buddha – that is, one who has become spiritually enlightened and ethically compassionate. But in this particular story the Jataka tale identifies the stag as the Buddha (*Suvannamiga-Jataka* #359). This identification of the Buddha with the victim is particularly powerful because it suggests that, from the ethical perspective created by the veil of ignorance of the wheel of death and rebirth (known as the wheel of samsara), violence against another is doing violence both against the Buddha and against oneself. For every animal is a potential future buddha and in some incarnation I might be, or have been, such a creature.

The Buddhist tale makes an ethical point that brings to mind yet another story, this one from the Gospel of Matthew, which presents a Christian version of the myth of history. In the cosmic story of Christianity no rebirths are envisioned. On the contrary, you only get one chance in this life, here and now, and at the end of it you will have to face a final judgment and then either reward or punishment. According to the Gospel of Matthew, Jesus (revered by Christians as "the Son of God ") tells the following parable.

The sheep and the goats: a Christian parable of final judgment

When the Son of Man comes in his glory, and all the angels with him, then he will sit on the throne of his glory. And all the nations will be gathered before him, and he will separate people one from another as a shepherd separates the sheep from the goats, and he will put the sheep at his right hand and the goats at the left. Then the king will say to those at his right hand, "Come, you that are blessed by my Father, inherit the kingdom prepared for you from the foundation of the world; for I was hungry and you gave me food, I was thirsty and you gave me something to drink, I was a stranger and you welcomed me, I was naked and you gave me clothing, I was sick and you took care of me, I was in prison and you visited me." Then the righteous will answer him, "Lord, when was it that we saw you hungry and gave you food, or thirsty and gave you something to drink? And when was it that we saw you a stranger and welcomed you, or naked and gave you clothing? And when was it that we saw you sick or in prison and visited you?" And the king will answer them, "Truly I tell you, just as you did it to one of the least of these who are members of my family, you did it to me." Then he will say to those at his left hand, "You that are accursed, depart from me into the eternal fire prepared for the devil and his angels; for I was hungry and you gave me no food, I was thirsty and you gave me nothing to drink, I was a stranger and you did not welcome me, naked and you did not give me clothing, sick and in prison and you did not visit me." Then they also will answer, "Lord, when was it that we saw you hungry or thirsty or a stranger or naked or sick or in prison, and did not take care of you?" Then he will answer them, "Truly I tell you, just as you did not do it to one of the least of these, you did not do it to me." And these will go away into eternal punishment, but the righteous into eternal life. (Matthew 25: 31–46)

This story from the Christian tradition, like those we have cited from Judaism (David and Nathan) and Buddhism (the parable of the stag, the doe, and the hunter), reveals the power of religious narrative to create a veil of ignorance in which it becomes true that the good or evil we do to another we do both to ourselves and to the "holy one" – however the "holy" is interpreted in each tradition, whether it be God, Christ, Buddha nature, or some other expression of the holy.

Having said this, we should note that there is a significant difference in the two stories from religions of the West (Judaism and Christianity) that we have cited and the one from the East (Buddhism). While all three reveal the power of narrative to create a "veil of ignorance" in order to evoke ethical consciousness by bringing the agent to identify with the one affected by his or her actions (who is in turn identified with the "holy"), each focuses the ethical imagination differently. In the Jewish and Christian parables, the focus is on the human realm and justice for the stranger. These traditions (as well as Islam) tend to emphasize the discontinuity between humanity and nature. In the Buddhist parable (and others we could have cited from Hinduism or the religions of China) the focus is on the continuity between humans and nature.

The strength of the biblical traditions has been in affirming the importance of human dignity and social justice. Consequently, these traditions have a strong orientation to the problems of human justice and injustice, but a weaker sense of ecological justice due to an inability to identify as readily with the pain and injury caused to animals and the environment. In contrast, Hinduism and Buddhism, as Eastern traditions shaped by the myths of rebirth, encourage the ethical imagination to identify with the suffering of nature. And yet the strength of the karmic view is also its weakness. This is in large part due to the fact that the stories of rebirth emphasize that whatever misfortune happens to you in this lifetime (whether as an animal or a human) is the result of your past misdeeds. Therefore, while beings suffer in this life they never suffer unjustly (this, as we shall see, is known as the moral law of karma in these religious traditions). From this perspective, stories of karma tend to blunt rather than sensitize the ethical imagination. In contrast, while the biblical religions are perhaps less sensitive to the natural order, they tend to experience the problem of human injustice more acutely since there are no past lifetimes to explain away the suffering of others as justly deserved. What this should suggest to us is that the narrative traditions and their accompanying spiritual disciplines may, in at least some important respects, have something to teach each other, and each one of us (in terms of both strengths and weaknesses), no matter what part of the globe we come from. Like Gandhi and King, we may discover that we can be deeply influenced by other traditions in a way that does not dilute, but rather complements and deepens our own tradition.

The paradox of conflicting stories

No religion tells just one story. Religious communities present us with a complex of often seemingly contradictory moral and ethical injunctions. On the one hand, religious traditions tell stories which suggest that it is in the self-interest of human beings to be good, because if they are they will be rewarded and if they are not, they will be punished. Philosophers call this an appeal to "prudential reason." That is, it is in our own self-interest to be good. On the other hand, religious traditions also typically tell stories that suggest that human beings ought to act selflessly for the good of others, indeed, for the good of the whole community, without any thought of the advantages or disadvantages to themselves. Philosophers call this an appeal to "moral reason." Thus religions like Judaism, Christianity, and Islam say that individuals will be judged by God and rewarded or punished with heaven or hell. Religions such as Hinduism and Buddhism say that there is a law of karma at work in the universe according to which those who do evil will be punished by a lower rebirth in their next life, while those who do good will be rewarded with a higher rebirth. And yet all of these traditions say that the ethical ideal is selfless care for the well-being of others.

If ethics is about acting selflessly, clearly there is a contradictory tension between these two approaches to the ethical life. Prudential reason seems to

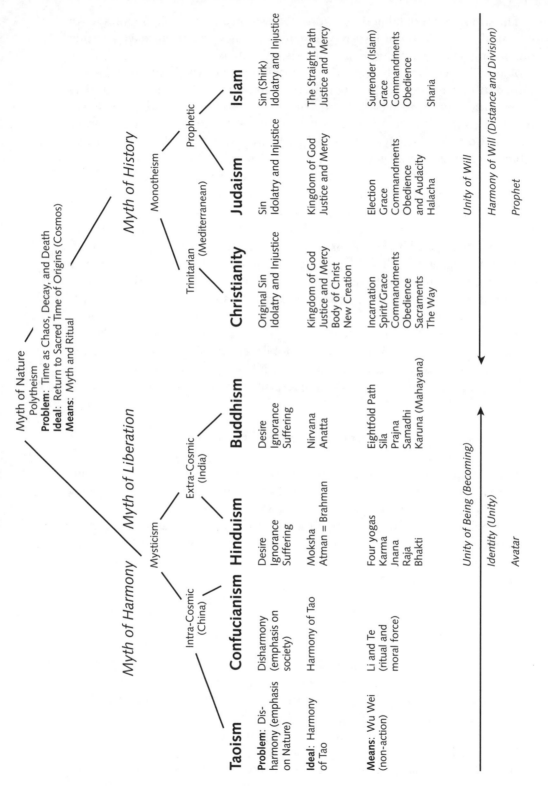

Figure 1.2 World Religions in Perspective

encourage persons to act ethically for unethical reasons of self-interest, while moral reason seems to ask persons to reject just such motivations as inconsistent with the moral life. The philosopher Ronald Green, in his book *Religion and Moral Reason* (1988), suggests that the key to resolving the paradox is to understand that ethical consciousness is a developmental achievement. He suggests that (1) prudential, (2) moral, and (3) religious reason mark the three stages of a spiritual and moral journey – a journey that leads individuals and communities out of an amoral state of consciousness through the moral and finally into the spiritual or religious. This third level brings about the transformation of personality needed to live the ethical life with selfless compassion.

A religious tradition must provide a comprehensive set of stories, rituals, and spiritual practices that will meet the needs of each individual at each of his or her stages in the process of spiritual growth. And of course, at any given time, different individuals will be at different stages in their life. Consequently, the seemingly contradictory advice offered by a religious community is really contradictory only if all of it is meant to be applied to every individual at all stages of life. But, of course that is not the case, for the stories of punishment and reward are meant for beginners in the moral and spiritual life, while the stories of selfless love and compassion are meant for those more advanced.

It is the task of myth and ritual performed in every religious tradition to keep the entire complex of stories and practices in existence so that that which is needed by each individual at each stage of his or her spiritual journey will be there when needed. This is one reason why ritual plays such an important role in religion. Ritual places the spiritual and ethical teachings of the tradition before all its adherents by constantly repeating those stories and practices needed for growth in the ethical and spiritual life, even though no one individual either needs or is ready to embrace all aspects of the wisdom of the tradition at any one time. Rather, the vast array of stories, practices, and beliefs of a given tradition offers the possibility of a pilgrimage whose goal is spiritual and ethical maturity – the kind of spiritual maturity we think is exemplified in the lives of people like Gandhi and King.

The Great Religious Stories of the World – An Overview

What we should expect, then, is both strengths and weaknesses in every religious tradition concerning the ability of each to promote the ethical transformation of consciousness. There are powerful ethical narratives to be found in all religions and cultures. And there are flaws in each of these narrative traditions. Comparing religious ethics, then, should help us gain the wisdom to appropriate the ethical guidance each can offer us without necessarily affirming the flaws in each. Our final task in this chapter is to survey, with a little more comparative detail, the major types of cosmic story (stories about what kind of world we live in) that have shaped the ethical imaginations of human beings around the world.

A casual survey of the history of religions leaves one with the impression of a chaotic diversity of religious stories that have emerged at different times and in different cultures throughout history. But while specific religious stories are indeed unique and diverse, we can group religious stories into four main types: the myths of nature, the myths of harmony, the myths of liberation and the myths of history. Refer to figure 1.2, World Religions in Perspective, as you read the remainder of this section on the types of religious expression. The figure compares the four types of religious symbolic stories or "myths" in their main varieties with respect to three things: (1) the fundamental *problem* of human existence as it is understood in that tradition (designated by a "P" on the left-hand side); (2) the fundamental *ideal* that the tradition holds up as the goal and fulfillment of life (designated by "I"); (3) the *means* (practices, experiences, etc.) by which humans are said to be able to overcome the problem and realize the ideal (designated by "M"). In this text we shall focus on the myths of liberation and of history that intersected in the lives of Gandhi, King, Heschel, Nhat Hanh, and Malcolm X.

The myths of nature

If one goes back far enough into the history of any culture, the earliest religious stories one will find are versions of the myths of nature. These are stories about the forces of nature that govern human destiny which portray them as either personal forces (gods, spirits, and ancestors) or impersonal magical forces (what anthropologists call *mana* types of religion). Such religions tend to see time as cyclical, like the seasons of the year, and myth and ritual as the means to erase the distance between "now" and the past so that it is possible to return to the time of origins "in the beginning," when the gods and ancestors first created the world fresh and new. In such stories the problem of life is time. Time is the enemy. Time brings decay. It brings old age, sickness, and death. The ideal of life is to return to the newness of life at the beginning of creation before time began, through the power of ritual. A return to the beginning renews the earth, erasing time and making all things new. The means for bringing about this return is to follow the way of the ancestors. For it is the ancestors who pass on the sacred wisdom that goes back to the time of origins. The performance of their sacred myths and rituals – retelling and reenacting the sacred stories of creation – leads to the ritual renewal of life, bringing it into harmony with the sacred rhythms of the cosmos manifested in the seasons of nature.

One of the most striking things about tribal cultures is that the living and the dead form a single ongoing community. Death is not the end of one's participation in a community but rather a change in status. One's influence increases rather than decreases at death. One becomes a sacred ancestor. One becomes the newest link in the ancient chain of those who mediate the sacred powers necessary to the health and well-being of the community. The ancestors embody the wisdom of the ages that sustains the well-being of the community. Morality is sustained through reverence for the sacred ways of the ancestors. As long as the community shows reverence for the ancestors and maintains their sacred ways, the community will thrive. But if the community shows disrespect for the ancestors and neglects to remember them in ritual and moral observance, then one can expect misfortune to come upon the community, for it will have lost contact with the sacred forces and sacred ways that give it life. Indeed, misfortune and disharmony in the community will typically be interpreted as being due to someone neglecting the ancestors and making them angry so that they bring these punishments upon the community. The injury done to the community will need to be repaired by appropriate rituals that will reestablish harmony with the ancestors and heal the tensions in the community, permitting a return to a faithful observance of the ways of the ancestors.

The great transition from the myths of nature to the myths of the great world religions

From about 8000 BCE the domestication of plants and animals made village life possible. Dating from approximately 3000 BCE, this agricultural skill made possible the emergence of cities, and this brought about a great transformation in human experience. Urban life drew human beings together out of different tribal cultures. In the tribe everyone lived in close harmony with the rhythms of nature, in extended families or clans that shared a common set of stories and rituals. Now, in the cities, human beings came together from different tribes, bringing with them different stories, different rituals, and different family identities.

Urban life also brought with it the specialization of labor. Whereas in tribal societies everyone shared the same tasks of hunting and gathering, in the cities the agricultural surplus created by the peasant farmers made it possible for others to become carpenters, blacksmiths, scribes, priests, etc. Society became more complex and differentiated into classes (peasants, craftsmen, noblemen, priests, and so on). Also, while in tribal oral cultures all knowledge was limited to the simple formulaic patterns of thought that people can hold in their memory, the emergence of writing in the new urban centers made it possible to store and retrieve information in great detail. All of this fundamentally transformed human identity. In the tribe identity was collective because everybody shared the same stories and actions. The cities, by contrast, were communities of strangers. The tribe emphasized sameness but in the cities tribal persons were confronted with differences that forced people to individuate their identities. In the cities, everything reinforced awareness of how one is different from another.

The loss of tribal collective life, with the emergence of large, impersonal, and often brutal urban city-states in Egypt, India, China, and Mesopotamia, ruled by ancient kings, who were considered either gods or representatives of the gods, was like being expelled from the garden of paradise into a world of suffering and cruelty. Life in these new urban city-states, where every person was a stranger, led to a threefold crisis of mortality, morality, and meaning. In the tribe identity was collective. The dead were the sacred ancestors who continued to dwell with the living in a single community. However, once persons under the impact of urban individuation began to be aware of themselves as individuals, death suddenly emerged as a personal problem so that life seemed even more cruel and uncertain. For once one has an individual self or identity, death becomes a problem that it never was before, namely the loss of one's "self."

Urban individuation also created the new problems of law and morality. In the tribe the "right" thing to do was the "rite" thing – the ritual way of the ancestors. In the city, people no longer experienced themselves as members of the same clan but rather as strangers, each looking out for his or her own good at the expense of others. Thus in the cities law emerged to set the minimum order necessary for human life and a need for ethics emerged to raise up the highest ideals of what human life could be. In the cities, once human identity was individuated, individuals experienced themselves as living in a world without morality where death (as the loss of self) was their destiny. This sense of mortality was only heightened by wars of conquest and the arbitrary rule of "divine" kings. Such a situation brings with it a crisis of meaning. Can life really have any meaning if it is filled with suffering and injustice, and ends in death? These are the great questions asked by *The Epic of Gilgamesh* (as we shall see in chapter 4) in the ancient Near East at the beginning of the Urban period (3000–1500 BCE) – an epic that expresses the anguish of the new urban individual.

It is to answer these questions that the great world religions emerged. Once city dwellers were individuated in their identities the old answer to the problems of mortality, morality, and meaning no longer worked. Individuation is a kind of loss of innocence. Once you have become an individual you cannot deliberately return to a collective sense of identity. Once death is experienced as the loss of the individual self, it is not possible to return to a collective sense of tribal identity as an eternal community in order to escape the burden of mortality. The only possible answer was to move forward and discover deeper wells of religious experience that could provide a new sense of human identity – one able to answer the new urban problems of mortality, morality, and meaning. This was the challenge that the great world religions tried to address as they emerged in three of the great centers of civilization in the ancient world after 3000 BCE – China, India, and the Middle East.

The world religions emerged in conjunction with the formation of great empires that united peoples of various tribes and city-states in a larger political unity. Such new political orders created a need for a new understanding of what it means to be human. In the tribe, to be human was to be a member of the tribal family who shared the same ancestral spirits. In the city-state, to be human was to serve the gods of the city. In both cases the ancestral spirits and deities were local, leaving problematic the human identity of those who lived elsewhere and served different spirits and deities. The great world religions attempt to redefine the meaning of being human in more universal terms, beyond the boundaries of the tribe and the city-state, seeking a higher unity to reality beyond the many gods and spirits that had been believed to govern human destiny in these smaller worlds. So, in China, all humans were said to share in common the Tao (the hidden power of harmony that governs the universe); in India, for Hindus it was the Brahman reality (the universal eternal self that underlies all things), or for Buddhists the emptiness of the Buddha nature (understood as the interdependent becoming of all things); and in the Middle East it was the realization that all were children of the one God (the source and creator of all things).

In these three centers of civilization, three great types of myth or sacred story emerged, each of which sought to expand the meaning of human existence and at the same time respond to the three fundamental problems raised by urban life (mortality, morality, and meaning). And each of these great stories broke down into a variety of alternative versions that gave rise to different religious traditions under the umbrella of a common story (see figure 1.2). In China the great story was the myth of harmony, of which there were two major versions, Taoist and Confucian. In India the great story was the myth of liberation, of which there were two major versions, Hindu and Buddhist. And in the Middle East, there was the myth of history, which generated three versions, Judaic, Christian, and Muslim.

China and the myths of harmony

In China there emerged the great cosmic story of the Tao. One's true self is the universal harmony of the Tao, the hidden harmony of the universe at work in the rhythms of nature. All of nature is made up of the opposites of yin and yang, of dark and light, of earth and heaven, of female and male. These opposites are never polar opposites, but rather each flows into the other with no absolute division, the way day flows into night and night into day, so that nothing is ever the total opposite of anything else. There is always a little day in every night, a little male in every female (and vice versa). The ideal of life, then, is balance and harmony. The great problem of existence is the disharmony that occurs when things are out of balance. To restore balance, two different religions emerged in China: Taoism and Confucianism. These two traditions offered different means to overcome the problem and realize the ideal. Taoism urged humans to seek harmony with the rhythms of nature through meditative simplicity (*wu wei*) first, and out of that harmony the harmony of society would flow spontaneously. Confucianism urged humans to seek to establish harmony in society through the practice of ritual (*li*) so that when social harmony is achieved, people will spontaneously be in harmony with the rhythms of the universe.

India and the myths of liberation

In India, like China, life was seen through the metaphors of the cycles and rhythms of nature, but unlike China, in India the rhythms were negated rather than affirmed. That is, human lives were thought to recapitulate the seasons and cycles of nature in an endless round of death and rebirth. Life was seen as suffering, not because there is nothing good about life, but because no matter how good it is, it always ends in old age, sickness, and death. The problem of life is that we humans are caught in an endless cycle of suffering, death, and rebirth because of an ignorance of our true identity. We suffer from the illusion that our self is identical with consciousness and bodily form. The ideal goal of life is to destroy the illusion of having a separate self that is fostered by our selfish desires, for only when all desire is eliminated will we be liberated from the wheel of death and rebirth. In that moment of liberation or enlightenment we will come to realize our true self. For Hinduism this true self is the eternal impersonal Brahman self (or alternatively, a cosmic *Purusha*, or personal self) which all beings share. For Buddhism it is the mysterious emptiness of the Buddha nature, understood as the interdependent becoming of all beings. Hinduism and Buddhism, as two versions of the myth of liberation, offer a variety of means for achieving this liberation, including meditation, the selfless performance of one's duties, spiritual knowledge and insight, and selfless love or devotion leading to compassion for all beings.

The Middle East and the myths of history

What the myths of nature, of harmony, and of liberation share in common is the use of the human experience of the rhythms and cycles of nature as the basis for the religious metaphors expressed in their sacred stories. What separated the myth of history from all these traditions is a shift from nature to history as the realm of human experience from which the primary metaphors for religious experience were drawn. While all religions communicate their traditions by telling stories, only the religions of the Middle East, beginning with Judaism, made "story" itself the central metaphor of religious expression. Unlike the rhythms of nature, which are eternally cyclical, stories have beginnings and endings. Ancient Judaism was the first to conceive of the cosmos as a great unfolding story told by a great, divine storyteller (God). Therefore, to make a play on words, the story of the cosmos is "his-story" (or today we would also say "her-story"). In the beginning God spoke, the world was created, and the story began. The story is the story of history – of the God who acts in time and leads his people through time toward a final fulfillment. The story begins with an initial harmony between God and humans, proceeds through a long period in which that harmony is disrupted by human idolatry and selfishness or sin, and looks toward a hopeful end of time in the future when all injustice, suffering, and death will be overcome and those wronged will be compensated – a time when the dead shall be raised and the whole of creation transformed.

There emerged three versions of this story in the Middle East – first the Judaic, then the Christian, and finally the Islamic. For each of these, we are all human by virtue of being children of the one God who created all things. All three traditions trace themselves back to the Patriarch Abraham, whom each considers to be the true model of faith, and to Adam and Eve as the first human beings. In all three, the problem of life is viewed as a combination of idolatry and human selfishness (sin), which leads to injustice; the ideal goal of life is the restoration of the rule of God, for when human wills are once more brought into harmony with the will of God, peace and justice will reign, and death will be overcome. The means for bringing this about vary, but include obedience to the will of God (and even debate with God, in the case of Judaism), the acceptance of divine grace or aid, and in the case of Christianity, the incarnation of God – and submission to the will of God in Islam. Thus, although the story of the cosmos has many ups and downs, many trials and tragedies, it is seen as the story of a journey which is headed for a happy ending. Time is promising and the future ultimately hopeful.

Conclusion

Each of the great narrative traditions sought to answer the problem of mortality by going beyond the answer of collective eternal identity provided by tribal life. In China and India the answer was essentially mystical: all selves in their true identity are either one eternal reality (the Brahman of Hinduism, the Tao of Chinese religion), or all selves are completely interdependent in their emptiness that transcends death (Buddhism). In the Middle East the answer was millennial (a millennium is a period of a thousand years of peace which precedes the end of time and the resurrection of the dead in the biblical tradition) rather than mystical; that is, all selves will be resurrected at the end of time. Each of these narrative traditions sought to answer the problem of morality as well, by helping the urban individual to get beyond self-centeredness and grasp the essential unity and interdependence of all human beings. Finally, each sought to provide human life with meaning by seeing individuals and communities as participating in a great cosmic story that gave drama and purpose to life. These were stories that were not interrupted and made absurd by death but rather, stories that transcended death.

We need to make a qualifying statement about the unity and diversity of religions. When we stand back at a great distance we can see the grouping together of religions under the four types of story outlined above. As we get closer we discover that each of these stories has diverse versions that express the differences of different religions (the major ones which we identified above).

And as we draw even closer to any one of these religions we will discover even more diversity. In fact, there is so much diversity in each tradition that it often overwhelms the unity. Those familiar with Christianity need only recall how many different kinds of Christianity there are. There is such a great difference between a simple Quaker service, an enthusiastic Southern Baptist service, and a formal high-church Episcopalian service, that it is sometimes hard to believe they are all examples of the same religion. That kind of diversity is true of every religious tradition. So by discovering some forms of unity in the diversity of religions we must not be fooled into thinking that we are rid of the diversity. The diversity is as important as the unity, and no form of human religiousness can be understood unless we take both into account.

A Postscript on Religious Language – A Word of Caution

One of the most challenging tasks facing anyone trying to understand the diversity of religious experience as expressed in myth and ritual is to grasp the nature of religious language. For to understand religious language literally is to misunderstand it. Religious language is inherently symbolic. For example, in Western religious experience, especially in the biblical tradition of the Psalms, adherents often say things like "God is my shepherd" or "God is my rock." We know this is not meant literally. God is literally neither a rock nor a shepherd. When we human beings use terms like this we are speaking metaphorically. A metaphor uses things that are more familiar to help us understand what is less familiar. Shepherds and rocks are something we know something about: God is a little more mysterious. So we use the familiar to help us understand the mysterious. When we say "God is our shepherd," we simply mean that God is like a shepherd, in the sense that God watches over us and cares for us in the same way that a shepherd does his sheep. Or when we say "God is our rock," we simply mean to say God is a reality as firm, solid, real, and dependable as a rock – a reality we can always rely on to be there to support us. We should not assume, however, that religion is only about overwhelming power. It can also be about paradoxical power, for some suggest that the ultimate reality operates not through coercion but through a gentler influence that will prove greater than all power.

Where do these metaphors and symbolic expressions come from? To answer this question requires a little imagination. Suppose that it is a beautiful, warm summer evening, the sky is clear as a bell and there are millions of stars shining brightly in the sky. It is so breathtaking that you decide to go for a walk in the rolling hills just outside the city. While you are on this walk you are suddenly overcome by an overwhelming experience. It is so overwhelming that it defies being put into words. After a short time, which seems like an eternity (and may have been), you return to your normal consciousness and wander back to the city where you run into a few friends at the local bar. You order a drink and then you say to them: "You will never guess what happened to me tonight. I had the most incredible experience, so incredible it defies description." Well, as you can imagine, the very first question you will be asked is: "What was it like?" As soon as that question is asked we have entered the realm of metaphor and symbolic language. The answer is metaphorical because it uses the familiar to illuminate the mysterious. It is symbolic because the metaphor that comes to mind is not purely arbitrary but seems to be evoked by the experience itself in such a way that just this metaphor is the only adequate one. That is to say, unlike metaphors, symbols seem to have a life of their own. We do not choose them; they choose us. Symbols seem to emerge from and speak to levels deeper than our conscious awareness.

Religious symbols conveyed in mythic stories take a great variety of forms, and not all are theistic. For example, Theravada Buddhists in ancient India refused to use the word "God" to describe their religious experiences. Instead they spoke of "emptiness" and "the void" and the inadequacy of all metaphors to explain their experience, which they called "nirvana." The word "God," which is so familiar to Western religious experience, is just one of a class of diverse terms used in different religions and cultures to express that which is ultimate in power, importance, and meaning. This class of terms includes not only the "God" of Western theism but also the impersonal Brahman reality of Hinduism, the mysterious Emptiness of Buddhism, and the impersonal nameless power of harmony at work in all things, called the Tao, in Chinese religions. And some of these terms are quite paradoxical. Some suggest the ultimate is personal and others that it is impersonal. While Brahman, Emptiness, and Tao seem impersonal, other types of religious experience reflect a personalism similar to that of Western theism, such as the all-highest cosmic Purusha (Person) revered in some forms of Hinduism, and the cosmic Buddha to which some Mahayana Buddhists pray. Indeed, the earliest forms of religious expression among tribal cultures also reflect this division into personal and non-personal by seeing in the forces of nature both personal spirits and impersonal forms of power. Anthropologists call these two animistic and mana types of religion, respectively.

All these expressions for what is truly ultimate and meaningful may in fact express diverse forms of religious experience, or they may be differing expressions for the same experience. The diversity may simply express the fact that people use the metaphors of their own cultural time and place to describe the indescribable. Since the times and places of such experiences are different, so are the metaphors. Therefore, it is not an easy task to discern whether differences of religious languages reflect experiences of different realities or different expressions of the same reality.

All of this is further complicated by the fact that religious language can take one of two forms: the way of analogy or the way of negation. The examples used above (e.g., "God is my shepherd" or "God is my rock") were examples of the way of analogy (*via analogia*). We used something familiar to create an analogy to something less familiar. However, there is another form of religious language, the way of negation (*via negativa*). This way of speaking religiously proceeds not by saying what God, or Brahman, or Tao (or whatever name we use for the ultimate in power, meaning, and value) is like but by saying what it is not. This approach is very typical of the mystical traditions. The mystic declares that God is "nothing." God is not this thing and not that thing, God is in fact no "thing" at all. God is beyond all finite things and hence no-thing. In general, Western theism has emphasized the way of analogy by saying God is, like us, able to "know" and to "love," but in a superior fashion. By contrast, Buddhism, of all the religions, has emphasized most strongly the way of negation, insisting that what is most valuable cannot be either named or imaged and is best expressed by terms like "emptiness." However, we should note that these two ways are not really in conflict, for the way of analogy includes the way of negation, and vice versa. For example, every time we say God is *like* some thing, we are at the same time saying God is *not* literally that thing. Every analogy implies a negation. And every negation must be a negation "of" something expressed in an analogy.

Our discussion of religious language should help us to appreciate just how challenging it can be to study and compare various religious traditions. Religious communities and religious traditions from different parts of the world use different metaphors and symbols, and they also mix the way of analogy and the way of negation in varying degrees. Therefore, it is possible that two different traditions may sometimes talk about the same human experience in two different ways – ways that seem to be total contradictions of each other. For example, it may seem that a Jewish theist and a Theravada Buddhist hold diametrically opposed religious beliefs, for Jews believe in a personal God and Theravada Buddhists do not. Theravada Buddhists say that the ultimate truth revealed in religious experience is "empty" or "void" – beyond imagination and naming. Yet when we look more closely at Jewish beliefs we discover that Jews believe that God can neither be named nor imaged. Perhaps theistic and non-theistic religious experiences are really not that far apart. However, it is also possible that they are really talking about truly different experiences.

How to resolve this type of question is a problem that has not yet been fully worked out by scholars of comparative religions. In general, we should begin by withholding judgment and simply try to understand how stories and rituals shape people's lives, their character, and behavior. From an ethical perspective, perhaps the real measure of comparison should be how people live their lives rather than in the apparently diverse images and concepts they hold. If both Jews and Buddhists, for example, are led by their religious experiences and beliefs to express compassion for the stranger, especially those who suffer or are in need, then perhaps there is more similarity than difference between them.

Questions for Discussion

1 What do we mean by the terms "religion," "myth," and "ritual," and how are they related?

2 In what sense can even seemingly secular moralities be said to have a religious dimension?

3 What is the significance of the terms "the sacred" and "the holy" as used by the authors of this text, and what is the significance of the distinction between them for ethics?

4 Why is narrative an especially appropriate form of expression for religious ethics?

5 How does the story of David and Nathan illustrate the nature of ethical consciousness, according to the authors?

6 In what ways can religious stories serve to create a "veil of ignorance," and why is this important for understanding religious ethics? Give examples.

7 Compare and contrast the major types of religious stories displayed in figure 1.1.

8 Why is the transition from tribal to urban life important for understanding the world's religions and their ethics?

9 What is the difference between the way of analogy and the way of negation as languages of religious experience, and how are they related to each other?

REFERENCES

Durkheim, Emile. 1973. *Emile Durkheim on Morality and Society* (ed. Robert N. Bellah). Chicago: University of Chicago Press.

Eliade, Mircea. 1957. *The Sacred and the Profane*. New York: Harper & Row.

Ellul, Jacques. 1973, 1975. *The New Demons*. New York: Seabury Press.

Green, Ronald. 1988. *Religion and Moral Reason*. Oxford: Oxford University Press.

Hauerwas, Stanley. 1977. *Truthfulness and Tragedy*. Notre Dame, IN: University of Notre Dame Press.

MacIntyre, Alasdair. 1984. *After Virtue*. Notre Dame, IN: University of Notre Dame Press.

Martin, Rafe. 1990. *The Hungry Tigress: Buddhist Legends and Jataka Tales*. Berkeley: Parallax Press.

The New Jerusalem Bible. 1966. Garden City, NY: Doubleday & Co., Inc.

The New Revised Standard Version Bible: Catholic Edition. 1989, 1993. New York: National Council of the Churches of Christ in the USA.

Otto, Rudolf. 1923. *The Idea of the Holy*. New York: Oxford University Press.

Rawls, John. 1971. *A Theory of Justice*. Cambridge, MA: Harvard University Press.

Tillich, Paul. 1957. *The Dynamics of Faith*. New York: Harper & Row.

Voegelin, Eric. 1952. *The New Science of Politics*. Chicago: University of Chicago Press.

Weber, Max. 1946. *From Max Weber: Essays in Sociology* (ed. H. H. Gerth and C. Wright Mills). New York: Oxford University Press.

2

STORIES OF WAR AND PEACE – ANCIENT AND POST/MODERN

Interpreting our own historical situation is a risky business, for we are still too close to the events. We do not have the distance needed to put everything into proper perspective. Nevertheless, without such an interpretation it is impossible to identify the ethical challenges that face us, so we must risk it. In this chapter we argue that two major trends unfolded in the twentieth century that are of significance for thinking about ethics: (1) the phenomenon of mass killing encouraged by sacred narratives that authorize "killing in order to heal," as symbolized by Auschwitz and Hiroshima, and (2) a cross-cultural and interreligious ethic of non-violent resistance or civil disobedience symbolized by figures like Gandhi and King – one that functions as an ethic of audacity on behalf of the stranger. The second, we suggest, offers an ethic of the holy in response to the sacred morality of the first.

The modern period, which began with a utopian hope that science and technology would create an age of peace, prosperity, and progress, ended in an apocalyptic nightmare of mass death, symbolized by Auschwitz and Hiroshima, leaving us with the task of creating a post/modern ethic that can transcend the techno-bureaucratic tribalism that expressed itself in two world wars. Techno-bureaucratic tribalism occurs when sacred narratives are combined with the technical capacity to produce mass death. While we do not pretend to offer an exhaustive explanation of the modern propensity for mass death, we do suggest two key elements: (1) the use of sacred narratives that define killing as a form of healing, and (2) the undermining of ethical consciousness by techno-bureaucratic organization through a psychological process of doubling (separating one's personal and professional identities), which enables individuals to deny that they are responsible for some of their actions. Through sacred stories, the stranger is defined as less than human and therefore beyond the pale of ethical obligation, as well as a threat to sacred order. At the same time, bureaucracies encourage one to engage in a total surrender of self in unquestioning obedience to higher (sacred) authority (whether God, religious leaders, or political leaders), so that when one acts as a professional self on behalf of an institution (the state, the military, the church, etc.) one can say, "It is not I that acts: a higher authority is acting through me, so I am not personally responsible."

Yet, despite the seemingly overwhelming dominance of techno-bureaucratic tribalism and mass killing in the twentieth century, a modest but important counter-trend also emerged – a cross-cultural and interreligious ethic of audacity on behalf of the stranger, linked to such names as Tolstoy, Gandhi, and King. The purpose of this chapter is to grasp the ethical challenge of modernity as symbolized by Auschwitz and Hiroshima. The purpose of the remainder of this book is to examine the potential of the ethical response to that challenge offered by the tradition of non-violent civil disobedience, symbolized by Gandhi and King, for a cross-cultural and interreligious post/modern ethic of human dignity, human rights, and human liberation.

Tales of Demonic Madness: From Auschwitz to Hiroshima

Auschwitz

In 1937, at the start of World War II, there were approximately sixteen million Jews in the world. By 1945 that number had been reduced by six million due to the mass extermination of Jews with systematic technical efficiency by the Nazis in death camps throughout Europe. This act of attempted genocide is usually referred to as the Holocaust. The nightmare of the death camps is vividly portrayed through a rich body of Holocaust literature, but undoubtedly the best known is Elie Wiesel's autobiographical novel – *Night*. In it, we get a glimpse into the horror of the struggle to stay alive and retain one's humanity and religious identity in a techno-bureaucratic world organized for the express purpose of destroying, first, the dignity, and then the life, of its victims. In one of the most often referenced incidents, Wiesel describes the execution of a young Jewish boy and two other prisoners who had been discovered harboring arms.

> One day when we came back from work, we saw three gallows rearing up in the assembly place, three black crows. Roll call. SS all round us, machine guns trained: the traditional ceremony. Three victims in chains – and one of them, the little servant, the sad-eyed angel. The SS seemed more preoccupied, more disturbed than usual. To hang a young boy in front of thousands of spectators was no light matter. The head of the camp read the verdict. All eyes were on the child. He was lividly pale, almost calm, biting his lips. The gallows threw its shadow over him. This time the *Lagerkapo* refused to act as executioner. Three SS replaced him. The three victims mounted together onto the chairs. The three necks were placed at the same moment within the nooses. "Long live liberty!" cried the two adults.

But the child was silent. "Where is God? Where is He?" someone behind me asked. At a sign from the head of the camp, the three chairs tipped over. Total silence throughout the camp. On the horizon, the sun was setting. "Bare your heads!" yelled the head of the camp. His voice was raucous. We were weeping. "Cover your heads!" Then the march past began. The two adults were no longer alive. Their tongues hung swollen, blue-tinged. But the third rope was still moving; being so light, the child was still alive. . . . For more than half an hour he stayed there, struggling between life and death, dying in slow agony under our eyes. And we had to look him full in the face. He was still alive when I passed in front of him. His tongue was still red, his eyes not yet glazed. Behind me, I heard the same man asking: "Where is God now?" And I heard a voice within me answer him: "Where is He? Here He is – He is hanging here on this gallows . . ." That night the soup tasted of corpses. (Wiesel 1958, 1960: 75–6)

The imagery of this story is powerful. And yet hanging was not the usual mode of extermination in the death camps. While it was useful as a dramatic exception to enforce camp discipline, it was too inefficient for perpetrating mass death. For that there were the gas chambers, followed by the ovens. Or worse, sometimes the children were thrown directly into the ovens – alive. Wiesel comes bearing tales of madness and death – the death of six million Jews, and perhaps the death of God, and of faith. What Wiesel said of his first night in Auschwitz could be said of all nights by all the death-camp prisoners.

Never shall I forget that night, the first night in camp, which has turned my life into one long night, seven times cursed and seven times sealed. Never shall I forget that smoke. Never shall I forget the little faces of the children, whose bodies I saw turned into wreaths of smoke beneath a silent blue sky. Never shall I forget those flames which consumed my faith forever. Never shall I forget that nocturnal silence which deprived me, for all eternity, of the desire to live. Never shall I forget those moments which murdered my God and my soul and turned my dreams to dust. Never shall I forget these things, even if I am condemned to live as long as God Himself. Never. (Wiesel 1958, 1960: 44)

Irving Greenberg has noted that it cost less than half a cent to gas each victim at Auschwitz and yet "in the summer of 1944, a Jewish child's life was not worth the two-fifths of a cent it would have cost to put it to death rather than burn it alive" (Greenberg 1977: 11). The ovens of Auschwitz seem to evoke the most powerful and disturbing images. Before Auschwitz, he says, when Jews heard about a cloud of smoke and a pillar of fire, they thought of the story of the Exodus – the story of the liberation of their ancestors by God from slavery in Egypt. But now, what Jew can hear of a cloud of smoke or a pillar of fire and not think of the smokestacks and the ovens of Auschwitz? All that was holy and life-giving seems to have been replaced by that which is demonic – that which is totally dehumanizing and destructive of life. The language of the holy has undergone a demonic inversion that seems to rob it of its spiritual and ethical power.

Trinity and Hiroshima

On July 16, 1945, at 5:30 in the morning, the first atomic bomb was exploded in the desert of New Mexico at a site named Trinity. A fireball "infinitely brighter than the sun, its temperature 10,000 times greater, began an eight-mile ascent . . . turning night into day" (Wyden 1984: 212). The awesomeness of the experience inevitably elicited a religious response from among the observers. One reporter overwhelmed by this tremendous display of power said he thought of "the Lord's command, 'Let there be light.'" Whenever human beings encounter a power which they believe governs their destiny, as we have suggested, they respond religiously with the ambivalent emotions of fascination and dread. The power of the bomb evoked emotions analogous to those of the holy. But the symbols of "light" and "life," drawn from the book of Genesis, were not really appropriate, for this event was no life-giving act of creation. It was rather a demonic inversion of the holy, revealing a power meant to produce total annihilation. It was J. Robert Oppenheimer, the scientific administrator of the Manhattan Project, who captured its meaning most accurately. He remembered the line from the Hindu scripture, the *Bhagavad Gita*, spoken by Krishna in his manifestation as the cosmic deity Vishnu, the lord of life and death: "Behold, I am become death, the shatterer of worlds."

On August 6, 1945, at 8:16 A.M., the bomb exploded over Hiroshima and the millennium that gave rise to science, technology, and the myth of progress came to a premature apocalyptic end. There are ironies to this event, for Hiroshima was historically the center of Christian missions to Japan and had the largest number of Christians in Japan – Christians who had steadfastly endured persecution and suppression. Moreover, August 6 was the date of the Feast of Transfiguration in the Christian calendar, a day which celebrates the revelation of Jesus as Son of God and provides a foretaste of his resurrection, recalling how Jesus and his disciples climbed to the top of a high mountain where he was transformed before their very eyes. In that moment, "his face shone like the sun and his clothes became as white as the light," a light so bright that his disciples covered their eyes and fell to the ground (Matthew 17: 1–8). The telling of this event in the New Testament itself alludes to Moses coming down the mountain with the Ten Commandments – commandments that offer life. Here too, "the skin on his face shone so much that they [the people] would not venture near him" (Exodus 34: 29–35). These events recall formative life-affirming moments in the history of Western religious and ethical experience. They recall the power of the Jewish God of history whose reality Christians sought to affirm with their own doctrine of the Trinity. But after Auschwitz and Hiroshima it seems as if the God of history has died. The symbols of "light" and "life" have been co-opted by the demonic and undergone an inversion of meaning. Now they promise death instead of life.

In an analogous way this is no less true for Buddhists than it is for Jews and

Christians. Once enlightenment meant to bring the light of insight that liberates the self from suffering and death through the experience of anatta, or no-self. But the total annihilation of all selves at Hiroshima brought about a demonic inversion of the experience of no-self. The *hibakusha* (literally "explosion-affected person"), or survivors of Hiroshima and Nagasaki, speak of themselves as *mugamuchu*, meaning "without self, without a center" (Lifton 1967: 26). However, they speak not of the humanizing experience of liberation or "no-self," which comes with Buddhist religious enlightenment, but the experience of total desolation, which comes with total immersion in the kingdom of death of which the survivors of Auschwitz were the first to speak. The dark night of Hiroshima brings no mystical fulfillment, only total immersion in the kingdom of death.

The observation of Irving Greenberg concerning the symbolic inversion of religious meaning after Auschwitz proves to be just as true with regard to Hiroshima. Thus "light" and "enlightenment" no longer symbolize life-giving enlightenment and spiritual liberation any more than the cloud of smoke and the pillar of fire by which Israel was led through the desert remind us of liberation and salvation. On the contrary, both call to mind the gas chambers of Auschwitz and the mushroom clouds of Hiroshima and Nagasaki. And Trinity no longer names the God of life but the place where planetary death was born. We live in a time of the demonic inversion of the holy. Now, when a commanding voice speaks from a burning fire it speaks not the language of being, "I Am Who I Am," but of not-being, "I Am Become Death."

Auschwitz and Hiroshima: The Formative Religious Events of the Post/Modern World

Although they stand side by side in the mythic imagination, Auschwitz and Hiroshima cannot be equated as historical events. Auschwitz expresses the linkage of two forms of the sacred – that of the technological mythos of efficiency with the ethnocentric tribalism of a sacred society that demonizes strangers – in this case the demonic tribalism of the Nazis. Hiroshima represents the halting of a similar linkage of technology and demonic tribalism of Japanese State Shintoism by the United States, which, for all its ethical failings, was shaped by a narrative tradition of welcoming, not annihilating, the alien and the stranger. Hiroshima stands as a warning, reminding us that if the Nazis or State Shintoists of Japan had had the bomb, techno-bureaucratic tribalism and genocide would have won the day. And yet, the triumph of the United States at Hiroshima is haunted by the profound moral question of whether it was really necessary to use the bomb at that stage in World War II; a decision perhaps tainted by the racial and nationalistic prejudices which were the heritage of nineteenth-century Western colonialism.

The parallel between Hiroshima and Auschwitz is only partial, and yet it is critical to understand, for it highlights the apocalyptic and demonic trajectory of modern technological efficiency. In sheer numbers, Auschwitz overwhelms Hiroshima and Nagasaki combined. At Auschwitz the death toll is in the range of two million, whereas the death toll from Hiroshima and Nagasaki combined probably did not exceed 400 thousand (Rhodes 1986: 734, 740; Dawidowicz 1975: 149). But the true measure of the immensity of Hiroshima is not in the total number killed but rather in the technical efficiency of the bomb. The bomb makes it possible to re-create the desolation of the Holocaust at a level of mind-boggling efficiency the Nazis could scarcely imagine. It took the Nazis several years to create their cities of the dead, but our technological genius now makes it possible to do so almost instantaneously. On average Auschwitz, as we calculate it, exterminated two to three thousand people per day. A record day might see the extermination of ten thousand. But at Hiroshima, tens of thousands died instantly. And even more died from the after-effects of the bomb. The atomic bomb makes the gas chambers seem pathetically inefficient by comparison. Today, a single one-megaton hydrogen bomb equals eighty Hiroshima bombs. The Hiroshima bomb was a world-shattering phenomenon, offering an apocalyptic promise of yet more terrifying things to come. It gave rise to the Cold War between Russia and the United States, which in turn led to an American nuclear policy of Mutually Assured Destruction (MAD), which was prepared to put the whole earth and all humanity at risk of total annihilation in order to "save" the democratic "Free World" from Communism. Both the democratic "Free World" and the Communist world were shaped by a sacral abhorrence of the stranger (i.e., each other), and sought to cleanse the world by eliminating the other. One of the extraordinary capabilities of this sacral techno-bureaucratic rationality was its ability to make madness seem reasonable.

What is striking about many of the responses to the Holocaust by Jewish authors is their linking of the particularity of the Jewish experience to the destiny of the whole human race, persistently drawing a connection between Auschwitz and Hiroshima. Again and again authors such as Irving Greenberg, Elie Wiesel, Eliezer Berkovits, Richard Rubenstein, and Arthur Cohen link Auschwitz to Hiroshima, not in order to draw exclusive attention to the plight of the Jews but, on the contrary, to interpret what happened to the Jews as a prophetic warning of the peril facing the whole human race.

Again and again, in the same breath as "Auschwitz" the name "Hiroshima" keeps coming up. The link between Auschwitz and Hiroshima turns out to be an inner link demanded by the analysis of those who were, directly or indirectly, the victims of the *Shoah* (a term for the Holocaust which means "desolation"). It is as if those who know something of the "desolation" of Auschwitz recognize that in some sense they have a kinship with those who know the "desolation" of Hiroshima. Moreover, there is a logical as well as a psychological link between the two. This link is the progressive unfolding of a secularized technological civilization that no longer holds anything sacred, not even human life –

nothing, that is, except the technical imperative: If it can be done it must be done. The death camps were technically feasible and they came to pass. The atom bomb was technically feasible and it came to pass. A final total apocalyptic nuclear annihilation of the earth is technically feasible . . . The threat of apocalypse, which erupted at Auschwitz, is no longer limited to the West. Hiroshima symbolizes the globalization of the demonic in technological form, a globalization which forces a meeting of East and West.

The movement from Auschwitz to Hiroshima is psychological, logical, and finally, mythological. For Auschwitz and Hiroshima have assumed the mythological status of sacred events that orient human consciousness the way events such as the exodus of Moses, the hijra of Muhammad, the enlightenment of the Buddha, and the resurrection of Jesus once did. Only they have seemed to accomplish what no great world religion has been able to do, for Auschwitz and Hiroshima have become transhistorical and transcultural events that are shaping a global public consciousness of our common humanity. The horrifying irony of this is that they are not manifestations of the divine but of the demonic, and the common awareness they are creating is one structured by dread. For Auschwitz and Hiroshima to become the orienting religious events of our time does not require that everyone understand these historical events, only that they are forced to live in a world of dread set in motion by these events. One of the most important tasks of comparative religious ethics is to discover, through interreligious and cross-cultural dialogue, a common hope to unite us as a global human community, one which can carry us beyond our common dread, one that may, perhaps, emerge out of a spirituality of passing over and coming back.

We who live at the turning of the millennium are the first generation to live in the shadow of the Holocaust. We are the first generation to live in the shadow of genocide. That a civilization of high culture, science, and learning could give birth to such a project – a rationally organized project to strip a subgroup of its population of its property and legal rights, transport them to death camps, and exterminate them with the most efficient technological methods available – leaves us overwhelmed. Like the experience of the mystic in the presence of an overwhelming God, the apprehension of this event fills us with both fascination and dread and leaves us speechless. We find ourselves doubting that we can find a language with which to adequately describe the event.

We are also the first generation to live in the shadow of Hiroshima. And while the dropping of the atomic bomb on Hiroshima was no act of genocide, it did give birth to a Cold-War era of conflict between Russia and the United States in which human beings were prepared to escalate the stakes from genocide to omnicide – the ending of virtually all life on earth. It was an era in which the mass extermination of human life and the destruction of the earth's ecology became thinkable as a "rational" and technologically feasible expression of foreign policy. And while the Cold War between Russia and the United States has thawed and melted, the use of nuclear weapons remains an option nations East and West refuse to eliminate. And it is an option that many fear will be adopted by terrorists around the globe, fueled by various sacral forms of racism, nationalism, and religious prejudice. The threat of apocalypse, which erupted at Auschwitz, is no longer limited to the West. Hiroshima symbolizes the globalization of the demonic in technological form, a globalization that forces a meeting of religions and cultures, East and West.

According to the testimony of mystics from many religions and cultures, in the mystical encounter with the immensity of the holy, language and imagination are defeated and individuals are left only with emptiness or imagelessness. As Robert Jay Lifton's comparative analysis of the survivors of both Auschwitz and Hiroshima confirms, today it is another kind of immensity which defeats the imagination – the immensity of the demonic. Every attempt to capture, in either word or image, the experience of immersion in the kingdom of death created by the Holocaust, Elie Wiesel has suggested, seems totally inadequate. Likewise, as one Japanese author-survivor of Hiroshima has put it: "there is no . . . category for the atomic bomb experience. . . . One can find no words to describe it." And another confessed that the immensity of the grotesque reality of death – the dead bodies, the smell, etc. – left him blocked, as Lifton reported it, "by a sense of the experience as sacred" (1967: 404, 408). Once silence was the paradoxical language of the mystical encounter with the source of life. After Auschwitz and Hiroshima, it has become the language of the encounter with the kingdom of death.

Auschwitz and Hiroshima are the formative religious events marking the transition from the modern to the "post/modern" world. What we mean by this requires some explanation. All civilizations began with religion explaining the world in terms of the myths or stories of the gods and sacred ancestors. Then in Europe in the seventeenth, eighteenth, and nineteenth centuries, science emerged and replaced the religious stories of the origin and destiny of the world with secular, rationalistic, non-religious stories. In the nineteenth and twentieth centuries this way of viewing the world was spread to virtually all cultures around the globe through colonialism – the European political and economic domination of the world's cultures. At the beginning of the nineteenth century, it seemed as if the great missionary movements of Christianity, which accompanied colonialism around the globe, would overcome all other religions. By the end of the century, it was beginning to look as if science was replacing all religions and that religion itself would soon disappear. In this world human beings were no longer supposed to be guided in their public life by their ancient sacred stories but by scientific and technical reason.

It is important to realize, however, that this secular view of the world is itself part of the history of religion in Western civilization. In the twelfth century a Cistercian monk and abbot from southern Italy, Joachim of Fiore (1132–1202), had a mystical vision of history – of the coming of a new heaven and a new earth. His vision profoundly shaped the "modern" secular understanding of history. In his *Everlasting Gospel*, Joachim suggested that history can be divided into three ages corresponding to the three persons of the Trinity in Christianity: the age of the Father (beginning with Abraham), which was superseded by the age of the Son (beginning with Christ), which would in turn be replaced by the coming of a third and final age – that of the Holy Spirit. Joachim thought of himself as living at the beginning of the final age of the Spirit. With the coming of the Spirit there would no longer be any need for the institutional religion – no need for a church and its clergy. The direct infusion of the Spirit, which Joachim expected, would create a natural spontaneous harmony between all individuals and render all institutions (including political ones) superfluous. The third age would be an age of perfection, of perfect freedom and harmony, which was destined to last a thousand years.

Joachim's symbolism of the three ages gave the modern period its great metanarrative. A metanarrative is an all-encompassing story that is meant to explain our origins and destiny, and hence the nature of reality. The ancient myths of the Greeks, Jews, Hindus, and others provided such metanarratives. Joachim's revision of the Christian metanarrative paved the way for the modern secular metanarrative of progress – history moves forward from the ancient period through the medieval and culminates in the modern age. For Joachim, the third age was identified with the triumph of mysticism over the institutional church. But his three ages became increasingly secularized during the Enlightenment in Western Europe, so that while the three-age model persisted it was no longer identified with the Trinity. For instance, Gotthold Lessing, the great Enlightenment scholar, held that the education of the human race passed through three phases: childhood, adolescence, and adulthood. The last, or third age, he identified with the age of Enlightenment, in which the autonomy of reason (instead of the Holy Spirit) would lead to a natural and rational harmony among human beings.

This vision of three ages was carried forward into the nineteenth century, where Auguste Comte, the founding father of sociology, divided history into the ages of myth (i.e., story), philosophy, and science. The great nineteenth-century philosopher of history, Hegel, provides yet another version with his view that the three ages of history lead to greater and greater freedom, a vision that Karl Marx revised, suggesting that the third age leads to the fulfillment of history in a classless society where all are equals. In every version of this story, the movement of history from the first, through the second, to the third age, is told as a story of progress – of leaving behind the ancient childhood of the human race with its superstitious religious stories to embrace the adulthood of the human race with its sophisticated, rational, and scientific worldview.

Two world wars, culminating in Auschwitz and Hiroshima, brought an end to the plausibility of such stories of history as progress. If anywhere, history now seems more likely to lead to apocalyptic desolation rather than some technological utopia. In this context, all movements that seek to move beyond modernity without reverting to pre-modern patterns can be considered post/modern. Our social-scientific understanding of history and society makes us aware that all societies are human cultural creations, and this makes it difficult to revert to pre-modern cosmological myths or metanarratives to guide human life and thought (although various fundamentalisms attempt to do so), even as our dis-illusionment with modernity after Auschwitz and Hiroshima makes it difficult to pretend that nothing has changed. And so human beings seek a yet-to-be defined "post/modern" alternative. Auschwitz and Hiroshima are the dramatic events which evoke in the human imagination a sense of the failure of moder-nity and its metanarrative of progress, and the need to go beyond the prejudice, hatred, and violence that have marked both pre-modern and modern human existence.

We caution that "post/modern" as used here should not be confused with "postmodernism." We do not have in mind any particular philosophical ideol-ogy (such as post-structuralism). Our spelling of "post/modern" with a for-ward slash is meant to separate our use of the term from such ideologies. The forward slash is meant to suggest that the line between modern and post/mod-ern is ambiguous and not yet clearly defined. The outlines of a world that will replace modernity are not entirely clear. What we do know is that after Auschwitz and Hiroshima, the age of modernity, with its utopian metanarrative of progress, is seriously compromised and no longer beyond question, and human beings around the globe are seeking new ways to be human. Our postmodern situa-tion, suggests Jean-François Lyotard, is characterized by the collapse of all our metanarratives (both religious and secular) (Lyotard 1984: 37). Instead we are forced to live in a world of diversity and diverse stories, with no single story being all-encompassing. The situation sets the context for our exploration of comparative religious ethics as a project in passing over and coming back. Gan-dhi and the spiritual children of Gandhi were and are engaged in such a project – one which rejects the metanarratives that support both pre-modern and mod-ern ideologies of racial, religious, gender, or national superiority, and seeks to construct a world of interdependence in which all life (human and non-human) is affirmed. Whatever the characteristics of the age that will follow modernity, if the experiment of the children of Gandhi can be taken as a clue, it will be an age that is no longer dominated by the modern West. It will be a post-European and post-Christian age. European thought, European ways of life, and Christi-anity, we suspect, will all find themselves de-centered but not rejected. Rather, what may emerge, ethically speaking, is a new appreciation for the interdepend-ence of all in the common web of life.

As a dividing line between modern and post/modern the events of Auschwitz and Hiroshima are paradoxically, at one and the same time, both sacred and profane. They have a profane, even demonic, face, and yet they elicit religious responses. Like the great classical events of religious history they define an his-torical era – the one in which we live. Once we divided history into before and after figures like the Buddha or Jesus. Now we divide history into before and after Auschwitz and Hiroshima – this is the modern–post/modern divide. How-ever, unlike the events of the Buddha's enlightenment, the exodus led by Mo-ses, or the resurrection of Christ, these sacred events are demonic – a demonic inversion of the holy. They do not bring life and enlightenment but death and dehumanization. Auschwitz and Hiroshima are the culmination of modernity, and whatever follows, whatever is post/modern, must radically reverse their demonic pattern if the world is to have a future. That is the ethical challenge of Auschwitz and Hiroshima.

Techno-bureaucratic Rationality and the Demise of Ethical Consciousness

The Holocaust

Techno-bureaucratic rationality and the demonic are closely linked. By the demonic we mean the seemingly overwhelming power of evil, which manifests itself in the capacity of some to dehumanize and annihilate others with a cold, calculated, technical and bureaucratic rationality devoid of all human empathy. Consequently, demonic movements treat their human victims as if their lives were no more valuable than those of insects. While that kind of cold, calculating rationality can exist apart from modern technology, techno-bureaucratic rationality seems to encourage it. The modern scientific and technological organization of society seems to amplify the human capacity for the demonic. In *The Cunning of History*, Richard Rubenstein argues that the Holocaust is not an aberration of history but rather the "expression of some of the most profound tendencies of Western civilization in the twentieth century" (1975: 21). Chief among these tendencies are the processes of bureaucratic rationalization. The turning point of the Nazi effort, he argues, occurred after *Kristallnacht* ("the night of broken glass," November 10, 1938), when Jews were subjected to random and pervasive mob violence in the streets. The Nazi leader Heinrich Himmler rejected and suppressed the further use of the mob violence that been promoted by his colleague Joseph Goebbels. Himmler reasoned that the only way to efficiently organize mass death was to remove the element of personal emotion and replace it with the cool and efficient operations of the impersonal techno-bureaucratic procedures that typified the death camps. Hatred is messy and inefficient. Unquestioning obedience to bureaucratic procedures would be necessary if killing on a mass scale was to be successful.

Between 1933 and 1945, Hitler and the Nazi (National Socialist) Party ruled in Germany and drew Europe and America into World War II (1939–45) – a war of expansion that was meant to give additional *Lebensraum*, or "living space," to what the Nazis considered to be the superior Aryan race of Germany. In the process, those deemed "not worthy of life" were to be "removed." The Nazis first developed gas chambers to eliminate the mentally and physically deficient, but it was the Jews of Germany, of Europe, and indeed of the whole world, who became the primary target of their "removal" campaign. The war that mattered most for the Nazis was the war against the Jews. This is best illustrated by the fact that even in the last days of the war, when Germany was losing badly and soldiers and supplies were desperately needed at the front, trains were still diverted to haul Jews in boxcars to the death camps. Hitler was more desperate to rid the world of Jews than he was to win the war.

The Holocaust was an unprecedented attempt in human history – a state-sponsored attempt at genocide. It was an attempt to eliminate an entire people simply because they existed. Unlike the millions of others who died in World War II, the Jews were not military combatants who died on the battlefront. The Jews of Germany and its conquered territories were not enemies, but citizens. There was no military or territorial advantage to treating them as the enemy. Their only crime was that they were not members of the pure Aryan race. Germans, defeated and humiliated in Word War I (1914–18), and suffering from extreme economic depression as a result of war reparations, sought a reason for their sufferings. Reverting to the stereotypes and prejudices of a long history of European Christian antisemitism, the Nazi Party offered an explanation: "The Jews," they said, "are our misfortune" – they are to blame. The Nazis portrayed them as a racial pollutant or a diseased growth on the healthy body of the German *Volk* (people) that had to be surgically cut out if the German nation was to be restored to the health and greatness that was its destiny.

Thus, once the Nazi Party came to power, the Jews were stripped of their citizenship and all their legal rights, and were herded off into boxcars and delivered to an elaborate system of death camps where they were either worked to death as slave labor or else murdered in specially designed gas chambers made to order for mass killing. The most infamous of the camps, Auschwitz, was established in Poland. In total, an estimated six million Jews were murdered during the Holocaust. The ultimate irony is that because they no longer had citizenship, Jews had no legal rights, and consequently no laws were broken at Auschwitz or any of the other death camps.

The Holocaust represents the merging of ancient religious prejudices (i.e., Christian anti-Judaism, which claimed that Jews were the killers of the son of God and therefore rejected by God and condemned to wander the earth without a home until the end of time) with modern racial prejudices and bureaucratic/scientific techniques so as to create a sacred society bent on using the most efficient means to exterminate an entire people for the sake of the "public good." This raises profound ethical questions. To a large degree, human beings tend to take their ethical cues from their society, its laws and customs. However, in the Nazi world all ethical norms were inverted. Killing Jews was considered good and saving their lives was considered evil. Moreover, the law was adjusted to reinforce these norms. One of the questions we must ask is: What stories made such an inversion possible, and how can we counteract such stories? The Holocaust provides us with a case study of the fundamental problem of ethics in the modern world: Are all ethical norms culturally relative and simply a reflection of a culture's arbitrary values? If so, how can the Holocaust be condemned? If not, then where do we turn to get our ethical norms when the whole of society, its laws, and even its religion have been corrupted? This is one of the key questions to be faced by any study of comparative religious ethics that seeks normative guidelines for right action in a world shaped by forces similar to the technical and bureaucratic forces that gave rise to Auschwitz and all the death camps of Europe.

The Manhattan Project

The scientific, technical, and bureaucratic aspects of the modern world that made the genocidal project of the Nazis possible are not peculiar to Germany. Indeed, they are part and parcel of the history of civilization, and especially of modern technological civilization. And religious prejudice, whether in the form of antisemitism or in other forms, is also all too common in the history of civilizations, both East and West. The combination can be ominous. There is something about technical bureaucracy that undermines ethical consciousness and deadens the human conscience, so that creating mass death seems not only thinkable but rational. This we see in the Manhattan Project, the American project to build an atomic bomb during World War II, which led, like Auschwitz, to a demonic inversion of religious and ethical sensibilities.

   With the surrender of Germany in 1945, the war in Europe came to an end, and some of the scientists who participated in the Manhattan Project to build the first atomic bomb tried to raise serious questions about the need to use it against the Japanese. They had thought the Germans were close to developing the bomb but they knew the Japanese were not. And yet a techno-bureaucratic logic, not unlike that which led to Auschwitz, prevailed. The death camps were a world unto themselves. The Nazis isolated their death-camp physicians from their families and the larger society in order to bring them into conformity with the sacred bureaucratic will of its genocidal program and its ethical imperative of unquestioning obedience. Too much exposure to differing points of view might have raised questions that might have undermined the efficiency of the operation. Likewise, the scientists of the Manhattan Project were isolated in the desert of Los Alamos, New Mexico. Initially, General Groves, who was in charge of the project, tried to bureaucratically compartmentalize the work of the scientists (for security reasons, he argued) to such a degree that most of them would have no occasion to talk to each other. Oppenheimer, the physicist who actually directed the project, had to immediately confront him and point out that as scientists they simply could not do the job they were being asked to do without the free exchange of ideas. A compromise set of bureaucratic security procedures were worked out.

In this environment the moral question of the use of the bomb came up for discussion only once. An attempt was made to hold a meeting of the scientists involved in the project at the Los Alamos site. Only a few scientists showed up. Oppenheimer made a point of being there and succeeded in suppressing any further questions. Oppenheimer, as a fellow scientist, was able to inspire trust in the military and political bureaucracy and induce the scientists to believe that "Once you know how to make the bomb it's not your business to figure out how not to use it" (Wyden 1984: 150). Robert Wilson, who had called the protest meeting, reflected in later years that it was as if they were automatons. Further questioning "simply was not in the air . . . Our life was directed to do one thing, it was as though we'd been programmed to do that. . . . We were the heroes of our epic . . . and there was no turning back" (Wyden 1984: 148–9). Indeed, when the presidential committee appointed by President Truman to decide the issue of the use of the bomb on Japan met on May 31, 1945, questions which would have challenged its use were never raised. Even the option of a demonstration use of the bomb or the dropping of the bomb on a non-urban target never came up for discussion in the official meeting, only in an unofficial ten-minute discussion by four members of the committee over lunch. Groves was very pleased to see the "mounting momentum for unquestioned use of the bomb" (Wyden 1984: 157).

It was not the scientists isolated in the desert whose conscience was awakened but those scientists who had been working in the city – the city of Chicago. There, Leo Szilard and James Franck both made desperate attempts, on behalf of the Chicago scientists, to awaken the conscience of the President and the Secretary of War. Szilard sent around a petition to be sent to the President which collected 67 signatures in Chicago, 88 in Oakridge, "and many more were ready to sign when the military authorities stepped in" and stopped the petition for "security reasons" (Wyden 1984: 176). At Los Alamos, Oppenheimer prevented the petition from ever being circulated. Special reports were also written, only to end up in dead-letter files, subverted by a bureaucratic process intent on reaching a preordained conclusion. The petitions, thanks to bureaucratic procedure, were never seen by President Truman. Not one of the four scientists at the May 31 meeting in Washington communicated any of the questions and moral doubts of the Chicago scientists. Technical experts were not supposed to raise ethical questions about mass death: they were supposed to follow orders with unquestioning obedience. Here, as in Germany and Japan, the bureaucratic procedures of decision-making proved themselves impervious to the demands of conscience.

Yet those who were to make the decisions (Secretary of War Stimson, General Marshall, and others) did not have the technical competence to fully appreciate what they were dealing with. They were totally unable to understand the technical details of the scientific reports on the bomb. The decision-makers were hopelessly dependent on technical specialists. In the end, the logic of technical autonomy won out – if it can be done, it must be done.

Doubling and the Myth of Life through Death: The Spiritual Logic of Mass Death in the Twentieth Century

The neo-paganism of the Nazi doctors

The Holocaust, says Eli Wiesel, demonstrated that "it is possible to be born into the upper or middle class, receive a first-rate education, respect parents and neighbors, visit museums and attend literary gatherings, play a role in public life, and begin one day to massacre men, women and children, without hesitation and without guilt. It is possible to fire your gun at living targets and nonetheless delight in the cadence of a poem, the composition of a painting. . . . One may torture the son before his father's eyes and still consider oneself a man of culture and religion" (1965: 10).

The power of evil, the power of total dehumanization and mass death displayed in events like Auschwitz and Hiroshima is overwhelming. When one looks at specific deeds of cold atrocity, it seems as if only someone who is overtly inhuman or demon-like could commit such deeds. But if we examine the lives of such persons we typically find that they were all too human.

Robert Jay Lifton's interviews with physicians who served in the death camps provides an intimate look into the lives and psyches of the professional physicians who played a major role in operating the camps. He tells of commenting to a survivor of Auschwitz that he was struck by how ordinary the Nazi doctors were. They seemed quite average, and hardly demonic. To which the survivor commented: "But it is demonic that they were not demonic." The lesson of Auschwitz is that ordinary people can commit demonic acts.

Lifton set out to answer the question of how this was possible for the Nazi physicians who were assigned to make the selections for the death camps. These doctors were typically separated from their families and removed to the strange new world of the concentration camps. There they were discouraged from maintaining regular contacts with the outside world. Although they were typically unprepared for their assignment and had some initial difficulty in carrying it out, by the end of two weeks most had adjusted to their new task and were performing quite effectively. This is remarkable when one considers these were all physicians who had taken an oath to heal and now had become practitioners of mass death. The transformation, Lifton argued, was made possible by two factors – a biomedical narrative that enabled them to think of killing as a form of healing, and a psychological process of "doubling," which enabled them to disown their own actions.

The narrative that enabled them to equate healing with killing was the neo-pagan myth of sacred ancestors, of blood and soil – the myth of the pure Aryan race recast in the language of modern medicine and biology. It was pagan in its reversion to a tribal identity that denied humanity to the stranger and neo-pagan in its conscious use of modern "scientific" evolutionary theory to justify it. This was a story that portrayed strangers (the Jews and others) as agents of pollution whose genetic inferiority (and therefore subhuman status) threatened the biological purity of the pure Aryan race through the mixing of the races and cultures. Viewing the Jews as less than human was not, in their eyes, a form of prejudice because for them it was based in the biological facts of evolution. As Lifton notes, "the nation would now be run according to what Johann S. [a Nazi physician] and his cohorts considered biological truth, 'the way human beings really are.' That is why he had a genuine 'eureka' experience – a sense of 'That's exactly it!' – when he heard Rudolf Hess declare National Socialism to be 'nothing but applied biology'" (1986: 129). The Jews were viewed as "agents of 'racial pollution' and 'racial tuberculosis,' as well as parasites and bacteria causing sickness, deterioration, and death in the host peoples they infested" (1986: 16). Just as the physician has to cut out a diseased appendage in order to restore the body to health, so the Nazi physicians had to cut out the Jews who were a cancerous decay on the healthy body of the German people. The death camps were portrayed as an exercise in public health built on the premise that *to kill is to heal*. And the authority of the physician as the embodiment of both modern scientific/technological and professional knowledge and skill was essential to legitimate this myth.

A psychological process of doubling accompanied this narrative as the means by which the physician was integrated into a new techno-bureaucratic social order. This was done through the development of a second identity. Alongside his previous self (as healer) the physician developed a second professional "killing self." By doing this the physician could say to himself – "I am a good man, a healer, and in my personal life I continue to be that. But when I go to work, I act not for myself but according to my public duties as a citizen and professional. In performing my duty I surrender myself in total unquestioning obedience to some higher authority who is in a better position than I to know what I ought to do. Therefore I have no choice. When I act, it is not I but some higher authority who is acting through me. Consequently, I am not responsible for what I do in my public and professional role. Moreover, what I do in my public role is not who I really am. Therefore, I can continue to think well of myself and I can go home and be loving and compassionate to my family and neighbors in the evening and go off to the camps the next day and continue the mass exterminations."

In exercising this logic, there is a kind of religious quality to the behavior of the Nazi physicians. They tended to surrender to "higher authorities" in the bureaucracy with unquestioning obedience, the way religious individuals sometimes surrender to the "higher authority" of the divine. The techno-bureaucratic order represented a kind of sacral order in which one participates by engaging in a total surrender of self in unquestioning obedience. The presence of the bureaucracy is (like God) experienced as awesome and overwhelming. The will of the bureaucracy was so massive and omnipresent that the Nazi physicians typically said they felt that their refusal to perform their duties would not change anything. The bureaucracy was impervious to individual choice. If they didn't do the selecting someone else would. Moreover, they said they did not feel responsible because the Jews who arrived in the camps were dead already. Their fate had been sealed by bureaucratic decisions long before they arrived. The physicians were merely cogs in the machine; instruments of a higher authority.

What doubling did was allow the individual physician to be integrated into the hierarchical order of a technical bureaucracy. Bureaucracy neutralizes our capacity to be ethical by separating ends and means. Unlike our personal life, where we choose both what we shall do (ends) and how we shall accomplish it (means), in a bureaucracy those higher up in authority are believed to be in the best position to see the big picture and choose the ends. Those technical experts lower down in the hierarchy are simply expected to use their knowledge and skill, with unquestioning obedience, to provide the means for carrying out ends chosen by others. Not having chosen the ends, they did not feel responsible for their actions. Again and again at the Nuremberg trials, Nazi bureaucrats argued: "I am not guilty. I had no choice. I was just following orders." Consequently, the demonic capacity to instigate mass death appears (at least in this instance) to be fostered by a total surrender to a sacred order in unquestioning obedience, through a process of doubling accompanied by narratives that reconcile killing and healing – a myth of life through death.

The parallel to Martin Luther's Christian ethics

For anyone familiar with the history of Germany as the seat of the Protestant Reformation led by Martin Luther, the precedents for "doubling" and "killing in order to heal" are striking. They reveal links not only to neo-paganism but also to Christianity. For while the Nazi story had a neo-pagan content, there are structural similarities between it and the Christian ethics of Martin Luther. Luther stood in a line of Christian thinkers, starting with Augustine or Hippo (354–430), who divided society into two realms – the religious and the secular. Augustine called these "the city of God" and "the city of man." The city of God represented the biblical tradition hidden within the larger history of civilization – the city of man. The church and its bishops represented the city of God on earth and the city of man ought to serve it in all things religious. However, in all things secular, the church ought to be subservient to the political order of the city of man, represented by kings and emperors. When this balance is maintained, God's rule is manifest in both spheres.

Luther expressed this by saying that God rules the world with both his right and his left hand. With the right he rules with grace, compassion, and forgiveness over the individual human heart through the Gospel proclaimed by the church. With the left hand, God rules with justice and wrath through the state in order to punish sinners. Paradoxically, God must always rule with both hands simultaneously, because at best human beings are always saints and sinners at the same time. The significance of this becomes clear for our reflections when we look at what Luther had to say about the role of the public executioner. He argued that one could be a loving, forgiving and compassionate Christian in one's personal life and still go to work every day as a hangman, conducting public executions. Unlike the medieval Catholic tradition, which argued that the public executioner must do penance after an execution, Luther argued that this was not necessary since, in his public role, the executioner was not acting for himself but for the state, and the state was acting for God. Thus it was not the individual but God who did the actual killing.

What is equally troubling is the narrative that accompanies Luther's ethic. Luther speaks of God as a hidden God with whom he wrestles (on the model of Jacob wrestling with the stranger in Genesis 32: 23–32) in an inner struggle. This God reveals himself paradoxically through opposites. Thus Luther tells us that:

> *When God brings to life, he does it by killing*, when he justifies, he does it by making guilty; when he exalts to heaven, he does it by leading to hell. . . . And finally, God cannot be God unless he first becomes a devil, and we cannot go to heaven unless we first go into hell, and cannot become the children of God, unless we first become the Devil's children. . . . We have spoken in extreme terms of this, and we must understand what is just as startling, that God's grace and truth, or his good-ness and faithfulness, rule over us and *demand our obedience*. . . . For a little while I must accord divinity to the Devil, and consider our God to be the Devil. But this does not mean that the evening lasts for the whole day. Ultimately, his steadfast love and faithfulness are over us. [Psalms 117: 2] (Ebeling 1964, 1970: 236–7, emphasis added)

This theme of bringing to life through killing did not originate with Luther but goes back to Augustine of Hippo (354–430), who, in his *Confessions,* inter-preted his own inner struggles as a wrestling with the God "who give[s] wounds in order to heal, who kill[s] us lest we should die away from you" (Augustine 1963: 42).

Parallels to the Bhagavad Gita

This pattern of total surrender in unquestioning obedience, doubling, and "killing in order to heal" has a cross-cultural significance that becomes apparent when we look at the story of the testing of the first atomic bomb. Robert Oppenheimer's recalling the words of the Hindu scripture, the *Bhagavad Gita*, at the Trinity test site is very revealing. It is as if in a moment of inverse enlight-enment or revelation, the religious symbols of East and West clashed and ex-ploded within his head, giving birth to a seemingly new type of religious experience, which we have described as a demonic inversion of the holy. It seems he chose the name "Trinity" for the experimental bombsite under the influence of the seventeenth-century poet John Donne, whose poetry explored the relationship of religion to death and suicide. General Groves wrote to Oppenheimer to ask why he chose the code name "Trinity" for the site. Oppenheimer responded: "Why I chose the name is not clear, but I know what thoughts were in my mind. There is a poem of John Donne, written just before his death ["Hymn to God My God, in My Sicknesse"], which I know and love. From it a quotation:

> As West and East
> In all flatt Maps – and I am one – are one,
> So death doth touch the Resurrection.
> *(Rhodes 1986: 571–2)* "

The poem, says Richard Rhodes in his recounting of the event, suggested to Oppenheimer the paradox that as "dying leads to death but might also lead to resurrection – as the bomb for [Niels] Bohr and Oppenheimer was a weapon of death that might also end war and redeem mankind." Oppenheimer, in his letter, admits "that still does not make a Trinity. . . . But in another, better-known devotional poem Donne opens, 'Batter my heart, three person'd God.' Beyond this, I have no clues whatever" (Rhodes 1986: 572).

Oppenheimer was not fully conscious of the connection between the two poems that haunted him, but the link is clear when the two are compared. For like the first passage, a reading of Donne's "Holy Sonnets" shows that it also explores the theme of redemption through destruction.

> Batter my heart, three-personed God; for You
> As yet but knock, breathe, shine, and seek to mend;
> That I may rise and stand, o'erthrow me, and bend
> Your force to break, blow, burn, and make me new.
> *(Donne 1962: 785)*

Donne's *14th Holy Sonnet* describes the narrative theme of wrestling with the God who wounds in order to heal and slays in order to make alive. It is the metaphorical appropriation of the biblical story of Jacob, wrestling with the stranger (Genesis 32: 23–32). However, unlike the Jewish (and also the literal biblical) account, the Christian version of that story, the version offered by two of the greatest thinkers of Christianity, Augustine and Luther, inverts the meaning of the biblical narrative so that it is said that God not only "wounds in order to heal" but also "slays in order to make alive." It is the version that allows the self (in this case, Oppenheimer) to deal with its uneasy conscience by doubling, in which the second or professional self, through an ethic of unquestioning obedience, will do what he must do no matter how distasteful this is to the first self.

Drawn to the imagery of Donne's poems, Oppenheimer found there a logic to justify his actions. Although the bomb would do unheard-of damage and unleash a terrible new power in the world, still the very awesomeness of the power of the bomb would bring an end to the war and make new life possible. However, on the day of Trinity, when the bomb became a reality, it was not the Christian Trinity but the words of Vishnu (in the Hindu scripture, the *Bhagavad Gita*), one of the deities of the Hindu Trinity, who brings cosmic destruction, that seemed more appropriate.

If we turn to the *Gita* passage Oppenheimer quoted from memory, we discover that the more typical translation is "Time am I" rather than "I am become Death." Either, however, is a legitimate translation, for time brings death. As the passage makes clear, time is the power of death, the destroyer of worlds. But what follows is especially interesting. Thus Vishnu says to Arjuna:

> Do what thou wilt, all these warriors shall cease to be,
> Drawn up [there] in their opposing ranks.
> And so arise, win glory,
> Conquer thine enemies and enjoy a prosperous kingdom!
> Long since have these men in truth been slain by Me,
> Thine is to be the mere occasion.
> *(Zaehner 1938, 1966: 297–8)*

We shall return to the *Bhagavad Gita* and the other stories mentioned in this chapter later on, where we will examine them in more detail. For now it is sufficient to know that Arjuna belongs to the Kshatriya caste of warriors and nobility. He is, however, a warrior who chooses not to go to war against his own relatives even though the war is just. He wishes neither to kill nor be killed. Krishna, his chariot driver, instructs him in the paths to Hindu enlightenment or spiritual insight. Krishna's goal is to convince him that it is his caste duty as a warrior to fight. As long as he is not "attached to the fruits of his actions" (that is, as long as he does not act from personal motives such as ambition or greed), but rather does his duty selflessly, he will not accrue any negative karma – that is, he will be ethically blameless. Indeed, "though he slay these thousands he is no slayer."

Krishna, it turns out, is really the human incarnation of the all-highest deity, Vishnu. And then, in chapter 11 of the *Gita*, Krishna reveals his true identity to Arjuna in an awesome vision. And what is his message? Arjuna need not feel any guilt for killing his kinsmen for he is not really their slayer. He, Vishnu, is the real slayer of all men. All he asks of Arjuna is that he do his duty selflessly and in unquestioning obedience. Here we have an archetypal example of the logic of doubling. This is the logic we found in Luther's hangman. We also found this same demonic logic among the Nazi doctors, only instead of God it was nature and bureaucracy that decreed life and death, and absolved these physicians of responsibility for their actions by declaring: "Long since have these men in truth been slain by Me, Thine is to be the mere occasion" (Zaehner 1938, 1966: 298).

The unconscious link that Oppenheimer made between Trinity and Vishnu is more than accidental. It symbolizes the meeting of East and West at Hiroshima, religiously and culturally, in the eruption of the demonic. And it points to the presence of the phenomenon of doubling in more than one religious and cultural tradition. The point is that whether we are speaking of religions East or West, the predominant language of religion has been that of total surrender in unquestioning obedience to higher authority – a language that encourages doubling and the eruption of the demonic in some form of "killing in order to heal." However, after Auschwitz and Hiroshima there must be no unquestioning obedience, not even to God, for, as Irving Greenberg argues, such obedience leads to SS-type loyalties.

The point to be grasped with regard to the convergence of religious experiences, East and West, at Trinity in the New Mexico desert is: whether we speak of the Hindu Trinity or the Christian Trinity, we are speaking of narrative traditions that sacralize death. Both the stories of Vishnu and of the Christian trinitarian God we have referred to differ from the Jewish stories of wrestling with God in one important respect. The religious visions of Arjuna, as well as Augustine, Luther, and Donne, envision a God who "wounds in order to heal and slays in order to make alive," while the God who comes as a stranger to wrestle with Jacob (Genesis 32: 23–32) "wounds in order to heal" but does not slay in order to make alive. In this story Jacob is accosted by a stranger who wrestles with him until daybreak. Jacob demands that the stranger identify himself but he will not. Instead, he requires Jacob to identify himself and then blesses him, and promptly changes his name to Israel, meaning *wrestler with God*, "for you have striven with God and with humans, and have prevailed" (Genesis 32: 28). And as the sun rises and the stranger flees, Jacob walks away limping, resolving to call the place Peniel, meaning "I have seen God face to face and yet my life is preserved" (32: 31). Donne, Luther, and Augustine invert the meaning of the biblical story so that the one who wrestles with God must lose, surrendering to become unquestioningly obedient. We shall explore the alternative ethical implications of the Jewish reading of the story shortly.

Parallels to Japanese Buddhism and neo-Confucianism

The myth of life through death played a defining role not only in Germany and America during World War II, but also in Japan. This point can be illustrated with the story told by the great eighteenth-century Buddhist Zen master, Hakuin.

> If you wish to attain the true Nonego [the Buddhist state of "no-self" or enlightenment] you must release your hold over the abyss. If thereafter you revive you will come upon the true ego of the four virtues. What does it mean to release one's hold over the abyss? A man went astray and arrived at a spot which had never been trodden by the foot of man. Before him there yawned a bottomless

chasm. His feet stood on the slippery moss of a rock and no secure foothold appeared around him. He could step neither forward nor backward. Only death awaited him. The vine which he grasped with his left hand and the tendril which he held with his right hand could offer him little help. His life hung as by a single thread. Were he to release both hands at once, his dry bones would come to nought. Thus it is with the Zen disciple. By pursuing a single *koan** he comes to a point where his mind is as if dead and his will as if extinguished. This state is like a wide void over a deep chasm and no hold remains for hand or foot. All thoughts vanish and in his bosom burns hot anxiety. But then suddenly it occurs that with the *koan* both body and mind break. This is the instant when the hands are released over the abyss. In this sudden upsurge it is as if one drinks water and knows for oneself heat and cold. Great joy wells up. This is called rebirth (in the Pure Land). This is termed seeing into one's own nature. Everything depends on pushing forward and not doubting that with the help of this concentration one will eventually penetrate to the ground of one's own nature. (Dumoulin 1963: 258–9)

Hakuin taught that true spiritual enlightenment occurs through a process which begins with the *Great Doubt*, proceeds to the *Great Death*, and ends in the *Great Joy*. In the first stage you are "overcome by a feeling of anxious, horrendous fear" as you doubt that life has any meaning – that there is a state of religious liberation. Even if there is such a liberation, you doubt that you can achieve it. In such a state you are stalemated and cannot proceed any further. The only way out is *Great Death*, the death of the ego-self, which in turn opens the gate to the *Great Joy* of spiritual enlightenment.

This Buddhist myth of life through death was embodied in the Bushido ethic of the Samurai warrior with its deep roots in the Zen Buddhist tradition, which shaped the national ethos of Japan. This ethic did for Japan what Luther's ethic of unquestioning obedience did for Germany. In his study of *Tokugawa Religions*, Robert Bellah argues that, while it began as a warrior ethic, through its amalgamation with Confucian morality it became the heart of Japanese national morality. Its central themes were militarism, especially absolute obedience to one's feudal lord, and a preoccupation with death and the ethic of honor as found expressed in the traditional ritual of *sepuku* (ritual suicide). "It is said, 'Bushido' means the determined will to die." A Bushido manual, the *Hagakure*, offers the following instruction: "Every morning make up thy mind how to die. Every evening freshen thy mind in the thought of death. And let this be done without end. Thus will thy mind be prepared. When thy mind is always set on death, the way through life will always be straight and simple" (Bellah 1957: 91).

Meditation on death is meant to purify the self of all selfish desires and prepare one for the total sacrifice of oneself, if necessary, for one's feudal lord. This ethic of obedience unto death was taken up into the new cult of the emperor which developed in Meiji Japan preceding World War II, giving the role of the

---

* A koan is a riddle given by a Zen master to a student to trick the mind into spiritual insight.

emperor a central political importance out of all proportion to the role he had played in the prior history of Japan. The new emphasis on the sacred role of the emperor was used to legitimate the new Japanese state. Through their Shinto, Confucian, and Buddhist narrative traditions the Japanese saw Japan as a country with a destiny, decreed by nature to rule the world. Kosuke Koyama describes the Japanese mentality that led to World War II in terms reminiscent of the Germanic Aryan mythology.

> The nation was paralyzed under the tyranny of the divine mythology. When the best of Japanese scholars were banned, the exercise of reason was condemned and the people were fed with unreasoned slogans which proclaimed that Japan was the righteous nation and her enemy was devilish. The world seemed divided into two camps, that of good people and that of the bad. The Japanese were good and the United States was the focus of all evil. (Koyama 1984: 34)

When one inserts the Bushido ethic into such a sacred cosmological–mythological story, the results are not dissimilar to those which occurred with the transformation of Luther's ethic of obedience in Nazi Germany under the myth of the pure Aryan race.

What Auschwitz and Hiroshima teach us is that the surrender to the myth of life through death in all its religious and even secular forms leads to "killing in order to heal" as a justification of mass death. The unconscious surrender to the sacral power of the ethnocentric techno-bureaucratic state has its training ground in the conscious surrender of one's will and one's whole being, advocated by the dominant forms of virtually all religions, East and West. After Auschwitz and Hiroshima, we can no longer afford the luxury of an unadulterated mythology of life through death, not even when it is sublimely transmuted, for instance, by Buddhist or Christian spirituality, into a language of self-transformation. We need not an ethic that sacralizes death but one that sanctifies life. We need not a sacral ethic but an ethic of secular holiness that champions human dignity, human rights, and human liberation against all mythologies of *killing in order to heal* with audacious tenacity.

The Way of All the Earth: Global Ethics and Tales of Divine Madness

From Abraham and Siddhartha to Tolstoy, Gandhi, and King

After Auschwitz, says Holocaust scholar Irving Greenberg, "nothing dare evoke our absolute, unquestioning loyalty, not even our God, for this leads to possibilities of SS loyalties" (1977: 38). The path from Auschwitz to Hiroshima and nuclear MADness only reinforces the truth of Greenberg's observation. Equating authentic religious self-transcendence with the total surrender of the self in unquestioning obedience is ethically and politically hazardous. Such an equation occurs within a narrative context that interprets life as warfare. The conditions of war are unique, in that during them we suspend ordinary ethical conventions and invert ordinary ethical norms so as to make a virtue out of killing. Narratives of warfare invert the symbolism of the holy so as to sacralize a particular way of life and render it more sacred than the dignity of the stranger. Narratives of warfare inevitably cast an impending conflict in apocalyptic terms, seeing the struggle as a sacred task whose purpose is to ritually purify sacred space by eliminating the profane other (the stranger) who threatens the sacred order of one's society.

However, an ethic of total self-surrender in unquestioning obedience is not the only option made available by the history of religions. For there are, in this history, not only narrative traditions of apocalyptic conflict but also narrative traditions of utopian audacity on behalf of the stranger – traditions as old as Abraham and Siddhartha, and as recent as Gandhi and King. If apocalyptic narratives require a demonic doubling so as to kill in order to heal, utopian narratives encourage dreams of a new world in which one welcomes the stranger and acts with audacity in defense of the stranger's dignity. Utopian stories will always seem mad, idealistic, and unrealistic in a world of violence. And such stories do in fact invite a kind of divine madness that inverts the meaning of sacred stories of war and transforms them into stories which encourage a non-violent struggle in defense of human dignity – even, and especially, if the stranger is one's enemy.

For not all forms of religious spirituality require unquestioning obedience. As we have already suggested, in opposition to the sacred society stand the traditions of holy communities that call into question the sacred order of things. Socrates said he was sent by God as a gadfly to the city of Athens to question its sacred morality. The Buddha said that no one should accept his teachings on his authority but rather question all things and seek direct insight. One of the most powerful of these alternative traditions of spirituality is the Jewish narrative tradition of audacity, or chutzpah. This is a narrative tradition that has its roots in the story of Abraham's confrontation with God over Sodom and Gomorrah, in which Abraham expresses audacity (chutzpah) in defense of the stranger. God declares his intention to destroy the city of Sodom because evil is rampant within its borders. Fearing that God will slay the innocent along with the guilty, Abraham has the audacity to argue with God, insisting: "Shall not the judge of all, also be just?" (Genesis 18: 25). Such chutzpah declares that no authority, whether sacred or secular, divine or human, may violate the dignity and integrity of another human being. For any authority to command such a violation is for it to undermine its own authority – even if that be God.

After Auschwitz and Hiroshima, what we need is an ethic of audacity. Every spirituality that asks for a total surrender of will or of self opens itself up to demonic possibilities. We fear that such spiritual disciplines are training grounds in fanaticism which blurs the distinction between God and the techno-bureaucratic state (or other finite authorities) and leads to the dehumanization of the chosen victims of such authority. And yet, as we proceed in this text, we will explore the possibility that this is not always the case. For if a sacral surrender leads to unquestioning obedience, it may still be that a surrender to the holy leads in just the opposite direction – that of audacity. The only authentic faith is one grounded in a spirituality of questioning, a faith prepared to call even God (or whatever is held either sacred or holy) into question. The difference between God or "the holy" and the idol is that idols do not tolerate dissent. The test of authentic spirituality is ethical – the possibility of dissent against all authority in order to protect human dignity.

Therefore the stories we have been telling about the way religion and technology have merged to create the apocalyptic madness of Auschwitz and Hiroshima are not the only stories that need to be told. If they were, we might all go mad. But alongside the apocalyptic madness of the modern and post/modern world we can trace the threads of another set of stories, stories of divine madness. For in the hands of some whose narrative imaginations have been shaped by the holy rather than the sacred, the stories of life through death have been transformed into stories of life against death – stories not of unquestioning obedience but of civil disobedience and audacity on behalf of the dignity of the stranger.

Such stories of divine madness are about audacity and civil disobedience on behalf of human dignity, human rights, and human liberation. To speak of human dignity, rights, and liberation is to suggest a vocabulary for a cross-cultural ethic in defiance of modern cultural and ethical relativism. It suggests that despite our cultural differences, all persons, in some sense, share a common humanity. Just how such an ethic is possible is precisely the issue we are about to explore. One can scarcely speak of human dignity, human rights, and human liberation in our world without thinking of the extraordinary accomplishments of the tradition of non-violence forged by three individuals from diverse religions and cultures: the Eastern Orthodox Russian author and novelist Leo Tolstoy, the Hindu spiritual leader Mahatma Gandhi, and the Southern Baptist preacher Martin Luther King, Jr. What the lives of these three individuals suggest to us is that it is possible for narrative diversity to generate a shared ethic without sacrificing the diversity of the particular traditions.

When one thinks of non-violence one thinks first of all of Mahatma Gandhi. It is no secret that Gandhi's encounter with Jesus' Sermon on the Mount was a major factor motivating him to turn to the great Hindu story of Arjuna and Krishna from the *Bhagavad Gita*, in order to find the message of non-violence within his own religion and culture. But people do not always recall that it was Gandhi's encounter with the writings of the great Russian novelist Tolstoy which drew his attention to the full power of the Sermon on the Mount.

Tolstoy came from the wealthy classes of landed gentry in Russia, and his novels brought him not only fame but fortune. And yet in the middle years of his life he experienced a great crisis and underwent a conversion. As a result he freed his serfs, gave away all his wealth, and spent the rest of his life serving the poor and attempting to live by the Sermon on the Mount. While Gandhi's Hinduism was clearly influenced by Tolstoy's Christianity, it is equally important to note that Tolstoy's Christianity in turn was deeply indebted to Buddhism. For Tolstoy's conversion was brought about in part by reading a story from the lives of the saints about a monk named Barlaam who brought about the conversion of a young Indian prince named Josaphat. The historian of religions Wilfred Cantwell Smith has traced the history of this story. He notes that Tolstoy was converted to the Christian life as spelled out in the Sermon on the Mount upon hearing a thinly disguised version of the life of the Buddha, which had made its way into the lives of the saints (Smith 1981: 6–11).

The story is that of Josaphat, a wealthy young prince who gave up wealth, power, and family in order to seek an answer to the problems of old age, sickness, and death. In the midst of his urgent quest he met a Syrian monk, Barlaam, who told him a parable about a man who fell into a well and is hanging on for dear life to two vines. Along come two mice, one white and one black, that begin to chew on the vines, so that before long the vines will be severed and the man will plunge to his death. This parable depicts the man's spiritual situation in which the mice represent night and day, the forces of time eroding his life and bringing him surely to his death. The paradox, spiritually speaking, is that instead of waiting for death to come he must learn to let go now, for if he no longer clings to his life but gives it up to God his spiritual death will lead to new life.

A century before Tolstoy, in Japan, the great Zen master Hakuin (1685–1768), as we have seen, told a similar story about a man who clung to the side of a cliff and had to learn to let go so as to experience the "Great Death" of enlightenment or non-attachment, a Great Death that paradoxically gives way to the "Great Joy" of achieving "No-Self" (Dumoulin 1963: 258–9). The parallel between these two stories is no accident, for the same story and the same parable made their way not only from India into China and Japan, but also from India through Persia into the Mediterranean world and eventually into Northern Europe. Versions of the story can be found in Greek, Latin, in Czech and Polish, in Italian, Spanish, French, German, Swedish, Norwegian, and Icelandic, as well as Arabic, Hebrew, and Yiddish. The story seems to have made its way into virtually all the world's religions. The Greek version came into Christianity from an Islamic (Arabic) version, which is how it passed into Judaism as well. The Muslims, in turn, got it from the Manichees in Persia, who got it from the Buddhists in India. The Latin *Josaphat* is a translation of the Greek *Loasaf*, which is a translation of the Arabic *Yudasaf*, which is a translation of the Persian *Bodisaf*, which is a translation of the Sanskrit *Bodhisattva*, which is a title for the Buddha. The parable of the man clinging to a vine appears to be even older than the story of the Buddha and may go back to Hindu, Jain, and even pre-Aryan sources (Smith 1981: 6–11). The story of the prince, Siddhartha (see chapter 6), who renounces the world, and of the accompanying parable, allows us to see the profound ways in which the narrative traditions of the world's religions can be interdependent. For if Gandhi came to appreciate the message of non-violence through exposure to the life and teachings of Tolstoy, it turns out that Tolstoy's conversion itself represents a convergence of the life stories of two of the greatest teachers of non-violence in the history of religions – Siddhartha Gautama and Jesus of Nazareth. But what Gandhi found lacking in Tolstoy's understanding of the Sermon on the Mount he found present in the *Bhagavad Gita*, namely, the notion of non-violence as an active rather than a passive virtue – that is, as capable of producing an active resistance to evil. The spiritual genius of Gandhi, as we shall see (in chapter 5), was to transform the metaphor of warfare in the *Bhagavad Gita* from one which authorized unquestioning obedience and killing in order to heal into one which authorized and demanded an audacity on behalf of the stranger. In so doing, Gandhi transformed the *Gita* into a story of non-violence on a par with the story of Jacob wrestling with the stranger and Jesus' Sermon on the Mount. Wrestling with the stranger does not have to lead to conquest any more than turning the other cheek has to lead to cooperation with evil. Both can be combined in an audacity on behalf of the stranger that is expressed in an active civil disobedience against unjust laws and on behalf of human dignity.

When Martin Luther King, Jr. embraced Gandhi's teachings on non-violence he was in fact drawing on the mystical and ethical insight of at least four great religious traditions: Hinduism, Buddhism, Christianity, and Judaism. Both Gandhi and King also explicitly drew on the Socratic witness to civil disobedience as an expression of audacity. What Tolstoy's, Gandhi's, and King's ethic of non-violence illustrates is that narrative traditions are not mutually exclusive worlds. People whose lives are shaped by dramatically different narratives can share a common ethical commitment to human dignity and human liberation. Moreover, what Gandhi's life illustrates (as we shall see) is that even narrative traditions of total surrender and unquestioning obedience can be rehabilitated and transformed into traditions of audacity, the way Gandhi transformed the *Bhagavad Gita* from a story authorizing killing in order to heal into a story of radical non-violent resistance (the audacity of civil disobedience) to evil.

Global ethics: the way of all the earth

The world as we know it is passing away. The great world religions like Judaism, Christianity, and Islam, or Hinduism and Buddhism, or Taoism and Confucianism, go back to the beginnings of civilization and are deeply bound up with the civilizations in which they emerged: the Middle East, India, and China. In the past these religions and cultures lived in relative isolation from one another. There were many histories in the world but no world history. Our situation is dramatically different. For today we live at the beginning of a new millennium that is marked by the emergence of world history. We are in the process of forging a global civilization.

The spiritual heritages of the human race have become our common inheritance, forming a rich ecology that can provide us with the wisdom we need to guide us into the coming millennium. The more complex an ecology is, the more stable it is. And the more simplified an ecology becomes, the more unstable it becomes, until it reaches a point where it is in danger of collapsing, unable to support life. The important thing to remember is that ecological diversity and complexity sustain life. This is as true for world culture as it is for nature. The time when a new world religion (or even a more secular metanarrative) could be founded – the time of a Moses, Jesus, Siddhartha, or Muhammad – says contemporary theologian John Dunne, has passed. The spiritual adventure of our post/modern world is different. Rather than taking our guidance from a single metanarrative derived from only one religion or culture, it must involve a search for ethical wisdom drawn from the narrative diversity of an emerging global civilization.

> The holy man of our time, it seems, is not a figure like Gotama [the Buddha] or Jesus or Muhammad, a man who could found a world religion, but a figure like Gandhi, a man who passes over by sympathetic understanding from his own religion to other religions and comes back again with new insight to his own. Passing over and coming back, it seems, is the spiritual adventure of our time. (Dunne 1972: ix)

What is required today is not the conquest of the world by any one religion or culture but a meeting and sharing of religious and cultural insight. Our common future depends upon our capacity to welcome the stranger, that is, our capacity for hospitality.

The spiritual adventure of passing over into the life of the stranger and coming back with new insight is a world-transforming process whose results have been keenly felt in the emergence of a global ethic of non-violent resistance to all assaults against the sanctity of human dignity. It illustrates the way in which comparative religious ethics can advance a normative ethic through cross-cultural dialogue without resorting to insistence that one exclusive metanarrative be embraced by all. If this is still, in some sense, a metanarrative, it is one that is self-negating. That is, it rejects exclusivity and authorizes diversity.

Alfred North Whitehead once estimated that approximately 10 percent of the European population participated in the Renaissance and yet the Renaissance transformed Europe. The global ethic we are seeking in this book is one that seeks to be post/modern in that it does not envision itself as a totalizing ethic in which everyone must adhere to the same story. Ten percent of the world's population, engaged in passing over and coming back, working through the presence of diverse holy communities – Buddhist, Jewish, Christian, and other kindred religious and secular communities – can be a saving remnant. This would be a remnant sufficient to create the public order necessary for the unity-in-diversity of a global civilization. That is, a public order that answers to the measure of human dignity, protects human rights, and brings about human liberation, even as it seeks to protect the earth itself.

The children of Gandhi surveyed in this book are members of the first generation after Auschwitz and Hiroshima. As such they represent the struggle of persons of conscience to create new modes of spirituality and ethics appropriate to a post/modern world – one that accepts the diversity of religions and cultures without succumbing to ethical relativism. They lived in the shadow of Auschwitz and Hiroshima and struggled to reverse the patterns of ethnocentric sacral prejudice and techno-bureaucratic rationality that led to these events; patterns that could lead to other such events if not contested with audacity. Their lives represent a rejection of the pre-modern and modern assumption that universality requires uniformity.

What their lives will teach us is that the ethical commitment to human dignity best thrives in the context of multiple communities and diverse stories, religious and non-religious, theistic and non-theistic. It is precisely this diversity in story and community (mythos and ethos) that can make a universal ethic of human rights possible as an ethic of human liberation, one capable of shaping public policy on a global level. If a human rights ethic were to be rooted in any one communal narrative alone, the danger of a religious and cultural imperialism would be grave. But the diversity of communal narrative traditions, provided they share one thing – a common commitment to welcoming the stranger – make it possible for them to create a mutually correcting, mutually balancing, moral ecology for an emerging global civilization. For if your story demands that you welcome the stranger, it contradicts the ethnocentric bias of all sacred stories, demanding that you recognize the human dignity of precisely the one who does not share your story. This recognition is a common characteristic of the "children" of Gandhi.

In the remainder of this book we shall explore comparative religious ethics as the practice of passing over into the stories and traditions of the stranger in order to return to one's own tradition with new insight. As we make the journey through the stories of the traditions of Part II, each of us must imagine ourselves to be in the situation of a Tolstoy, a Gandhi or a King, seeking shared spiritual insight as the basis for a cross-cultural ethic that can put an end to the apocalyptic madness and create a utopian new beginning for a global civilization of shared wisdom. Then, in Part III, we shall conclude with a discussion of how the inclusion of the missing voices of women is contributing to this wisdom by bringing East and West together in an ethic that defends not only human dignity, but the ecological integrity of our natural environment, without which there can be neither humanity nor dignity. Our goal is to find a way that promotes life rather than death for *all* the earth.

Questions for Discussion

1   What does it mean to say that Auschwitz and Hiroshima are formative religious events that represent the demonic inversion of the holy? Give examples.

2 How does techno-bureaucratic organization function to undermine ethical consciousness? Give examples.

3 Explain the narrative and psychological–organizational aspects of demonic doubling by comparing Luther, the Nazi doctors, and Oppenheimer.

4 In what sense can the Nazi doctors be considered to have engaged in a religious surrender of will?

5 In what ways can Auschwitz and Hiroshima be said to symbolize the ethical challenge of modernity?

6 Explain why Auschwitz is, and Hiroshima is not, an example of genocide.

7 What is the link between the narrative of Jacob wrestling with the stranger and narratives of "killing in order to heal"?

8 What is the difference between an ethic of obedience and an ethic of audacity (give examples), and why is the latter of special significance after Auschwitz and Hiroshima?

9 Why do narratives of war have a particularly problematic impact on the moral life?

10 Why are the lives of Tolstoy, Gandhi, and King significant for studying ethics after Auschwitz and Hiroshima?

11 Explain the processes of "passing over" and "coming back" and their significance for creating a post/modern ethic.

12 In what sense do "passing over" and "coming back" express a spirituality that facilitates an ethic of hospitality to the stranger, and how does this spirituality contribute to the emergence of a cross-cultural and interreligious ethic?

References

Augustine, St. 1963. *Confessions*, trans. Rex Warner. New York: Mentor-Omega.

Bellah, Robert. 1957. *Tokugawa Religions: The Cultural Roots of Modern Japan*. New York: Free Press.

Cohen, Arthur A. 1981. *The Tremendum*. New York: Crossroad Books.

Dawidowicz, Lucy. 1975. *The War Against the Jews*. New York: Holt, Rinehart, & Winston.

Donne, John. 1962. "Holy Sonnets." In *The Norton Anthology of English Literature*, Vol. 1. New York: W. W. Norton & Co.

Dumoulin, Heinrich, SJ. 1963. *A History of Zen Buddhism*. Boston: Beacon Press.

Dunne, John S. 1972. *The Way of All the Earth*. Notre Dame, IN: University of Notre Dame Press.

Ebeling, Gerhard. 1964, 1970. *Luther: An Introduction to his Thought*. Philadelphia: Fortress Press.

Greenberg, Irving. 1977. "Cloud of Smoke, Pillar of Fire; Judaism, Christianity, and Modernity After the Holocaust." In Eva Fleischner (ed.), *Auschwitz: Beginning of a New Era?* New York: KTAV Publishing House.

Hoyt, Edwin. 1986. *Japan's War*. New York: Da Capo Press.

Koyama, Kosuke. 1984. *Mount Fuji and Mount Sinai: A Critique of Idols*. Maryknoll, NY: Orbis Books.

Lifton, Robert Jay. 1967. *Death in Life*. New York: Basic Books.

——. 1986. *The Nazi Doctors: Medical Killing and the Psychology of Genocide*. New York: Basic Books.

——. 1987. *The Future of Immortality*. New York: Basic Books.

Lindsey, Hal, with C. C. Carlson. 1970. *The Late Great Planet Earth*. New York: Bantam Books.

Lyotard, Jean-François. 1979, 1984. *The Postmodern Condition*. Minneapolis: University of Minnesota Press.

Prabhavananda, Swami and Isherwood, Christopher (trans.). 1944, 1951, 1972. *The Song of God: Bhagavad-Gita*. New York: Mentor, New American Library.

Rhodes, Richard. 1986. *The Making of the Atomic Bomb*. New York: Simon & Schuster.

Rubenstein, Richard. 1975. *The Cunning of History*. New York: Harper & Row.

Smith, Wilfred Cantwell. 1981. *Towards a World Theology*. Philadelphia: Westminster Press.

Wiesel, Elie. 1958, 1960. *Night*. New York: Hearst, Avon Books.

——. 1965. *One Generation After*. New York: Avon Books.

Wyden, Peter. 1984. *Day One: Before Hiroshima and After*. New York: Simon & Schuster.

Zaehner, R. C. (trans.) 1938, 1966. *Hindu Scriptures*. New York: Dutton & Dent, Everyman's Library.

PART II

WAR AND PEACE: ANCIENT STORIES AND POST/MODERN LIFE STORIES

INTRODUCTION: ETHICS AFTER AUSCHWITZ AND HIROSHIMA

After Auschwitz and Hiroshima, neither the Western explanation of suffering as divine punishment for sin nor the Eastern explanation of suffering as the result of one's own karma (the result of the evil deeds of one's past lives) seem plausible. Both end up blaming the victims for their own suffering. What is needed, we argue, is a sense of outrage against unjust suffering that results in ethical action to prevent it. Masao Abe argues that Buddhism, Christianity, and Judaism offer three different models of the relationship between religion and ethics. In Buddhism there is a mutual negation between religion and ethics. Spiritual enlightenment results in ethics being left behind to be replaced by universal compassion which, Abe insists, transcends the judgmental character of ethics. In Christianity ethics (doing good) cannot lead to religion or salvation because the human will is corrupted by sin and cannot freely will to do what is good. However, spiritual conversion through the grace of God can heal the human will and make it possible for one to do what is good. So religion can make the ethical life possible. In both Buddhism and Christianity the self cannot know the highest good apart from a spiritual transformation of identity, so the self must be slain in order to be healed. However, in Judaism, Abe argues, there is a two-way street between religion and ethics – God can demand justice of humans and humans can have the audacity to demand justice from God. Consequently, he says, there is no death of the self in Judaism. This spiritual audacity, we have argued in chapter 2, is an important premise for all ethics after Auschwitz and Hiroshima if there is to be a meaningful protest against all sacred authorities that foster injustice and unjust suffering. These three types of relation between religion and ethics offer us a beginning hypothesis for comparative religious ethics, one that will have to be modified after careful study.

The modern story of human existence tells us that humanity is on a journey of progress through history. It is this enlightened age of critical scientific rationality which will guarantee the progress of the human race. But the secular Enlightenment belief in science, rationality and the inevitability of historical progress has been dealt a devastating blow by the events of Auschwitz and Hiroshima. It is no longer possible to believe, as modern advertising once promised, that because of modern technology "every day, in every way, our life is getting better and better." Science, technology, and reason have led, not to a utopian world of perfection, but to the pillar of fire and cloud of smoke which arose out of the abyss of mass death.

And if secular scientific and technical reason has failed us, it is tempting to seek an answer in a return to religion and the sacred. But after Auschwitz and Hiroshima, it is also an open question whether any religious vision of the world can survive unscathed. It is not only the Western belief in the providence of God as the Lord of history that founders on the rocks of Auschwitz and Hiroshima but also the Asian narrative traditions of karmic rebirth embraced by Hindus and Buddhists. Karma plays the role in their worldview (the myths of liberation) that Providence does in the myths of history that came out of the Middle East. It answers the question: Why do we each undergo the particular fortunes and misfortunes that we do? Religious ways of viewing the world deny that the events of people's lives are pure meaningless chance. Both the myths of history and the myths of liberation, for example, argue that there is a hidden purpose at work in all human lives. In the myth of history this purpose is explained as the "will of God." The world is a just world, because the God who governs it is just. At the end of one's life a final judgment will occur in which punishment and reward will even out the injustices of this life. In the Hindu and Buddhist myths of liberation, people are thought to have more than one life. What happens to one in any given lifetime is explained in terms of the cosmic law of karma. Fortune and misfortune come to one in this life because of good or evil deeds done in past lives. The universe is always just, for everybody always gets exactly what they deserve. The events of Auschwitz and Hiroshima seem to call both these types of cosmic stories, as well as the ethical assumptions that flow from them, into question.

For many, it is difficult to believe in the God of Moses or Jesus or Muhammad – the God who leads his people through history toward the day of resurrection – after Auschwitz and Hiroshima. Why would a God who is all good and all loving lead people into the kingdom of death? It seems like work more fitting for the devil. How can this be the work of divine providence, that is, of a God who provides for his creatures? And even if God did not actively lead the Jews into the kingdom of death, why did he allow it to happen? In past misfortunes, pious Jews argued that they suffered in punishment for their sins. But this argument does not work for the Holocaust. As the Jewish philosopher Emil Fackenheim has argued, it was not faithless Jews being punished for their sins who died at Auschwitz but some of the most pious and observant Jews of Eastern Europe. Why did God not rescue them as he did when they were slaves in

Egypt? Likewise, the victims of Hiroshima seem to have suffered out of all proportion to any crime one could imagine in their past lives. "Indeed, Hiroshima and Auschwitz seem to have destroyed any kind of [belief in] Providence" (Fackenheim 1970: 6). Even the appeal to justice, punishment, and reward in a life after death seems hollow and inadequate. What state of affairs after death could possibly make up for the suffering and devastation of the victims of an Auschwitz or Hiroshima?

If, as Emil Fackenheim suggests, the idea of divine providence seems untenable after Auschwitz, the idea of karmic justice seems equally problematic. For example, Zen Buddhist scholar Masao Abe has sought to come to grips with Auschwitz and Hiroshima through a discussion with both Jews and Christians. We shall examine Buddhist ethics in some detail later. For now, it is sufficient to note that Buddhists hold that all things are constantly changing (the doctrine of *anicca*, or impermanence), and therefore nothing is eternal. This means, among other things, that there is no eternal self or soul and there is no eternal God. Rather, all things are constantly coming into being and going out of being in interdependence with all other things. The primary illusion of human beings is to think they have their "own being" (*svabhava*), that is, that one's own being is independent of what happens to all other beings. Spiritual enlightenment occurs when we experience that all things are really *empty* of their own being (they are anatta, or no-self, meaning no eternal self) because all things arise in interdependence (*paticca-samuppada*), and therefore nothing has its being independent of all other things.

Masao Abe interprets the law of karma within the context of the realization of interdependence and arrives at some startling conclusions. He insists that karma is not just individual. It is always more than personal – it is social and collective as well. Therefore, he argues:

> From the perspective of the Buddhist doctrine of karma, I am not free from responsibility for the Holocaust in Auschwitz. I must accept that "Auschwitz is a problem of my own karma. In the deepest sense I myself participated as well in the Holocaust." . . . The Holocaust is *ultimately* rooted in the fundamental ignorance (*avidya*) and the endless blind thirst to live inherent in human existence in which I am also deeply involved through my own individual karma. . . . I believe that only through . . . fundamental enlightenment as the realization of fundamental ignorance, can one properly and legitimately cope with such a historical evil as the Holocaust. (Abe 1990: 50, 51)

Abe goes on to argue that to look at Auschwitz from an ethical perspective in terms of "justice" is counterproductive, since ethical judgments lead to accusations and the accused parties tend to respond with counter-accusations, producing endless conflict. Such conflict only leads to the accumulation of further negative karma for everyone involved. In order to deal with events such as Auschwitz properly, Abe argues, one must achieve a level of spiritual insight that takes one beyond the level of ethics.

The Buddhist goal, says Abe, is to finally see the emptiness and relativity of the ethical dimension from a perspective that lies beyond it – the religious dimension of enlightenment (1990: 47). Abe believes Christianity, to some degree, shares such a relativizing attitude toward ethics; that is, both the Buddhist and Christian stories call for the spiritual death of the self, which Abe interprets as taking one beyond ethics. He sees the "self-emptying" of Christ as an analogue to the Buddhist experience of emptiness. He takes Paul's Letter to the Philippians 2: 5–8 as the key text – where Christ is described as not clinging to equality with God, rather he empties himself, taking on the form of a servant and "becoming obedient *even* unto death, yea, death of the cross" (1990: 9). Buddhism and Christianity find some of their deepest affinities, he perceptively suggests, in this ethic of obedience brought about by the realization that the total death of the self (the Buddhist "Great Death" and its parallel "Dying with Christ") leads precisely to a new level of consciousness (the Buddhist "Great Joy" and its parallel rising with Christ to become a new creature).

On this new plane of consciousness one engages in a kind of "teleological suspension of the ethical," to use a term coined by the Western philosopher Soren Kierkegaard. One must achieve a perspective beyond all ethical judgments of good and evil. From his Buddhist perspective, says Abe, "there is no continuous path from ethics to religion. In order to enter the realm of religion, human ethics must be overcome. Ethics must 'die'" (1990: 181). At the level of Buddhist-enlightened consciousness there are no dualistic ethical distinctions or judgments of good and bad, even as the Gospel narratives suggest that God's love, like the rain, falls equally on the just and the unjust alike (1990: 48, 49). To respond constructively to the Holocaust, we are told, one must get beyond the dualism of love and hate and realize its (i.e., the Holocaust's) "relationality and . . . nonsubstantiality" (1990: 52).

As Abe unfolds the full implications of karmic interdependence, this transmoral perspective, which relativizes all ethical judgments, leads to the problematic claim that somehow the victims of the Holocaust have in some way contributed to their own suffering and deserve what happened to them.

> In the ethical and relative dimension, responsibility for the Holocaust clearly resides in Nazi, not in Jewish, individuals. But the same Buddhist doctrine of karma teaches us that . . . in an immeasurable way, even the uttermost evil of the Holocaust is related to the innumerable events in the past and present of human history in which all of us, assailants *and victims* alike are involved. When we are victims of a horrible suffering such as what occurred in Auschwitz or Hiroshima, *we tend to absolutize the evil involved as if it happened to us passively, unrelated to our own karma.* (1990: 52; emphasis added)

What Abe is saying is that the suffering of the victims is related to their own karma. That is, if the victims of Auschwitz or Hiroshima suffer it must be because they deserve it because of some evil they have done in their past lives. However, this argument, like that Western argument that the victims were be-

ing punished for their sins, rather than convincing us, tends to have the opposite effect. Such explanations that blame the victims for their suffering seem
blasphemous in the face of the depth of that suffering. It is as if we need to find
meaning in the world so badly that we would rather believe all people deserve
the evil that happens to them than accept that there is no justice or meaning in
the world. But, we would argue, this makes the price of meaning too high.
After Auschwitz and Hiroshima, the lines between sacred and profane, religious
and non-religious, believer and non-believer, may have become blurred – but
not the line between good and evil. If anything, that line must become clearer
and no religious narrative vision must be exempted from that demand. At the
moment when the bomb dropped on Hiroshima, one survivor said: "I thought,
'There is no God, no Buddha . . . There is no God, no help'" (Lifton 1967:
373). This was not her last word: as time passed she was able to express some
faith and hope again. But whenever she recalled her experience at Hiroshima,
remembering those she was not able to help or save, Robert Lifton reports,
these reaffirmations would be overcome by her sense of death guilt – a phenomenon that survivors of both Auschwitz and Hiroshima manifest. This is a
profound feeling of guilt for having survived when so many others did not. The
survivor vacillates between moments of faith and hope and moments overwhelmed by the hopeless abyss of the demonic. This vacillation is similar to that
reported in Irving Greenberg's description of Jewish faith after Auschwitz as
"momentary faith," in which moments of renewed faith and hope alternate
with moments of hopelessness and despair and neither can be definitively eliminated (1977: 27). Indeed, Lifton describes the psychological state of Hiroshima survivors in just this way.

After Auschwitz and Hiroshima it would seem that the karmic narrative traditions of Buddhism and/or Hinduism cannot survive intact any more than the
biblical narratives of divine providence. All affirmations of meaning will have to
stare meaninglessness in the face. We humans may have to settle for, at best, a
partially meaningful world. The extraordinary passion for justice and human
dignity, which is uniquely emphasized in the biblical tradition, through the
prophets and the book of Job, has its roots, to a large degree, in the fact that the
biblical narrative traditions provide a much less adequate meaning system than
that provided by the narrative traditions of karmic rebirth found in Hinduism
and Buddhism. The difference between the Asian narratives of karma and the
Mediterranean narratives of divine providence at work in history illustrate the
trade-offs of different religious stories that are used to interpret human existence.

The karmic story of death and rebirth provides a good example of our claim
that our understanding of good and evil is shaped by the kind of story we think
we are in and the role we see ourselves playing in that story. Karmic narratives
provide a vision of multiple lifetimes through which perfect justice is always
accomplished, for everyone always gets exactly what he/she deserves. If someone is poor, or suffers injustice in this life, it is assumed that he or she deserves

it as a punishment for evil deeds done in a previous life. All suffering therefore is viewed as just. This means that such narratives undermine the possibility of experiencing suffering as unjust and therefore of experiencing the kind of moral outrage and indignation expressed in the biblical stories of an Abraham or a Job (see chapter 6 on Judaism). Affirming a belief in a God who is in charge of human destiny and lacking a notion of karmic rebirth, biblical narratives, we would argue, were never successful in explaining why people suffer. When you find yourself in a narrative that understands human existence as a single journey through time from birth to death, guided by a personal God, the level of unexplained suffering increases dramatically. Suffering becomes experienced, as in the book of Job, as an undeserved injustice. Job's audacity to question even God and to demand justice (as we shall see in chapter 6) is rooted in such an experience.

The Mediterranean traditions (Judaism, Christianity, and Islam) attempted to alleviate this threat to meaning by promising life beyond death. But, unlike the karmic vision of Asia, this promise is never able to adequately explain why suffering was necessary in the first place. Any attempt to identify the cause of all suffering as sin in these myths of history is dashed on the rocks of Auschwitz and Hiroshima. It superficially saves meaning – nothing happens without a good and just reason. But it does so at a very high cost. Like the karmic view, it requires the view that everyone who suffered or died at Auschwitz or Hiroshima did something so awful in their lives that they deserved what they got. It is not only implausible but blasphemous. It violates the victims a second time, by taking away their good name. Moreover, it makes God appear to be a vindictive tyrant. As in the story of Job, the survivors of Auschwitz and Hiroshima have a right to take offense at such a cheap solution.

In Masao Abe we see the continuing power of the mythic narrative of life through death. He sees strong similarities between the Buddhist understanding of emptiness and the Christian understanding of *kenosis* as the self-emptying of a Christ who is obedient even unto death on the cross (Philippians 2: 1–11), and profound dissimilarity between these two traditions and Judaism (Abe 1990: 181). In response to a challenge from the Jewish scholar, Eugene Borowitz, concerning his interpretation of the Holocaust, Abe argues:

> It is also stated in Exodus that God told Moses he could not see his face without dying. We can encounter God not directly but only through death – a spiritual death. In Buddhism the great death . . . the death of the ego is emphasized as the necessary moment for awakening. In this regard, religion is not an extension of ethics . . . As the key characteristics of Judaism, Borowitz emphasizes divine forgiveness, the responsibility and capability of all people to turn from evil, and the creation of holiness through righteous living. Learning this, I have realized that in Judaism the relation between ethics and religion is not understood to be discontinuous but distinctively continuous. Judaism is clearly different from Buddhism, a tradition in which there is no continuous path from ethics to religion or from religion to ethics, for in Buddhism ethics and religion are dialectically connected

through mutual negation. It is also significantly different from Christianity in which there is a continuous path from religion to ethics . . . but there is no continuous path from ethics to religion. . . . This characteristic of Judaism is all the more evident when Borowitz states that "because God is holy/good, Jews are to be holy/good" (Borowitz 1990: 82). This means that in Judaism the realization of spiritual death . . . and great death (the complete death of the human ego) are absent. (1990: 181, 185)

Abe presents us with a typology or set of alternative models for the relation between religion and ethics in at least three different religious traditions – Judaism, Christianity and Buddhism (see figure 3.1). He argues that the Buddhist model sees the religious level of insight as higher than the ethical and requires the negation and transcendence of ethics. One has to abandon ethics to achieve the highest spiritual insight. The Christian model also sees the religious level as higher than the ethical, he says, but believes that once you achieve this religious level of insight, it can then raise up and transform the ethical – bringing it up to its level. Thus while ethics is not a bridge to religion, religion is a bridge to ethics and ethics need not be negated by religion.

Both Christianity and Buddhism, in Abe's view, share the myth of life through death, that is, of the death of the self as essential to religious insight and transformation. By contrast, he observes, Judaism appears to reject the myth of life through death and affirms that the relationship between religion and ethics is a two-way street. The highest ideals of both religion and ethics are the same – justice. In this model the self does not seek to annihilate itself in total surrender but rather engages in the audacity (chutzpah) to argue with God, or whatever is held most sacred or holy, in order to protect and defend human dignity against all injustice. Abe clearly prefers the story of life through death to the

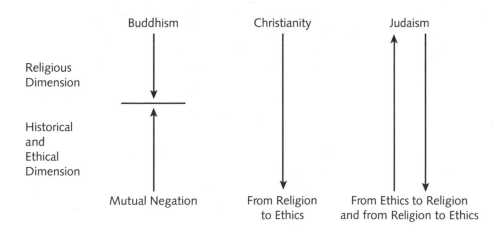

Figure 3.1 Abe's Models of Religion and Ethics

story of audacity. However, as we have already seen in chapter 2, there are serious problems with such a choice and good reason to make just the opposite selection.

What Abe tries to do is to incorporate Auschwitz and Hiroshima into the traditional frames of religious reference as if nothing has changed. The bottom line is that ethics, whether religious or secular, cannot be studied in the same fashion after Auschwitz and Hiroshima – as if nothing momentous had happened in human history. For these events have called into question human confidence in all worldviews and all ethical frames of reference, whether pre-modern or modern – whether religious or non-religious. This situation places us in a post/modern frame of reference in which we are looking for a post/modern mode of ethical thinking adequate for an emerging global civilization.

In the chapters that follow we will be experimenting with "the way of all the earth" as a possible post/modern way of engaging in comparative religious ethics after Auschwitz and Hiroshima. Using Tolstoy, Gandhi, and King as our models, we shall pass over into the stories and traditions of different religions and cultures in a quest for shared insight and ethical wisdom adequate to deal with the complexities of our techno-bureaucratic civilization – the very kind of civilization that gave birth to Auschwitz and Hiroshima. We shall be engaged in what Gandhi called "experiments with truth." To do this we shall immerse ourselves in some of the pre-modern stories that have shaped the narrative imagination of adherents in each religious tradition. Then we shall assess the ancient wisdom of each from a post/modern perspective by looking at a contemporary figure in each tradition who has drawn upon the ancient traditions, stories, and spiritual practices, in a new way in order to more adequately address the challenges of a post/modern world after Auschwitz and Hiroshima.

Our purpose in doing this will not be to catalog the beliefs and practices of the world's religions. Our purpose is far more urgent. We are on a quest for wisdom. We are asking how we might live wisely and compassionately after Auschwitz and Hiroshima. We are asking how we ought to live so as to prevent the forms of prejudice and technological amoralism that led to these events from leading to similar events in the future. And we are hoping that by pursuing the way of all the earth, we shall find such wisdom in the dialogue between the great religions of the post/modern world, especially among their saints, heroes, and heroines.

In the process of doing this we shall ask if a set of comparative models such as that proposed by Masao Abe can be established for studying comparative religious ethics. We shall suggest that while there is some validity to Abe's comparisons, they are too rigid. In principle, if not always in fact, these options for understanding the relationship between religion and ethics may not so much define differences between religions as different options within any given religious tradition – indeed, any narrative tradition, whether religious or non-religious. Nevertheless, beginning with his models will be a useful way of getting at the complexity of our subject matter, even if, in the end, we have to modify or even abandon them. So let us begin or journey into the recesses of the mythic past and the stories of Gilgamesh and Socrates and see where the odyssey of our journey from story to story, religion to religion, culture to culture, takes us.

REFERENCES

Abe, Masao. 1990. "Kenotic God and Dynamic Sunyata," and "A Rejoinder." In John B. Cobb, Jr. and Christopher Ives (eds.), *The Emptying God: A Buddhist–Jewish–Christian Conversation.* Maryknoll, NY: Orbis Books, 3–68, 157–202.

Borowitz, Eugene. 1990. "Dynamic Sunyata and the God Whose Glory Fills the Universe." In John B. Cobb, Jr. and Christopher Ives (eds.), *The Emptying God: A Buddhist–Jewish–Christian Conversation.* Maryknoll, NY: Orbis Books.

Fackenheim, Emil. 1970. *God's Presence in History.* New York: Harper Torchbooks.

Fasching, Darrell. 1993. *The Ethical Challenge of Auschwitz and Hiroshima.* Albany: SUNY Press.

Greenberg, Irving. 1977. "Cloud of Smoke, Pillar of Fire; Judaism, Christianity, and Modernity After the Holocaust." In Eva Fleischner (ed.), *Auschwitz: Beginning of a New Era?* New York: KTAV Publishing House.

Lifton, Robert Jay. 1967. *Death in Life.* New York: Basic Books.

3

THE RELIGIOUS QUEST
AND THE BIRTH OF
ETHICS

The transition from tribal to urban life created a profound shift in human identity – the individuation of human consciousness (see chapter 1, pp. 30–38). A tribe is an extended family sharing a collective identity. A city is a community of strangers in search of a common identity. In the tribe, the right way (morality) is the rite way (tribal ritual). In the city, law and ethics replace ritual as the mediator of relationships between strangers. Two ancient stories present us with the primordial or archetypal issues of the quest for the ethical life – the story of Gilgamesh and the story of Socrates. Both address the relationship between ethics and mortality. The story of Gilgamesh, the oldest recorded human epic, reflects the crisis of morality, mortality and meaning that arose in the new urban environment. It is a story that combines two of the most significant themes of religious story: (1) the quest for an answer to the problems of old age, sickness, and death, and (2) wrestling with the stranger – both of which have a profound impact on the human quest for the good life and justice in a world of strangers. With his arrogance tempered by a knowledge of his mortality, as well as his friendship and respect for the stranger (his "double," Enkidu), Gilgamesh returns from his failed quest and rules Uruk with wisdom and justice. The story of Socrates is also about the intersection of ethics and mortality – in this case when, paradoxically, the religious obligation to doubt and question the sacred order of urban society leads to his being executed for impiety toward the gods and the corruption of youth. It is Socrates' insistence that in order to live the ethical life one must conquer the fear of death (which was expressed in his act of civil disobedience to Athenian law) which provided an important model to twentieth-century social activists such as Gandhi and King.

Long before human beings wrote stories they told stories. Then, somewhere around 3000 BCE, writing was invented by the Sumerians, who recorded the first great human epic – *The Epic of Gilgamesh*. In Sumer, the misty recesses of time began to clear as tribal and village life gave way to urban civilization and written records. Among the records we find fragmentary references to the story of a great king by the name of Gilgamesh. But it is from their neighbors along the Tigris and Euphrates rivers, the Babylonians, that we get the most vivid and complete stories of Gilgamesh. These come from the first half of the second millennium BCE. *The Epic of Gilgamesh* is the oldest story we have of the human quest to make sense out of life. It is a story of the awakening of human self-awareness to the truth of our common mortality – of old age, sickness, and death. And it is the story of a great quest to find an answer to the problem of our mortality – a quest that lies at the root of all the great world religions and separates them from all that went before. But let us not get sidetracked into history and theory just yet. Rather, let us begin with the story and its power to move our hearts and minds as we identify with the dilemma and the quest of the heroic yet tragic figure of Gilgamesh.

The Story of Gilgamesh: The Crises of Morality, Mortality, and Meaning

[A retelling of *The Epic of Gilgamesh*. All quotations are from a translation by N. K. Sandars, *The Epic of Gilgamesh* (Penguin Books 1960, 1964, 1972). Some details also rely on the translation found in *The Ancient Near East: An Anthology of Texts and Pictures* (Princeton University Press, 1958), edited by James B. Pritchard, 40–75.]

Wrestling with the stranger – the encounter with Enkidu

"I will proclaim to the world the deeds of Gilgamesh. This was the man to whom all things were known; this was the king who knew the countries of the world. He was wise, he saw mysteries and knew secret things, he brought us a tale of the days before the flood. He went on a long journey, was weary, worn-out with labour, returning he rested, he engraved on a stone the whole story" (61). So the story of Gilgamesh begins, a story whose origins go back to the beginning of civilization in Ancient Mesopotamia (3000–1500 BCE), a story that tells of the loss of innocence that occurred when human beings first left the tribal world oriented to the rhythms of nature – the rhythms of eternal return – to become city dwellers, and there discovered both their individuality and their mortality.

The gods, we are told, created Gilgamesh, two-thirds god and one-third human, with a beauty surpassing all others. Gilgamesh built himself a city, Uruk (in Mesopotamia, near Babylon), with fortified walls and a temple for the sky god Anu and the goddess of love, Ishtar. But the citizens of Uruk were not happy with Gilgamesh, for he ruled with an arrogance that knew no bounds. He took the sons of his subjects for his army and their daughters for his bed. So the citizens cried out to the gods for help. Then the gods decided to create an equal for Gilgamesh, in order to teach him the meaning of humility and of justice. Thus the highest deity, Anu (the sky god), heard the cry of the people and ordered the goddess of creation, Aruru, to create an equal for Gilgamesh: "Let it be as like him as his own reflection, his second self, . . . Let them contend together and leave Uruk in quiet" (62). So the goddess created Enkidu. He was the image of Gilgamesh except that he was slightly shorter and stockier. However, unlike Gilgamesh, he was uncivilized – a wild man with a long mane of hair, he was untamed, living in the wilderness in natural harmony with the animals.

One day a hunter ran into him at a watering hole. This happened three times, and each time the hunter was struck with fear at this awesome and fierce being who seemed to be both man and beast. Enkidu, it seemed, had thwarted the hunter's attempts to trap animals, protecting them and freeing them. So the hunter went to his father to ask his advice on how to trap Enkidu. His father sent him to see Gilgamesh, to ask him for a prostitute to take back with him to the wilderness to use as bait to trap the wild Enkidu. The plan was to have her strip naked and sit by the watering hole to attract him when he came for a drink. And so the hunter brought back with him an alluring woman whom he placed by the watering hole. And when Enkidu appeared, the hunter instructed her to bare her breasts without shame and welcome his amorous advances. And so it was that Enkidu was attracted to the prostitute and made love to her for six days and seven nights. And when it was over the animals no longer trusted Enkidu but rather fled from his presence. So he returned to the woman, who told him that now he had become wise like a god. And the woman proceeded to teach him how to be human. As he set out with her on a journey to Uruk, she taught him the customs of civilized people – how to wear clothes, how to hunt, and so on. So Enkidu set out for Uruk convinced that he was the strongest man alive, and prepared to challenge Gilgamesh for the rule of Uruk.

Meanwhile, an omen came to Gilgamesh in a dream, for he told his mother that he had dreamt that a meteor fell from heaven and it was too large for him to lift. Moreover, he was attracted to it as if to the love of a woman, and in the dream his mother told him that the meteor was his brother. When his mother heard this, she interpreted the dream to mean that a man was coming who would challenge him as an equal and whom he would come to love with the love he had only felt previously for a woman.

Soon Enkidu arrived at the gates of the city and the people gathered round, noticing how much like Gilgamesh he looked. Then Enkidu confronted Gilgamesh at the gate of the city, and they entered into a mighty wrestling match, like two bulls, whose clash shook the foundations of the buildings of the city. The two wrestled to exhaustion. Although Gilgamesh just barely managed to best Enkidu, it did not lead to his defeat but rather to a deep respect and friendship, a friendship in which each recognized the other as his equal. After that, Enkidu and Gilgamesh embraced and their friendship was sealed. They became closer than brothers. Then Gilgamesh and Enkidu went off to share many adventures together. Although they knew that only the gods live forever, many times the two defied death in their heroic adventures, seeking to make a name for themselves, so that they should at least live on in song and story.

Wrestling with the goddess: the encounter with death

During one of their adventures Gilgamesh attracted the attention of the goddess Ishtar and she fell in love with him. So she invited him into her bed and at the same time proposed marriage. But her reputation for "loving them and leaving them" had preceded her and Gilgamesh had no desire to be her next conquest. So Gilgamesh spurned her advances, reminding her of her reputation. At this, Ishtar fell into a rage and she went to her father, the sky god Anu, and her mother, the goddess Antum, and demanded that Gilgamesh be taught a lesson. While at first reluctant, Anu finally relented and gave her the Bull of Heaven to use as the instrument of her vengeance. The bull came down to earth and snorted, and cracks opened up in the earth like a great earthquake and hundreds fell to their death. Then the bull attacked Gilgamesh and Enkidu. But Gilgamesh managed to slay the bull with his sword and he sacrificed the bull's heart to his own protector, the sun god Shamash. However, this only enraged Ishtar even more and she sought her revenge another way. That night, while the two slept, Enkidu had a dream which he revealed to Gilgamesh in the morning. In the dream he saw all the gods in council debating how to punish them for slaying the Bull of Heaven. So it was decided that one of them must die. Shamash tried to intercede on their behalf, but to no avail, and Enkidu was struck down with an illness.

The dream was indeed prophetic and Enkidu became ill. As Enkidu lay dying he said to Gilgamesh: "So dear as you are to me, brother, yet they will take me from you. . . . I must sit down on the threshold of the dead and never again will I see my dear brother with my eyes" (89). At first Enkidu cursed the prostitute who seemingly brought him to this destiny by luring him out of nature and into the tragic world of civilization, but the god Shamash reminded Enkidu of all the good that had come of this, for without her Enkidu would never have met Gilgamesh, whom he loved as a brother and whose glory he had shared. And so Enkidu repented of his curse and blessed the prostitute.

Then Enkidu related to Gilgamesh another of his dreams. In this dream Enkidu encounters Death. He stands alone before an awesome and terrifying man-bird with a vampire's face, the feet of a lion, and hands like the talons of an eagle. This creature smothers him with his embrace and he is transformed into a birdlike creature who is then led away to the House of Darkness, where none who enter ever leave – a place from which there is no return. In this place there is no light and everyone eats dirt and clay. At hearing this Gilgamesh stripped off his clothes and wept. He then told Enkidu that no one had greater wisdom than he had just revealed. The dream, he said, was marvelous but also terrifying and "we must treasure the dream whatever the terror; for the dream has shown that misery comes at last to the healthy man, the end of life is sorrow" (93). For twelve days Enkidu lingered in his suffering and then he died. Gilgamesh was beside himself with grief. He could not feel the beat of the heart of his friend and his eyes no longer opened. Still he refused to accept his death. He held him in his arms for seven days until a worm fell out of Enkidu's nose. Finally he accepted that his friend would not awaken and buried him. Then he built a statue to his friend and went off tearing out his hair and weeping as he wandered the steppes. Gilgamesh said to himself: "How can I rest, how can I be at peace? Despair is in my heart. What my brother is now, that shall I be when I am dead" (97). Gilgamesh wept not only for his brother but for himself, because he did not wish to be laid in the earth, to be covered in darkness. He wanted only to live in the light, his eyes beholding the sun. And so he set out on a quest to find Utnapishtim, who he believed had an answer to the problem of human mortality – the problem of old age, sickness, and death.

The quest for an answer to the problem of mortality

Utnapishtim and his wife dwelt in the land of Dilmun, the land of the rising sun. They were the only mortals who knew the secret of eternal life. Gilgamesh resolved that he would journey to the land of the rising sun to gain this secret. So he set out, and eventually his journey brought him to the great mountain that guards the rising and setting of the sun. At its gate the Scorpions, beings who are half-man and half-dragon, stood guard. These beings recognized that Gilgamesh was no ordinary mortal but a child of the gods (two-thirds god and one-third man), and they treated him with respect. They asked him why he sought passage, and he told them that he came out of grief for his friend Enkidu and for all humanity who suffer from the sting of mortality. Thus he sought a cure for death – the secret that only Utnapishtim knew. The Scorpions warned him that this required a dangerous journey into the darkness which no other mortal had ever made. Nevertheless, they allowed Gilgamesh to continue his journey.

Gilgamesh then passed through a darkness so dense that he could see nothing. He walked for twelve leagues in this darkness. The time seemed infinite, the darkness suffocating and terrifying. And then, just when he thought he could go on no more, he walked into a flood of sunlight and he stood in the garden of the gods, where rich gemstones hung like fruit from the trees and vines. Here the sun god, Shamash, happened upon him unexpectedly and was startled to see a mortal in the precinct of the gods. He warned Gilgamesh that he would not be successful in his quest to find an answer to the problem of death. Gilgamesh then headed for the shore of the sea that separated him from Utnapishtim, where he met the winemaker Siduri. She asked him why he seemed to be in despair. He answered: "Because of my brother I am afraid of death, because of my brother I stray through the wilderness and cannot rest" (101). He went on to explain that he sought Utnapishtim and an answer to the problem of death. But Siduri warned him that he could never be successful, for "when the gods created man they allotted to him death, but life they retained in their own keeping" (102). And so she recommended that he eat, drink, and be merry, for tomorrow we die – that is the lot of humankind.

But Gilgamesh refused to give up his quest and resolved to cross the ocean of death and enter the land of the rising sun where Utnapishtim lives eternally with the gods. Thus he sought out Ursanabi, the boatman for Utnapishtim, to see if he would take him across the murky waters of death. Ursanabi agreed to ferry him across. After a journey of many days they arrived at Dilmun, the land where Utnapishtim dwells. There he met Utnapishtim and explained the despair that caused him to make this journey and his hope of being given the secret of immortality, explaining that this was the reason he had made so long and dangerous a journey. Risking his life, he killed the hyena, the lion, the panther, and the tiger along the way and now he had arrived haggard and weary, but filled with hope.

Utnapishtim told Gilgamesh that there is no permanence in life; nothing lasts – all things perish. The fate of every human being is sealed by the gods. Gilgamesh demanded to know how he became an exception to this rule. So Utnapishtim told him the story of the flood. In a past time the gods became angry with human beings because they were too noisy and unruly, always disturbing the peace of the gods. So the gods decided to destroy all human beings in a flood. But one of the gods warned Utnapishtim of the coming disaster and instructed him to build a boat for himself and his family and take as many living creatures as possible into the boat as well. Then the rains came for seven days and all life was destroyed. The boat finally came to rest, grounded on the top of a mountain for six days. Then on the seventh day he sent out several birds who all returned, finding no dry land on which to rest. Finally he sent out a raven that did not return.

Then Utnapishtim knew that the danger was over and he made a sacrifice to the gods on the mountaintop, and the gods swarmed around like flies when they smelled the sweet odors. When the storm god, the mighty warrior Enlil, arrived he was angry to discover that some mortals had survived. But the god Ea spoke in defense of the mortals, arguing that the gods had exacted too hard a punishment upon humankind. Enlil was moved by Ea's speech and took Utnapishtim and his wife each by the hand, had them kneel before him, and conferred upon them the gift of immortality.

When Utnapishtim finished telling Gilgamesh his story, he asked him, "Who will assemble the gods for your sake?" (114). Gilgamesh pleaded with Utnapishtim, "What shall I do . . . Where shall I go? Already the thief in the night has hold of my limbs, death inhabits my room; wherever my foot rests, there I find death" (115). But Utnapishtim seemed untouched by his pleas. He gave him no answer but only some fresh clothing. Then he sent him away to return to the land of mortals.

However, just as his boat was about to cast off, the wife of Utnapishtim felt compassion for Gilgamesh and prevailed upon Utnapishtim to reveal the secret of eternal life which Gilgamesh so desperately sought. Utnapishtim then proceeded to tell him of the secret "mystery of the gods," namely, that there is a special plant found at the bottom of the sea which has the capacity to restore a human being to youth. He instructed him that on his journey back he was to dive to the bottom of the sea and get this plant. He warned him that, like the rose, it had thorns that would make it difficult to grasp. So Gilgamesh did as he was instructed. Tying stones to his feet, he dove into the water and sank to the bottom where he retrieved the plant, loosed the stones, and returned to the surface, where a heavy current carried him ashore.

Gilgamesh named the plant "The Old Men are Young Again" and he rejoiced to think he could now regain his youth. Then Gilgamesh and the boatman Ursanabi began the long journey back to Uruk together. After a long day's walk they stopped for the evening. There Gilgamesh saw a pond of cool water in which to bathe, and so he disrobed, laid his magical plant on a rock, and dove in. While he was bathing a snake came along who was attracted by the sweet smell of the plant. This snake carried off the plant and consumed it. Immediately the snake sloughed its skin and was made young again. When Gilgamesh discovered that the plant was missing he sat down and wept. He had had eternal life within his grasp and had lost it. So he and Ursanabi had to return to Uruk empty-handed. There he surveyed the city he had built and had to rest content with his human accomplishments.

> O Gilgamesh, this was the meaning of your dream. You were given the kingship, such was your destiny, everlasting life was not your destiny. Because of this do not be sad at heart, do not be grieved or oppressed; he [the god Enlil] has given you power to bind and to loose, to be the darkness and the light of mankind. He has given unexampled supremacy over the people, victory in battle from which no fugitive returns, . . . But do not abuse this power, deal justly with your servants in the palace, deal justly before the face of the Sun. (118)

So Gilgamesh ruled Uruk in glory. Such is the story of Gilgamesh, "the king who knew the countries of the world. He was wise, he saw mysteries and knew secret things, he brought us a tale of the days before the flood. He went on a long journey, was weary, worn-out with labour, . . . returning . . . he engraved on a stone the whole story" (61). And when the time came, this great king died like all other mortals.

Urbanization, Doubling, and Death

Since the beginning of time religion has been about the need to enter into the experience of death in order to experience a rebirth. This is the narrative theme of primal or tribal culture, emphasizing animism and veneration of the ancestors – myths of "eternal return," as Mircea Eliade describes them. Even early archaic civilization (characterized by the emergence of the city-state and polytheism) still appealed to this mythic theme. In ancient Babylonia of the early second millennium BCE, the great New Year's Akitu festival was still being celebrated as a ritual of cosmic death and rebirth. The King, the symbol of cosmic order, was dethroned and a festival period of chaos (a kind of Mardi Gras) followed, which culminated in the retelling and reenacting of the creation story in which the god of the city, Marduk, slew the dragon-goddess of chaos, Tiamat, and out of her slain body created the world. Thus through death new life comes into being. The New Year festival represented the turning point in the cycle of seasons, the transition from winter and death to spring and new life. Without the ritual reenactment of the creation it was believed the universe would disintegrate into chaos and oblivion. The ritual enabled the Babylonians to pass through the death of winter and reconstitute their world anew in the rebirth of spring, at which point the King could be restored to his throne and cosmic order reestablished in society.

The Babylonian New Year festival still operated within the primal sphere of collective identity. But Babylonia was an archaic urban culture whose complexity was already altering and individuating human consciousness. Reflecting this situation, *The Epic of Gilgamesh*, in its second millennium BCE versions, records the emergence of a new "urban self" through a process of doubling closely tied up with the encounter with individual mortality.

Robert Jay Lifton suggests that doubling is produced by a radical change in social environment. One of the most radical changes in social environment in the history of humanity was the move from the tribe to the city. It is probable that doubling first occurred when human beings made that move. Such doubling is a central theme in the story of Gilgamesh. We find it helpful to distinguish between primary doubling and secondary doubling. Primary doubling is the mysterious experience of reflexive self-consciousness – the ability to stand apart from ourselves and look at our own actions without which ethical reflection would not be possible. This is a kind of alienation from one's self by which one comes to see one's own actions as if through the eyes of a stranger. We actualize this capacity in secondary doubling, which is assuming a particular social role or identity through which we can look at ourselves as we act in our other role or roles. Our capacity for doubling (primary doubling) is always actualized in some specific role that we assume (secondary doubling). When Gilgamesh comes to see himself through the eyes of Enkidu as a friend, rather than through his identity as a prince, he begins an ethical journey. The eyes of

Enkidu become the mirror for Gilgamesh's soul, through which he comes to see and understand himself and his relationships to others. Through his relationship with Enkidu, Gilgamesh achieves reflective self-awareness. Through wrestling with the stranger, Enkidu, Gilgamesh gains humility and wisdom.

The Epic of Gilgamesh represents the situation of the newly individuated person of the urbanized world. A self no longer clothed in a collective tribal identity and a collective *myth of eternal return* but stripped naked and exposed to his mortality as an individual. The impact of the shift from tribal to urban life upon human identity is symbolized in the story of Gilgamesh, and his double, Enkidu, who is both like Gilgamesh and yet slightly different (slightly shorter), represents the differentiated other who is the mirror for Gilgamesh's own self. Enkidu becomes the symbol of Gilgamesh's self-consciousness – his ability to imagine himself through the eyes of his friend and to imagine his own personal mortal destiny through the mortality of his friend.

Without doubling as a form of self-reflection the ethical life would not be possible. Doubling becomes demonic only when this capacity for self-reflection is avoided through self-deception, so that responsibility for the actions of the self in particular circumstances are denied (claiming, for example: "I had no choice"). Significantly, unlike the doubling of the Nazi doctors, which allowed them to disown their own actions, as if done by another, Gilgamesh's doubling enables him to reflect on his actions, become self-aware and compassionate, and return to his city to rule no longer with arrogance but with justice. The story of Gilgamesh tells us that doubling does not automatically lead to demonic acts. It can, under the right circumstances, lead to responsibility and compassion.

Enkidu, as the bearer of Gilgamesh's ego, symbolizes the emergence of the urban self from the collective myths and rhythms of nature. No longer participating in the eternal rhythms of nature, Gilgamesh can no longer find comfort in them. Having become a self, the myths of collective participatory tribal identity no longer speak to him. He is left with the burden of his own mortality – the burden of anticipating the loss of his own self in death. That is the situation symbolized by his failed quest for immortality. Primal animism and archaic polytheism have no answer to the problem of death as the loss of one's own self, except the answer of collective consciousness to which Gilgamesh, having fallen into individuated self-consciousness, can never return. Gilgamesh, it seems, has been banished from paradise, just as Enkidu had been when he was "domesticated" by the prostitute (of civilization).

Primal (tribal) and early archaic (urban) societies were collective, monistic, this-worldly and optimistic in their orientations. Religious myth and ritual were oriented towards assuring prosperity, longevity and fecundity (e.g., many offspring). But in India and the Mediterranean, with urbanization, a new pessimism emerges about life in this world. Whereas before life was focused on the fertility of mother earth as symbolized by the mother goddess, now life loses its savor. The formation of the "inner self" of reflexive consciousness enables the self to imagine its own death as a loss of "self." The burden of death as the loss of one's self seems to empty life of its sweetness, and life in the flesh comes to be viewed as suffering. And the answer to the problem of life as suffering becomes imagined as liberation from the earth and the seductive power of the flesh, which can only lead to death and decay.

The great world religions, we have argued, emerged precisely in response to the traumatic shock of urbanization that left human beings with three fundamental and seemingly insoluble problems: mortality, morality, and meaning. The great myths of history, of liberation, and harmony, in the Ancient Near East and in Asia, succeeded where Gilgamesh failed. They too, as we shall see, offer stories of wrestling with the stranger and of the quest to find an answer to the problems of old age, sickness, and death as the path to spiritual and ethical wisdom. And because their stories also provided an answer to the problem of death, wherever these great religious visions emerged they swept through, transformed, and surpassed the prevailing animistic and polytheistic worldviews – and so transformed the face of the earth. They offered experiences and stories that not only transcended death but enabled strangers to see and understand that they shared a common identity – a realization that gave birth to new moralities and new meanings.

In the chapters that follow we shall be passing over into some of the key stories and practices of these new moralities and meanings as we engage in our own quest for wisdom in the face of our mortality. But before we proceed on that quest, we need to make one more stop in this initial phase of our journey. And that stop is in Athens, Greece, in the second half of the first millennium BCE, where the stories of Socrates' quest for an answer to the problems of mortality, morality, and meaning gave birth to ethics as the result of a powerful and distinctive religious experience – the experience of possession by a God who compelled him to question and to doubt the sacred morality of Athenian society. There may be many ways of thinking ethically, but the fact that we call certain ways of thinking and questioning "ethical" is due to the powerful historical influence of the Socratic religious experience which gave birth to philosophy.

The Story of the Trial of Socrates

[A retelling of the trial of Socrates based on Plato's *Apology*. All quotations are from "The Trial of Socrates: The Apology," in *The Last Days of Socrates* (Penguin, 1954, 1959, 1969), edited and translated by Hugh Tredennick.]

The nature of the Socratic religious experience and its powerful social implications are well illustrated in Plato's retelling of the story of Socrates' trial – *The Apology*. The situation is that Socrates, who has spent his life instructing the youth of Athens how to engage in the quest for knowledge and virtue, is accused of impiety toward the gods of the city and corrupting the youth. If he is found guilty, it may cost him his life.

The trial of Socrates represents one of the first recorded acts of civil disobedience whereby the sacred law and order of society were called into question in the name of a Good that transcends sacred order. Civil disobedience differs from ordinary lawbreaking in that the one who engages in it deliberately breaks the law but does not seek to escape the consequences of that action. On the contrary, such a person uses the occasion to call into question the justice of the law in the name of some higher vision of the good life. Socrates, standing accused of impiety toward the gods and corrupting the youth, pleaded not guilty and insisted that his accusers had misrepresented his teachings and told outright lies about him. He assured the jury of 501 Athenian citizens that from him they would hear the truth in plain speech with none of the artificial rhetorical flourish of his opponents.

Socrates described himself as a complete stranger to the procedures of the law court. At the age of 70, he told his jurors, he finds himself in a court for the first time in his life. He asked his jurors not to be distracted by his plainness and inexperience but simply to give him a fair hearing. He pointed out to the jury that he had to defend himself against two sets of accusers. The first were his official accusers, led by Anytus, Meletus, and Lycon. They, he said, did not trouble him nearly as much as the second, the rumormongers, who always remain nameless, and who no doubt had been filling the minds of the jurors with false stories about him since their youth. Against the first group, Socrates felt he could mount a defense. Against the second, it was almost impossible to do so, since their accusations were vague and their identities obscure and they were not available to be cross-examined.

Let us imagine we are at the trial and listening in on Socrates as he speaks. If we had been there we would have heard him say something like this. What is the accusation against me? It is that I inquire into sacred matters "below the earth and in the sky," which mortals are not supposed to intrude upon, and that I do so using specious arguments that make the weaker argument seem as if it were the stronger and in so doing set a bad example. Much of this is fueled by the plays of Aristophanes who delights in making fun of me. But there is no truth to any of it. Nor is there any truth to the claim that I attempt to educate people, charging exorbitant fees. There are indeed experts in many subjects for which it would be legitimate to charge a fee, but who is the expert at perfecting human beings? Certainly not I.

So, then, how did I gain such a false reputation? It is odd since I certainly do not claim to have the kind of wisdom and expertise that my opponents would have you believe that I claim. My strongest witness on my behalf is the famous oracle of the god at Delphi. Now Chaerephon, my friend, went to Delphi once and asked the god if there was anyone wiser than Socrates. And the priestess who interprets for the god replied, no one is wiser than Socrates. Now when I heard this I asked myself what could this mean? I know that I have no special claim to wisdom and yet the god does not lie, so how am I to explain this? The only thing I could come up with occurred to me after questioning one of our politicians who thought of himself as very wise indeed. Well, after only a few questions, which he could not answer, I showed him that although he thought he knew something, in fact he did not. Needless to say this was resented. After that encounter I realized I was certainly wiser than this man, not because I knew more than he but because "he thinks he knows something which he does not know, whereas I am quite conscious of my ignorance" (50). This has happened with many such individuals – not only politicians, but poets and skilled craftsmen, and others – and after a while I realized I was doing myself harm because people were wrongfully considering me their enemy. However, I could not stop myself from engaging in such conversations, for I was compelled to do so out of a sense of religious duty to discover the meaning of the oracle's declaration.

Now one of the reasons that those whom I questioned have been so hostile to me afterwards is that they assume that because I was able to show how little they know, that meant I claimed to know everything. Nothing, however, could be further from the truth. Real wisdom belongs to God alone. The oracle was simply telling us that human wisdom has little substance to it. The essence of human wisdom is a knowledge of ignorance, and that, my dear jurors, I do claim to have. "That is why I still go about seeking and searching in obedience to the divine command." And I must say that following this command has not made me rich: on the contrary, "my service to God has reduced me to extreme poverty" (52).

Undoubtedly there is one other factor that has created prejudice against me and led to false accusations. There have been some wealthy young men who have found it amusing to hear me cross-examine people in authority and may have done so themselves in a frivolous manner for their own amusement. The victims of such misbehavior no doubt were annoyed and probably blamed me, even though these were not my students and had never been so encouraged by me. Anyway, such victims, no doubt unfamiliar with my actual teachings, likely complained about me as one who was stirring up the youth, teaching them atheism and other forms of impiety and disrespect. It is this kind of thing that most likely fueled the attacks of Meletus, Anytus, and Lycon against me. How can one really defend oneself against this kind of rumor and innuendo?

Now let's take a closer look at the formal charges made by Meletus. I supposedly corrupt the minds of the youth by leading them to believe in gods I myself have invented rather than the gods of the state. Now when I ask Meletus who has a positive influence on young people, he tells me the members of the jury surely do, and all those citizens in attendance here for this trial surely do, and all of our political leaders surely do. In fact, I cannot find anybody who Meletus thinks corrupts our youth except me. This I find both astonishing and suspect. Can it really be that I alone am the cause of all the corruption of our young people? I assure you I have never intentionally done so and if I ever unintentionally did so it is not a crime punishable by death under our laws. At best it is a misdemeanor.

As to the charge that I teach belief in new gods instead of those honored by the state, I was not clear as to whether Meletus thought me a complete atheist, as he sometimes suggests, or just somebody who simply believes in different gods, as he has suggested at other times. However, Meletus clarified that for me – it seems my crime is that I believe in no gods at all. But surely it is clear from his testimony in this trial that he has accused me of both believing in gods and not believing in gods. Such contradictory accusations are obviously frivolous and should not be taken seriously. It is no different than his accusation that I teach the youth to believe in spurious supernatural activities and at the same time that I do not believe in supernatural beings. He cannot have it both ways. Meletus is nothing more than a bully seeking to throw his weight around.

Now some of you may wish to know whether I regret my actions, which have clearly put me in danger of receiving the death penalty. No person who is worth anything ought to make his or her decisions based on whether or not they lead to life or death. The only criterion must be whether one's actions are right or wrong. I did not think about living and dying when I served in the military defending our cities and colonies. I faced death bravely, and "when God appointed me, as I supposed and believed, to the duty of leading the philosophic life, examining myself and others," I could do no less (60). To fear death is just another form of our ignorance, for it supposes one knows what one does not know. For we do not know whether death is the greatest evil or the greatest blessing that can happen to us.

What I do know is that it is wrong to disobey my superior, whether that be God or man. If you offered to acquit me on the condition that I stop philosophizing (that I stop loving and pursuing wisdom), warning me that if I did not then I would be executed, then I would respond: "I owe a greater obedience to God than to you; and so long as I draw breath and have my faculties, I shall never stop practicing philosophy and exhorting you and elucidating the truth for everyone that I meet" (61). I shall never give up challenging those who care more for money, power, and reputation than they do for truth and goodness. I shall never stop questioning such individuals and exposing their hypocrisy. No one, whether young or old, stranger or fellow citizen, can be exempt from such questioning. This "is what my God commands; and it is my belief that no greater good has ever befallen you in this city than my service to my God" (62). Goodness is more important than wealth, both for the individual and for the state. How can this message corrupt the youth?

I cannot be threatened into conformity. You may put me to death, or banish me or deprive me of my rights as a citizen. But I do not think these are such great calamities. It is far worse to put an innocent man to death. So I do not plead on my own behalf but on yours. I only wish to save you from abusing God's gift to this city by executing me. "If you put me to death, you will not easily find anyone to take my place. It is literally true (even if it sounds rather comical) that God has specially appointed me to this city" (62) as a kind of gadfly to sting you and wake you up. I am just a pesty little fly sent by God for your benefit. You ought to spare me but I suspect you will "finish me off with a single slap; and then you will go on sleeping till the end of your days, unless God in his care for you sends someone to take my place" (63). You may doubt that God sent me, but what other explanation is there for my having neglected my own well-being and that of my family, living in poverty, in order to spend my time encouraging goodness? I have never taken a fee for this and my poverty is my proof.

If you ask me why I do this, I can only answer that "I am subject to a divine or supernatural experience" (63). Since my childhood "a sort of voice comes to me and . . . it always dissuades me from what I am proposing to do, and never urges me on." This voice forbid me to enter politics, for in politics I should have surely perished long ago without doing much good. "The true champion of justice, if he intends to survive even for a short time, must necessarily confine himself to private life and leave politics alone" (64). During the time I was on the council of the city, you know that I refused to condone illegal executions even though most of you cried out for blood, for I thought my duty was to be on the side of law and justice even if that meant death for me. I can do no other than follow the path of a lover of wisdom (a philosopher), as the God has commanded me through oracles and dreams. As for the charge that I have corrupted the youth, the parents and siblings of many of my students are here today and my enemies have not been able to produce one who will verify this accusation. If I had corrupted these youth surely the youth themselves would not accuse me, but most certainly their relatives would – but they do not.

With this I rest my case. I do not plead with you tearfully like a woman asking for mercy, nor do I bring my relatives to plead on my behalf. I ask only for justice based on facts and arguments. To plead with the jury would be to corrupt them and ask them to put justice aside in favor of my special pleading. I will not do that. "I leave it to you and to God to judge me as it shall be best for me and for yourselves" (69).

At this point the council voted by secret ballot and Socrates was found guilty. Socrates responded, saying: I am not disappointed or upset by your decision. I expected it. I am only surprised at how close the vote was. Only thirty votes more and I would have been acquitted. I am supposed to suggest a penalty for my crime of having encouraged people to live the examined life. My dear fellow citizens, the unexamined life is not worth living. Therefore, for encouraging the examined life, I believe I should be rewarded with a salary from the state for the rest of my life. That, of course is not what you want to hear. So let me tell you I can only suggest a modest fine, for, being a poor man, I can afford no more than 100 drachmae. Wait – my friends say they will put up 3,000 drachmae.

The jury rejects this proposal and mandates a death sentence, and Socrates responds to them: I know, dear jurors, that I am condemned not because my arguments were unsound but because I did not plead for my life and show you proper deference, and I was unrepentant about leading the philosopher's life. I do not fear death enough to seek life at any cost. "The difficulty is not so much to escape death; the real difficulty is to escape from doing wrong, . . . When I leave this court I shall go away condemned by you to death, but they [those who voted for Socrates' execution] will go away convicted by Truth herself of depravity and wickedness" (73). However, I wish to assure those jurors who voted for my acquittal that my fate is not a sad one, for always in the past the prophetic voice of my God has warned me if I was taking the wrong course, yet on this day when I face what many consider the worst of fates, this voice did not come. Therefore, I suspect what is happening to me is a blessing and that death is truly no evil. In any case either death is the end of consciousness and I will experience no more tribulations or it is an entry into another life and I will taste its joys. This I do firmly believe, "nothing can harm a good man either in life or after death, and his fortunes are not a matter of indifference to the gods" (76). Thus I do not blame those who voted against me. I ask only one thing, namely, "when my sons grow up," if they should put "money or anything else before goodness, take your revenge by plaguing them as I plagued you; . . . Now it is time that we were going, I to die and you to live; but which of us has the happier prospect is unknown to anyone but God" (76).

The Socratic Invention of Ethics and the Way of Doubt

Philosophy was invented by the ancient Greeks and it is Socrates who is gener-ally credited with being the father of philosophy, giving it its distinctive ques-tions and classic form. Socrates believed in philosophy as a form of conversation, of questioning, and answering. He never wrote a word and it is primarily due to the admiration of his student Plato that we know anything about his life and thought. For some seventy years he taught philosophy in Athens, and he taught it in a most unsettling manner. For Socrates believed that the beginning of wisdom is a knowledge of ignorance, and therefore he taught people to ques-tion everything they took for granted. He did this in order to get them to realize how little of what they thought they knew was really knowledge. This, of course, can be exceedingly disturbing because human beings like security and order, and questions tend to make people feel insecure – and that can be very socially disruptive. It can be very distressing to any community to have their way of life questioned, and the ancient Athenians were no different in this re-gard. For this reason, after decades of sharing his wisdom with the citizens of Athens, Socrates was arrested and put on trial for his impiety toward the gods and for corrupting the youth. He was found guilty and was executed for his crime.

    To understand why Socrates was viewed by so many of his fellow-citizens as a threat to society we need to understand the socially disruptive nature of his questions. When we are asked why we live a certain way and not some other, our first inclination is to say "because that's the way we have always done it." This is the same as saying "it's customary" or "these are our customs." However, no people looks upon its customs as if they are perfectly arbitrary, as if one way is as good as another. "Customs" is a loaded word, for in every culture many of the customs are viewed as sacred. They represent a sacred way of life. People live and die for what they hold sacred, especially their "way of life," as the countless wars of recorded history amply demonstrate. Thus, if you press a people with further questions as to why they have always done things this way, they will tell you something like: "because in the beginning the gods and/or the sacred ancestors created our world this way. Therefore, this is the right way to be human." This answer works for a culture, whether the "beginning" it traces itself back to is the creation of the world at the beginning of time or the re-creation of their world in some later revolutionary moment of time, such as 1776.

Sociologists call the way human beings answer such questions the social *legitimation* of a society's way of life, and they call the strategies whereby that way of life is put into question the *delegitimation* of a society. As we have already noted, the Greek term from which we get our word "ethic" (*ethos, ethike*) is the word for the "customs" of the people – the sacred customs. In tribal societies these customs were held in common but the emergence of cities in the ancient world disrupted that pattern by bringing people together from different tribal communities having different customs and stories. Therefore, urban societies had to supplement ritual with law, and ethics in the Socratic sense. Law, in ancient societies, in part supplemented and in part replaced ritual. Like ritual, law too received its legitimacy from sacred stories that traced its beginnings back to sacred ancestors and gods. Like ritual, it is a conservative force in society. It functions to protect the sacred order of the way of life of a people and insure at least the minimum order necessary for people to live together.

Up until the time of Socrates, law and custom in ancient Greece reinforced the sacred order of society, and ethics was identical with the customary morality or the sacred customs of the people. In a sacred society like that of Athens, the human city was seen as *the cosmos writ small*, that is, the social order is seen as an embodiment in miniature of the sacred order of the cosmos created by the gods and the sacred ancestors. Knowledge of that sacred order is communicated through the myths (sacred stories) and rituals of that society. In such a cosmological society "*the way things are* (i.e., the sacred customs) is the way they ought to be" and to disrupt or change them was not only a personal sin but a crime, a violation of public order.

In a sacred society everyone who shares the same stories, customs, and identity (everyone who is the same) is considered sacred and human, and anyone who is different or who dares raise questions about the possibility of being different – of engaging in a different way of life – will be considered the enemy of everything sacred and human. In Athens, Socrates became the enemy. The revolution that Socrates introduced was to dare to question the sacred stories and the sacred customs of the people and suggest that what everybody thought was right and good might not really be right and good. He dared to ask: "Is what people say is good, really the good?" To raise that question was to threaten public order, the sacred order and way of life of the Athenian people. He was accused of impiety toward the gods and corrupting the youth, because to question the Athenian way of life meant he had to question the authority of the gods who legitimated that way of life. And to teach the youth to raise such questions, of course, was to encourage their own impiety, and to encourage them not to follow in the sacred ways of their ancestors – hence, corrupting them.

During his trial Socrates is accused of being an atheist because he questions the gods. But Socrates responds by saying he is not an atheist but that he is responsible to another god, his own *daimon*, who apparently speaks within him and compels him to question all things. Therefore, despite the accusation, Socrates is not so much an atheist as a new kind of theist. He is not irreligious but religious in a new way, one which compels him to question the sacred order of things in the name of an "Unseen Measure." The God to whom he answers is not like the gods who dwell "out there" in the sky, and forests and rivers of nature. This is a God who can only be encountered "within the self" through the inner life of the soul. By turning inward Socrates discovered a "wholly other God," a God who was beyond this world and whose very existence called this world and its sense of justice into question. In the name of this experience of a God or a Good which radically transcended (to "transcend" means literally "to go beyond") this world, Socrates introduced an other-worldly "Ought" into this world, suggesting that the way things are is not necessarily the way they ought to be. For Socrates it is not enough for society to be the sacred order of the cosmos writ small, it must also (and primarily) be the human writ large. Thus he argued that the true measure of a just society is not the way things are (the sacred customs or sacred order), but rather the human is the measure of all things.

A just society is one in which the human is the measure, Socrates argued, provided we understand (as the Sophists did not) that the measure of the human is the Unseen Measure. No society is truly just that makes sacred order (law and order) more important than justice for human beings. Law and order must answer to a higher standard, the Unseen Measure of a wholly other God or Good. Thus Socrates was neither an atheist nor irreligious. On the contrary, he was responding to another God, another Good than that of the sacred society. And in responding to this wholly other God, he invented ethics as we now understand it, namely, ethics not as observance of the "sacred customs" but rather as the questioning of sacred customs and sacred order.

Ethics, so conceived, is both a religious and an impious activity (one that secularizes all sacred societies) at the same time. It is religious in that it is rooted in an inner experience of a wholly other dimension of being and value (wholly other than that of a sacred society and the order of nature). This experience sets one apart from this world and its values. We have called this type of experience an experience of the holy. This experience is the experience of a radical opening of the self (soul) to the infinite that is manifest in the compulsion to doubt and question. Answers present us with finite and particular understandings, our questions keep us open to the infinite. We always have more questions than answers. By questioning the sacred order of society (its answers), a community is continually transformed by its questions and kept open to the infinite.

The experience of being open to the infinite separates or alienates the human self from the way things are. This experience of the holy is what separated Socrates from the society around him. It made him a stranger within his own society, setting him apart from it and giving him an alternate perspective and an alternate understanding of the good rooted in a divine compulsion that disclosed itself as the Unseen Measure, which touched his soul, providing an infinite measure for his humanity. To be human, to be a person of virtue, was to reflect this Unseen Measure and prod one's community into living up to its highest requirements.

Such experiences of the holy create not only alienated individuals but holy communities. In ancient Greece these communities were, for a brief time, the philosophical schools. A holy community is made up of members who share the experience of the wholly other dimension of normative meaning that sets them apart from the larger community around them, even as it binds them to each other. These communities function as alternate communities or countercultures within the larger society. Their task is not to eliminate sacred order but to modify it so as to ensure that society is not only the *cosmos writ small* (reflecting sacred order) but also the *human writ large* (reflecting the Unseen Measure). Without the presence of holy communities constantly questioning and acting as gadflies in relation to the larger society, society no longer remains open to the infinite, justice disappears, and life becomes "dehumanized." The sacred order of every society must be questioned in the name of human justice, a justice that respects the indefinable mystery of being human, namely, that the human is in the image of the unseen measure and exceeds all measure. Therefore, any society that treats those who are different as less than human is guilty of placing a measure on what cannot and must not be measured.

To define the humanity of someone and confine him/her to that definition is to dehumanize him/her. Today we call it "stereotyping" another person. Putting it in contemporary terms, we would say that the crime of all racism, all sexism, and all religious and ethnic prejudice is to define those who are different, strange or alien to us as "by nature" less than human, and force them to occupy some diminished place within the sacred cosmic order of things. To do this is to replace the Unseen Measure with our own biased measure for defining the human while pretending that we are not prejudiced because not we, but (the sacred order of) "nature," created us all as we are. Therefore, women come to be viewed as "by nature" inferior to men, or blacks "by nature" inferior to whites, and so on.

It is well known that the philosophical schools that derived from Socrates through Plato and Aristotle did not view everyone in terms of the Unseen Measure, most notably women and slaves were not accorded their full humanity. And yet, to the degree that it can be shown (as it certainly can) that all classes of people are capable of openness to the infinite (of doubt and questioning), the implications of the Socratic experience of the Unseen Measure contribute to the development of the modern notion of human dignity. Such a conclusion is inevitable because the Socratic compulsion to question knows no bounds (which is why we say it is an experience of the infinite) and eventually leads to a questioning of the limitations in vision of even the most venerable (sacred) questioners. In this sense, Socrates' accusers were right. His questions, when pursued to their logical conclusion, will subvert every sacred order.

Because ethics is rooted in a form of religious experience, namely "the holy" (the experience of the infinite or wholly other), which separates us from the world around us, ethics is rooted in the individual experience of alienation. To be alienated is to experience oneself as a stranger in one's own world, much as Socrates did. That is exactly what has to happen in order for the criticism of the sacred order of society to occur. As long as persons experience themselves as at home in their world they will not question its customs. Socrates' experience of being under the influence of an alien God or *daimon*, a God who demanded that he doubt and question, made him experience himself as a stranger within Athenian society. The holy communities created by this type of experience are composed of those who experience themselves as strangers to their societies: people who hold alternate understandings of the good, through which they seek to criticize the society around them. The contemporary individuals (Gandhi, King, and others) we will study, each in their own way, exemplify both the model of Gilgamesh's wrestling with the stranger and the model of holiness and alienation that leads them to become, like Socrates, ethical gadflies sent to transform society.

Questions for Discussion

1   In what sense is the story of Gilgamesh a story of religious quest?
2   How does "wrestling with the stranger" function as an ethical theme in the story of Gilgamesh, so as to illustrate the positive side of "doubling"?
3   In what sense is Socrates' ethic a religious ethic?
4   In what ways does the story of Socrates express an ethic of the holy?
5   Compare and contrast the relation of death to ethics in the stories of

Gilgamesh and Socrates.

6   Why is it important that every society be not only the "cosmos writ small" but also the "human writ large," and how does Socrates' act of civil disobedience reflect the importance of both?

REFERENCES

Pritchard, James B. 1958. "The Epic of Gilgamesh." In *The Ancient Near East: An Anthology of Texts and Pictures*. Princeton: Princeton University Press.

Sandars, N. K. (trans.). 1960, 1964, 1972. *The Epic of Gilgamesh*. London and New York: Penguin Books.

Tredennick, Hugh. 1954, 1959, 1969. "The Trial of Socrates: The Apology." In *The Last Days of Socrates*. London and New York: Penguin Books.

4

HINDU STORIES – ANCIENT AND POST/MODERN

The cosmic story of ancient Hinduism saw human existence as lived on a great cosmic wheel of samsara, the wheel of death and rebirth, which is governed by the law of karma. This law says that one's future reincarnations will be better or worse, depending on the moral quality of one's actions in one's present life, and one's moral obligations are largely determined by the caste one is born into as a result of previous karma. The wheel of samsara is the realm of impermanence governed by playful illusions of individual self-identity that are rooted in selfish desire. Liberation (moksha) from the wheel of samsara and all rebirth occurs when one is freed from all desire and realizes one's true identity in which one's "atman" or "self" is the same as the universal eternal self, the Brahman reality that underlies all things. In the formative story, the *Bhagavad Gita*, Arjuna is faced with conflicting moral duties. As a member of the Kshatriya caste, he is a warrior who is obligated to go to war to reestablish justice, but he is also obligated not to do harm to members of his own caste, his cousins whom he faces across the battlefield. His chariot driver, Krishna, proceeds to instruct him in the paths that lead to knowledge of his true eternal and undying identity (atman = Brahman) and then Krishna displays his true identity as Vishnu, the lord of life and death. In the end, Arjuna learns that he can enter into war and even kill his relatives if the cause is just, provided he does so selflessly (without thought of personal gain), for it is Vishnu who really determines who lives and dies. Consequently Arjuna stands up to fight. In the life story of Gandhi, we learn how a great contemporary social activist, through a process of "passing over and coming back," drew upon and transformed this story of war into a story of peace teaching non-violent resistance. The terrifying power of stories of war is that they authorize the inversion of morality, so that killing becomes good, and not killing, evil. Gandhi's life and his spirituality of *brahmacharya* show how a sacred narrative of war can be transformed by a life of holiness – a life that significantly altered the religious traditions of Hinduism. In our comparative reflections we ask whether Gandhi meets the challenges of our post-Holocaust world.

Cosmic Story: The Myth of Liberation

Beginning around 1500 BCE, Aryan tribal migrations, using new advances in travel technology – namely, the domestication of the horse and the invention of the chariot – made their way from the steppes of Central Asia into both Europe and India. In India these migrations brought about a syncretistic merger between the pre-Ayran religiosity of the Indus River valley and the religiosity of the new Aryan invaders. The Aryans developed a rich Vedic literature out of which Hindu and Buddhist teachings emerged – the former in direct continuity, the latter through significant revision. Between 1200 and 900 BCE four great ritual collections had emerged: The *Rig Veda*, the *Yajur Veda*, the *Sama Veda* and the *Atharva Veda*. These scriptures became the sacred knowledge (*Veda* is Sanskrit for "knowledge"), or "eternal dharma" – the sacred truths of Hinduism upon which everything else was built. The Vedas contained many stories of the origins and destiny of the world, and elaborate directions for performing sacred rituals that would bring good fortune to those who paid to have them performed on their behalf. The rituals were in the hands of a priestly caste known as brahmins (because they were specialists in the sacred power known as "Brahman"), who were keepers of the sacred knowledge of the scriptures.

According to the *Rig Veda*, the universe comes into existence through the primordial sacrifice of the cosmic self (Purusha) by the gods. And from the sacrifice of this person the four castes were formed: "The Brahmin was his mouth, the arms were made the Prince [Kshatriya], his thighs the common people [Vaishya], and from his feet the serf [Shudra] was born" (Zachner 1966: 10). Out of this sacrifice the sacred cosmic order (*rita*) is born and with it the dharma – the order of ritual and duty which conforms human beings to the sacred order of things. The right way (of morality) is the rite way (of ritual and sacred custom). In the Vedas it is the brahmin priests who maintain the sacred order of the universe through their karmic skill with ritual.

From about 900 BCE the Upanishads emerged as a tradition of commentary on the Vedas that suggested that the many types of "brahman" (power) of the gods were really manifestations of one single power, "Brahman." With this shift to seeing a higher unity behind the diversity, the rudiments of Hinduism as a great world religion began to form. In the Upanishads, a fully developed Hinduism emerged over the next several hundred years in which karma came to be understood primarily as ethical power rather than ritual power and dharma as moral duty rather than ritual duty. This sacred order of dharma focused attention on the right moral order (including caste) that sustained the universe.

The Upanishads are imbued with the sense that life is transitory, governed by endless cycles of death and rebirth, and filled with playful illusions that hide the true nature of reality. Because of these illusions people suffer needlessly. How-

ever, one should not misunderstand: life is unsatisfactory not just because bad
things happen to people, but rather because no matter how good life is, it never
lasts – it always ends in old age, sickness, and death, and death just leads to
rebirth and a new round of life and death. During the Upanishadic period,
individuals, known as forest dwellers, went on a quest, like Gilgamesh, in search
of an answer to the problems of old age, sickness, and death. These forest dwellers,
however, claimed a more successful outcome to their quest. In the Upanishads
the view emerged that the self (*jiva*) that is lost in death, only to be reborn, is
ultimately an illusory self. One's true self (atman) is never born and never dies.
Consequently, the way to liberation from the transitoriness of life and problems
of old age, sickness, and death is to come to a direct experiential insight into
one's true self in order to realize, through one's experience, that one's true
atman (self) is the same reality as Brahman – the ultimate, unborn, undying,
eternal power that underlies all things.

When the Upanishadic sages tried to imagine their situation in the cosmos
they used the familiar image of the chariot wheel. Life, they said, is the great
wheel of samsara – the wheel of illusory transitoriness in which death is always
followed by rebirth. Everything is always changing, but in a circular fashion like
the cycles of nature (spring, summer, fall, winter, and then spring again) – being born, growing to maturity, then old age, suffering, and death – only to be
born again. Everything undergoes a constant round of change. Everything, that
is, except Brahman, the eternal unborn, undying, unchanging reality that underlies all things. Moreover, since death only brings another rebirth, and rebirth brings another round of old age, suffering, and death – the only answer to
the problem of transitoriness is to be liberated from the wheel of death and
rebirth altogether. The story of life as a quest for liberation from the wheel of
death and rebirth is the great cosmic drama that both Hinduism and Buddhism
share. However, as we shall see, each offers a unique version of the story, leading to distinct ethical and social consequences.

Both Hinduism and Buddhism share a vision of life as lived within the great
cosmic wheel of samsara and both agree that the fundamental problem of life is
illusion rooted in selfish desire. To put this in the context of our story of
Gilgamesh in Mesopotamia, if the problem of old age, sickness, and death
emerged with urbanization and individuation as consciousness of having an
individual self, then in order to be rid of the problems of old age, sickness, and
death one must get rid of this self. Drawing on the wisdom of the Upanishads,
both Hinduism and Buddhism say that the conscious bodily self is a fundamental distortion of our true identity – a distortion that is created by greedy desires
(specifically, selfishness).

Desire divides and separates one being from another. As soon as I allow the
experience of "I want x" to dominate my consciousness I have created the
illusion that "I" am a separate being pursuing my own desires, with no essential connections to others. Thus, under the illusion of being a separate self, I
set out to pursue what is good for me without regard for the harm it may do

to others. So desire creates illusion and illusion creates suffering. Each reinforces and generates the other. Desire functions to tie me to the wheel of samsara. Desire is like a sticky glue that, if still present in my consciousness at my death, keeps me stuck to the wheel of rebirth. But if I succeed in eliminating all such desires from my "self," then at death all trace of "self" (jiva) will disappear and I will experience a final liberation from the wheel of death and rebirth.

The self that disappears is the individualized self (jiva) created by urbanization. When the fiction of that self is exposed, one gains insight into the true nature of the self (atman). The dissolution of the illusion that my true self is the same as my body-consciousness allows me to become aware that what remains is the universal, eternal, undying self – the atman that is the same as Brahman. It is as if each person was an iceberg and the tip of the iceberg was bodily self-consciousness. The illusion would be for the iceberg to think that body-consciousness is all there is to itself. *Moksha*, or liberating enlightenment, we might think, would occur when the tip of the iceberg becomes directly aware of the hidden immensity of its being (the ice below the water level) as its own self. But that is not quite the analogy we are looking for. For the iceberg might still think that it is separate from all other icebergs floating in the sea, not realizing that ice is simply frozen water. To realize that ice is the same as water is to realize atman is the same as Brahman. True moksha would occur when the iceberg achieved this further realization.

To make a difference, this awareness must be more than theoretical, it must occur in our concrete experience as a direct insight. Only this experience enables me to realize that my self and the selves of all other beings are one self – one reality, Brahman. To actually experience this is to undergo a profound ethical transformation, in which I do not need – and so do not desire – to take from another, for I and the other are not competing realities. Indeed, to do violence against another in order to fulfill "my" desires no longer makes sense, for to do violence against another is to do violence against myself.

And so, in this new state of liberated consciousness I am without desire and without self and so do not cling to the wheel of rebirth. But being without desire does not mean being emotionless. Quite the contrary: being liberated from selfish desire, one experiences a universal compassion for all beings who share the same universal self. To achieve such a state of selfless compassion for all beings would be to achieve the state of final liberation, or moksha. No longer ruled by the desires that create illusion and suffering, one would be free of all rebirth. One would become one with the Brahman reality that is unborn and undying in a state of bliss that transcends the wheel of rebirth.

In the Upanishads, over a period of several hundred years (900–400 BCE), four major strategies for arriving at such experiences were developed – the yogas, or spiritual disciplines leading to unity with Brahman. The earliest were the yogas of knowledge (*jnana yoga*) and caste duty (*karma yoga*). Then, in the fifth century BCE, the royal path of *raja yoga* was developed among the forest dwellers. This was the path of inward meditation, stilling the mind in order to break through the illusions of self. Finally, around the second century BCE, the path of love and devotion, or *bhakti yoga*, emerged among the popular cults of theistic piety in Hinduism. These four paths articulate types of spiritual practice that are found not only in Hinduism but throughout the world's great religions.

As you engage in the quest for liberation from one life to the next, your destiny is governed by the laws of karma. Karma is the cosmic law of justice at work in the universe that guarantees that everyone gets exactly what they deserve – not within the confines of a single lifetime, but over many. Thus those who are selfish and who do evil in one lifetime will return in a lower rebirth, where they will be required to learn the lessons they failed to learn in their past life. If they do so, then in their next life they will have a higher rebirth, leading them ever closer to their final liberation, or moksha. Thus nothing that happens in life is accidental. Every event has a meaning and a purpose. The good fortune or misfortune one suffers in one's life is exactly what one deserves in the light of one's past lives. There is something to be learned from every event, and every event leads one either closer to or farther from one's goal of final liberation. One's life is part of a larger cosmic drama, a quest that at journey's end brings liberation and fulfillment.

Talk of higher and lower rebirths within this dramatic story suggests that there is a hierarchy of better and worse, higher and lower, to be encountered in one's rebirths. Indeed, animal rebirths are usually thought to be lower than human rebirths, and within the realm of human rebirths there is a social hierarchy defined by the Hindu caste system. The caste system, which is thought to be the product of the merging of Aryan and non-Aryan peoples, originally defined by skin color (the word for caste is *varna*, meaning "color"), eventually developed into a hierarchy of social positions, each with its appropriate duties and obligations with the priests (*Brahmin*) at the top, followed by nobility (*Kshatriya*), skilled workers (*Vaishya*), and manual laborers (*Shudra*) at the bottom. And beyond the bottom were those completely beyond all status – the outcastes. Caste governed both one's profession and one's social relations – determining what work one could do and whom one might marry or associate with. In general, physical contact and interaction were severely restricted between persons of higher and lower castes. Caste was seen as part of the sacred cosmic or natural order of things (rita) and the mixing of castes as endangering the stability of that sacred order that made life possible.

One was not free to change castes, for caste identity was given at birth and was thought to be the result of one's past-life karma. However, by performing the duties of one's caste (one's dharma) one facilitated a more fortunate rebirth in a higher caste for the next life. According to the teachings of the brahmins, their caste stood at the pinnacle – one had to be eventually reborn into the brahmin caste – and as a male – in order to achieve final liberation. Other strands of Hinduism, especially those shaped by popular devotion (*bhakti*), rejected such a rigid view and held that the truly devout servant of the gods can achieve liberation in this lifetime, no matter what caste or gender.

The moral obligations of *dharma* (sacred truth and duty) fall into two categories: *sadharanadharma* and *svadharma*. The first are the obligations one has to all persons regardless of station in life – such as *ahimsa*, or not injuring others, telling the truth, exercising forgiveness and good will toward others, as well as living a pure life. Svadharma are those obligations that are specific to one's station in life as defined by the *varnashrama dharma* system. In the ancient brahmanic tradition these latter obligations superseded the former. But in other strands of Hinduism (such as Vedanta) it is just the opposite. The varnashrama dharma system defined the fundamental ethical obligations of every Hindu by tying their karma not only to their caste (varna) status but also to the stages (*ashrama*) of life, which were four: student, householder, forest dweller, and sage. As a member of one of the top three castes, at a young age one would enter the path of the student, where one's obligation would be to study the wisdom of the Vedas, and then proceed on to the stage of the householder, where one's obligation would be to raise a family and play a role in society by fulfilling one's professional caste responsibilities. For many lifetimes these two stages might define one's whole life. Eventually, however, one might achieve a rebirth that merited proceeding to a stage beyond that of a householder to that of the forest dweller. The forest dweller is one who, in old age, leaves behind responsibilities in the world to seek enlightenment. This quest might take yet many more lives before one achieves a rebirth that permits one to move beyond the stage of the forest dweller to achieve the wisdom of the sage, that is, the wisdom of final liberation (moksha) from the wheel of death and rebirth.

By tying the varnashrama dharma system to the great myth of the cosmic wheel of death and rebirth (the wheel of samsara – of endless change and suffering) through the cosmic law of karma, Hinduism exemplifies the essential meaning of the term religion – "to tie or bind." For the great cosmic story of karma/samsara ties or binds every adherent into the drama of life as a quest for final liberation, and gives each a sense that his or her own life is an unfolding drama, filled with purpose and meaning. And most significantly, for our purposes, this story defines the moral obligations of every member of Hindu society according to their caste and station. It provides Hinduism with a sacred morality or way of life. Thus the myth of liberation tells every adherent what kind of story they are in and what role they are playing in that story, and so defines for them the meaning of good and evil – of right and wrong.

The Hindu myth of liberation contains elements of both the sacred and the holy. On the one hand, the varnashrama dharma svadharma system governed by the law of karma created a sense of sacred order in which members of each caste were morally obligated to perform the duties of their caste. To mix the castes or to attempt to perform the duties of another caste were considered the gravest of sins. The caste system created a sacred hierarchy founded on ritual purity that viewed casual contact with the stranger from another caste as polluting the sacred order of things. Therefore the caste system built hierarchical inequalities of high caste and low caste (and even untouchables) into the very structure of society understood as part of the order of nature. This hierarchical order functioned normatively – the way things are is the way they ought to be.

And yet, if the sadharanadharma system is given primacy, the story of karma and rebirth serves as "a veil of ignorance" that encourages every individual to identify equally with the well-being of every other creature, for karma and rebirth remind you that you may be reborn in the role of any other being in your next lifetime. Therefore the law of karma encourages every person to identify with the well-being of even the humblest member of society. Indeed, if you abuse another creature, you may be reborn as just such a victim in your next life so that you can learn the lesson of compassion and undo any future such patterns of abuse. In this aspect, the story of liberation expresses the ethic of the holy with its commitment to human dignity and equality as expressed in an ethic of hospitality to the stranger.

Therefore, different aspects of the Hindu myth of liberation promote both equality and inequality – both the ethics of the holy and of the sacred. And because both patterns are present in the narrative imagination that governs Hindu storytelling, we will find that its narratives are capable of encouraging both unquestioning obedience that justifies discrimination against the stranger and an audacity on behalf of the stranger that justifies questioning and challenging all authority in the name of human dignity. No more dramatic example of these counter-tendencies can be found than in the alternative interpretations of the *Bhagavad Gita*. To fully appreciate this we must look first at the story of Arjuna and Krishna in the *Bhagavad Gita* and then at the way in which Gandhi retold this story in order to address the challenges of the modern and post/modern world.

Formative Story: Arjuna and Krishna

[A retelling of the story of Arjuna and Krishna as found in the *Bhagavad Gita*. All quotations are from the translation by Swami Prabhavananda and Christopher Isherwood, *The Song of God: Bhagavad-Gita* (New American Library, 1944, 1951, 1972)].

Introduction

If life is just a bowl full of stories, the Hindu tradition provides a rich collection of stories through which to see and understand human existence. If the cosmic drama of the wheel of samsara provides the background for all of its stories, a wide variety of other tales provide the foreground. Indeed, in the period following the Upanishads, two great collections of epic literature came to define the religious imagination of adherents to the eternal dharma – the *Ramayana* and the *Mahabharata*.

Out of the latter comes one of the greatest and most influential of Hindu stories – the *Bhagavad Gita,* which means, "The Song of God" or "Song of the Lord." The story of Gilgamesh combined two of the most influential types of stories in the history of religions – the stories of quest for an answer to the problems of old age, sickness, and death, and stories of wrestling with the stranger. The *Bhagavad Gita* presents us with another powerful example of the latter. For the *Gita* is really about Arjuna wrestling with his friend, Krishna, and ultimately also himself and his god, Vishnu. It teaches an important lesson of this type of story – namely, whenever we wrestle with the stranger (in this case Krishna) and with ourselves about the meaning and purpose of life, and about our responsibilities, we end up wrestling with the deepest mystery of life – in this case portrayed as the god Vishnu.

The *Gita* was probably written in the second century BCE at a time when religious movements emphasizing popular devotion (*bhakti*) began to offer an alternative to the traditional Upanishadic paths to liberation from the wheel of samsara through knowledge (jnana yoga), duty (karma yoga), and meditation (raja yoga). For these latter three paths were all very demanding. They were paths that attracted the religious specialist who could devote his or her whole life to pursuing liberation. Bhakti, the expression of love and devotion towards some deity, however, was a more democratic path open to even the busiest and most worldly practitioner.

The *Bhagavad Gita* is *smriti* and not *sruti* – which means that it is not technically a "sacred scripture" (sruti) of Hinduism, for it does not belong to the canon of the Vedas and the Upanishads. Nevertheless, it has for all practical purposes scriptural status since it is viewed as a summary statement of the wisdom of the Vedas. While ancient commentaries exist on the *Gita*, its status in Hinduism grew considerably in the nineteenth and twentieth centuries, perhaps because its emphasis on action and the struggle for justice made it a natural vehicle for the Indian struggle against colonial domination by the British. This is a theme to which we shall return in our discussion of Gandhi.

The story of the *Gita* is actually part of a much larger epic story, the *Mahabharata*, the world's longest epic poem. This epic is about the adventures of the great king Bharata and his descendants, including King Pandu and his five sons. When Pandu died, his brother Dhritarashtra succeeded him on the throne and raised Pandu's five sons along with his own 100 sons. The eldest of these 100 sons, Duryodhana, became very jealous of Pandu's sons and sought to murder them but they escaped. Eventually a compromise was reached and the Pandavas received half the kingdom – the worse half. Nevertheless, the Pandavas made the most of it, clearing the land and building a great city. Unfortunately, they lost their half of the kingdom to Duryodhana in a dice game and were forced into exile for twelve years. However, provided they could remain in hiding without being discovered, the Pandavas were supposed to get their kingdom back at the end of the exile. Although they successfully avoided detection for the specified period, when the time came to return their half of the kingdom, Duryodhana refused. So the Pandavas (sons of Pandu) went to war against the sons of Dhritarashtra, dividing all of India against itself. The battle lasted eighteen days and in the end the Pandavas won.

The story of the *Gita* is the story of one of Pandu's sons, the young prince Arjuna. It is set on the day the battle is scheduled to begin and depicts Arjuna in his chariot with his chariot driver, Krishna. They are lined up with the other Pandavas on the battlefield facing their own relatives in what may be a battle to the death. Arjuna sees no point to killing his own kinsmen, and as the *Gita* opens he declares that he would rather die than fight. The remainder of the *Gita* is then a dialogue between Arjuna and his chariot driver Krishna, in which Krishna and Arjuna wrestle with each other over the issue of whether Arjuna should fight or not. Krishna seeks to persuade him that it is his religious and ethical duty to fight. As the story proceeds we learn that the cosmos goes through infinite cycles of death and rebirth and that in every age, when "goodness grows weak, when evil increases," an Avatar (incarnation of God in human form) is sent to reestablish righteousness (dharma) and help human beings find the path to liberation (moksha). In the *Gita* we learn that Krishna is such an Avatar and that he has come to instruct Arjuna on his duties (karma yoga) and on the path to true liberation from the wheel of death and rebirth. The story of the *Gita* is related by Sanjaya, the clairvoyant chariot driver for Dhritarashtra. He is able to see and hear everything that is going on in Arjuna's chariot, even though he is at a great distance, and he relates it all to Dhritarashtra.

A matter of conscience – Arjuna wrestles with himself

As the *Gita* opens, Arjuna is greatly distraught. His limbs are weak, his mouth is dry, he is trembling, and the bow he is carrying slips from his hand. He tells Krishna that he can see no sense in killing his own grandfathers, brothers, and uncles, just for the sake of retaining the kingdom. And he declares that even if they should seek to slay him, he can do them no harm. Arjuna has found himself caught in the middle of a terrible ethical dilemma. One the one hand, he is a member of the Kshatriya caste, and as such he has a moral obligation to perform the duties of a warrior and lead his men in battle to fight for a just cause. On the other hand, those whom he is called to do battle against are members of his own family and caste, and caste morality (which is also part of his dharma or duty) forbids him to take the life of members of his own caste. The sacred cosmic order of society is reflected in the caste system and must never be breached by such internal violence, for when families are broken, the rites are forgotten and the mixing of castes follows; then the ancestors are forgotten, nothing re- mains sacred and the world disintegrates into chaos. Thus Arjuna is damned if he does and damned if he doesn't go to war. No matter what he does, it seems, he violates an ethical obligation and accrues negative karma.

Karma, as we have noted, is a moral concept. It suggests that human beings create punishment or reward for themselves in their next lifetime by their selfish or selfless actions in their present lifetime. To accrue negative karma means that Arjuna will be reborn lower on the scale of life, perhaps as a low-caste Shudra. It may take him many lifetimes to work his way back up the ladder of the caste system to be reborn as a nobleman or Kshatriya warrior or to the highest caste of the priests or brahmins, where he can achieve liberation from the wheel of death and rebirth altogether. Because karma yoga is the practice of those duties and obligations which one has because of one's caste status, Arjuna does not know which is worse: to kill or be killed, to win the war or lose it. So he tells Krishna: "I cannot see where my duty lies . . . I am your disciple. I put myself in your hands. Show me the way" (35).

The path to liberation – Arjuna wrestles with Krishna

It is from this ethical double bind that Krishna seeks to release him by leading him to insights into the true nature of his self and his obligations, insights that will allow him to fight without accumulating negative karma. Krishna tells Arjuna to shake off his cowardice, stand up, and fight. In chapters 2 through 10, Arjuna wrestles with Krishna intellectually and spiritually, as Krishna tries to convince him to stand up and fight. In order to accomplish this, Krishna presents arguments for the traditional yogic paths of Hinduism as the means for providing him with the insight he needs in order to see his duty clearly. These are the paths of knowledge (jnana yoga), duty (karma yoga), meditation (raja yoga) and devotion (bhakti yoga). Then, in an awesome mystical vision in chapter 11, Krishna pulls out all the stops and reveals his true identity as Vishnu, the cosmic lord of life and death. It is this awesome experience that is decisive, convincing Arjuna to stand up and fight, which he declares himself ready to do at the conclusion of the *Gita* in chapter 18.

Arjuna fears dying and he fears killing others, so Krishna tries to get Arjuna to use his capacity for insight (jnana yoga) to penetrate the illusion of living and dying by realizing that his true self is eternal. It is only when we are under the illusion that the self is the same as the body and its self-consciousness that we are filled with anxiety about living and dying, thinking that this name and this form is all we are and therefore we must preserve it or lose it. One must ask, however, how it is that one can say "I" at different stages of life – as a child, a youth, an adult, and in old age – and still have it be the same "I." Is it not because, unlike the body, which undergoes radical changes at each stage of life, the "I" is eternal and unchanging? Thus Krishna argues: "the truly wise mourn neither for the living nor for the dead. There was never a time when I did not exist, nor you, nor any of these kings. Nor is there any future in which we shall cease to be. . . . Bodies are said to die but that which possesses the body is eternal. . . . Therefore you must fight" (36). The atman (self) is truly "unborn, undying, never ceasing, never beginning, deathless, birthless, unchanging forever" (37). The eternal self assumes and sheds bodies like worn-out suits of clothes, in an eternal round of death and rebirth, until it is finally liberated from all desire and illusion which keeps it tied to the wheel of suffering (samsara), the wheel of death and rebirth.

Arjuna is torn by the conflict he feels over his caste duty, so Krishna reminds him that his caste duty (karma yoga) as a Kshatriya warrior is to fight. To not fight is to be disgraced, to fight is either to die and win heaven or conquer and win the earth. However, Krishna is aware of Arjuna's fear of accruing negative karma by killing his kinsmen, so he goes directly to the point. In what is one of the central teachings of the *Gita* – non-attachment to the fruits of one's actions – Krishna helps Arjuna see that the traditional definition of a *sannyasi* (one who renounces the world), as one who withdraws from the world of action to live a pure life in the forest, is faulty. The true sannyasi, he argues, is not the one who withdraws from responsibilities in the world but one who acts in the world selflessly without any desire for personal gain or loss. The correct practice of karma yoga is to do one's duty selflessly, without any personal ambition. If Arjuna fights in order to gain wealth and power then his actions are unworthy and accrue negative karma. But if Arjuna fights for the right reason, to reestablish justice and to fulfill his caste obligation as a warrior, he accrues no negative karma. The key to the correct practice of karma yoga is to do one's duty selflessly. People who do so are true sannyasin. There is no higher obligation than one's caste duty: even if one could perform someone else's duties from another caste better than they, one should not do it, says Krishna, one must always remain faithful to one's own karmic obligations. Anything else will violate the sacred order of the cosmos and lead to the mixing of castes and the disintegration of the sacred order which sustains life.

Arjuna may be listening to Krishna. He may be wrestling with him, struggling to understand what Krishna is saying to him, but his mind is in too much turmoil to really grasp what Krishna is saying. So Krishna attempts to instruct him in the third yogic path of meditation (raja yoga) in order to bring the stillness and calmness to his mind and so prepare the way to insight. Only the yogi who turns inward shall discover the reality of Brahman, the eternal, unborn, and undying reality that sustains all things and which is identical with one's true atman or self. The secret, he says, is mastery of the senses – shutting out the outer world, fixing one's gaze where the eyebrows converge, looking inward, following one's breathing, and in this process stopping the ordinary, everyday workings of the mind that allow it to spin a web of illusion and suffering rooted in selfish desire. When the mind is thus under control and free of all desires it becomes totally one with Brahman, then atman (self) and Brahman (universal eternal being) are one and the same reality. He who practices yoga, says Krishna, shall not only come to true knowledge but also receive "direct spiritual experience, besides" (70).

Finally, Krishna proceeds to instruct Arjuna on the path of devotion (bhakti yoga), the fourth yogic path. Although only direct mystical experience truly knows it, the entire universe is pervaded by the reality of Brahman in the form of a cosmic deity or person (person, or Purusha, is often referred to as *Saguna Brahman*, which means "Brahman with personal qualities"). Devotion to this highest person, says Krishna, is itself a powerful path leading to liberation from the wheel of death and rebirth. The simplest act of devotion; the offering of fruit, or water, or a flower, if done selflessly out of love and devotion to the cosmic Purusha, can lead directly to liberation (moksha). Even if one performs this rite of devotion (*puja*) to one of the millions of other Hindu deities beside Vishnu it counts, for these gods and goddesses are but the million faces of the one ultimate reality. Thus, says Krishna, if you perform such an act of devotion,

> you will free yourself from both the good and the evil effects of your actions. Offer up everything to me. If your heart is united with me, you will be set free from karma even in this life and come to me at last. . . . Though a man be soiled with the sins of a lifetime, let him but love me, rightly resolved, in utter devotion: I see no sinner. That man is holy. . . . Even those who belong to the lower castes – women, Vaishyas and Shudras too – can reach the highest spiritual realization, if they will take refuge in me. . . . Fill your heart and mind with me, adore me, make all your acts an offering to me, bow down to me in self-surrender . . . and you will come into my being. (84–5)

The cosmic vision – Arjuna wrestles with Vishnu

The cumulative force of Krishna's arguments begin to have an effect on Arjuna, but he is still not ready to make this total devotional surrender. Arjuna says to Krishna that his lips have confirmed the true understanding of self and he says to him: "my heart bids me believe you" (88). "Nevertheless, I long to behold your divine Form" (91). Arjuna knows the truth abstractly, but until he knows it by direct personal experience he will not be transformed and ready for action. Krishna tells him that he cannot see this truth with ordinary mortal eyes and so he gives Arjuna the gift of divine sight to see, with a spiritual eye, the true nature of reality. The vision that follows is awesome and terrifying. Krishna is transformed into the cosmic deity Vishnu, a being with "innumerable mouths" and "myriad eyes." Arjuna sees the entire universe, including the gods, embraced in the body of this cosmic deity, the God of the gods. Arjuna is awestruck and terrified and the hair on the back of his neck stands up. He sees Vishnu with his "mouths agape and flame-eyes staring" and he is filled with dread. Then he sees the warriors from both sides of the battlefield being chewed and crushed between the "wide-fanged jaws" of Vishnu as he spews out their mangled heads. "Swift as many rivers streaming to the ocean, rush the heroes to your fiery gullets: mothlike, to meet the flame of their destruction, headlong they plunge into you, and perish. Licking with your burning tongues, devouring all the worlds, you probe the heights of heaven" (94). Thus Vishnu declares: "I am come as Time [or Death], the waster of all peoples [or, destroyer of all worlds]. . . . All these hosts must die; strike, stay your hand – no matter. Therefore strike, win kingdom, wealth and glory. Arjuna, arise, . . . seem to slay. By me these men are slain already" (94).

Arjuna finds his voice and speaks to Vishnu: "Carelessly I called you 'Krishna' and 'my comrade,' took undying God for friend and fellow-mortal, overbold with love, unconscious of your greatness. . . . I have seen what no man ever saw before me: Deep is my delight, but still my dread is greater. Show me now your other Form, O Lord, be gracious" (95). And so, mercifully, Vishnu returns to his human form as Krishna, a form that Arjuna can bear to look upon. And Krishna reminds him that the vision he had just experienced cannot be had by studying the Vedas, nor by practices of self-denial nor charity toward others, nor by ritual, but only by bhakti – intense, loving devotion.

Now Arjuna has experienced the truth of his own being and of all being, he knows his true self is the same as the eternal undying Brahman/Purusha of all beings and he no longer fears death either for himself or for others. Nor does he fear negative karma. He realizes that whoever acts selflessly, without attachment, "though he slay these thousands, he is no slayer" (122). He now knows it is not he who determines who lives and dies but the lord of life and death, Vishnu. His obligation is simply to do his duty selflessly in total surrender and unquestioning obedience. He now knows that it is vain to say he will not fight; it is in his very nature as a Kshatriya to fight – that is his karma and his destiny. And so Arjuna declares to Krishna: "By your grace, O Lord, my delusions have been dispelled. My mind stands firm. Its doubts are ended. I will do your bidding" (130).

And so it happened, and so Arjuna went on to fight and win the battle. And so Sanjaya concludes his story by saying: "Ever and again I rejoice, O Kin, and remember [the] sacred and wonderful truths that Krishna told to his comrade. Ever and again I am glad and remember, rejoicing" (130).

Life Story: Mohandas K. Gandhi and the Way of Brahmacharya

India and colonialism

Mediated through the life of Mohandas K. Gandhi, the *Bhagavad Gita* demonstrates the extraordinary ethical and political power a story can have. For, through the life of Gandhi, the *Gita* literally brought the British Empire to its knees and changed the course of history. To appreciate this, one must first understand a little of the history of the British in India. In the wake of the Protestant Reformation, and the scientific and industrial revolutions that brought modernity, a new and largely Protestant European civilization engaged in dramatic global expansion. Capitalism sought foreign markets through the colonization of the Americas, Africa, and Asia by European nations and their international business corporations. At its peak in the nineteenth century, virtually all the nations of the world, except Ethiopia and Japan, were under European control. Japan was the one Asian country engaged in colonialism. If the acceptance of colonialism and Western/European values was typical of the modern phase in world history, the rejection of Western rule and European values typifies the emergence of a post/modern phase. In this sense, the Indian campaign for *swaraj* or "independence" was, in part, a post/modernist rejection of Western modernity, and Gandhi's movement, rooted in non-violent civil disobedience, an interesting experiment in post/modern ethics.

The British were the dominant force in the history of colonialism. As in Africa, they were a major presence in Ceylon (Sri Lanka) and India, controlling them from the mid-nineteenth to the mid-twentieth century. In 1800 there were more people under British rule in India than in any other colonial area and by 1890 there were more under British rule in India than in all the rest combined. The British relationship with India began as an economic one, through the British East India Company, and gradually escalated into one of political domination. By the 1850s the British East India Company was in control of virtually all of India. A revolt against foreign domination broke out in 1857 and was quelled after slightly more than a year. In 1858 the British government officially took over the rule of India, developing the country's infrastructure (creating a railway system, developing modern industries, adopting Western administrative systems, and so on) for the purpose of bringing it into the international economy. This resulted in a sevenfold increase in foreign trade between 1869 and 1929.

In the process, Britain grew wealthier while per capita income in India declined. Concomitant with these developments was the emergence of a new indigenous administrative elite made up of professionals and administrators, trained in Western-style educational institutions needed to run businesses and the country. Foreign dominance led to a Hindu backlash seeking to recover and raise up Hindu values through independence movements like the Brahmo Samaj and the Arya Samaj. The Indian National Congress was created in 1885 as a political avenue for the expression of Indian national consciousness. An extreme wing of this movement began to question the right of the British to rule India. In 1915, Mahatma Gandhi returned from South Africa, where he had refined the methods of non-violent civil disobedience, to lead India toward the independence that was finally achieved in 1947, the year before Gandhi's assassination.

The early years

Gandhi was born on October 2, 1869 in Porbandar in the state of Gujarat, to Banya parents – that is, members of a Vaishya merchant caste. His parents were Vaishnava Hindus – followers of the deity Vishnu. His father was not particularly religious but his mother was devoted to the lord Krishna. His father was an important official in local government and Mohandas grew up in a pluralistic world where family friends were Jains and Muslims as well as Hindus. His first encounters with Christianity were quite negative, with overzealous missionaries who viciously criticized Hindu religion and culture. He was a serious child, who, from an early age, was deeply committed to honesty and the truth. Indeed, he saw a childhood confession of dishonesty to his father as an early turning point in his lifelong commitment to the truth – a commitment he came to call *satyagraha*.

Another formative event of his early years related to his arranged marriage to his wife, Kasturbai, when both were 13 years old. Gandhi's father's health was quite poor by this time and he died when Gandhi was about 15. His father's death was a source of considerable guilt, for although he was quite attentive to his father's needs during his illness, it happened that he left his father's bedside shortly before his death in order to go to the bed of his bride. It was during this time that his father died and Gandhi felt that, because of his own lust, he had failed to be with his father in his last moments. His sense of guilt for this was overwhelming and he interpreted the death of his next child as a just punishment for his behavior. This event taught him the necessity of bringing the needs of the flesh under a strict spiritual discipline. Perhaps because of this, the way of asceticism or self-denial through fasting, prayer, and self-discipline played a central role in his life.

England, law school, and theosophy

At age 19, Gandhi was given permission by his mother, with deep reservations, to go to London to study law with the hope that three years of such training would ensure his advancement when he returned to India. Gandhi tried to secure the permission of his Banya caste elders, but they refused. They felt that it was impossible for a Hindu to remain faithful to his religion in England. Gandhi, however, made vows in his mother's presence, promising to refrain from wine, women, and eating meat, and refused to be deterred. He set sail for England in 1888. For this, he was declared an outcaste by the Banya. Strangely enough, Gandhi's journey to England led him not away from his Hinduism but more deeply into it. For it was in England that Gandhi came to discover the *Bhagavad Gita* and to appreciate the spiritual and ethical power of Hinduism. Because he had promised his mother that he would remain vegetarian, he took to eating his meals with British citizens who had developed similar commitments to vegetarianism through their fascination with spirituality and with India. In these circles he came into contact with Theosophists, most importantly Madame Blavatsky and her disciple Annie Besant, both of whom had a profound influence upon him. His associates also included Christian followers of the Russian novelist Leo Tolstoy, who, after his midlife conversion, had embraced an ethic of non-violence based on Jesus' Sermon on the Mount.

At the invitation of his Theosophist friends he read the *Bhagavad Gita* for the first time, in an English translation by Sir Edwin Arnold, entitled *The Song Celestial*. It was only much later that he took to a serious study of it in Sanskrit. He was also deeply impressed by Arnold's *The Light of Asia*, recounting the life of the Buddha. Thus, through the eyes of Western friends, he was first moved to discover the spiritual riches of his own Hinduism. The seeds were planted in England, nourished by more serious study during his years in South Africa, and brought to completion upon his final return to India in 1915.

From his Theosophist friends he not only learned to appreciate his own religious tradition but came to see Christianity in a new way. For unlike the evangelical missionaries he had met in his childhood, the Theosophists had a deeply allegorical way of reading the Christian scriptures that allowed them to find in the teachings of Christ a universal path of spiritual truth that was in harmony with the wisdom of Asia. The power of allegory lay in seeing in the literal stories of the scripture a deeper symbolic meaning based on what they believed was profound universal religious experience and wisdom. From the Theosophists, Gandhi took an exegetical principle that has its roots in the writings of St. Paul – "the letter killeth, but the spirit giveth life." This insight would eventually enable him to read the *Gita* in the light of his own deep religious experience and find in it the profound truths of non-violent civil disobedience.

South Africa, humiliation and the courage of non-violence

In December of 1890 Gandhi passed his Bar examinations and received his law degree. In June he was officially called to the Bar, permitting him to begin his career as a lawyer. Gandhi returned to India in 1891, deeply influenced by Western ways. He tried to live, dress, and act more English than the English. As a lawyer, he was a failure. His education in English law did not adequately train him for the practice of law in India and so he had to further apprentice himself to learn his trade. And on the one occasion where he actually had a client, he was so nervous that he had to abandon his post in court to a law clerk due to his inability to speak. Gandhi credited two humiliating experiences with changing the direction of his life. The first occurred in India, when he was physically thrown out of the office of a British political agent when he tried to use his influence as a British-trained lawyer. It made him realize that he did not want a bureaucratic career kowtowing to the British in India and he began looking for alternatives. It was at this time that he was offered a job as a legal representative for a Muslim businessman in South Africa. Gandhi, desperate to find a direction for his life, took the offer.

Shortly after arriving in Durban, Gandhi was asked to make a business trip to Pretoria. He purchased a first-class train ticket by mail and began his journey. However, on the journey he was ordered out of his first-class compartment by the train steward at the demand of a white man who objected to sharing a compartment with a "colored" man. Gandhi was ordered to the baggage compartment and when he refused he was thrown off the train. He spent the night in the train station and resolved never to let fear rule his life again. It was a decisive turning point on the road that led him to become the man who brought British imperialism to its knees. What began as a short business assignment in South Africa in 1893 turned into a twenty-one-year stay. In South Africa the timid Indian lawyer was transformed into the fierce spiritual and political leader who returned to India to lead it in its successful bid for swaraj, or independence from the British.

It was in South Africa that Gandhi had his first successful experience as a lawyer. It was successful because he was able to get the two parties to bypass an expensive legal battle and submit to his arbitration. In the process he began to see another way to practice law, one which was to build on his true talent as a negotiator and reconciler of social and political differences. At the same time, Gandhi began a campaign to limit and reverse the laws of discrimination that had been inflicted on Indians and native Africans in South Africa, and he proved himself to be eloquent, courageous and tireless. By the time his business in South Africa had been completed, leaders of the Muslim and Hindu communities from India clamored for him to remain and lead them in the fight for justice on their behalf. Gandhi agreed to remain. Over the next twenty years he developed the techniques of social protest and civil disobedience that would prove decisive when he finally returned to India.

It was in South Africa that Gandhi first began to study the *Gita* intensely. He set up a routine of memorizing a fixed number of verses every day until he had committed it all to memory. It was at this time, too, that he gave up an insurance policy he had taken out as he grew in the conviction that his life and that of his family were in the hands of God, and that ought to be sufficient. Then he read a book by John Ruskin (*Unto This Last*) that changed his life. It motivated him to establish a community in a farm setting where people could live simply and in harmony with nature. So he founded Phoenix Farm, from which he edited a weekly magazine, *Indian Opinion*.

A major turning point for Gandhi in South Africa was the Zulu Rebellion that began in 1906. Gandhi led an ambulance corps into the areas of conflict, where he was profoundly moved by the suffering of the Zulus at the hands of the South Africans. He came back from that experience with the resolve to spend the rest of his life in service to humanity. The spiritual transformation he had been undergoing seemed to take a definitive shape after this event in a way of life defined by (1) brahmacharya, or ascetic self-sacrifice and celibacy, (2) satyagraha, or "soul force," and (3) ahimsa, or non-violence. These three became the defining characteristics of Gandhi's spirituality. Gandhi's experiment with truth now drew him into asceticism, into a more severely self-disciplined life of fasting and prayer. And yet his development of a spiritually disciplined life was never a goal in itself, but always a means to be of service to others, much the way parents make sacrifices to make things better for their children. Thus when Gandhi made his final commitment to celibacy at age 37, it was as part of a pattern of brahmacharya, or self-sacrifice and self-discipline, which he came to feel was necessary if he was to extend his capacity to love beyond his biological family to embrace all human beings.

Despite the service of Indian Hindus and Muslims in the ambulance corps again during the Zulu War, they remained discriminated against by South African law. Gandhi and his family settled in Johannesburg and he confronted South African law once more. The Asiatic Registration Act introduced in 1906 restricted Indians dislocated during the Boer War from returning to the Transvaal and also forbade all new immigration. Indians currently living in the Transvaal were fingerprinted and given certificates which they had to carry at all times proving their right of residence. Gandhi led the opposition to this new law through civil disobedience, declaring that although the government might imprison him or even kill him, they would only have his body, not his obedience. After two weeks General Jan Christian Smuts, the Minister in Charge of Indian Affairs, offered Gandhi a compromise – all prisoners would be released and the law repealed if Indians would voluntarily register. Gandhi kept his word but Smuts went back on his, at which point over two thousand Indians gathered for a public burning of their certificates. Gandhi and others were again arrested, served a two-month sentence, were released and rearrested for the continued resistance, serving another three months.

In 1910 South Africa achieved self-rule as a dominion of the British empire. Despite Gandhi's trip to England to lobby against anti-Indian laws, they remained on the books. It was at this time that Gandhi wrote *Indian Home Rule,* which both criticizes violent overthrow of the empire and yet suggests Indians must find a non-violent way to free themselves from Western colonialism and materialism. It was the beginning of a strategy that would eventually unseat British power in India. About the same time Gandhi struck up an active correspondence with Tolstoy, who seems to have seen him as his spiritual heir, and founded Tolstoy Farm, twenty-one miles outside of Johannesburg.

In 1913 further insult was given to the Indian community by a judge's ruling that non-Christian marriages could not be recognized in the Union of South Africa. This was compounded by a new law barring Indian immigration to South Africa. Gandhi responded with his first massive strategy of civil disobedience. Gandhi warned the government of their intention to break the immigration laws and led some five to six thousand protesters on a march to Charlestown. Gandhi was arrested and his followers were taken by train to a hastily con-. structed internment camp. This in turn inspired a new round of strikes by thousands of Indians. The headlines reached England and India, and Gandhi used the press to create public pressure.

Another public march was planned but Gandhi called it off when an unrelated European railway-workers' strike paralyzed the country. Gandhi insisted that he would not press his adversaries in their time of weakness. General Smuts recognized the integrity of Gandhi's actions. While he felt no compunction about responding to the railway strikers' violence with violence he admitted that Gandhi's strategy of non-violence "reduces us to sheer helplessness." In June of 1914, Gandhi negotiated an agreement with General Smuts that recognized non-Christian marriages, and suspended discriminatory taxes. However, the immigration restrictions remained in force. Gandhi, who had no official political standing, had negotiated an improved, if not perfect, situation for Indians in South Africa. And he had demonstrated that satyagraha, or civil disobedience, could be an effective political tactic. This event was the culmination of twenty-one years in South Africa – a sojourn that had transformed Gandhi from a timid lawyer into a mature spiritual and political leader. Following this, Gandhi and his family set sail to return to India.

The return to India: the journey to self-rule (swaraj) and liberation (moksha)

After a brief stop in England he reached Bombay in January of 1915 at age 45. He established his first community, "Sabarmati Ashram," in India outside of Ahmedabad on the Sabarmati River. His community included many who had followed him from Phoenix Farm in South Africa. His first test was accepting a family of untouchables as part of the community. There was resistance both within the ashram and in the surrounding community whose donations kept the ashram going. It appeared that the ashram would be forced to close down until a gift from an anonymous donor saved the day.

During World War I Gandhi cooperated with the British in recruiting volunteers for the British army despite his own commitment to non-violence. He hoped that demonstrating the loyalty of Indians to the British empire would hasten the day when India would receive its independence. But after the war the British passed the Rowlatt Act (March 1919), which imposed severe restrictions on Indian freedom. Gandhi called for a general strike on April 6 in protest. However, hostility to the British was such that uncontrolled violence broke out. Gandhi tried to call off the strike but it was out of control. A ban on public meetings was proclaimed by the British on April 11. On April 13 over five thousand Indians gathered in protest at Jallianwalla Bagh. General Dyer ordered troops to open fire, and in ten minutes 400 people were killed and 1,200 injured. Gandhi blamed himself for calling the people of India to satyagraha before they were spiritually ready.

Gandhi now advocated complete non-cooperation with the British and urged Indians to abandon Western dress and wear *khadi* (Indian-woven cotton cloth rather than British factory-made cloth) as an expression of the national identity. Gandhi himself took to wearing only a *dhoti* (loincloth) made of handwoven Indian cotton, the traditional garb of a Hindu forest dweller – to emphasize his Indian identity. The goal was swaraj, or Indian self-rule. In 1920 the Indian National Congress adopted non-cooperation as an official policy and a new constitution drafted by Gandhi. By January of 1922 some thirty thousand Congress workers were jailed for non-cooperation. The British were beginning to feel the weight of the challenge. In March they arrested Gandhi, who told the judge that he had disobeyed an unjust law and willingly was prepared to pay the penalty. He was sentenced to six years. He was released after twenty-two months to undergo an appendix operation.

In 1930 the Indian National Congress began another push for self-rule. Gandhi chose to defy the salt laws enacted by the British as a means of forcing the self-rule issue. Salt is a very important part of the diet in a country as hot as India. The British forbade Indians from making their own salt (easily done for those who lived by the sea) and then taxed them for the salt they purchased. Gandhi set out with members of his ashram and the press for a 200-mile walk to the sea, at Dandi, to defy the salt laws. After almost a month they arrived at the sea, where he collected salt water for conversion to salt, in defiance of the law.

At first the British tried to ignore his actions, but the world press made that impossible and the movement of defiance spread, with new salt marches. In May Gandhi was finally arrested. By midsummer some one hundred thousand protestors were in jail. Gandhi agreed to call off the protests and go to England for a round table conference, and Irwin agreed to release most of the protestors and allow Indians to make their own salt. In England Gandhi was a media sensation, but he returned to India empty-handed.

In August of 1942 Gandhi launched another mass civil disobedience campaign, demanding that the British "quit India." Gandhi and others were arrested and mass violence broke out. Gandhi entered into a twenty-one-day fast. Finally, on May 6, 1944 Gandhi was released from jail for the last time – having spent, over a lifetime, some five and a half years behind bars, at the end of which he lost his wife, who died in jail on February 22, 1944.

In 1946 the British finally began making plans for a return of India to Indian rule. The Muslims campaigned heavily for a separate country for Muslims. Gandhi opposed dividing India. From the beginning he insisted that the struggle for independence had to be subordinated to the task of spiritual regeneration, without which the oppressed only succeed in becoming the oppressors. That is why, even when Indian independence was finally achieved, he considered his life a failure because it led to a violent split between Hindus and Muslims. He had worked all his life to unite Muslims and Hindus as one people. He lost this final struggle. On August 15, 1947 India was granted its independence and the Muslim state of Pakistan was created. This was not Gandhi's vision. He felt his life's work had ended in failure. He found nothing to celebrate in this outcome. Within months his life came to an end.

On January 30, 1948 in New Delhi, Gandhi was assassinated by a radical Hindu, Natharum Vinayak Godse, who objected to Gandhi's efforts to bring about a reconciliation between Muslims and Hindus in India. Godse saw Gandhi's toleration of Muslims as undermining Indian nationalism. Moreover, he too saw himself as a follower of the *Gita*, which he interpreted as authorizing him to kill in order to heal; that is, to kill even one's own kin, if necessary, in order to save India for Hindus. Needless to say, his was a reading of the *Gita* totally at odds with that of Gandhi. Godse's reading of the *Gita* revealed an imagination shaped by the sacred that turns the stranger into an enemy who is less than human. Gandhi's reading reveals an imagination shaped by the holy, committed not only to hospitality to the stranger but also to audacity on behalf of the stranger. Gandhi died as he had lived, defending the dignity of the stranger. His death sent the nation and the world into mourning. His final gift to the world was the legacy of satyagraha – a cross-cultural and interreligious ethic of non-violent civil disobedience.

Gandhi's ethic and the spirituality of brahmacharya

The emergence of modern secular Western society was largely the result of the Enlightenment and the emergence of science as the new language of public truth – a language that had no need of the "God hypothesis." As a result, religion was privatized. It was reduced to a matter of personal opinion and personal preference that should be kept out of the public realm. Persons may be privately religious but public life should be secular. Colonialism, especially British colonialism, spread the modern worldview around the world. But every culture invaded by colonialism eventually went through a phase of rejecting (either in whole or in part) colonialism and its modern worldview. This anti-colonialism could take either a pre-modern or a post/modern form. Or more likely, as in Gandhi's case, a combination of the two. For, on the one hand, he urged a reversion to pre-modern forms of economy for India (e.g., hand-woven cloth rather than machine-made) while at the same time urging a post/modern vision of a united India of Muslims and Hindus free from British rule.

The way Gandhi interpreted the *Bhagavad Gita* in thought and action exemplifies this post-European post/modernism in which religion is once more understood as a public and political reality, yet free of pre-modern tribalism. On this Gandhi was unequivocal: "I can say without the slightest hesitation, and yet in all humility, that those who say that religion has nothing to do with politics do not know what religion means" (Mehta 1976: 69). For Gandhi, to be religious was to be political. But political action that was deeply religious had to be deeply ethical, and that meant satyagraha, or non-violent civil disobedience.

Gandhi's religious ethic was organized around the three key themes of his spirituality: brahmacharya, satyagraha, and ahimsa. The Brahmachari is one who seeks God as the *Gita* demands – by transcending all love and hate. Such a state is not, as it may seem, a state of emotionlessness but rather a new level of openness and compassion for all beings. This can only occur when one no longer looks upon other beings with the self-centered love and hate that comes from judging all others in terms of whether they please one's own self. To go beyond such ego-centered love and hate is to be able to love each being for itself instead of for how it is related to one's own needs. Bramacharya is the practice of the self-sacrifice and self-discipline (for example, through celibacy, poverty, and fasting) that leads to this universal selfless compassion.

For Gandhi, religion and politics became one through the practice of brahmacharya. For only selfless compassion for the well-being of others can inspire the trust that makes political leadership possible. Brahmacharya, as the commitment to celibacy, was for him the beginning of such a life lived for others. This kind of selfless compassion which renounces all wealth and power, he proved, can transcend the cynicism of politics-as-usual and turn politics into a spiritual and ethical enterprise. Like Socrates, Gandhi took poverty as a sign of a divine calling. His commitment to living simply and communally was proof of his genuineness to those who followed him.

It was in South Africa that Gandhi perfected the link between brahmacharya and satyagraha – that is, "soul force" as the power of truth. Truth – the truth of our essential oneness and humanity – operates through spiritual rather than physical force. Truth can never be coerced, it must win our minds and hearts on its own merit. Therefore, for Gandhi, truth can only be known through a commitment to ahimsa, that is, non-violence. Such truth can have an extraordinary political impact because it manifests itself not in a will to have power over others but through the sacrifice of all desire for such power. As soon as truth needs violence to protect it, it has become a lie.

For Gandhi, political action, in order to be viable, had to be committed to non-violence. If cynical politics proceeds by a willingness to sacrifice others, and so creates yet more cynicism, the politics of satyagraha demands that one always proceed in such a fashion that it is oneself rather than others who will be asked to suffer. Because politics is carried on by fallible human beings, Gandhi argued, that is the only kind of political action that has ethical integrity and spiritually transformative power. Satyagraha is founded on the notion that self-sacrifice is redemptive and transformative – capable of touching not only the mind but also the heart of one's opponents. Responding to violence with violence only escalates violence. By returning love for hate, non-violence for violence, one seeks to reach the conscience and awaken the humanity of one's opponent.

Gandhi argued:

> Passive resistance is a method of securing rights by personal suffering: it is the reverse of resistance by arms . . . If by violence I force the Government to repeal the law, I am employing what may be termed body-force. If I do not obey the law and accept the penalty for its breach, I use soul-force. It involves sacrifice of self. . . . Moreover, if this kind of force is used in a cause that is unjust, only the person using it suffers. He does not make others suffer for his mistakes. (Gandhi 1970: 5–6)

It is symptomatic of the spiritual adventure of the post/modern world that Gandhi first seriously encountered the *Bhagavad Gita* not in India but in England. His encounters with Theosophists and the followers of Tolstoy's radical Christianity awakened in him memories of his own childhood and a desire to find in the spiritual depths of the *Gita* parallels to the ethic of the Sermon on the Mount.

> I remember how one verse of [a] Gujarati poem, which as a child I learnt at school, clung to me. In substance it was this: "If a man gives you a drink of water and you give him a drink in return, that is nothing; Real beauty consists in doing good against all evil." As a child, this verse had a powerful influence over me, and I tried to carry it out in practice. Then came the *Sermon on the Mount*. . . . Of course, I knew the *Bhagavad Gita* in Sanskrit tolerably well, but I had not made its teaching, in that particular, a study. It was the New Testament which really awakened me to the rightness and value of Passive Resistance. When I read in the *Sermon on the Mount* such passages as "Resist not him that is evil; but whosoever smiteth thee on thy right cheek turn to him the other also," and "Love your enemies and pray for them that persecute you, that ye may be sons of your Father who is in Heaven," I was simply overjoyed, and found my own opinion confirmed where I least expected it. The *Bhagavad Gita* deepened the impression, and Tolstoy's *The Kingdom of God is Within You* gave it a permanent form. (1970: 1)

By passing over into another religion and culture Gandhi came back with new insight and appreciation for his own. This was true for Gandhi in relation not only to Christianity but also to other religions, such as Buddhism, Jainism, and Islam.

> I have endeavored in the light of a prayerful study of other faiths of the world and, what is more, in the light of my own experiences in trying to live the teachings of Hinduism as interpreted in the *Gita*, to give an extended but in no way strained meaning to Hinduism, not as buried in its ample scriptures but as a living faith speaking like a mother to her aching child. (1971: 30)

Gandhi found truth in all the great religions and that truth always drove him back deeper into his own tradition, even as it opened his communities and ashrams not only to all castes and outcastes but also to persons of every religion and culture. His communities were models of hospitality to the stranger. They were models for a post/modern community of unity-in-diversity.

Concerning the *Gita*, two things were clear to Gandhi from the beginning. First, the *Gita* was not history but allegory, consequently it was meant to be understood not literally but symbolically. Second, all scripture, including the *Gita*, had to be tested in experience, and the touchstone of that test was ethics. And the test of ethics was ahimsa, or non-violence. "Any conduct that is contrary to truth and ahimsa is to be eschewed and any book that violates these principles is not a shastra [sacred scripture]" (Jordens 1998: 133). In this spirit, Gandhi went so far as to deny the authority of any Hindu scripture that supported "untouchability."

The fact that the *Gita* was not historical did not trouble Gandhi. He knew that the story of the *Bhagavad Gita*, and of the *Mahabharata* from which it comes, were not verifiable by the canons of modern historical method. But he saw these scriptures as stories of the soul whose truth was meant to be verified through ethical experience. Moreover, his own ethical sensibility was deeply shaped by his experience of humiliation when he was thrown off the train for sitting in the first-class section as a "colored" upon first arriving in South Africa. He knew what it was like to be treated as "untouchable" and it gave him the ethical touchstone – nothing is truth, no matter how sacred, that violates human dignity.

Gandhi knew that his interpretation of the *Gita* appeared problematical to many. But he marshaled a forceful argument for his position.

> I do not agree that the *Gita* advocates and teaches violence in any part of it. . . . The fact is that a literal interpretation of the *Gita* lands one in a sea of contradictions. . . . Many of us make the very serious mistake of taking literally what is accepted as scriptures, forgetting that the letter killeth and the spirit giveth life. . . . [The *Gita*] is pre-eminently a description of the duel that goes on in our own hearts. . . . It deals with the eternal duel between good and evil. (1971: 4–6)

Gandhi was aware that he was offering a "new" interpretation of the *Gita* but it was an interpretation forged out of a lifetime of religious and ethical commitment. "Let it be granted that according to the letter of the *Gita*, it is possible to say that warfare is consistent with renunciation of fruit," he said.

> But after 40 years' unremitting endeavor fully to enforce the teaching of the *Gita* in my own life, I, in all humility, feel that perfect renunciation is impossible without perfect observance of Ahimsa in every shape and form. . . . If it is difficult to reconcile certain verses with the teaching of Non-violence, it is far more difficult to set the whole of the *Gita* in the framework of violence. (1971: 26, 16).

"What . . . I have done," said Gandhi, "is to put a new but natural and logical interpretation upon the whole teaching of the *Gita* and the spirit of Hinduism" (1971: 30). If the message of spiritual realization in the *Gita* is that all beings share the same self (whether understood as Brahman or Purusha), then how could the *Gita* be literally advocating violence? For to do violence against another would be to do violence against oneself. The self-contradictions of a literal interpretation, in Gandhi's way of thinking, forces the mind into an allegorical mode where it can grasp the true spiritual intent of the *Gita*'s meaning. Reading the *Gita* allegorically, Gandhi put his argument this way:

> I regard Duryodhana and his party as the baser impulses in man, and Arjuna and his party as the higher impulses. The field of battle is our own body . . . Krishna is the Dweller within, ever whispering in a pure heart. . . . After the first mention of fighting, there is no mention of fighting at all. The rest is a spiritual discourse. . . . The fight is there, but the fight as it is going on within. . . . The message of the *Gita* is to be found in the Second Chapter of the *Gita*, where Krishna speaks of the balanced state of mind, of mental equipoise [i.e., non-attachment to the fruits of action]. In 19 verses at the close of the Second Chapter . . . Krishna explains how this state can be achieved. It can be achieved, he tells us, after killing all your passions. It is not possible to kill your brother after killing all your passions. . . . These verses show that the fight Krishna speaks of is a spiritual fight. (1971: 17– 18, 31–2)

The command given to Arjuna by Krishna to stand up and fight may be a "spiritual" command, but if one understands Gandhi's philosophy of satyagraha, it should be apparent that this does not mean (as it usually does in "modern" terms) that the struggle is purely inner (private) and personal. On the contrary, spiritual means replacing "body force" (violence) with "soul force" – the practice of non-violent civil disobedience through satyagraha and ahimsa. As the *Gita* suggests, there really is injustice in the world and therefore there really is an obligation to fight injustice and even to go to war to reestablish justice. One must be prepared to put one's body on the line, but do so non-violently.

Comparative Reflections: The Paradoxes of War and Peace

In this section and the questions that follow we invite you to pass over into the life of Gandhi and wrestle with Gandhi, and with our conclusions. We draw comparisons and suggest conclusions for your reflection with the hope that they will provoke discussion and the sharing of insight.

Gandhi's spiritual interpretation of the *Gita* is the opposite of the modernist tendency to psychologize and privatize religious experience. Ethics is about what one does with one's body in relation to the public order of society. Soul force is about using one's body to call the public order of society into question in the name of justice and human dignity. Soul force is just as public and just as political as body force, but is committed to the politics of non-violent civil disobedience instead of violent revolution. Like Socrates, Gandhi's ethic is both spiritual and political. Like Abraham, the heart of his ethic is rooted in spiritual audacity rather than to surrender in unquestioning obedience. It shares a common ethos with the Socratic way of doubt and the Abrahamic way of audacity. Gandhi's life story suggests an ethic that questions the sacred order of things and has the audacity to engage in civil disobedience in the name of justice and on behalf of the stranger. And the religious and cultural diversity exemplified in communities and ashrams he founded were models of post/modern spirituality and ethics – a spirituality and an ethic that is cross-cultural and interreligious.

Taken at face value, the *Bhagavad Gita* is a story that reinforces the sacred order of Hindu caste society and teaches unquestioning obedience to Vishnu, the Lord of Life and Death. A central message of the *Gita*, from this perspective, is that the highest duty of every individual is to carry out the duties of the caste they were born into. And provided they do so selflessly and with unquestioning obedience, they will accrue only positive karma, even if their caste duty, like Arjuna's, is to kill others on the battlefield of life. Why is it that Arjuna will accrue no negative karma? Because when he kills another as a result of selflessly performing his caste duty, it is not he who does the slaying but Vishnu, who acts through him. Thus Arjuna is absolved of all guilt because he is not acting for himself but selflessly. He can say – It is not I who acts but Vishnu who acts through me: He, not I, is the true slayer. This is the logic of doubling that we discussed in chapter 2 – the logic that absolves one of the feeling of responsibility for one's actions. It is a logic that is rooted in a spirituality of total surrender of self in unquestioning obedience, as we noted in our discussion of mass death. The force of this logic, then, is to lead Arjuna to accept his caste duty as a warrior and stand up and fight. Thus, taken at face value, the moral purpose of the story of Arjuna and Krishna in the *Bhagavad Gita* seems clear. Its purpose is to justify war and the necessity of violence as a means of establishing justice.

In our discussion of religion and story we have noted two types of story that have been found in many religions and cultures – stories of the quest for an answer to the problems of old age, sickness, and death, and stories of wrestling with the stranger. There is another type of story that is pervasive across cultures – stories of war. These types are not mutually exclusive. Stories of war are stories of wrestling with the stranger that have been infected by a sacral dualism. The *Gita* is both a story of wrestling with the stranger and a story of war. Perhaps no other type of story has a more disturbing impact on human behavior than that of war. For stories of war invert normal ethical orientations. While in most cultures people would normally say that killing is evil and not killing is good, in times of war these admonitions are inverted. Within a story of war, killing is considered good and not killing is considered evil. Indeed, not killing will be considered cowardly and unpatriotic.

All it takes to invert a culture's moral orientation is the adoption of a story of war. The implications of this inversion are profound. Once we believe that we are in a story of war and see ourselves as soldiers prepared for battle, everything that was once forbidden to us becomes permitted. For our understanding of good and evil is shaped by the kind of story we think we are in and the role we see ourselves playing in that story. In times of war the very activities that would normally horrify our ethical sensibilities come to be seen as our highest ethical obligation – calling for the highest sense of duty and self-sacrifice for the good of our community. Moreover, the war we perceive ourselves to be engaged in need not be a literal war. For war easily becomes a useful metaphor for all kinds of situations. So people speak of the war on poverty, the war on drugs, the war on crime, the war against illiteracy, business competition as a kind of warfare, and so on. Through such metaphorical transfers, we open the gates to ethical inversion in even the most peaceful of cultures.

Having said that, it is all the more remarkable that Gandhi was able to find in the story of the *Gita*, a story about war, an ethic of non-violence. What the life of Gandhi teaches us is that the sacral imagination can be redeemed by the experiences of the holy. It is possible to transform stories of war into stories of peace. How is this possible? Because the meaning of a story is shaped by the narrative imagination of its listener and the narrative imagination of the listener is shaped by his or her own religious experience – whether that of the sacred or that of the holy. Gandhi's assassin, for instance, read the *Gita* as a sacred story that obligated him to slay those who would pollute the sacred order of Hindu society by advocating the integration of Hindus and Muslims in one community. Gandhi read the *Gita* as offering a vision of the holy, in which to do violence against another was to do violence against oneself.

Gandhi argued that his interpretation of the *Gita* was superior to others because the *Gita* was not a theoretical book but a story of action, and only someone who tried to live as a karma yogin would be in a position to truly understand it. Gandhi asserted that his qualification for interpreting the *Gita* was that he had "experimented with truth" by trying to live by the teachings of the *Gita* for over forty years. These forty years, he said, taught him by experience that those intepretations of the *Gita* that understand it to be advocating violence against one's enemy fall into self-contradiction and cannot be valid, while his own non-violent interpretation grasped the heart of its truth – the oneness of all humanity.

In offering such a view Gandhi established one of the most important principles for the comparative study of religions after Auschwitz and Hiroshima – namely, that the test of religious truth must be, first of all, ethical. For Gandhi, any understanding of the sacred dharma of Hinduism that allows one to violate the dignity of another human being is a false understanding of dharma, no matter how high the end or purpose for which this is done. For Gandhi, what the *Gita* taught was not "unquestioning obedience" but the audacity to question all authority, even to the point of civil disobedience to the laws of society. He was convinced that commitments to violence and to human dignity were incompatible. You cannot use the one to promote the other. And he was convinced that the deepest insights of the *Gita* affirmed this truth.

Gandhi's commitment to non-violence was so profound that he even suggested that the most appropriate response of Jews to Hitler would be non-violent civil disobedience. The Jews, of course, were largely non-violent, but they did not engage in organized civil disobedience. His critics have suggested that he did not fully appreciate the difference between the Nazis and the British. This is probably true. Gandhi expected the British to imprison protestors, but he was sure they would not engage in mass executions, so long as the protests were non-violent. Would he have persisted in civil disobedience if it meant the death of six million Hindus? That is an open question. Certainly, Gandhi was a tactician who knew when to press his enemy and when to back off – as his negotiations with the Afrikaners and the British in South Africa and in India testify. And, paradoxically, he was willing to campaign for the enlistment of Indian men in the military during World War II because, he said, it was wrong to accept the protection of the British empire and not participate in its defense. Certainly the brutality of the Nazis stretched Gandhi's optimism about human nature and the potentiality for converting one's enemy to a near breaking point. Indeed, "if there ever could be a justifiable war in the name of and for humanity," he said, "a war against Germany, to prevent the wanton persecution of a whole race, would be completely justified. But I do not believe in any war. A discussion of the pros and cons of such a war is, therefore, outside my horizon or province" (1951: 91).

For Gandhi, war is outside the horizon of consideration, because one cannot engage in violence without becoming the same as one's enemy and therefore, from an ethical point of view, even if you win you lose. But his statement makes clear that he understands why, in the face of genocide, others might view war as justified. In making this statement, Gandhi alludes to the "just-war" tradition in ethics. According to this tradition, at least as it is formulated in Christianity, the use of violence for personal self-defense or in order to gain territory or power is always wrong. The only justification for the use of violence is the protection of the weak and the innocent. In the *Gita*, Arjuna is told that if the cause is just and he acts selflessly to reestablish justice, then violence can be justified. There may be situations such as those presented by Nazi Germany where violence, if not right, is at least the lesser of two evils. We shall return to a full discussion of this issue in chapter 8, when we discuss the challenge of Malcolm X to the Gandhian tradition of non-violence advocated by Martin Luther King, Jr.

Quite apart from the principles involved, there is the pragmatic question of whether non-violent resistance could have worked for the Jews. Gandhi was probably wrong in his belief that Jewish non-violent resistance would have stopped Hitler. Both Gandhi and King had some success with non-violent resistance because they were able to mobilize a sympathetic majority in their respective cultures. Jews, however, were a small minority in an overwhelmingly Christian civilization, who could not count on rousing such a majority because of long centuries of Christian hatred and prejudice toward them (accusing them of being "children of the devil," "Christ killers," etc.). Indeed, not only were German citizens unsympathetic to the fate of the Jews, but even the allied nations who fought Hitler showed no great interest. For example, Britain turned down an opportunity to bargain supplies for Jewish lives and the United States made Jewish emigration so difficult that it did not even fill its very limited immigration quota for Jews during World War II. Nor could the Jews count on the Nazis limiting themselves to actions that fell short of mass murder.

Nevertheless, we would still argue that Gandhi was not wrong to suggest that some form of non-violence could have stopped Hitler. Yet it was not the Jews who were in a position to do that, but European Christians. Gandhi rightly described the Jews as the outcasts of Christian society. Exploiting centuries of Christian prejudice against Jews, Hitler was able to draw popular support by exploiting Christian hatred and mistrust of Jews, blaming the Jews for the political and economic misfortunes of Germany. Had Christians rejected anti-Jewish stereotypes and lived by the Sermon on the Mount, especially as Tolstoy and Gandhi understood it, they could have stopped Hitler through non-cooperation. The time to have acted was in the beginning when Hitler was seeking to curry favor by appeals to prejudice and hatred in order to gain support and votes. Once Hitler assumed power, non-violence could have far less impact. This is not to suggest that non-violence should only be used tactically (when one is likely to succeed) but only that it would be wrong not to try to foresee what the real costs of non-violent resistance might be. Whether one chooses to use violence or chooses non-violent resistance, both choices are agonizing, for the consequences in either case can be quite tragic.

One of Gandhi's most lasting contributions to a cross-cultural ethic after Auschwitz and Hiroshima was his development of techniques for forcing bureaucracies to accommodate the ethical demands of conscience. Although Gandhi lived through World War II, including the atrocities of Auschwitz and Hiroshima, his mature insight into the *Gita* and civil disobedience predates those events. And yet his ethic of satyagraha, or non-violent civil disobedience, is directly applicable to the ethical issues raised by a post-Auschwitz and Hiroshima world. This is because, in forging his ethics of non-violence, Gandhi was responding to the same type of challenges. The conjunction of techno-bureaucracy and ethnocentrism that lies at the heart of modernization is present both in the spread of European colonialism around the world in the nineteenth and early twentieth centuries (including India), and in the events that led to Auschwitz and Hiroshima. Moreover, techno-bureaucracy and ethnocentrism both remain universal characteristics across cultures in contemporary technological civilization. The real power of bureaucracy, we have argued, is in its ability to undermine the ability of persons to raise ethical questions. What is required is the audacity to question and subvert bureaucratic authority. Thus the spiritual audacity of Gandhi's strategy of satyagraha against British bureaucratic colonialism is transferable, especially if applied to developing trends that have not yet escalated out of control.

Finally, Gandhi's life shows us that religious traditions and religious stories are not static, eternal, and unchanging but evolve in response to the ethical challenges of time and place without becoming purely relativistic (simply reflecting the sacred morality of the surrounding society). Gandhi shows us how ancient wisdom remains relevant and can be transformed into post/modern insight and action, contributing to a cross-cultural and interreligious ethic after Auschwitz and Hiroshima.

Questions for Discussion

1   In what ways does Gandhi's ethic violate the modernist paradigm of the privatization of religion?
2   How does the contrast between the sacred and the holy, or morality and ethics, appear in Gandhi's life and thought?
3   Does the concept of human dignity play a role in Gandhi's thought? If so, how?
4   In what sense does Gandhi transform the *Bhagavad Gita* from a story of war into a story of peace, and on what basis?
5   Describe Gandhi's spirituality and explain how it functions in relation to his ethic of non-violence.
6   How does Gandhi's ethic address the ethical challenges of a techno-bureaucratic society?
7   Was Gandhi right to think that the practice of non-violent civil disobedience by the Jews could have worked in Nazi Germany?
8   In what ways does Gandhi's life illustrate one way in which a religious tradition can undergo transformation?
9   How would you characterize Gandhi's Hindu ethic in terms of Masao Abe's models of religion and ethics (see figure 3.1)?
10 How is the post/modern spirituality of "passing over" and "coming back" illustrated in Gandhi's life story, and what is its ethical significance?

REFERENCES

Edgerton, Franklin. 1944. *The Bhagavad Gita*. New York: Harper & Row.
Fischer, Louis. 1954. *Gandhi, His Life and Message for the World*. New York: Mentor, New American Library.
—— (ed.). 1962. *The Essential Gandhi: An Anthology of His Writings on His Life, Work and Ideas*. New York: Random House, Vintage Books.
Gandhi, M. K. 1951. *Selected Writing of Mahatma Gandhi*. Boston: Beacon Press.
——. 1970. *The Science of Satyagraha*. Bombay: Bharatiya Vidya Bhavan. Distributed

by Greenleaf Books, Weare, NH.

——. 1971. *The Teaching of the Gita*. Bombay: Bharatiya Vidya Bhavan. Distributed by Greenleaf Books, Weare, NH.

Isherwood, Christopher and Prabhavananda, Swami (trans.). 1944, 1951, 1972. *The Song of God: Bhagavad-Gita*. New York: New American Library.

Jordens, J. T. F. 1998. *Gandhi's Religion: A Homespun Shawl*. New York: St. Martin's Press.

Mehta, Ved. 1976. *Mahatma Gandhi and His Apostles*. New Haven, CT: Yale University Press.

Zaehner, R. C. (trans.). 1966. *Hindu Scriptures*. New York: Everyman's Library.

5

BUDDHIST STORIES – ANCIENT AND POST/MODERN

We begin with the formative story of the life of the Buddha rather than the cosmic story, because the Buddha's own enlightenment experience led to important changes in the cosmic story of the myth of liberation as found in Hinduism. This is noted in the section "The Cosmic Story Revised". Then we turn to the life story of Thich Nhat Hanh, which shows how the ancient stories take on new ethical implications in his "socially engaged Buddhism." The story of the Buddha is a story, like Gilgamesh's, of wrestling with the stranger (in his case, four strangers) and a quest to find an answer to the problems of old age, sickness, and death. The difference is that the Buddha returns with an answer, the experience of "no-self" or "emptiness" expressed in his understanding of the interdependent co-arising of all things. This is the basis for the Buddhist revision of the cosmic story of death and rebirth, for the Buddha asserted that when he had his enlightenment experience he realized that *all* things are impermanent and therefore there is no universal eternal (Brahman) self. Buddhist compassion, therefore, is not rooted in the experience of sharing a common self with all beings but rather in the experience of being interdependent with all beings. The essence of illusion is a sense of "own being" (*svabhava*), which is thinking that I have my being independent of all other beings and so can pursue my good without thinking of others. Such an illusion, based in selfish desire, is the root of all suffering, while enlightenment is the dissolution of this false division between self and all other beings, which then gives rise to universal compassion. The life story of Thich Nhat Hanh provides a contemporary life story of a social activist who, during the Vietnam War, transformed the understanding of these ancient stories so as to give rise to a "socially engaged Buddhism" shaped by a spirituality of meditative mindfulness. In our comparative reflections we take up the issue of a possible disagreement between Thich Nhat Hanh and Gandhi on the meaning of loving one's enemies.

Formative Story: Siddhartha

Introduction

Like the story of Gilgamesh, the story of the Siddhartha Gautama, known as the Buddha or "Enlightened One," is also a story of a quest to find an answer to the problems of old age, sickness, and death. And like both the stories of Gilgamesh and of Arjuna, Siddhartha's story is one of wrestling with the stranger – a wrestling that leads to a confrontation with his own mortality. If we can place the evolving story of Gilgamesh in the early stages of the urbanization process, somewhere between 3000 and 1500 BCE, Siddhartha Gautama (563–483 BCE), the Buddha, or "Enlightened One," appears at least a millennium later in India, where urbanization was intensifying at a pace which parallels that of the Mediterranean. Gilgamesh is a transitional figure in the shift from tribal to urban society in the ancient world. He represents the naked urban self that has been stripped of its tribal myths but has not yet fully developed a language of inner experience. He has not yet glimpsed the dizzying depths of his own inwardness and discovered his openness to the infinite. Consequently, Gilgamesh can only seek an answer to old age, sickness, and death outwardly, in the world around him. So he seeks to recover a plant of eternal youth that can be found by diving into the depths of the sea. Unlike Gilgamesh, who ended up empty-handed, Siddhartha is said to have turned "inwards" to dive deep into the murky depths of the self, penetrating its illusoriness and returning enlightened with an answer to the problem of death as a loss of self.

Siddhartha Gautama was born in northern India in a period of rapid urbanization and social change in the sixth century BCE. The alienation of the urban experience, as we have noted, produces a new world of psychological and sociological suffering characterized by a threefold crisis of morality, mortality, and meaning. Alienated from both neighbor and cosmic meaning, the self experiences life as burden of suffering. Both Hinduism and Buddhism emerged as answers to the problem of alienation produced by the individuation and the doubling of the new self-conscious urban self. Both, in part, handle the problem of doubling or self-consciousness by suggesting that the self we are conscious of is an illusion created by craving or desire. By extinguishing the fires of desire one eliminates alienation and the doubling of self-consciousness, overcoming the problems of mortality, morality, and meaning.

Siddhartha, like Gilgamesh, belongs to the class of those born to be warriors and rulers (Kshatriya) rather than priests (Brahmins). In an urban world, warfare escalates into a major activity and the warrior is on the frontline of those to first experience the prospect of death as a loss of self. We saw this in the *Bhagavad Gita*, where Arjuna, a Kshatriya (member of the warrior class), agonizes over prospects of slaying and being slain just prior to an important battle and is led to a prolonged reflection on the self and death. It should not be surprising that religious leadership in a newly urbanized world comes from this warrior class. In a period in which the Upanishads were still being written and the Brahmanic tradition of Hinduism was still forming, Siddhartha's story offered an alternative path. When Siddhartha left his family to enter the forest seeking an answer to the problems of old age, sickness, and death, he embraced a branch of the shramanic tradition of forest dwellers who, like others such as the Jains and the Ajivakas, rejected Vedic scripture, caste, and the Brahmanical sacrifices. Let us turn to the story of his quest that is formative for all Buddhist paths.

Siddhartha's quest

[A retelling of the story of the life of the Buddha, based on the *Buddhacarita* of Ashvagosha and on earlier sources from the Pali Canon, especially those cited in *The Life of the Buddha as Legend and History* by Edward J. Thomas (Routledge & Kegan Paul, 1927.) All quotations are from the *Buddhacarita* as edited and translated by Edward Conze in *Buddhist Scriptures* (Penguin Books, 1959).]

Life in paradise – the palace years

Like the story of Gilgamesh, the story of the Buddha is a tale about a young prince who wrestles with the stranger and with death, and as a result sets out on a journey – a quest to find an answer to the problems of old age, sickness, and death. Unlike Gilgamesh, however, Siddhartha returns from his quest with an answer to share with humankind – the path to Nirvana, the ultimate liberation from the wheel of death and rebirth.

Once there lived a great king of the Shakya clan (sixth century BCE), Shuddhodana, and his wife Maha Maya. The couple conceived a child whom they would name Siddhartha. This child was conceived out of pure love, untainted by selfish desire. Before the actual conception, Maha Maya had a dream. She dreamt that a huge white elephant entered her womb without causing any pain. Indeed, her whole pregnancy was painless and trouble-free. As the time for her delivery drew near, she and the King went for an outing in the countryside to a delightful spot called Lumbini grove. There she realized that her time had come and she gave birth to the future Buddha miraculously from her side, without any pain or discomfort. "He did not enter the world in the usual manner, and he appeared like one descended from the sky" (35). His appearance was as dazzling as the sun to those who looked upon him. Instantly, upon his birth, he took seven long strides, surveyed the four quarters of the universe and declared: "For enlightenment I was born, for the good of all that lives. This is the last time that I have been born into this world of becoming" (36).

After his birth, the great visionary Asita came to the palace, and upon seeing him declared that this child had the potential to be either a great world ruler or a great world savior, and he predicted that he would give up his kingdom for the latter path and would discover the secret of the extinction of rebirth to the benefit of all humankind. He had come, he said, to proclaim the dharma (teaching) of liberation. Like a sun he would remove the darkness of delusion, freeing the world from the bondage of all craving and suffering, and from old age, sickness, and death. Having said this, Asita lamented that he was too old to see the day when that would occur.

Queen Maya died shortly after Siddhartha's birth and the boy was raised by her sister. The boy had a happy childhood without illness or suffering. He was extremely intelligent, learning in days what it took others years to master. His father, Shuddhodana, hoped his son would succeed him on the throne. He also wanted Siddhartha to have a perfect life, free of all pain and suffering, and therefore he restricted him to life within the palace gates where he could protect him and ensure his every pleasure. Thus the young prince lived as if in the midst of paradise, in a world of wealth, rich foods, and sensuous young maidens. There, his every need and desire were met and suffering was unknown to him. At the appropriate time, his father arranged his marriage to a beautiful young woman, Yashodhara, and they had a son whom they named Rahula. And so Siddhartha lived in blissful happiness, without a care, for the first twenty-nine years of his life.

Paradise lost – wrestling with the four strangers

As time passed, however, Siddhartha began to wonder what the world was like outside the palace gates, even though he was forbidden by his father to leave the palace grounds. And so he resolved that he would make such a journey. Thus on four separate occasions he secretly took a chariot-drive through the countryside. Each time he met a stranger who had a profound impact on his life. On the first such occasion he encountered an old man who was bent over with age and could barely see or hear. He was shocked at this encounter because he had been protected from all knowledge of aging and had not seen what it could do to a human being. Greatly disturbed by this sight, he immediately returned to the palace, where he paced anxiously and could find no peace. However, he resolved to make a second journey. On this journey he encountered a sick man. Again, he found himself greatly disturbed by the knowledge of the pain that can come upon a person stricken with disease and returned to the palace in turmoil. And still he resolved to make a third trip. This time he encountered a dead man lying by the side of the road. He was thunderstruck by this encounter. He had been protected from all personal knowledge of death. He did not know that this was the destiny of all humankind. He looked at the dead man and saw his own destiny. He was filled with revulsion and terror and he swiftly returned once more to the sheltered life of the palace.

When Siddhartha returned to the palace he was beside himself. All the joys and pleasures of life seemed hollow and specious in the face of his knowledge of death. How could anyone be protected from old age, sickness, and death? Wealth was no protector, nor was power. Old age, sickness, and death come to all human beings regardless of their station in life. Truly they are the great equalizers. Now the prince withdrew from the pleasures of life in the palace as one who had lost all taste for such things. He thought to himself: "When I consider the impermanence of everything in this world, then I can find no delight in it" (40). The world now seemed to him to be caught up in the swirling passions of delusion, ablaze with the "all-consuming fire" of false desires that could never result in any lasting fulfillment. What is the point of wealth, of sensual pleasure, indeed, of happiness, when they only attach you to things that will eventually be taken away from you by old age, sickness, and death?

Siddhartha no longer felt either safe or content within the palace walls. In the midst of this great crisis that had come upon him in the middle of his life, he made yet a fourth journey outside the palace. As he traveled through the countryside he noticed the field plowed up for planting and he thought of the death of the grass and the insects and small creatures that had been caused by this seemingly innocent act. And he looked upon the faces and bodies of the farmers working in the fields. The sun, the wind, and long hours of labor had each taken its toll on their bodies, as had time itself. Time, it seemed to him, was unceasing change, an endless succession of generations, none of which had found any safe haven from its ravages. Generation after generation was born to no destiny other than to suffer and die. Everywhere he looked he saw old age, sickness, and death. He was overwhelmed and yet filled with compassion for the lot of all living things. He was humbled by these thoughts and no longer felt himself to be better than others simply because he was a prince. He realized he shared a common lot with all living things and he longed to find a path of liberation that would free all creatures from the world of samsara, the world of suffering and impermanence.

As he was having these thoughts while traveling through the countryside, he came upon a fourth stranger who changed his life forever – a monk. Siddhartha stopped to talk to this stranger, who was dressed in a simple robe, and discovered that he too had been terrified by the knowledge of old age, sickness, and death. This monk also had been confronted with the meaninglessness of life. As a result, he had left the world and set out on a quest to find a blessed state in which death was overcome, a state of mind in which "kinsmen and strangers mean the same to me, and greed and hate for all this world of sense have ceased to be" (43). And so, this monk explained that he now sought to live a simple life; owning nothing, desiring nothing, expecting nothing.

Siddhartha, profoundly moved by this encounter, returned to the palace one last time, with the thought firmly planted in him that he too must take this path. Siddhartha wrestled with himself late into the night, surveying his comfortable life, but he could no longer find any pleasure in the wealth, the women, or the power. In the middle of the night he roused his groom, Chandaka, and ordered him to bring him his horse Kanthaka. They rode together until they reached a hermitage where Siddhartha gave Chandaka all the jewels he was wearing and then dismissed him. He sent Chandaka back to his father with a message. He instructed him to say that he was leaving the palace and his family, and giving up his rightful claim to the throne in order to take up the homeless life and discover an answer to old age, sickness, and death. He did not, therefore, want his father to grieve for him or think that he was leaving in anger or resentment. He knew that his father would think he was too young to be abandoning life in the world for the path of a forest dweller but he thought to himself: "There is no such thing as a wrong season for Dharma. . . Death confronts me all the time – how do I know how much of life is still at my disposal?" (44). Chandaka tried to dissuade him from this course of action, but Siddhartha responded by reminding him that all relationships end in parting, if not brought about by events and circumstances, then by death itself. Moreover, he tells him, his parting now has the higher purpose of putting an end to all such partings by finding a path of liberation. And so Chandaka returned to the palace without him.

The quest for an answer to the problem of mortality

With his entry into the life of a forest dweller, Siddhartha became a sannyasi – one who has renounced the world. For the next seven years Siddhartha pursued his quest for enlightenment, seeking the experience and insight that would provide him and all humankind with an answer to the problem of old age, sickness, and death. During the years of quest, he first studied how to meditate with two of the great masters of meditation in the forest-dweller tradition, namely, Alara Kalama and Uddaka Ramaputta. However, these studies did not bring him to the insight he sought. So he left these teachers and joined a band of five monks who were fasting in order to rid themselves of all desire. For if it is true that desires attach us to the sensory world of impermanence with the delusion that this world can fulfill these desires (a delusion that can only end in suffering, separation, and death), then surely the path to liberation is one that eliminates all desire.

For six years Gautama pursued the path of austerity and self-denial, seeking to defeat all desire and achieve liberation. But although he fasted and starved himself until you could see his backbone through his rib cage, the only thing he achieved was dizziness and headaches. He began to realize this was not the path to liberation either, for just as the attempt to fulfill our desires only makes us desire even more, so the attempt to deny our desires only makes us more obsessed with the absence of that which we desire. In both cases the self and its selfish desires are only reinforced. Surely, Siddhartha thought, there must be a middle way between these extremes. As he was thinking this, a young maiden came along carrying food and drink, and when she saw how emaciated he was she offered it to him. Siddhartha saw her offering as a good omen, for the night before he had had five great dreams that led him to believe that he was about to become a buddha, that is, an enlightened one. Therefore, he kindly accepted her offer, resolving to regain his health and strength in order to give his body sufficient energy to pursue the middle way.

Then Siddhartha went off and set himself down to meditate beneath a fig tree and resolved he would not get up until he had achieved enlightenment. He remembered an experience he had had as a child, when he once spontaneously entered into a trance state of consciousness while sitting under a rose-apple tree watching his father plow a field. Taking that state of consciousness as a clue, he sought to reduplicate and deepen it, sure that it would lead to enlightenment. With that conviction he meditated on into the darkest hours of the night. During the night the great master of temptation and illusion, Mara, the Evil One, sought to tempt, intimidate, and dissuade him from his goal. Mara and his army sought to threaten and distract Siddhartha, terrifying him with wind and storm, so as to break his concentration, and when that didn't work he sent his daughters to seduce him. But all to no avail, for Siddhartha would allow nothing to distract his concentration, and Mara was defeated.

With Mara defeated, Siddhartha passed into successively deeper states of consciousness and insight with each of the four watches of the night. During the first watch he achieved personal recollection of his past lives and he realized that he had lived many times before, each lifetime bringing him closer to this moment of final liberation. Then, at the second watch, he came to understand the law of karma that governs the death and rebirth of all beings according to their merits and demerits, that is, according to whether their actions were selfish or selfless in their past lives. And he realized that there is nothing substantial or eternal one can cling to in the world of samsara, the world of impermanence and suffering. Then, during the third watch of the night, he grasped the secret of nirvana or liberation, namely, the extinction of all desire through the path opened up by the four noble truths and the eightfold path. "He passed through the eight stages of Transic insight and quickly reached their highest point. From the summit of the world downwards he could detect no [eternal] self anywhere. Like the fire, when its fuel is burnt up, he became tranquil" (50). The truth of enlightenment is that there is no eternal self to be found anywhere in the universe, only the interdependent co-arising of all things in a constant sea of change (samsara). Finally, with the fourth watch and the coming of the dawn, he achieved full enlightenment. At that moment the earth shook, the sky lit up, and thunder resounded through the air like mighty drums. Then "rain fell from a cloudless sky, flowers and fruits dropped from the trees out of season. . . . At that moment no one anywhere was angry, ill, or sad; no one did evil, no one was proud; the world became quite quiet, as though it had reached full perfection" (51). And joy spread everywhere throughout the universe and everyone was pleased except Mara.

Siddhartha, now the Buddha or enlightened one, remained in this state of nirvanic consciousness for seven days. In this state he experienced his final temptation, for he was tempted not to proclaim and teach what he had discovered for fear that it could not be put into words. However, his great compassion for the world overwhelmed this last great temptation and he resolved to spend the remainder of his life sharing the dharma, the teachings that lead down the path to final liberation. For he thought, "having myself crossed the ocean of suffering, I must help others to cross it" (54). Siddhartha assumed his destiny as a buddha, the destiny prophesied by Asita at his birth, that he would become a great world savior.

The proclamation of the dharma

Siddhartha then made his way to the deer park at Kashi where he encountered the five monks he had joined in fasting when he first entered the path of a forest dweller. Now he preached to them his first sermon and they became his first disciples. He explained to them how he had found the middle way between luxury and asceticism, the way of the four noble truths and the eightfold path. These truths are that 1) life is suffering, 2) desire is the cause of suffering, 3) the extinction of desire (nirvana) ends suffering, and 4) the eightfold path is the way that leads to the extinguishing of desire. If the Buddha had been tempted not to teach the path opened up by his enlightenment it was no doubt because it could not be put directly into words. All he could do was tell them what nirvana or liberation was not, and then show them by what path they could come to discover for themselves what it is. Thus to become a follower of the dharma or teachings of the Buddha it was not enough to hear and memorize them. On the contrary, one had to make a threefold act of faith; taking refuge in the Buddha, the dharma (his teachings) and the sangha (the Buddhist community). Only one who trusted in the Buddha and his teaching as imparted by his community, the sangha, could find the way that leads to final liberation.

It is only in the Buddhist community, led by those who have trod the middle path and so can show the way, that the novice or new seeker can learn the meaning of the eightfold path as an actual set of practices. This is the path of 1) right understanding, 2) right thought, 3) right speech, 4) right action, 5) right livelihood, 6) right effort, 7) right mindfulness, and 8) right concentration or meditation. These eight steps along the path are grouped by the Buddhist community into three basic categories: (1) wisdom (*prajna*) for the first two, (2) morality (*sila*) for the next three, and (3) meditation (*samadhi*) for the last three. In the sangha one learns the basic insights and intentions that lead to nirvana, one learns to lead the compassionate and truthful life that prepares one for liberation, and finally one learns the meditation practices which actually bring about the liberating insights of enlightenment. So the Buddha taught his first disciples the truth of the fire sermon, namely, all the world is burning, burning with desire, and only by "cooling down" or "blowing out" the flame of desire (the literal meaning of "nirvana") can human beings be liberated from the eternal cycle of death and rebirth on the wheel of samsara, the wheel of suffering and impermanence.

What the Buddha experienced in his enlightenment that set him apart from the Hindu path of the Upanishads was that everything in the universe is anicca (impermanent), therefore nothing is eternal. This means there is no eternal Brahman-self pervading the universe as the Upanishads suggest. And that means that the atman (self) is not the same as Brahman. On the contrary, all selves are anatta, that is, empty of all eternal self. The ultimate illusion of the self is that it has its "own being" (svabhava) independent of all other beings. The truth revealed by the Buddha's enlightenment is that the self has neither permanence nor an absolute boundary: instead all selves are constantly changing and all selves (and all beings) are changing and becoming in interdependence.

The experience of enlightenment transforms ethical consciousness by bringing this interdependence and its implications to conscious awareness. Because all beings are empty of separate self and interdependent, I cannot do harm against another creature without doing harm to myself. Enlightenment leads to compassion for all living beings and a life of non-violence. Moreover, because all things are empty of self (*sunyata*), the Buddha called into question the sacred order of the Hindu caste system which had created a hierarchical ordering of human identity that treated members of the upper castes as more valuable than the lower castes and outcastes. Those who took refuge in the Buddha and his dharma also took refuge in his sangha – the Buddhist holy community where all selves were treated as equal because all selves are equally empty. Thus, there was no caste status within the sangha. The Buddha, therefore, converted many people from all walks of life – from the greatest priests (Brahmins) and royalty (Kshatriya) to the average craftsman (Vaishiya) and the lowest castes (Shudra), and even outcastes. Within the Buddhist community all were to be equal.

The final liberation

The Buddha Siddhartha Gautama lived to a ripe old age of 79. He died from accidental food poisoning. Yet his was not an accidental death, for three months earlier he predicted his final entry into nirvana. No one took his life from him, he said, he gave it up willingly, having brought salvation to the world. As the time of his death approached "the earth staggered like a drunken woman, and in all directions great fire brands fell from the sky. Indra's thunderbolts flashed unceasingly on all sides. . . . Everywhere flames blazed up, as if the end of the world with its universal conflagration had come" (59). And a mighty wind swept through the earth, mountains crumbled, trees fell and thunder filled the air. Then "in full sight of his disciples he lay down on his right side, rested his head on his hand and put one leg over the other. At that moment the birds uttered no sound, and, as if in trance, they sat with their bodies all relaxed. The winds ceased to move the leaves of the trees, and the trees shed wilted flowers, which came down like tears" (60). The Buddha then instructed his disciples not to grieve but rejoice in his final liberation from all death and rebirth and he faced his departure with a deep peace. Finally, he reminded his disciples that whoever sees his dharma sees the Buddha. The dharma was his parting gift to the world. Then the Buddha entered into a deep trance and died into the everlasting peace of final nirvana (*Pari-Nirvana*). At his death the moon's light disappeared in a cloudless sky, the rivers boiled over, and flowers grew out of season on the tree above his deathbed. Afterward, his followers cremated his body and his bones were preserved as sacred relics. These were divided into eight portions and given to the rulers of prominent kingdoms for the edification of their subjects.

The Cosmic Story Revised: The Myth of Liberation

Theravada stories

After the time of the Buddha many schools, with different understandings of his teachings, emerged. The oldest to survive was Theravada – the Buddhism of the elders. Later (in the second century BCE) another major school emerged, known as Mahayana, which means "the greater vehicle." Mahayana saw itself as having a superior understanding of the Buddha's message and therefore called Theravada by the name "Hinayana," meaning "lesser vehicle." Theravadins, however, rejected this designation, insisting that they, not Mahayanists, followed the authentic teachings of the Buddha. Theravadins embraced the cosmic story of liberation as it was developing in the Upanishadic tradition of Hinduism but altered it based on their understanding of the Buddha's enlightenment. They too saw the fundamental problem of life as an endless round of death and rebirth on the wheel of samsara. They too saw life rebirth as caused by illusion rooted in ego-centered desire, although they emphasized more strongly the suffering that arises because of desire and illusion. And they too saw the goal or ideal of life as liberation from the wheel of death and rebirth. And they, like their Upanishadic counterparts before the emergence of the Bhakti movements in the second century BCE, saw three basic means to overcome the problem and achieve the ideal: prajna, wisdom or right views (parallel to jnana yoga), sila, or morality (parallel to karma yoga), and samadhi, or meditative concentration (parallel to raja yoga). But they denied that these means would lead to the experience of an eternal self or Brahman.

The story of the Buddha intersects with the story of Gilgamesh around a key insight – as Utnapishtim says to Gilgamesh: "There is no permanence in life, nothing lasts – all things perish." Nirvana means to "blow out" or "cool down." What is extinguished is the fire of desire that creates illusion and suffering on the wheel of impermanence. In perhaps his most famous sermon, the fire sermon, Siddhartha proclaimed that all the senses are on fire: "And with what are these on fire? With the fire of passion, say I, with the fire of hatred, with the fire of infatuation; with birth, old age, death, sorrow, lamentation, misery, grief, and despair are they on fire" (Burtt 1955: 97; from the *Maha-Vagga* in the Pali Canon).

For Siddhartha, nothing is eternal, so surrender to Vishnu or identification with Brahman are also forms of illusion that keep one attached to the wheel of samsara, the wheel of suffering and rebirth. Nirvana or liberation can only occur when even this illusion is given up. Only then does moksha truly become nirvana or true liberation – a state that cannot be defined. One cannot say what it is – only what it is not.

For Siddhartha, the final truth about the self is that there is no self. This does not mean that the self does not exist, rather it is a denial that there is anything eternal in the self. All selves are "empty" of an eternal self. This claim also entails a denial that any being has its "own being" (svabhava) independent of all other beings. To believe that one has one's own being involves one in the deepest of ethical illusions, namely that one can pursue one's own good independent of any concern for the good of others. For the truth, as the Buddha taught it, is that all things in the universe, although impermanent, come into existence and go out of existence in complete interdependence. No being is ever isolated and independent of any other.

Both the Hindu and the Buddhist traditions agree that the bodily ego-self is an illusion. The Upanishadic traditions of an emerging Hinduism had been speculating for some time that the self we are conscious of is an illusion. However, those traditions suggested that beyond the illusory self there was a *true* self: eternal, universal, unchanging. From infancy to old age the body goes through radical changes and yet it is possible for the child of eight who becomes the old man or woman of eighty to say "I" throughout his or her life and still mean the same "I." How is this possible? The body changes, the Upanishads speculate, and all else changes as well, except the eternal self within – the eternal "I" or "atman" that is identical with "Brahman," the universal eternal reality that underlies all things. This provided one kind of answer to the problem of death. The self that dies is not the true self (atman), only the illusory self (jiva). Once we know and experience this true self then we realize in our own experience that in our true identity we transcend death and rebirth and are liberated from the wheel of old age, sickness, and death, the wheel of change, of suffering and rebirth – samsara.

In Brahmanic Hinduism the experience of ultimate reality remains tied to the imagination. The Brahman-self is ineffable, it cannot be sensed but it can be imagined as an invisible essence that sustains all things. And because it can be imagined it can be *tied and bound* up with a cosmological order socially embodied in the caste system. Within this cosmological story, caste duty is the karmic path that the self must traverse, through many lifetimes, in order to realize its true Brahman-self. That is, one must perform one's caste duty as a required step to achieving moksha. In this way, the religious imagination of ultimate reality (Brahman) is used to legitimate (make obligatory) the sacred hierarchical order of society (the caste system).

It is precisely this conjunction of imagination of ultimate reality and societal legitimation that the Buddhist experience of enlightenment denied. Nagasena, a Theravadin Buddhist monk, in the *Questions of King Milinda,* explains "no-self" to the Greek King Milinda as follows: There is no such thing, he says, as a chariot. A chariot is made of non-chariot components. "For it is in dependence on the pole, the axle, the wheels, the framework, the flagstaff, etc., that there takes place this denomination 'chariot,' this designation, this conceptual term, a current appellation and a mere name." In the same way, "Nagasena" is a mere name for the interdependent moments of energy (dharmas) that make up body and mind in interdependence with all other dharmas that make up the universe (Conze 1959: 148–9). Neither the chariot nor Nagasena have their own independent being.

The conclusion here is not that the self has no reality at all but rather that it is an impermanent reality that is manifested in the interdependence of the parts. The true self is empty of svabhava, that is, of its own (essential and/or eternal) being. It has neither eternality nor independence. Rather, the self's true reality can only be expressed negatively as the absence of self (no-self). This means that the sense of boundary between myself and others, which is part of my sense of individual identity, is an illusion. There is no absolute boundary between my self and all other beings. The self has its reality only in radical interdependence with the becoming of all things known as "dependent co-arising" (*pratitya samutpada*).

Thus the Buddha did not need to appeal to a universal self in order to teach that doing violence against another is doing violence against oneself. Rather, the Buddha taught non-violence based on the awareness of the interdependence of all things. For once I realize that all things are interdependent (and that "own being" or svabhava is an illusion) there is no way I can imagine doing violence against another without doing harm to myself. In the moment of enlightenment, self-interest and altruism coincide to create ethical consciousness expressed as compassion for all beings.

Structurally, Buddhist enlightenment resembles Hindu enlightenment. Both agree that life is suffering, that desire is the cause of suffering and that liberation occurs when desire is extinguished. Both seek a destruction of the illusory self (the double) through the extinguishing of desire. But when we come to the essence of enlightenment, there is an important distinction between the ineffability of Brahman and the "emptiness" of the Buddhist experience of nirvana.

The difference between the two types of religious experience (Buddhist and Brahmanic) is evinced in the creation of a Buddhist holy community – the sangha. Unwilling to use the language of imagination (analogy, metaphor) as its primary language, Buddhism resorts to the language of negation – the language of no-self and emptiness. This has immediate sociological implications. If everything is impermanent and interdependent and all selves are empty then there is no Brahman reality that legitimates (makes something seem sacred and authoritative) the hierarchical cosmological social order of the caste system. Consequently all selves are equal by virtue of their emptiness. The radical break with the Brahmanic religious imagination was at once both a religious and a political act with direct sociological consequences. It gave rise to an alternate or separate community, the sangha as a community of those who were aware of their equality and interdependence. It may well be that the Buddhist sangha is the first community to embrace the notion of the equality of all human beings.

The sangha was a public and forceful presence, an alternate community living an alternate way of life in the world, one which called the sacred Brahmanic vision of Hindu society into question. The force of the Buddha's teaching was to call into question all claims to authority, whether sacred or profane, including his own: "Just as the experts test gold by burning it, cutting it and applying it on a touchstone, my statements should be accepted only after critical examination and not out of respect for me" (Unno 1988: 129–47). The internal structure of the monastic community took the form of a democratic republic or representative democracy, in which each monk had an equal vote. This inner structure expressed the Buddhist consciousness of the equality of all selves and stood in stark contrast to the hierarchical and monarchical structure of the larger caste-structured society of India.

The sangha, as a community set apart, sought to provide an ethical model for Buddhist laity and also for monarchical political authorities. In the eightfold path of the Buddha, sila (morality) precedes and prepares the way for samadhi (enlightenment) and the ethical life of compassion. There are 227 rules that govern the monastic life of Buddhist monks. The core of this Buddhist morality is summed up in ten precepts that govern monastic life. The precepts forbid (1) taking life, (2) stealing, (3) sexual impropriety, (4) lying, and (5) all intoxicants that might cloud the mind. These first five comprise the essential morality for lay persons as well. However, in addition, monks are forbidden to (6) eat after midday, (7) take part in amusements such as dancing, singing, and theatre, (8) wear ornaments or dress extravagantly, (9) sleep in comfortable beds, (10) accept money. Monks and lay persons live in an interdependent relationship in which lay persons receive great karmic merit by supporting the life of the monks through giving food, clothing, and other necessities, and monks provide lay persons with the example and counsel needed to pursue the holy life. Perhaps most extraordinary was the Buddha's first precept, which required a life of ahimsa or non-violence in relation to all sentient creatures. This meant that certain ways of life were forbidden. For example, one could be neither a butcher nor a soldier.

The stellar example of the power of Buddhist morality to transform society occurred during the reign of Ashoka. As emperor of the Mauraya empire, which included almost the whole subcontinent of India, he was the most powerful ruler anywhere in the world at that time. Early in his reign as emperor in India (270–230 BCE), Ashoka converted to Buddhism as a result of a war of conquest against his neighbors that left him revolted by the great bloodshed. Embracing the teachings of the Buddha, he vowed never again to shed the blood of any creature. And he committed himself to ruling according to the teachings (dharma) of the Buddha. His rule was marked by tolerance toward all religions and a compassionate concern for the welfare of all his subjects. His policies included free medical care for all his subjects and a reform of the legal system to make it more just. He also promoted vegetarianism through official government policies. Buddhism grew and flourished under his reign and he sent Buddhist missionaries to Sri Lanka and also into the Hellenistic world.

Mahayana stories

Religious traditions, like all things, are never static. They are constantly changing traditions of storytelling and story dwelling. The stories and teachings of Theravada Buddhism are contained in the Pali Canon composed of three baskets – the Tripitaka. The baskets are collections of writings: The *Vinaya*, or rules of the monastic community, the *Sutras*, or teachings of the Buddha and his followers, and the *Abhidharma*, the psychological/metaphysical principles for the right interpretation of the Vinaya and Sutras. By the first century BCE a new movement was sweeping both Hinduism and Buddhism in India – the Bhakti movement. Bhakti, as we learned in the last chapter, is the path of love and devotion. It represents a popular revolt against the dominance of religious specialists who focus on knowledge of the sacred writings or the rigors of meditation. Bhakti is the path that is open to all persons, no matter how unlearned and unsophisticated. Bhakti is the path of lay persons as opposed to that of the priests (brahmins) and forest dwellers (*shramanas*). Bhakti added a new path to both traditions – that of love or devotion.

Thus, even as the *Gita* and the epic literature of *Ramayana* and *Mahabharata* swept Hinduism with the spirit of bhakti, presenting stories of the gods to move the human heart to devotion, so this same spirit also swept through Buddhism, giving birth to the Mahayana or "greater vehicle" that was open to all the people, not just to monks. The sacred writings of Mahayana are contained in the *Prajnaparamita* (Perfection of Wisdom) literature, thirty-eight books formulated roughly between 100 BCE and 600 CE. And just as the essence of Upanishadic wisdom is thought to be summed up in the *Bhagavad Gita*, so the essence of the *Prajnaparamita* literature is thought to be summed up in the *MahaPrajnaparamita Sutra*, whose wisdom is said to be further condensed in the *Diamond Sutra* and distilled into its essence in the even shorter *Heart Sutra*.

Mahayana accounts for its origins in one of its most popular scriptures, the *Saddharmapundarika* or *Lotus of the True Law*. In the Lotus Sutra, the Buddha reveals his cosmic presence to his followers. For Theravada Buddhism the highest goal is to become an Arhant, which is one who has reached his/her last rebirth and will achieve enlightenment like the Buddha, never to be reborn or heard from again. The Lotus Sutra, however, presents quite another understanding. Now in the Lotus Sutra, the Buddha reveals that his earthly body (*nirmanakaya*) is not his true body (*dharmakaya*). For only when he entered nirvana did he assume his true identity or dharmakaya (truth body) by which he is present always and everywhere. Now in the Lotus Sutra we discover that Siddhartha's enlightenment-quest was a drama enacted to inspire others to seek enlightenment, since as the cosmic Buddha who assumed an earthly body (nirmanakaya) he was already enlightened from the beginning. Indeed, according to the Lotus Sutra, there is not just one Buddha but in fact many buddhas. In a doctrine that parallels the Avatar doctrine of the *Gita,* we learn that every cosmic age has its buddha and that there are myriads of universes coexisting, each of which has its own buddha.

In addition to the earthly body and the truth body of the Buddha there is also the heavenly body of the Buddha (*sambhogakaya*). This is the form that a buddha takes when he has finished his life in the earthly realm but wishes to remain on the wheel of samasara out of compassion, in order to help all other beings achieve enlightenment. Indeed, a key doctrine of Mahayana is the doctrine of the *Bodhisattva.* To appreciate the doctrine of the Bodhisattva one must understand the difference in the stages on the path to enlightenment in Theravada. In this tradition, after many rebirths, an individual may move closer to the goal of achieving nirvana, finally winning rebirth as a "stream winner." This means he or she is on the path that will end in enlightenment. Then, in a future incarnation, the stream winner will become a "once returner" who, in his or her next life, will actually achieve enlightenment. In that last rebirth one has become an Arhant – one who will be enlightened in this lifetime and liberated from the wheel of samsara, never to be reborn again.

However, according to Mahayana teachings, the Arhant of the Theravada tradition has not really achieved enlightenment. The proof of this is that the Arhant thinks that he can enter enlightenment all by himself as if he had his "own being" (svabhava) and can achieve his own enlightenment without concern for the good of others. Such a view of enlightenment is just a spiritual form of selfishness, Mahayanists argue. The truly enlightened is one who recognizes the interdependence of all beings and, out of compassion for the suffering of the world, vows not to enter final nirvana until all beings – indeed "the last blade of grass" – are enlightened. That is the vow of a truly enlightened being, one who is called a Bodhisattva. In short, a Bodhisattva is a buddha who remains on the wheel of samsara out of compassion, in order to help others achieve enlightenment. Instead of leaving the wheel of samsara the Bodhisattva assumes a heavenly body (sambhogakaya), so that as a heavenly buddha he can remain on the wheel of samsara and assist those who pray to him or her.

Thus with Mahayana, we discover that there is not just one Buddha, Siddhartha, but many buddhas, and that buddhahood is a goal offered not just to monks but to the laity as well. Therefore, rather than there being just one Buddha – Siddhartha Gautama – there are many earthly and heavenly buddhas (in the form of nirmanakaya and sambhogakaya). Moreover, the goal of every Buddhist, whether lay or monk, should be to become a buddha, or rather, a Bodhisattva. The compassion of the Bodhisattva is powerfully expressed in the *Siksasamuccaya Sutra:*

> All creatures are in pain, he [the Bodhisattva] resolves, all suffer from bad and hindering karma . . . so that they cannot see the Buddhas or hear the Law of Righteousness or know the Order. . . . All that mass of pain and evil karma I take in my own body . . . I take upon myself the burden of sorrow; I resolve to do so; I endure it all. I do not turn back or run away, I do not tremble . . . I am not afraid . . . nor do I despair. Assuredly I must bear the burdens of all beings . . . for I have resolved to save them all. I must set them all free, I must save the whole world from the forest of birth, old age, disease, and rebirth, from misfortune and sin, from the round of birth and death, . . . I shall give myself into bondage, to redeem all the world from the forests of purgatory, from rebirth as beasts, from the realm of death. I shall bear all grief and pain in my own body, for the good of all things living . . . I must so bring to fruition the root of goodness that all beings find the utmost joy, unheard of joy, the joy of omniscience. (de Bary 1969: 84–5)

What the doctrine of the Bodhisattva did was to raise up love (*metta*) and compassion (*karuna*) as central doctrines of Buddhism, transforming Buddhism into a religion that made a place for liberation not only through meditation but also through divine aid (grace or assistance) offered by the many heavenly buddhas who are Bodhisattvas. One of the most popular of these Bodhisattvas is Amida (Amitabha) Buddha. Those who repeat the name of Amida and have faith in Amida will be reborn in the "pure land," a heavenly realm which hastens the day of one's final liberation. Another is Avalokitesvara (Chinese *Kuan-yin*, Japanese *Kannon*). In China, Kuan-yin was transformed from a male Bodhisattva into a female Bodhisattva – a kind of divine mother who looks after her children.

The most radical change wrought by Mahayana Buddhists was to transform the Theravada understanding of the cosmic wheel of samsara – the wheel of death and rebirth. The Mahayana tradition stood the view of the wheel of samsara shared by Hindus and Theravada Buddhists on its head. They did this by denying that moksha or nirvana removed one from the wheel of death and rebirth. Samsara and nirvana, they argued, are not two different worlds, and liberation is not going from one to the other. Rather, samsara and nirvana are two different ways of experiencing the very same world. The basis for their interpretation was a radical understanding of the doctrine that all things are empty.

According to Mahayana wisdom, the mistake of Theravadins was to treat the dharmas, the continually coming into being and perishing atomic units of energy whose interdependence make up all things, as if each such dharma had its own being. But if all things are empty (*sunya*) of their own being (i.e., have no independent reality but are in fact interdependent), then samsara is also empty, and so is nirvana. Even the buddhas are empty. According to the Diamond Sutra: "Although innumerable beings have thus been led to Nirvana, in fact no being at all has been led to Nirvana. . . . 'Tathagata' [a name for the Buddha] is called one who has not gone to anywhere and who has not come from anywhere" (Conze 1959: 164, 166). "If you meet the Buddha, kill him," is a Zen saying meant to drive home the emptiness of Buddha nature. The Buddha is not some being to be met along the roadway but the true nature (suchness) of the interdependent becoming of all things.

Nirvana is not escaping the wheel of death and rebirth but rather seeing and experiencing its true nature as empty. When one achieves enlightenment and no longer clings to the dharmas (achieves non-attachment) the wheel of suffering becomes the wheel of liberation and joy, right here and now. Suffering is rooted in ego-centered desire. When the illusion of self is penetrated in the enlightenment experience then the suffering of samsara disappears as well. One no longer sees the world of samsara through the eyes of greed and desire that distort one's perception. One no longer sees the world in terms of dualisms like samsara and nirvana or "my good" versus the "good of others." Yet one refrains from affirming monism – which would deny the otherness of others – embracing instead a non-dualism. In so doing, one sees things as they really are instead of as one needs them to be in order to satisfy one's desires. One sees them in their interdependence (*pratitya-samutpada*) and "suchness" (*tathata*) – just as they are.

In the experience of enlightenment, emptiness and the Bodhisattva ideals of love (*metta*) and compassion (*karuna*) merge. For the enlightened self experiences the interdependence of all things that destroys the illusory boundaries of self, so that all things are loved for what they are in themselves in their "suchness" rather than for how they please or displease the individual ego. There is a well-known Zen Buddhist story that illuminates the ethical implications of the realization of emptiness. "Zen" is a Japanese term for "Ch'an," which is the Chinese term for the Sanskrit "Dhyana," which means meditation. While Mahayana Buddhism began in India, it grew and flourished in China and Japan, especially in its Pure Land and Zen forms. Zen represents the other extreme from that of Pure Land Buddhism. For if Pure Land emphasizes faith and the help of the heavenly Bodhisattvas, Zen emphasizes the need to achieve enlightenment or "satori" through one's own diligent efforts, especially through the practice of meditation.

According to a Zen story, once there were two monks walking through the countryside. As they walked along they approached a stream. Standing near the stream was a young woman distressed by the prospect of having to get wet in order to cross. As the two monks approached her, the elder of the two offered to carry her across. The young woman kindly accepted his offer of assistance and he carried her across the stream. On the other side, the two monks bid the woman farewell, and continued their journey in silence for about two miles. Then the younger monk spoke in anger to the older monk, saying: "Why did you pick up that young woman, you know monks are not supposed to go near women?" To which the older monk replied: "You mean you are still carrying her? I left her at the stream."

The difference between the two monks is the difference between a mind that has experienced the emptiness of the dharmas and one that has not. The young monk is still clinging to the dharmas. Indeed, he is still holding onto the woman even though she is long gone. And as a result he has missed the wonder and the beauty (the suchness) of the last two miles of his journey. He does not see the woman for who she is and what she needs. Rather, he is caught up in spiritual pride over the observance of sacred rules. The older monk, in contrast, has no thought for himself and is unwilling to place sacred rules above a person in need. He acts out of compassion for the woman and having done so "lets go" of her, in order to be present in his next experience with equal openness and compassion. The younger monk illustrates the power of self-centered desire to cause one to try to stop time and hold onto the past and the suffering this causes. The older monk illustrates the non-attachment of the enlightened self. Such a self clings neither to the past nor to the future but lives fully in the present. He is able to be compassionate because he is always mindful; that is, he is always wholly attentive to his present experience.

Life Story: Thich Nhat Hanh and the Way of Mindfulness

The problem of compassion and social change in Mahayana Buddhism

Despite a definite change in emphasis and some exotic elaboration of the Buddhist cosmology, all of the key elements of Mahayana ethics – such as emptiness and interdependence, love and compassion – are present in Theravada as well. However, the path of Mahayana, it would seem, brings the ethical dimension of Buddhism into sharper relief with its emphasis on the Bodhisattva ideal of sacrificing oneself out of compassion for the good of others. As we have seen in chapter 1, Ronald Green argues that the ethical point of view requires achieving "omnipartiality" – seeing one's actions from the viewpoint of all others and a willingness to sacrifice one's own good for the welfare of others.

The Bodhisattva ideal of Mahayana Buddhism understands enlightenment as producing just such a perspective – one becomes the other and experiences one's own actions through the eyes of the other. The goal of meditation is to bring about such an enlightenment in which you experience the relativity of the boundary between self and other (no-self or interdependence) so as to become the other. According to the *Bodhicharyavatara* of Santideva:

> All have the same sorrows, the same joys as I, and I must guard them like myself. The body, manifold of parts in its division of members, must be preserved as a whole; and so likewise this manifold universe has its sorrow and its joy in common. . . . By constant use the idea of an "I" attaches itself to foreign drops of seed and blood, although the thing exists not. Then why should I not conceive my fellow's body as my own self? . . . I will cease to live as self, and will take as my self my fellow-creatures. We love our hands and other limbs, as members of the body;

then why not love other living beings, as members of the universe? By constant use man comes to imagine that his body, which has no self-being, is a "self"; why then should he not conceive his "self" to lie in his fellows also? ... Then, as thou wouldst guard thyself against suffering and sorrow, so exercise the spirit of helpfulness and tenderness towards the world. (Burtt 1955: 139–40)

The emphasis on compassion (karuna) and on enlightenment as seeing this world rightly rather than leaving the world of suffering (samsara) would lead one to expect that Buddhism, especially Mahayana Buddhism, would have historically been a powerful religious force for social justice and the ethical transformation of society.

And yet, as in other religious traditions, that has not really been the case in the past. Before the modern period, Mahayana was a socially and politically conservative force. In Japan during the Meiji period that led to World War II, for example, Mahayana Buddhism blended into Japanese Neo-Confucianism and Shintoism in support of state imperialism, colonialism, and aggression against other Asian nations, as well as aggression against the West. Nor did it prove itself to be the champion of the poor and oppressed in the feudal societies of China and Japan.

The ethical failure of the goal of compassion in the Bodhisattva ideal was largely due to an almost totally spiritualized interpretation of the meaning of compassion. That is, the way one showed compassion was to provide spiritual help and guidance that would lead others to enlightenment rather than through actions that sought to correct social injustice. This failure was not unique to Buddhism. It can be found in the pre-modern ethics and spirituality of other religions as well. It is only with the transformation of our understanding of the socially constructed nature of the social order that emerged with the social sciences in the modern and post/modern period that religious compassion has been channeled into the reform of societies and their institutions as an essential task of ethics. And yet, of all religions, one might have expected Buddhism to have pioneered this approach. For, as we have seen, for a brief period, under the rulership of Ashoka, such an approach did exist. But Mahayana (and Theravada too) retreated from that ideal into a more purely "spiritual" understanding of compassion.

Thich Nhat Hanh and socially engaged Buddhism

In the post/modern period, however, that has begun to change with the emergence of *socially engaged Buddhism*, primarily in response to the injustices of Western colonialism, while at the same time availing itself of the new ways of looking at history and society that emerged out of Western modernization. Nowhere has the emergence of socially engaged Buddhism been more dramatic than in Vietnam, especially in response to the Vietnam War against the background of the colonial presence of the French and later the United States. The key leader of that movement is the Buddhist monk Thich Nhat Hanh. Nhat Hanh, who was nominated for the Nobel Peace Prize by Martin Luther King, Jr., came to international public attention as the leader of the Vietnamese Buddhist peace delegation to the Paris negotiations that sought to end the war in Vietnam. He is a Zen master (one who has achieved satori, or enlightenment, and now teaches others the way) who has written more than sixty books on poetry, spiritual guidance, meditation and Buddhist social action in the contemporary world. He lives in exile in France where he writes, teaches, and assists other Vietnamese refugees. He is the leading international figure in the movement for socially engaged Buddhism.

Thich Nhat Hanh was born the son of a minor government official in Nguyen Xuan Bao in South Vietnam in 1926. When he was 17 years old he entered the Tu Hieu monastery in Hue, in central Vietnam. His teacher was Thich Chan That, a Zen master of the Rinzai tradition. His training exposed him to both Zen and Pure Land, and also the Theravada tradition that is widely practiced in the south of Vietnam. He was ordained a monk in 1949. His own name was inspired by a medieval monk by the name of Van Hanh – which means "ten thousand actions." "Nhat Hanh," by contrast, means "one action."

Thich Nhat Hanh proved himself to be a "modern" monk when, as a monastic student, he led a movement to include more philosophy, literature, and foreign languages in the curriculum of the Bao Quoc Institute for student monks. When his request was denied, he left and moved to Saigon, where he studied at the university and supported himself by writing novels and poetry. After he graduated with honors, he was asked to return to Bao Quoc Institute under a new policy that permitted the inclusion of modern secular knowledge in the curriculum. However, his ideas were too radical for his elders and he again left to co-found the Ang Quang Temple in Saigon (1950), which later became An Quang Buddhist Institute, the leading center of Buddhist studies and social activism in Vietnam. Then, in Dalat in 1956, he founded a new monastic community, Phuong Boi. He also taught at a local high school and became the Editor-in-Chief of *Vietnamese Buddhism*, the official magazine of Vietnamese Buddhism. It is as editor of this magazine that he began to formulate his understanding of a socially engaged Buddhism. Then in 1961 Nhat Hanh made his first journey to the United States, where he studied at Princeton. In 1963 he lectured on Buddhism at Columbia University. He returned to Vietnam in 1964 to join other Buddhist radicals after the fall of Diem. At this time he began work to establish Van Hahn University in an effort to develop a Buddhist approach to higher education. He also founded the School of Youth for Social Service as an instrument for Buddhist social activism. He was also part of a project to establish a Buddhist publishing house and edited a weekly called *Sound of the Rising Tide*. His articles, books, and poems were found threatening by both the South and North Vietnamese governments, who banned some of his poetry such as *Prayers for the White Dove of Peace to Appear*. Then, in 1965, Thich Nhat Hanh founded the Tiep Hien Order, which translates as the "Order of Interbeing," as a new Rinzai branch expressing the philosophy of engaged Buddhism.

To appreciate the significance of these initiatives it is necessary to understand that Thich Nhat Hanh was a participant in the Buddhist movement in protest against the war in Vietnam and American involvement in the war. America had taken the side of the South against communist North Vietnam. Most of the Buddhist movements that protested the war were neutralists. They came out neither in favor of the South (the Saigon government) nor the North (the Hanoi government and the NLF, or National Liberation Front), but rather sought to find a path to peace for all Vietnam. Neither side, however, was prepared to accept their neutrality, and both North and South accused Buddhists of being on the "other side." In this situation the American government, under the leadership of President Lyndon Johnson, tended to see the Buddhists as anti-American and pro-North Vietnam.

In the spring of 1965 Thich Nhat Hahn survived an assassination attempt and left Vietnam on May 22, invited by the Fellowship of Reconciliation to present the Buddhist cause to Americans. This invitation led to an international tour and unknowingly was the beginning of his exile from Vietnam.

The International Fellowship of Reconciliation sponsored Thich Nhat Hanh on an international speaking tour of nineteen countries, including the US, where he met with Secretary of Defense Robert McNamara. On June 1, 1966 he made a "Five Point Proposal to End the War" in Washington, DC. On the same trip he met Martin Luther King, Jr. and a friendship was formed between them. This encounter helped King come out publicly against the Vietnam War. In January of 1967 King nominated Thich Nhat Hanh for the Nobel Peace Prize. It was the year that Nhat Hanh published a book *Vietnam: Lotus in a Sea of Fire* to explain the Vietnamese Buddhist position to the West. It was published in eight languages. About this time Thich Nhat Hanh also met the famous Christian monk and social activist Thomas Merton, who spoke of Thich Nhat Hanh as "my brother." And later, in Rome, he met with Pope Paul VI and solicited Catholic support for the peace movement in Vietnam.

In 1969 Thich Nhat Hanh became the head of the Vietnamese Buddhist peace delegation that worked to influence the Paris peace talks. After the peace agreements were signed, the Saigon government would not allow these monks to return to Vietnam and the delegation committed itself to the work of reconciliation in exile. Thich Nhat Hanh has been living in exile ever since. From his community in the south of France, known as Plum Village, he has led an international movement for the development of socially engaged Buddhism.

As Thich Nhat Hanh looks back at his visit to the US under the sponsorship of the Fellowship of Reconciliation in the mid-1960s, he sees it as a spiritual turning point, opening the door to a new understanding of Christianity and its significance for him as a Buddhist. In his book, *Living Buddha, Living Christ* (1995), he recalls sharing the Eucharist with the Catholic Vietnam War protestor Father Daniel Berrigan, much to the shock and surprise of both their Buddhist and Christian friends. This occurred on April 4, 1968, the day that Martin Luther King, Jr. was assassinated. Thich Nhat Hanh says that meeting Christians like Berrigan, Merton, and of course, Martin Luther King, Jr., made him realize that there is another side to Christianity. Up until then his encounter with Christians had been under the conditions of French colonialism and the efforts of Catholic missionaries. This was a Christianity very much shaped by a sense of the sacred, a Christianity that equated itself with Western civilization and saw no place for the stranger. But when, for example, he met Martin Luther King, Jr., he was startled to discover a very different kind of Christianity. "I knew," he says, "I was in the presence of a holy person. Not just his good work but his very being was a source of great inspiration for me. And others, less well known, have made me feel that Lord Jesus is still here with us" (1995: 5, 6).

Through the lives of such persons, says Thich Nhat Hanh, he has been able to "touch Jesus Christ and his tradition" so that thirty years later he has on the altar in his hermitage images of both the Buddha and Jesus, whom he reveres equally as his "spiritual ancestors." What he has come to discover, he says, is that sometimes one has more in common with deeply spiritual persons in other traditions than with many in one's own. By living deeply in one's own tradition and listening deeply to others we discover the beauty in both. Seeing all things as interdependent, he goes on to explain that "Buddhism is made only of non-Buddhist elements, including Christian ones, and Christianity is made of non-Christian elements, including Buddhist ones" (1995: 11). And so we discover ourselves in the lives and stories of others. "Dialogue must be practiced on the basis of 'non-self.' We have to allow what is good, beautiful, and meaningful in the other's tradition to transform us" (1995: 9). In his own way, Thich Nhat Hanh has embraced the post/modern spirituality of passing over and coming back, for as a Buddhist he insists that sharing one's tradition with another "does not mean wanting others to abandon their own spiritual roots and embrace your faith. . . . We must help them return to their tradition," whether it be Christian, Jewish, etc. (1995: 196).

Thich Nhat Hanh's ethic: non-dualism and the way of mindfulness

The heart of Thich Nhat Hanh's Buddhism is the same non-dualism that we have already encountered in another Zen Buddhist, Masao Abe. As we noted in the Introduction to Part II, Abe proposes a Buddhist model for comparative ethics that sees the ethical point of view as distinct from the religious point of view and inferior to it. There is no direct path from ethics to religion in Buddhism, he asserts, because ethics involves making judgments of good and evil and all such judgments presuppose a dualistic frame of mind that reflect not enlightenment but illusion. The problem with ethical judgments, he says, is that they are made from the point of view of the offended party and thus have not really achieved the consciousness of omnipartiality (i.e., seeing the viewpoint of all parties) that is the mark of enlightened consciousness. Therefore, to achieve a higher viewpoint, the self must be emptied of all its dualistic assumptions. Enlightenment brings about a kind of "teleological suspension of the ethical" (to use Kierkegaard's phrase).

Thich Nhat Hanh shares this Mahayana philosophy of non-dualism. This is clearly demonstrated in one of his most famous poems, "Call Me By My True Names:"

> Don't say that I will depart tomorrow–
> even today I am still arriving.
>
> Look deeply: every second I am arriving
> to be a bud on a spring branch,
> to be a tiny bird, with still fragile wings,
> learning to sing in my new nest,
> to be a caterpillar in the heart of flower,
> to be a jewel hiding itself in a stone.
>
> I am still arriving, in order to laugh and to cry,
> in order to fear and to hope,
> the rhythm of my heart is the birth and death
> of every living creature.
>
> I am the mayfly metamorphosing
> on the surface of the river.
> And I am the bird,
> that swoops down to swallow the mayfly.
>
> I am the frog swimming happily
> in the clear water of a pond,
> and I am the grass-snake
> that silently feeds itself on the frog.
>
> I am the child in Uganda, all skin and bones,
> my legs as thin as bamboo sticks.
> And I am the arms merchant,
> selling deadly weapons to Uganda.
>
> I am the twelve-year-old girl,
> refugee on a small boat,
> who throws herself into the ocean
> after being raped by a sea pirate.
> And I am the pirate,
> my heart not yet capable
> of seeing and loving.

I am a member of the politburo,
with plenty of power in my hands,
and I am the man who has to pay
his "debt of blood" to my people,
dying slowly in a forced-labor camp.

My joy is like spring, so warm
that it makes flowers bloom all over the Earth.
My pain is like a river of tears,
so vast that it fills up all four oceans.

Please call me by my true names,
so I can hear all my cries and laughter at once,
so I can see that my joy and pain are one.

Please call me by my true names,
so I can wake up
and open the door of my heart,
the door of compassion.

(Nhat Hanh 1993: 107–9)

We see in this poem the key elements of Mahayana Buddhist insight. The underlying theme is emptiness of the self that is expressed in the interdependence of all things, which dissolves the boundaries of self (into "no-self") such that Nhat Hanh becomes the other through his compassion. He cannot separate himself from either the good or the evil that is found in the world, whether in the world of nature or of human society. Indeed, when the self comes to know its emptiness and interdependence the very categories of "good" and "evil" disappear. Is the bird evil because it eats the mayfly? Is the snake evil because it eats the frog? In a like manner, Nhat Hanh asks, is the pirate evil because he has raped the girl? Nhat Hanh expresses the omnipartiality of enlightenment, refusing to judge others – an enlightenment that carries him beyond dualistic judgments of good and evil.

Thich Nhat Hanh says that he was inspired to write the poem in 1976 when he first heard about the rape and suicide of the twelve-year-old girl spoken of in the poem. "I learned," he says, "after meditating for several hours that I could not just take sides against the pirate. I saw that if I had been born in his village and brought up under the same conditions, I would be exactly like him. Taking sides is too easy" (1993: 107). If you take the side of the little girl, he argues, you will want to get a gun and shoot the pirate (1987: 62). But if you realize that had you been raised under the circumstances of such a pirate you too would probably do what he did, then you realize that you too could be that pirate. To do violence against the pirate is to do violence against oneself, just as surely as the pirate's doing violence against the girl is also doing violence to himself. Such is the nature of the interdependence of all things.

At the heart of Thich Nhat Hanh's ethic of non-dualism is the spiritual practice of mindfulness. Mindfulness is a mode of consciousness illustrated by the
story of the two monks who come to the aid of the young woman at the river,
told above. It is a mode of consciousness in which our awareness is always fully
in the present moment of experience. Thus Zen Buddhism teaches that when
you eat just eat, when you walk just walk, and when you sleep just sleep – that
is true enlightenment. This sounds simple but in practice is very difficult, for
our minds are very often not one with our actions. While doing one thing we
are thinking of another. So instead of tasting and savoring our food when we
eat, we are clinging instead to some past moment we can't seem to let go of
because we are emotionally attached to it by our desires, like the young monk
who felt slighted when he did not get the opportunity to do a "good deed."
And if we are not brooding about our past, we are likely to be fantasizing about
our future – our hopes and fears for what tomorrow will bring. As a result we do
not even taste our food. Now if we multiply this by every experience we have in
a given day, we soon discover that we are going through life always somewhere
else than where we are, being dragged around by our self-centered hopes and
fears and so unable to be compassionate in this present moment, as the opportunity arises. It is as if we were sleepwalking through life and the Buddhist call
is to "wake up."

The Zen practice of mindfulness that Thich Nhat Hanh teaches is meant to
teach a person how to live with full awareness in every moment of one's life and
so gain the spiritual wisdom that comes from being fully alive. The self, we
might say, is just a bundle of emotions, a bundle of fears and hopes that keeps
us distracted from experiencing life and creates the illusion that our individual
well-being is a private matter unrelated to that of others. When we can learn to
be without self or self-less (anatta), then, for the first time, we experience life in
its "suchness" – as it really is in its concrete interdependence with all things.
When we are without self, the dualism of "self and other" disappears and we
discover that our body is not limited by our skin. Our bodies exist only through
interdependence with the rich ecology that sustains us. Thich Nhat Hanh calls
this the truth of "interbeing." We have no body without the sun that makes
plants grow, for plants make the oxygen we breathe and the food we eat, sustaining our bodily selves. How can one be a being without "interbeing?" The
unity cannot exist without the diversity. "When we understand that we inter-
are with the trees," says Thich Nhat Hanh, "we will know that it is up to us to
make an effort to keep the trees alive" (1993: 130). To neglect or destroy them
is to neglect and destroy ourselves. To know this is to feel the suffering of all of
nature as our own. The sun, the plants, the earth, and the universe in all its
complexity are one's body; without them, not one of us can be. We can only be
by interbeing.

When we think abstractly about the world we divide it up into self and not-
self, but when we keep our consciousness directly immersed in our direct experience of the world, the difference between self and other disappears in our

actual experience of the interdependence of all things. Mindfulness is the practice of keeping one's consciousness attentive to one's experience. The heart of Zen is the practice of mindfulness, first in sitting meditation, but then in everything one does. The essence of this spiritual practice is simply following one's breath. Breath, says Thich Nhat Hanh, is the link between mind and body. Following one's breathing, immersing one's consciousness in the natural rhythm of the body's breathing, stills the mind and allows the suchness of reality to break into one's consciousness. As one sits in meditation the mind will wander, fretting about yesterday, worrying about tomorrow. The task is not to suppress such thoughts but rather not to cling to them. One must note them, and then let them go. This is non-attachment. By not clinging one learns to keep one's consciousness at one with each new moment of experience as it comes up.

And so one takes this practice into all the activities of one's life. When walking, walk. When working, just work. When playing, let go of work and just play. Every act, says Thich Nhat Hanh, should be a ritual of mindfulness awakening us to our true identity of interbeing. "True mind is our real self, is the Buddha: the pure one-ness which cannot be cut up by the illusory divisions of separate selves, created by concepts and language" (1975, 1976: 42). True mind is the consciousness of interbeing which "floods the heart with compassion" (58).

For Thich Nhat Hanh, the practice of mindfulness releases not only compassion but the perseverance to act against all odds. In 1976 he was part of a rescue operation in the Gulf of Siam to save the "boat people" fleeing persecution in Vietnam. The governments of Malaysia, Thailand, and Singapore were refusing to allow them to land and sending them back into the sea and almost certain death. Many died, but Nhat Hanh and others rescued around 800 people. In one case a group of Vietnamese landed in Malaysia and destroyed their boat so that they could not be forced back to the sea. Nhat Hanh and his companions manned rescue boats, struggled with government bureaucrats, and alerted the international press. They struggled mightily to do everything in their power to save lives. At one point the authorities in Singapore arrested them and refused to allow them to give the boat people any further aid. He reports: "The suffering we touched doing this kind of work was so deep that if we did not have a reservoir of spiritual strength, we would not have been able to continue. During those days, we practiced sitting and walking meditation, and eating our meals in silence in a very concentrated way. We knew that without this kind of discipline, we would fail in our work. The lives of many people depended on our mindfulness" (1993: 103).

In the middle of his helplessness and despair, Thich Nhat Hanh turned to meditation on peace and, he reports, a calm came over him and his fears departed. With his mind clear he turned to the French Embassy for assistance and five minutes before he was to be expelled he was granted an extension to stay and make the needed arrangements for those he was aiding. "As long as I live," he said, "I will never forget those seconds of sitting meditation, those breaths, those mindful steps during that night and that morning. . . . I vowed that if I could not have peace at that moment, I would never be able to have peace. If I could not be peaceful in the midst of danger, the kind of peace I might realize in easier times would not mean anything." As a result of these mindful efforts, the US increased its quota for Vietnamese refugees from seven thousand to a hundred thousand in 1977.

Comparative Reflections: Gandhi and Thich Nhat Hanh

In this section and the questions which follow we invite you to pass over into the life and thought of both Thich Nhat Hanh and Gandhi and wrestle with both, as well as our conclusions, and come back with your own insights. We draw comparisons and suggest conclusions for your reflection with the hope that they will provoke discussion and the sharing of insight.

Thich Nhat Hanh's ethic of non-dualism and spirituality of mindfulness clearly opens up a path of great ethical significance. However, the problem of ethics and spiritual enlightenment as defined by Thich Nhat Hanh, and by Masao Abe, sees ethical thinking as a form of dualistic consciousness (dividing the world into good and evil) that must be transcended by religious consciousness through enlightenment, and this raises important questions. We must ask whether Thich Nhat Hanh's non-dualism, with its argument that we must not blame the pirate for raping the girl, is perhaps making the same point that Masao Abe was trying to make about the question of responsibility for the Holocaust. But Abe makes the point about which Thich Nhat Hanh remains silent in his poem – namely that in some way the victims, too, are responsible for what happened to them, due to the karma of their past lives. However, as we have argued, after Auschwitz and Hiroshima, it is just such claims that must be questioned.

Nor is it clear that the law of karma should be used to exonerate evildoing, as Nhat Hanh seems to imply in his commentary on his poem *Call Me By My True Names*. For, it can be argued, even from Buddhist premises, the conditions of our life do not alone make us who we are. There is also the element of choice concerning what we do about the conditions we find ourselves in. Therefore, it is not certain that we would do exactly as the pirate did if raised in the same circumstances. Karma is rooted in choice, not fate. That is what makes us responsible for our karma. If this were not true, the Buddhist striving for enlightenment, which requires insight into our past karma, would be pointless. Everything would be purely determined by past circumstances. But, as the story of the Buddha itself suggests, our present karma is the result of past decisions, not just of past circumstances. This means that decisions we made in the present can alter our future karma, and that we can transcend the circumstances in which our decisions are made.

Moreover, the thesis of Abe that in Buddhism there is no path from ethics to enlightenment – meaning that the ethical stage must be left behind in embracing the "higher" stage of religious consciousness – is itself called into question by some scholars of Buddhism. Damien Keown, in *The Nature of Buddhist Ethics*, argues that a close examination of the Pali Canon of Theravada Buddhism would show that there is another Buddhist perspective from which the continuity of ethics and enlightenment is affirmed rather than denied (Keown 1992).

Among those who argue for the disjunction between ethics and enlightenment, the most common analogy drawn from the teachings of the Buddha is that morality is like a raft that carries one across a river to nirvana on the other shore. Once the other shore is reached, the raft is left behind. By analogy, therefore, ethics is left behind once one achieves enlightenment. Keown, however, examines nine such references to a raft that he has been able to find in Theravada scriptures and notes that only one could be plausibly interpreted in such a fashion (and even that passage does not seem to necessitate such an interpretation), whereas the other eight all support the view that morality is part of enlightenment. Thus, in the *Incremental Discourses* of the Buddha, it is said, for example, that: "Taking what is not given is the near shore; abstaining therefrom is the further shore. Sexual misconduct is the near shore; abstaining therefrom is the further shore" (Keown 1992: 95). Thus in Keown's view sila (morality) and samadhi (enlightenment) coexist on the further shore. Nor is this pattern exclusive to Theravada, since he notes that it can be found in Mahayana Buddhism as well. If this be the case, then the perspectives of Masao Abe and Thich Nhat Hanh, while offering a Buddhist perspective on ethics, do not offer the only Buddhist perspective on ethics.

Why is this concession important? Because, after Auschwitz and Hiroshima, we have argued, we must be suspicious of every form of the myth of life through death. This myth involves a total annihilation of the self in surrender to a higher authority that suspends our sense of personal responsibility. When religion becomes separated from genuine ethical consciousness it lends itself to demonic and totalitarian purposes far too easily, as the role of Buddhism in Meiji Japan illustrates. After Auschwitz and Hiroshima, we must never again allow that to happen.

Finally, we should ask whether Gandhi's ethic of non-violence might have something to say about this problem. We think so. Although Thich Nhat Hanh acknowledges a debt to Gandhi in his commitment to non-violence, his understanding of the spiritual and ethical requirements necessary to live non-violently are significantly different.

Both Masao Abe and Thich Nhat Hanh argue that non-dualism offers a higher perspective than that of the ethical level of the judgment of right and wrong, because non-dualism avoids the pattern of accusation, counter-accusation, conflict, and the negative karma generated by such interactions. That is, ethical judgments create a dualistic frame of mind (us versus them). If you blame the pirate, Nhat Hanh argues, you want to get a gun and shoot him. Non-dualistic, non-judgmental love occurs, he says, "when we are able to love our enemy, [then] he or she is no longer our enemy" (1993: 76). But Gandhi offers another way of resolving this issue; namely, that the *Gita* teaches that there really is such a thing as injustice and we must be prepared to make judgments about the unjust actions of another, and that we really do have enemies whom we must go to war against. However, for Gandhi, we can go to war against them without picking up a gun. To love one's enemies, therefore, is not to deny that they are enemies but rather to love them in spite of their actions, seeking through non-violent resistance and personal suffering to bring about a conversion of the heart of one's enemy. The message of the *Gita*, as Gandhi reads it, is that judgment does not have to lead to negative karma. If in judging them, one resists them non-violently, one does not accrue negative karma. Moreover, according to Gandhi, if one makes an error in judgment (and all humans are fallible) in defining the other as an enemy, the only one who suffers is the protestor. Violence, in Gandhi's view, leads to irreversible actions (e.g., killing the other), whereas non-violent actions, respecting human fallibility, are reversible.

Questions for Discussion

1   Compare and contrast the themes of wrestling with the stranger and the quest to find an answer to old age, sickness, and death in the *Epic of Gilgamesh* and the life of the Buddha. What is the ethical significance of these themes in each story?
2   How does Thich Nhat Hanh's ethic relate to the modernist paradigm of the privatization of religion?
3   How does the contrast between the sacred and the holy, or morality and ethics, appear in Thich Nhat Hanh's life and thought?
4   Compare and contrast Gandhi and Thich Nhat Hanh's ethics of non-violence. Are they really in disagreement?
5   Does the concept of human dignity play a role in Thich Nhat Hanh's ethic? If so, how does it relate to Gandhi's understanding of dignity?
6   Compare the spirituality of Gandhi with that of Thich Nhat Hanh, and explain how each functions in relation to their respective ethics.
7   How does Thich Nhat Hanh's ethic address the ethical challenges of a techno-bureaucratic society?
8   Does Thich Nhat Hanh's ethic fit Masao Abe's models of religion and ethics for Buddhism (see figure 3.1)?
9   How is the post/modern spirituality of "passing over" and "coming back" illustrated in Thich Nhat Hanh's life story, and what is its ethical significance?

RESOURCES

Burtt, E. A. (ed.). 1955. *The Teachings of the Compassionate Buddha*. New York: Mentor, New American Library.

Conze, Edward. 1959. *Buddhist Scriptures*. London and New York: Penguin Books.

de Bary, William Theodore. 1969. *The Buddhist Tradition in India, China and Japan*. New York: Random House, Vintage Books.

Dharmasiri, Dunapala. 1986. *The Fundamentals of Buddhist Ethics*. Singapore: Buddhist Research Society.

Ingram, Catherine. 1990. *In the Footsteps of Gandhi: Conversations with Spiritual Social Activists*. Berkeley: Parallax Press.

Jayatilleke, J. N. 1979. "The Practical Policy of Buddhism Towards Racism and Caste." In *Facets of Buddhist Thought*. Kandy, Sri Lanka: Buddhist Publication Society.

Keown, Damien. 1992. *The Nature of Buddhist Ethics*. New York: St. Martin's Press.

Ling, Trevor. 1973. *The Buddha*. New York: Penguin Books.

Nhat Hanh, Thich. 1975, 1976. *The Miracle of Mindfulness: A Manual of Meditation*. Boston: Beacon Press.

——. 1987. *Being Peace*. Berkeley: Parallax Press.

——. 1993. *Love in Action*. Berkeley: Parallax Press.

——. 1995. *Living Buddha, Living Christ*. New York: G. P. Putnam & Sons, Riverhead Books.

Queen, Christopher and King, Sallie. 1996. *Engaged Buddhism: Buddhist Liberation Movements in Asia*. Albany: State University of New York Press.

Thomas, Edward J. 1927. *The Life of the Buddha as Legend and History*. London: Routledge & Kegan Paul.

Thurman, Robert A. F. 1988. "Social and Cultural Rights in Buddhism." In Leroy S. Rouner (ed.), *Human Rights and World Religions*. Notre Dame, IN: University of Notre Dame Press.

Unno, Taitetsu. 1988. "Personal Rights and Contemporary Buddhism." In Leroy S. Rouner (ed.), *Human Rights and World Religions*. Notre Dame, IN: University of Notre Dame Press.

6

JEWISH STORIES – ANCIENT AND POST/MODERN

All religious traditions communicate their insights through story, but in Judaism story itself is the key metaphor of religious experience. The cosmos does not go through endless cycles of death and rebirth, but, like a story, has a beginning and an ending. Jews imagine God as the divine storyteller and the unfolding drama of cosmic history as God's story. At the core of this drama are the stories of covenant and exile. The covenant between God and his people, established at Sinai, expresses an ethic of the holy, demanding justice for the orphan, the widow, and the stranger. This covenant is a two-way street – God demands justice from human beings but human beings can, like Abraham arguing with God over the fate of innocent strangers in the city of Sodom, also have the audacity or chutzpah to demand that God be just. Like Jacob wrestling with the stranger, one can wrestle with God and win, if it is in the name of justice. The legitimacy of wrestling with God and questioning God is the lesson taught by the formative story of Job and echoed in the Talmudic and Hasidic traditions, as well as in the post-Holocaust writers of Judaism. After Auschwitz there must be no unquestioning obedience, not even to God. In the life story of Abraham Joshua Heschel, a Hasidic Jewish scholar who marched with Martin Luther King, Jr. on behalf of the rights of African-Americans and who was a leader in the Vietnam War protests, we find this ethic of spiritual audacity on behalf of the stranger exemplified. In our comparative reflections we raise the question of significant differences in the understanding of justice between Thich Nhat Hanh's ethic of omnipartiality and Heschel's ethic of audacity on behalf of the stranger. We also raise a question about the myth of life through death (killing in order to heal) in Buddhism and Judaism.

Cosmic Story: The Myth of History

Creation as the story of history

While all religious traditions pass on their vision of reality through stories, story plays a unique role in the religiousness of Jews. The great religions of Asia, for instance, have told stories that draw on the metaphors of nature to explain religious experience. The cycles of nature are used to explain the wheel of death and rebirth in the myths of liberation from India and the rhythms of yin and yang in the myths of harmony from the religions of China. In Judaism, while analogies from nature are not absent, there is a clear shift from nature to history. And in the approximate period in which the Upanishads were being written in India (900 BCE to 200 CE), to speculate metaphysically on the nature of the cosmos and ultimate reality, the "biblical" stage of Judaism was taking shape not through metaphysical speculation but through historical imagination. That is, in the story told by Judaism, if you want to understand who "God" is, you do not look primarily to nature and metaphysics (for example, Prakriti and Brahman in the Upanishads) but to story and history – history as the story of the people – Israel's journey with God through time.

Indeed, for Judaism, God is the divine storyteller and the unfolding of creation in history is God's story. In the beginning "God said: Let there be light" and the story began. Creation does not end when the cosmos is formed; the story of all humanity and especially of Israel continues the creation story. And the story unfolds in history until God brings it – despite many trials and tribulations – to a happy ending when the dead shall be raised to enjoy a new heaven and a new earth at the end of time.

The story of Israel leads from the creation of the first man and woman – Adam and Eve – and the near annihilation of humanity because of their sins, as related in the story of Noah and the Flood, through the division of humans into many language groups at the tower of Babel, to God's call to Abraham to be a father of many nations (c.2000 BCE), and his promise to give the land of Canaan to his descendants – the tribes of the people Israel. It moves on to the descent of the tribes of Israel into Egypt during the time of Joseph and the famines. It relates how the tribes became enslaved in Egypt, how God sent Moses (c.1250 BCE) to deliver them from slavery in the Exodus, and how God brought them to Sinai to form a covenant: "You shall be my people and I will be your God."

The story goes on to tell how the tribes of Israel wandered in the desert for forty years, and only after the death of Moses did they enter the land of promise under the leadership of Joshua. For the next 200 years, during the period of the Judges, the tribes lived on the land as a loose confederation. However, as the threats of military conquest from their neighbors became more frequent, many among the tribes began to demand that Israel have a king like other nations, with a standing army to protect Israel. Others, however, argued that there can be only one king over Israel – the God of Abraham, Isaac, and Jacob. God, according to the story, tolerant of their weakness, agreed to appoint a king. And so Saul was anointed with oil by the prophets, as a sign that God (not the people) chose the first king over Israel (c.1020–1004 BCE). Indeed, the concept of messiah (*mashiah*) has its beginnings here, for a "messiah" is an "anointed one" chosen to rule over the kingdom of God, the kingdom of Israel. It was David (1004–965 BCE), the second king over Israel, who established Israel as a great nation – he and his son Solomon (965–928 BCE), who built the first temple as a place of grandeur for the God of Israel.

However, after the time of Solomon there was quarreling about the succession to the throne and Israel was divided into two kingdoms: Israel in the north and Judah in the south. At this time, prophets like Amos and Hosea (c.800 BCE) arose, introducing an ethical voice into Israel; calling into question its sacred way of life. They reminded the people that ever since they gave up their nomadic ways and became an agricultural and urban people, they had been drifting further and further away from the ethic of the tribal covenant made at Sinai. In the cities the people acted as if they were strangers to each other, and the rich mistreated the poor. So the prophets warned that God wants more than animal sacrifices in the temple. What God wants most of all is the sacrifice of a pure heart committed to deeds of justice and mercy.

It is with the prophets that Jewish monotheism becomes fully formed. For in the tribal days of the time of Moses, Israel's religion was "henotheistic" – it held to one God above all others. Thus the commandment "I am the Lord your God . . . you shall have no others beside me" did not mean there were no other gods but only that Israel was forbidden to follow them. God was their tribal God. But after Israel was established as a great nation in the time of David, the prophets forced Israel to see that they did not own God; that indeed, their God was the God of all the nations, one who would use the other nations to punish Israel if she did not keep the covenant. From the time of the prophets Israel began to think of God in the manner that came to be expressed in the Book of Genesis – as the Creator of all things and all peoples. From this time forward, Israel would become progressively convinced having "no other gods" required more than loyalty. It required seeing that all other gods were false gods – idols. Out of the prophetic experience came the pure and simple creed of Judaism, the *Shema*: "Hear O Israel the Lord is our God, the Lord alone" (Deuteronomy 6: 4). This confession is completed by reminding the members of Israel to love this God with all their heart, soul and strength; to pray the Shema on arising and retiring; and to bind it on their hands, forehead, and doorposts so that the awareness of the one true God might permeate their every thought and action.

The prophets warned the people that if they did not return to the covenant, this God, who is Lord of all creation and history, would punish them. And that is exactly how the misfortunes of Israel and Judah came to be interpreted, for, in 721 BCE, the Assyrians conquered the kingdom of Israel and carried its inhabitants off into slavery. In 621 BCE, King Josiah discovered what he believed to be an ancient lost book (the Book of Deuteronomy) in the temple. This book echoed the teachings of the prophets about the need to practice justice in order to please God. On this basis he initiated a reform that included a renewal of the covenant and required that all worship be done only at the temple in Jerusalem. However, according to the story, the reforms were not observed conscientiously and God again allowed the people to be punished. In 586 BCE the Babylonians conquered the Assyrians and their territories and carried off the inhabitants of the southern kingdom of Judah into exile and slavery.

In exile in Babylonia, the people-Israel had to learn how to sustain their religious identity without the land and without their temple. It is likely that the tradition of the synagogue as a community of study and prayer first arose in exile as an institutional vehicle for keeping the faith of Israel alive, apart from the land and the temple. During the exile another generation of prophets arose – Jeremiah, Ezekiel, and Isaiah – who confirmed that God was indeed punishing them for their failure to keep the covenant, but then added that the punishment was only for the purpose of teaching them a lesson. They would soon be permitted to return to their land and rebuild their temple. Indeed, the Persians, under Cyrus the Great, conquered the Babylonians and after only fifty years of exile, Israel was permitted to return to the land (538 BCE).

When the first wave of exiles returned to the land a modest second temple was rebuilt (520–515 BCE), but the leadership was weak and the people lacked a clear direction. It was not until Ezra and Nehemiah led a second wave of exiles (458 BCE) in a return to the land of Israel that a clear pattern for a post-exilic Judaism was laid down. If it was the prophets who put monotheism and ethics (the demand for justice for the orphan, the widow, and the stranger) at the center of the Jewish tradition, it was the priestly reforms of Ezra and Nehemiah that linked monotheistic ethics to holiness. For the word for "holy" – *qadosh* – means "to separate" or "set apart." And that is exactly what the priestly reforms demanded of the people. They understood the lesson of the exile to be that to worship the God who alone is holy one had to be holy as well. Consequently, they demanded that the people repent of their past mistakes of consorting with other nations, other gods, and other ways of life, in order to purify themselves as a holy people by separating themselves from their neighbors and rededicating themselves to the one true God and the covenant way of life – the covenant of Sinai that had made them a holy people. This meant, for example, that all those who had married foreign wives had to abandon them or be cut off from their own people. Israel must once more be a holy people, set apart from other nations in its commitment to faithfulness to the one true God and to justice and compassion for neighbor and stranger. It is with this priestly reform that Judaism adopted the experience of *exile and return* as the normative story through which to interpret all its future experiences, providing a normative pattern for all post-biblical forms of Judaism. In this sense, the Babylonian exile and return to the land of Israel gave birth to Judaism as a religious tradition.

The Exodus: covenant and ethics

The most important creation story in the biblical tradition is not that of the creation of the world but of the creation of Israel as a holy people – the story of the Exodus from Egypt and the covenant at Mount Sinai. For it is only after Israel came into existence as a people that it came to ask questions about the ultimate creation of all things and how its existence as a people related to creation as a whole.

The Exodus is a story about how a people enslaved by the Egyptians achieved their liberty against insurmountable odds and were led into a new land that was given to them by their God, in keeping with a promise made to their ancient ancestor Abraham (c.2000 BCE). According to the biblical stories, the tribes of Israel, descendants of Abraham, wandered down into Egypt during the time of a serious famine. For many generations they lived peaceably among the Egyptians, but as they grew in numbers the Egyptians began to mistrust them as intrusive outsiders who might turn against them. So the Egyptians enslaved them and cruelly oppressed them. And still their numbers grew, so that eventually the Egyptians initiated a savage policy of population control – ordering the slaying of every male child born among them. However, one mother saved her child by putting him in a basket and floating him downriver into the arms of the Pharaoh's (the ruler of Egypt) daughter, who instantly fell in love with him and adopted him, naming him Moses, which means, according to the story: "I drew him out of the water."

Moses grew up as the adopted son of the Pharaoh's daughter but under the care of his mother who served in the daughter's household. As a young man, Moses had to flee Egypt when he killed an Egyptian who abused an Israelite. In the desert Moses encountered the God of Abraham, Isaac, and Jacob in a burning bush and was commanded to return to Egypt and free his people. Moses reluctantly did as he was commanded and confronted the Pharaoh with the demand that the tribes be freed. However, only after God devastated Egypt with ten plagues did the Pharaoh finally consent to let them go. And even as Israel fled, he changed his mind and sent his armies to stop them, only to have his soldiers drowned in a sea that miraculously parted to let the tribes of Israel through and then closed over their pursuers.

This God then led Israel into the desert, leading them in a cloud by day and a pillar of fire by night. In this way, according to the story, the God of Israel brought his people out of Egypt to Mount Sinai in the desert, where he entered into a covenant with them:

> And Moses went up to God, and the Lord called to him from out of the mountain, saying, "Thus shall you say to the house of Jacob, and tell the people of Israel: You have seen what I did to the Egyptians, and how I bore you on eagles' wings and brought you to myself. Now therefore, if you will obey my voice and

keep my covenant, you shall be my own possession among all peoples; for all the earth is mine, and you shall be to me a kingdom of priests and a holy nation. These are the words which you shall speak to the children of Israel." (Exodus 19: 3–6)

These words are taken from the story of the creation of the people-Israel as recounted in the Book of Exodus in the Torah – the Bible of Judaism. They are the words said to have been spoken by the God of Abraham to his prophet Moses as he prepared to enter into a binding relationship, called the *covenant*, with a people he had *chosen* as his very own and rescued from slavery in the land of Egypt. This agreement took the form: I will be your God and you will be my people. I will guide and protect you and you will obey my commandments so that you may live long upon the earth and be a model for other nations. This covenant is understood on the model of a marriage contract as an intimate ethical contract of love and commitment obligating both parties. It is a set of mutual expectations and obligations, and, as such, it is a two-way street. Jews are obligated to walk in the way of Torah, the way of life embodied in the Ten Commandments given at Sinai. God is obligated to guide and protect his people. The intimacy of this relationship is such that each party has the right to make a claim upon the other. God has a right to demand obedience to the covenant, but Jews have a right to expect care and protection on the journey through time.

The covenant is expressed in ten commandments (Exodus 20: 2–14, Deuteronomy 5: 6–18) that make it clear that the heart of the way of Torah is a life of ethical commitment to justice and mercy. The commandments are said to be divided into two tablets – the first expressing obligations to God and the second expressing obligations to other human beings. The first demands that the holiness of God be honored such that adherence to all other gods is forbidden, as is the making of any image of God. For, unlike the idols of other nations, the God of Israel, in whose image all humans are made, is a God without image. That is what sets God apart as transcendent and holy, and makes God different from the gods of other nations. And the second tablet then demands that all human beings be treated with the respect of creatures created in the image of God. If one's neighbors are in God's image then one cannot steal from them, slander them, harm, or kill them without also committing a crime against God. The two tablets are traditionally divided as follows:

Tablet One

1. I am the Lord your God who brought you out of Egypt, you shall have no other gods before me
2. You shall make no graven images
3. You shall not take the name of the Lord your God in vain
4. Keep holy the Sabbath

Tablet Two

5. Honor your father and mother
6. You shall not kill
7. You shall not commit adultery
8. You shall not steal
9. You shall not bear false witness against your neighbor
10. You shall not covet your neighbor's house, wife, or manservant

By living according to the covenant and its commandments Israel became a holy people, a kingdom of priests. For as the Hebrew word for "holy" (qadosh) suggests, to be holy is to be "set apart." In this case, set apart from the sacred society of the Egyptians. Israel was *chosen* out of all the nations and *set apart* to be God's people – a people whose very way of life would set them apart from all other peoples as a witness to the reality of the one true God, the God of Abraham and Sarah. Israel's "chosenness" was, therefore, not one of privilege but responsibility – to be a model of justice and compassion.

So this people wandered through the desert for forty years, guided by God in the form of a cloud by day and a pillar of fire by night. And then, finally, just after Moses' death, they entered the land of promise. Moses spent his life making possible the liberation of his people, and when the goal was about to be realized he died in the land of Moab, knowing that his efforts were not in vain. Joshua, son of Nun, led them into the land of promise.

Wrestling with God and the stranger: three stories

The binding of Isaac

If the story of Moses and the Exodus recounts the creation of Israel as a holy people of the covenant, the stories of Abraham, his son Isaac, and his grandsons Jacob and Esau, present equally powerful ethical themes.

Undoubtedly the most profound test of Abraham's faith in the promise of God, to create a great nation through Isaac, was the command that came from God to take Isaac and sacrifice him as a burnt offering on a mountaintop. Hearing and obeying this command, Abraham set off with Isaac, two assistants, and a donkey bearing wood for the offering. After three days Abraham came to the mountain. Then Abraham took the wood and Isaac, his son, and set out for the mountaintop, leaving his assistants behind to tend the donkey. Isaac carried the wood, Abraham the fire and the knife. On the way, Isaac asked Abraham where the lamb for the sacrifice would come from. Abraham replied simply that God would provide. And when they got to the mountaintop, Abraham tied up his son and placed him on top of the firewood. Then he raised his knife to kill his son. But at that moment an angel of God intervened saying: "Do not lay your hand on the boy or do anything to him; for now I know that you fear God,

since you have not withheld your son, your only son, from me" (Genesis 22:
12). And Abraham saw a ram caught in some bushes and offered it instead of
his son. And Abraham called the place "The Lord will provide." And because
Abraham was willing to sacrifice his son at God's command, trusting in God's
promise in spite of all, God promised to make Abraham's descendants through
Isaac as numerous as the stars, and through them all the nations of the earth
would be blessed.

Israel: Wrestler with God

When Isaac grew into a young man he married Rebekah and she conceived
twins who would be named Jacob and Esau. Rebekah had a very difficult pregnancy. From the beginning, the two were at war with one another, struggling
and wrestling with each other in her womb. And so it would be between them
throughout much of their lives. They were extremely competitive and jealous of
each other. So Rebekah complained to God, and God responded: You have
two nations quarreling within you. "One shall surpass the other, and the older
shall serve the younger" (25: 23).

When they were young men and Isaac was very old, and with very poor eye-
sight, Jacob disguised himself as Esau and deceived his father into giving him
the blessing and inheritance meant for Esau. When Esau found out, Jacob had
to flee in fear for his life. He went to a distant land where he prospered. After
many years he decided to return home to the land of his parents. So he sent a
message to his brother Esau saying that he had become prosperous and would
like to return home, implying that he would be happy to share his wealth if his
brother would look on his return favorably.

So Jacob sent one half of his entourage ahead with instructions to say to his
brother Esau that all the flocks and wealth with them were a gift from his brother
Jacob, hoping in this way to win his favor. Then as night began to fall Jacob
camped by the Jabbok River and sent his remaining family and flocks across the
river while he remained alone. In the night a strange man attacked him and wrestled with him until dawn. The stranger found that he could not defeat him, but
he did manage to injure Jacob's thigh. As the dawn began to break, the stranger
demanded to be released but Jacob said he would not let the stranger go until he
blessed him. So the stranger asked for his name. And when Jacob gave it to him,
the stranger replied by saying that he would no longer be called Jacob but Israel
(which means wrestler with God), for he had wrestled with God and with humans and yet had prevailed. In return, Jacob asked the stranger's name but the
stranger refused to give it; however, he did bless him as he departed. So Jacob
called the place Peniel and as the sun rose, Jacob limped off saying: "I have seen
God face to face . . . yet my life has been spared" (32: 31). That very day Esau
finally met Jacob and embraced him, weeping as he kissed him. And Jacob responded, saying: "To come into your presence is for me like coming into the
presence of God, now that you have received me so kindly" (33: 10).

This is the story of how the children of Abraham became "Israel" – a people of faith. For the people-Israel regarded themselves as descendants of Abraham through the lineage of Isaac and Jacob. It is a powerful story that illuminates the fundamental presupposition of the covenant tradition: that the relationship between God and human beings is a two-way street in which you can wrestle with God and win, as long as you do so in the name of justice and mercy. Jacob is returning to establish justice by seeking mercy and forgiveness, making things right for the way he wronged his brother. When he wrestles with the stranger, he wrestles at the same time with the God who is without name or image, with himself, and with his brother. Because his intent is to reestablish justice, he wins the blessing of the stranger who will not give his own name while giving Jacob a new name – Israel, or "wrestler with God."

Abraham's audacity

In Judaism, this story, along with that of Abraham's argument with God over the city of Sodom, gave rise to a tradition of chutzpah (boldness or audacity) – arguing and wrestling with God over questions of justice as an essential component of the life of faith. According to the story in the book of Genesis, chapter 18, Abraham has the chutzpah to challenge God's justice in order to protect innocent strangers. The citizens of Sodom are known for their wickedness and God, it seems, intends to destroy the entire city and all its inhabitants. Abraham does not know the citizens of Sodom but he fears that God will destroy the innocent along with the wicked. So Abraham wrestles with God, arguing: "Will you indeed sweep away the righteous with the wicked?" (Genesis 18: 23) ". . . Shall not the Judge of all the earth do what is just?" (18: 25). Here Abraham not only wrestles with God, he wins. For he gets God to agree that the city will be spared if as few as ten just men can be found.

What this story tells us is that if the God of the covenant is the God of justice, then God is not above justice. Justice is where the life of God and of human beings must coincide. God can demand justice of human beings but the reverse can also occur. Abraham has the chutzpah or audacity to demand that if God is going to be God, then justice must be done. God is no more free to act arbitrarily and unjustly than are human beings. So Abraham bargains with God on behalf of these strangers whom he has never even met. This stand by Abraham is all the more powerful because it is on behalf of strangers. For hospitality to the stranger is the most often repeated commandment in the Torah. To welcome the stranger is to welcome either God, God's messiah, or at the very least an angel (messenger of God). Consequently, to do violence against the stranger is to do violence to God. Justice that is only for one's friends is not justice. It is only when the image of God is recognized in the stranger that justice can be done. Hospitality to the stranger is the ultimate measure of justice in the biblical tradition.

The paradox is that the Jewish tradition contains stories that seem to teach contradictory moral lessons. On the one hand, the story of the binding of Isaac seems to make unquestioning trust and obedience the test of faith, whereas the story of Sodom seems to make chutzpah – the audacity to question all authority, even God, in the name of justice – the test of faith. Rather than deciding between these two, Judaism seems to have embraced both. Obedience in faith is highly valued, and yet it can never be an absolute – neither the actions of God nor those of human beings are beyond question. Faith and obedience are held in tension with the demand for justice.

Formative Story: The Audacity of Job

After Auschwitz, perhaps no story has had more meaning for Jews than the story of Job. We select Job as the formative story for Judaism from this post-Holocaust perspective. For it is Job who had the audacity to challenge the justice of God in the face of his unjust suffering. We preface our account of the Job story with brief accounts of both Talmudic and Hasidic Judaism to show that even before the Holocaust, the tradition of audacity was alive and well.

Rabbinic Judaism, Hasidism, and the spirit of audacity

Between the time of the priestly reformation of Ezrah and Nehemiah (c.458 BCE) and the end of the first century CE, the Judaism of ancient Israel underwent a profound transformation that led to the emergence of Rabbinic Judaism as the normative model of Judaism in history. During this period a number of new movements emerged, offering alternative visions of the way in which the Jewish life ought to be lived. These included the Sadducees, the Pharisees, the Hellenists, the Samaritans, the Zealots, the Essenes, and the Nazarenes. From among these, Rabbinic Judaism developed out of the Pharisaic movement.

The word "rabbi" means "teacher." It was a term used by the Pharisees to identify those who were learned in the wisdom of the two Torahs, the "Torah" being the "teachings" concerning the revelations of the will of God. In the ancient world, oral tradition – the passing on of religious wisdom by word of mouth from one generation to the next – dominated religious life everywhere. But with the invention and spread of writing (c.3000 BCE), an alternative had emerged – the written word set down in the form of scriptures or sacred writings. Within Judaism this led some, called Sadducees, to assert that the revelation of God's will can only be found in the written text of the Torah – the five books attributed to Moses (from Genesis to Deuteronomy). Rather than claiming the opposite and more ancient oral tradition exclusively, the Pharisees sought to compromise by offering the view that God's revelation is both written and oral – hence the doctrine of the dual Torah. According to their teachings, when

God revealed his will to Moses on Mount Sinai, he gave Moses both written tablets and oral explanations of what was written down, and the two together comprise the Torah of God. This was necessary, they argued, because the written word always needs an explanatory context to make sense out of it. Therefore, apart from the Oral Torah, the Written Torah would make no sense.

In the first century CE, one Jewish movement, the Zealots, tried to inaugurate a revolt against Rome. Rome responded by sending in troops and in 70 CE destroyed the second temple and drove the Jews out of Jerusalem. After this, the Pharisees diplomatically sought to mend fences with the Romans and succeeded in getting permission to start academies for the study of the Torah. In the academies they created the dual scriptures of Rabbinic Judaism: the *Tanak* (Hebrew Bible) and the *Talmud*. "Tanak," in Hebrew, is essentially an anagram of three letters – T, N, and K – which stand for the three parts of the Jewish Bible: Torah (teachings/revelation), Neviim (prophets), and Ketuviim (writings/wisdom literature). The basic shape of the Bible in both Judaism and Christianity (which added a "New Testament" and called the Tanak the "Old Testament") was created by these decisions of the Pharisees.

With the written Torah now established, the Pharisees or rabbis then set about a second task, the paradoxical task of putting the Oral Torah into writing. This came to be known as the Talmud. How does one commit an oral tradition to writing without destroying its oral nature? The rabbis had an ingenious solution. The Talmud that they created was not a book organized around a series of stories the way the Bible is. Each page of the Talmud is made up of diverse sections written by different persons in the history of Judaism, presenting arguments and counter-arguments about what the way of Torah requires with regard to the various aspects of human existence – such as commerce, marriage, and family relations.

The genius of the Talmud is in preserving the character of the Oral Torah despite its written form. For a typical page of Talmud (see figure 6.1) is made up of diverse and distinct parts, all of which coexist on the same page. At the core of the page you may find a statement (A) from the Mishnah of the second century outlining the opposing points of view of two great Pharisees, Hillel and Shammai, on some question of appropriate behavior. Then above that, on the same page, a section of the Gemara (B), from a period two or three hundred years later, relating the Mishnah to relevant passages from the Tanak and to the diverse opinions of the Amoraim (its authors), who comment on the meaning of the Mishnah in light of the scriptures and of the opinions of the Tannaim (e.g., Hillel and Shammai). Then you will also typically find a section (C) devoted to the commentary of the greatest of the Rabbinic Talmudic scholars, Rashi, from the eleventh century. In yet another section (D), you will find the commentaries of the students of Rashi from a collection known as the Tosafot (twelfth and thirteenth centuries). Each of these expresses its own views of the meaning of the passages of the Mishnah in light of the comments of the others, and in light of additional commentaries and writings that supplement the tradi-

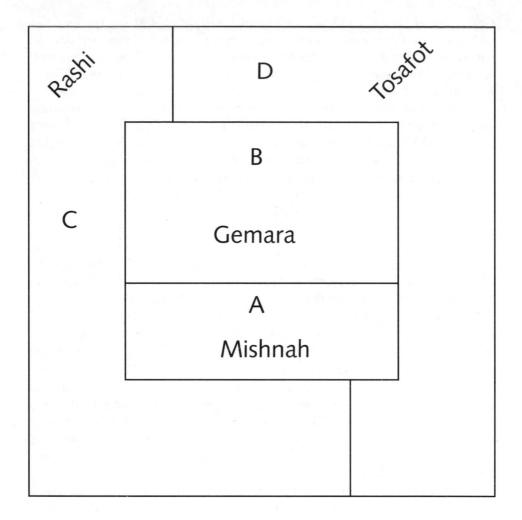

Figure 6.1   A Page of Talmud

tion. You cannot just sit down and read the Talmud as you would a book. Its very structure requires you to enter a debate that spans the centuries.

If the prophets put ethics at the center of monotheism it was the Pharisees who succeeded in putting ethics at the center of everyday Jewish life – reminding Jews that God set before them the choice between life and death and made it possible for them to choose life by choosing *to walk in the way of God* (the literal meaning of the word for God's law or commands – *Halakah*), giving them 613 commandments (good deeds, or *mitsvot*) by which to embody, in their lives, the justice and mercy of God as a model for all nations. In the view of the Judaism of the dual Torah, the world does not so much need to be saved as sanctified or made holy. To be holy is to belong to the God who makes all life flourish. To sanctify life is to rescue life from the forces of sin and death and bring it into a life-giving harmony with the will of God as revealed in Torah. To be a Jew is to walk with God, even wrestle with God, on the journey through life, in order to make all life holy, so that sin and death may be diminished and life might flourish.

Over the centuries the distilled wisdom of the rabbis on ethical issues was collected to provide a guide to the ethical life – the most authoritative being *Shulkan Aruk* from the sixteenth century. Although Talmudic decisions are made to guide the life of the Jewish community, it would be a mistake to think that the whole point of Talmud study is to reach a conclusion. There is a wonderful story in the Talmud that conveys the spirit of the rabbinic debate and the profound sense of authority that this ongoing argument carried within the tradition. According to the Talmud, Rabbi Eliezer ben Hyrcanos began to prove his interpretations of the Talmud by working miracles. Other scholars, however, challenged and chided him for such tactics and invited him instead to "wrestle with us over the text." Finally, Rabbi Eliezer called on heaven to vindicate his interpretation and a heavenly voice responded: "What do you want already with Rabbi Eliezer? The *Halakah* [God's commandments or laws] is always as he says." However, Rabbi Yoshua stood up and cried out "You, Yourself God, told us on Mt. Sinai to follow the community of those who agree on the truth." After this God was silent. Later the prophet Elijah was asked to interpret that silence and "he smiled . . . and said, 'My children have defeated me. My children have defeated me!' " (Lane 1986: 568, citing the Babylonian Talmud, Baba Metzia, IV, 59b). The meaning of the Halakhah is not to be determined by miracles or even the voice of God. Even God is bound to accept the meaning the rabbis come to understand through wrestling with his Word. The Talmudic way is the way of Abraham and of Jacob – or arguing and wrestling with God and man and winning. For the Talmudic tradition sanctifies the capacity to doubt and to criticize. "The wonder of the Talmud is its toughminded claims in behalf of the intellect, not in search, but in the service, of God" (Neusner 1973: xviii). God is found in the "thrust and parry of argument." Talmudic debate is a ritual for experiencing God through the questions. And yet, although the Talmudic scholar is vigorous and bold in his questions, his questioning is never divorced from faith. Faith and audacity, as we have suggested, paradoxically go together.

This same spirit of chutzpah can be found in Hasidic Judaism. Hasidism is a spiritual revolution that originated in the eighteenth century. The Hasidic movement first emerged in Poland with the activities of Israel ben Eliezer, who was called the *Besht* by his followers – an acronym for the *Ba'al Shem Tov*, or "Master of the Divine Name." The Besht was an ecstatic healer who worked miracles using magic, amulets, and spells. He taught that joy *(simhah)* is the appropriate response to the world no matter how much suffering Jews experience. The Besht was a charismatic figure who drew a circle of followers around him who hung on his every word and gesture, and who formed a prayer circle characterized by ecstatic singing and dancing, and deeply moving spiritual talks by the Besht around the Sabbath dinner table. The Besht taught that the essence of the way of Torah is to be found in devotion (*kavanah*), burning enthusiasm (*hitlahavut*), and attachment or clinging to God (*devekut*), rather than study of the Talmud.

The Besht became a model for the Hasidic notion of the *Tzaddik*, or "Righteous Man," and his followers were known as Hasidim. For the Hasidim, the Tzaddik was no ordinary person but one especially chosen by God as a direct link between heaven and earth. He was revered as a savior figure whose holiness was considered so powerful that, like Moses (Exodus 32: 11–14), he could intervene on behalf of the faithful and literally change the mind of God. Like the rabbis, the Tzaddik was a religious virtuoso; however, he was not a Talmudic virtuoso but a virtuoso of mystical piety. His virtuosity was said to be spontaneously contagious. Just being near him could enable the Hasidim to catch his piety as the spark to light their own. Like the Bhakti movement in Hinduism and Buddhism, it offered a way for even the poor and unlearned to move from the periphery into the heart of their religion as they understood it.

In spite of its emergence in an era of *pogrom* (mass violence against Jews), for the Hasidim, there was no greater sin than melancholy or sadness (*Atzut*). For sadness is the root of all sin. It emerges out of a fundamental ignorance of the pervasive and immanent presence of God in all things. Without this awareness humans go astray. According to a story of the Besht, this world is like the palace of a great king who is visited by both foolish and wise servants. The foolish servants are bedazzled by the splendor of the palace and spend all of their time gathering the gold and jewelry found in its many rooms. They are so caught up in gathering wealth that they never get to the throne room to see the King himself. The wise servants, on the other hand, are not distracted by all the material benefits of the palace and rush to the throne room to behold the King's glory. And once they behold the King, they realize that the palace and all its treasures were really a magical illusion. Just so, said the Besht, God hides himself in his creation. In fact, all of creation is created out of the reality of God. Therefore, there is no distance between God and humanity for those who have the eyes to see. And once you do see, there can be no excuse for sadness but only simhah, or joy – deep, pervasive, passionate joy and celebration. For this reason, asceticism or self-denial is not an appropriate religious response for a Jew so long as each remembers that to enjoy the creation is not a goal in itself but a way of enjoying God. The Hasidic way of Torah is to sanctify the secular by sanctifying the natural impulses – directing them toward God.

In Hasidic teaching, the Jewish proclamation of the Oneness of God means not just that God is without equal but also that God is all there is. This God created the world through a cosmic act of humility whereby he withdrew (*tzimsum*) his power and might into himself so as to create a space for his creatures. Creation then emanates from the humility of God, who hides himself in his creation. God is in exile from himself in order to be present in his creation, so as to bring his creatures to union with him. God pervades all things and apart from God all things are nothing. Moreover, nothing happens that is not the will of God who, being hidden in all things, is the cause of all things.

Realizing this calls for a corresponding humility (*shiflut*) on the part of human beings. This is achieved through meditative prayer (kavanah) in which one experiences an annihilation of all thought and finally of all self – to be replaced by attachment or clinging to God (devekut). Humility is not thinking less of oneself but rather not thinking of self at all – for in truth, there is no self, only God. The Hasid who achieves this spiritual realization is filled with not only joy (simhah) but a burning enthusiasm (hitlahavut), which leads to the performance of mitzvot (deeds of loving kindness) spontaneously and with a pure heart. For it is not deeds performed out of a sense of duty, but rather out of a sense of love and devotion, that sanctify and repair the world (*tikkun olam*) by liberating the divine spark in all things to be reunited with the divine itself.

The biblical spirit of audacity or chutzpah that we found in Talmudic Judaism is also found in Hasidism. The Hasidic master, Rabbi Levi Yitzhak of Berdichev, tells a story of how one day he asked a poor tailor to speak of the argument he had had with God that day in his prayers. The tailor responded:

> "I told the Master of the Universe, . . . today is the Day of Judgment. One must repent. But I didn't sin much. I took a little left-over cloth from the rich. I once drank a glass of brandy and ate some bread without washing my hands. These are all my transgressions. But *You*, Master of the Universe, how many are *Your* transgressions? You have taken away small children who had not sinned. From others you have taken away the mothers of such children. But, Master of the Universe, I shall forgive You Your transgressions, and may You forgive mine, and let us drink *L'Hayyim* [to life]!" That year Reb Levi-Yitzhaq proclaimed that it was this tailor with his argument who had saved the Jews. "Ah," he added, "but if I had been in his place, I would not have forgiven the Master of the World such great sins in return for a little left-over cloth. While I had Him, I would have asked that He send us His Messiah to redeem the World!" (Lane 1986: 581)

Job and the spirit of audacity

When the subject of ethics comes up in Judaism, the first impulse is to turn to the prophets of ancient Israel and the Deuteronomic reforms that placed ethical monotheism at the center of Judaism. One thinks of prophets like Amos (5: 24) who speak for God, proclaiming: "let justice roll down like waters, and righteousness like an everflowing stream." But the formative story we have chosen does not come from the prophetic books but from that portion of the Tanak known as the "Writings" which contains the wisdom literature of ancient Israel. We choose this story for three reasons. First, more than the prophetic books, the book of Job has the flavor of the Talmud. It is constructed as an argument between Job and three friends who come to comfort him in his misfortune.

They thrust and parry in a dazzling exchange, in a quest for knowledge of the will of God. Then later, a fourth friend arrives with a new set of arguments, which scholars believe were probably added much later by someone who edited the book. So, like the Talmud, the Book of Job is a wrestling with both God and man that spans more than one generation.

The second reason for choosing the book is that what Job and his "comforters" are wrestling with is the question of whether God is just. It is this question that goes to the heart of biblical ethics and evokes the tradition of chutzpah or audacity. The prophets assume that God is just and that human beings must respond to the demand of God to be just. But Job, like Abraham at Sodom, confronts a situation that makes him legitimately doubt that God is just. Thus the Book of Job is the ethical book *par excellence* in the biblical tradition, for, as we have argued, ethics is about questioning whether what we say is the good is really the good. Morality applies sacred norms to behavior; it questions the behavior but not the norms, precisely because they are sacred and unquestionable. But ethics questions the norms themselves, even if the norm be "God." Thus, were it not for the tradition of chutzpah, the Bible might offer a moral tradition, but it would not offer an ethical tradition.

The third reason for choosing the Book of Job is that after the Holocaust, the question of Job and the question of many Jews has become one and the same. For many Jews have asked deep and troubling questions not only about the goodness of human beings but also about the goodness of God. The chutzpah to question even God, which is as old as Abraham and as venerable as the Talmud, has, since the Holocaust, become a central theme of Jewish thought and existence and the story of Job has assumed new prominence in the tradition.

The post-Holocaust Jewish theologian, Emil Fackenheim, has raised the fundamental question: Where was God at Auschwitz? Like many other Jews he rejects the pious traditions of the past that accounted for misfortune by suggesting that "it is punishment for our sins." The Jews who died in the death camps, he argues, were overwhelmingly Jews from the most pious and observant communities in Eastern Europe. God cannot be exonerated that easily. So where was God? And how can one continue to be Jewish in the face of God's seeming abandonment of his people in the death camps? In response to these questions, Fackenheim says:

> There is a kind of faith which will accept all things and renounce every protest. There is also a kind of protest which has despaired of faith. In Judaism there has always been protest which stays *within* the sphere of faith. Abraham remonstrates with God. So do Jeremiah and Job. So does, in modern times, the Hasidic Rabbi Levi Yitzhak of Berdiczev. He once interrupted the sacred Yom Kippur service in order to protest that, whereas kings of flesh and blood protected their peoples, Israel was unprotected by her King in heaven. Yet having made his protest, he recited the Kaddish, which begins with these words: "Extolled and hallowed be the name of God throughout the world . . ." Can Jewish protest today remain within the sphere of faith? . . . In faithfulness to the victims we must refuse com-

fort; and in faithfulness to Judaism we must refuse to disconnect God from the holocaust. Thus, in our case, protest threatens to escalate into a totally destructive conflict between the faith of the past and faithfulness to the present. (Fackenheim 1970: 76)

It is this spirit of audacity in the face of overwhelming suffering and injustice that post/modern, post-holocaust Judaism shares with the rabbis, the Hasidim and with Job.

The first story of Job: unquestioning obedience

[A retelling of the story of Job based on the biblical story of Job. All quotes are from Pope 1965.]

Once there was a man named Job who lived in the land of Uz. He was a good man, blameless in the eyes of God. And he was a prosperous man with a large family of seven sons and three daughters. He owned much property, a great house, many servants, and large herds of sheep, oxen and donkeys. Daily he prayed to God in thanksgiving, and for the well-being of his family.

One day the members of God's heavenly court were meeting when one of them, the Satan, entered. Yahweh, the God of all creation, asked him where he had been and he responded "roaming the earth" (Job 1: 7). So God asked him if he had seen his servant Job. God boasted about how good and how pious Job was, saying: "there is none like him on earth" (1: 8). To which the Satan replied: of course he is good and pious, he has everything he could want. But he has never been tested. Send him a little misfortune "And he will curse you to your face" (1: 11).

Now God thought about this for a moment and then said: OK, I will put him in your hands. You can do anything you want to him short of harming him personally. Then the Satan struck Job with fury, bringing upon him a series of misfortunes. His crops were destroyed, his herds plundered by his enemies, and his children were killed in a storm when their house collapsed. Job was devastated. And yet, despite it all, Job refused to blame God. Instead he said: "Naked I came from my mother's womb, and naked shall I return there. Yahweh gave, Yahweh took away. Blessed be Yahweh's name" (1: 20).

Then the members of God's court gathered once more when the Satan returned to report on Job. God thundered at the Satan: So, now what do you think of my servant Job? "He still holds fast to his integrity. Though you incited me against him to destroy him without cause" (2: 3). To which the Satan replied: Maybe, but "all that a man has he will give for his life. Reach out and strike him, touch his bone and flesh, and he will curse you to your face" (2: 4). So God once more succumbed to the Satan's taunts and gave him permission to bring Job physical suffering, so long as he didn't actually take his life.

So the Satan returned to the earth and afflicted Job with a "foul pox" from head to foot and Job found himself sitting in ashes, scraping his boils in utter misery. Then his wife said to him: "Do you still maintain your integrity? Curse God and die." But Job said to her: "You talk like a foolish woman. Shall we accept good from God, and not accept evil?" (2: 10). And Job continued to refuse to blaspheme God. Then three of Job's friends (Eliphaz, Bildad and Zophar) came to comfort him. When they saw him, each wept and tore his robe. And they sat with him in silence for seven days and seven nights.

Then God, being immensely pleased with Job's unwavering piety and trust restored twofold everything the Satan had taken from Job. He now had twice as much wealth and twice as many children. And Job lived to be 140 years old and then he died, very happy with his life.

The second story of Job: wrestling with God

There are two stories in the Book of Job. One tells us of a pious man put on trial by God to test his faith, the other tells us of a man of integrity who puts God on trial to test God's commitment to justice. The first is found in what has been called the "framing story" which is composed of Chapters 1 and 2 and 42: 10–17. It reflects very ancient traditions of storytelling about the importance of piety and patient suffering in the Near East. In this story, Job is a model of true faith and piety who never questions God, no matter what happens to him. For this he is greatly rewarded. That is the story we just heard (above).

The second story, however, is very different. The ancient storyteller (or story-tellers), who gave us our present version of the book of Job, took this ancient story, split the beginning (1, 2) from the ending (42: 10–17), and sandwiched between them a second story (3–42: 9), which stands in dramatic contrast and contradiction to the story we have just told.

Chapter 3 begins abruptly and emphasizes the contradiction. "Job spoke out and said: Damn the day I was born" (3: 1–3). "Why did I not die at birth?" (3: 11). "What I most feared has befallen me, what I dreaded has o'ertaken me. I have no rest, no quiet, no repose, but continual agony" (3: 25–6). Job is angry. He feels he suffers unjustly. If, in the framing story, God put Job on trial, now in the inner story, it is Job who puts God on trial. "What have I done to you, man watcher?" he cries (7: 20). "Show me where I have erred" (6: 24). He accuses God of injustice and demands: "Relent, for my cause is just" (6: 29).

Job demands a trial before God to prove his innocence but he does not believe he will get a fair hearing. "How can a man be acquitted before God?" he asks (9: 2). Already Job foresees what will actually happen to him when God appears to him in the whirlwind (as described in Chapters 38–41). "If I summoned and he answered, I do not believed he would heed me. He would crush me with a tempest . . . Though righteous, his mouth would condemn me; though guiltless, he would declare me perverse. I am innocent . . . [Yet] I am already found guilty" (9: 16–17, 20–1, 29). Job goes on: "He is not, like me, a man whom I could challenge, 'let us go to court together.' Would there were an umpire between us to lay his hand on us both. Let him put aside his club, let his terror not dismay me, then I would speak and not fear him. But I am not so with him" (9: 32–5). For Job, God has become an enemy: "You are changed to a tyrant toward me . . . you lift me up and mount me on the wind, you toss me about with a tempest" (30: 21, 22). And yet Job resolves, "I will defend my conduct to his face. This might even be my salvation" (13: 15, 16). He asks for only two things: (1) not to be intimidated by the sheer terrifying power of God and (2) that if he has committed any offenses deserving of his suffering that he be told what they are (13: 21–3).

While God remains silent before Job's demands until the very last minute, the friends who have come to comfort him do not. These friends who sat in quiet compassion with Job in the first story now speak up but do not offer much comfort. In fact, they accuse Job of deserving everything that has happened to him. If Job has become the prosecuting attorney who has put God on trial, they have become the defense attorneys, bent on exonerating God by making Job seem guilty and so deserving of his suffering. So Eliphaz argues that the innocent do not suffer, only those who deserve it (4: 7, 8). And Bildad argues that God is by definition just, so Job must be guilty. All he has to do is admit this guilt and he will be forgiven (8: 3–7). And Zophar argues that Job may genuinely believe he is innocent but God can reveal his hidden guilt – guilt he has perhaps repressed or forgotten (11: 4–7). And so the arguments go on and on, as they each take turns attacking Job again and again. Then a new figure appears in court, Elihu (in Chapters 32–7). From him one might expect something new, but all he does is rehash the old arguments all over again, as if the strategy is simply to wear Job down until he finally submits.

Job, however, does not take these attacks on his integrity lightly. He lashes back at his so-called friends, saying; "Galling comforters are you all. Have windy words a limit? What moves you to prattle on?"(16: 2–3). Would that they were in his place and he in theirs, then they would know what it is like to be unjustly accused. They are not true friends, their answers offer no comfort. Having never experienced this kind of suffering, they are too sure of themselves. Their answers are too pat, as if they had God in their hip pocket (12: 5, 6). They are nothing but frauds who seek to curry God's favor by telling lies about him. "Is it for God's sake you speak evil, for him that you utter deceit?" For this, Job warns, God will rebuke you "quack healers" (13: 4–12).

The conversation between Job and the comforters abruptly comes to an end with the appearance of God, who answers him out of the midst of a great storm. God booms forth his challenges, calling Job to account for his words. "Gird your loins like a hero, I will ask you, and you tell me. Where were you when I founded the earth?" (38: 3, 4). God proceeds to do just what Job predicted he would do if ever they met – overwhelm him with his sheer power without ever once explaining what Job had done to deserve his suffering. So God continues to thunder down his challenges: Who laid the cornerstone of

Creation? Who was it that contained the sea? Have you ever commanded the dawn? Can you throw a lightning bolt? "Can you thunder with a voice like this?" (40: 9). "Would you annul my judgment, condemn me that you may be justified?" (40: 8).

It is all as Job predicted – he is being tossed around as in a storm by a God who does not answer for the justice of his actions but chooses to intimidate instead. So God declares: " 'Will the contender with Shaddai yield? He who reproves God, let him answer for it.' Job answered Yahweh and said: 'Lo, I am small, how can I answer you? My hand I lay on my mouth; I have spoke once, I will not reply; twice, but I will say no more' " (40: 2–5). Job is completely intimidated by the sheer awesome power of God and is cowed into submission: "I know that you can do all things" (42: 1). "I had heard of you by hearsay, but now my own eyes have seen you; so I recant and repent in dust and ashes" (42: 5, 6).

The final act and the moral of the story

The story seems to be over. Job said he would not get a fair hearing and he did not. Job said God would simply rely on his power and wouldn't even bother to answer his questions, and that is what happened. Job said he would be intimidated by the power of God, and he was. And just when we think the story is over and everything has happened just as predicted, suddenly – in three little sentences – the whole meaning of the story is stood on its head. For the words of repentance are barely out of Job's mouth, when God speaks again, but this time to the friends of Job who sought to "comfort" him with false accusations. For God spoke to Eliphaz and his friends, saying: "My anger burns against you and your two friends; for you have not spoken truth of me, as did Job, my servant. So, now, take yourselves seven bullocks and seven rams, and go to Job, my servant, and make a burnt offering for yourselves, and Job, my servant, will pray for you, for I will accept him, so that I may not do anything rash to you; for you have not told the truth of me, as did Job, my servant." And the comforters did as they were commanded and "Yahweh accepted Job and restored Job's fortune when he prayed for his friends and increased what he had twofold" (42: 7–11).

There is a great and powerful irony in this conclusion. For it is the friends who have been saying all along that God is just and therefore Job must be guilty of something, even if they do not know what. And it is Job who has been saying that he is innocent and that therefore God is unjust. And now, no sooner has God forced Job to repent and recant than he turns around and declares to the so-called friends of Job that it is Job who has spoken the truth of him and not the friends.

What are we to make of this? The book of Job does not really answer the question of why there is undeserved suffering in the world. But in these final words of God to the comforters it does undermine the notion that all people deserve the suffering that comes to them. It does not explain the coexistence of God and suffering but it does say that God always stands on the side of human integrity and justice, even if God has to testify against himself in order to affirm the dignity of those who suffer unjustly.

Finally, the book of Job gives human beings permission to argue with God and suggests that one can argue with God and win. For Job may have lost the battle but he won the argument – by God's own admission. The book of Job stands squarely within the covenant tradition that holds both God and humanity accountable to each other. This covenant is expressed in the narrative tradition of chutzpah, the tradition of wrestling and arguing with God, which goes back to Abraham and Isaac and forward through the Talmud and the Hasidic tradition and into our post-Holocaust world. It is this tradition that dares to ask with Abraham and Job: "Shall not the judge of all, also be just?" (Genesis 18: 26).

Life Story: Abraham Joshua Heschel and the Way of Audacity

A life story of holiness and audacity

Susannah Heschel begins a retelling of the story of her father's life by quoting a telegram that Abraham Joshua Heschel sent to President John F. Kennedy. It was on the occasion of a White House meeting with religious leaders in 1963 to discuss the civil rights crisis. It read:

> TO PRESIDENT JOHN F. KENNEDY, THE WHITE HOUSE, JUNE 16, 1963
> I LOOK FORWARD TO PRIVILEGE OF BEING PRESENT AT MEETING TOMORROW AT 4 P.M. LIKELIHOOD EXISTS THAT NEGRO PROBLEM WILL BE LIKE THE WEATHER. EVERYBODY TALKS ABOUT IT BUT NOBODY DOES ANYTHING ABOUT IT. PLEASE DEMAND OF RELIGIOUS LEADERS PERSONAL INVOLVEMENT NOT JUST SOLEMN DECLARATION. WE FORFEIT THE RIGHT TO WORSHIP GOD AS LONG AS WE CONTINUE TO HUMILIATE NEGROES. CHURCH [AND] SYNAGOGUES HAVE FAILED. THEY MUST REPENT. ASK OF RELIGIOUS LEADERS TO CALL FOR NATIONAL REPENTANCE AND PERSONAL SACRIFICE. LET RELIGIOUS LEADERS DONATE ONE MONTH'S SALARY TOWARD FUND FOR NEGRO HOUSING AND EDUCATION. I PROPOSE THAT YOU MR. PRESIDENT DECLARE STATE OF MORAL EMERGENCY. A MARSHALL PLAN FOR AID TO NEGROES IS BECOMING A NECESSITY. THE HOUR CALLS FOR HIGH MORAL GRANDEUR AND SPIRITUAL AUDACITY.
>
> Abraham Joshua Heschel

For her father, Susannah Heschel recalls, "politics and theology were always intertwined. After the civil-rights march in Selma [in which he marched with Martin Luther King, Jr.], he said, 'I felt my legs were praying.' Even as social protest was for him a religious experience, religion without indignation at political evils was impossible: 'To speak about God,' he said, 'and remain silent on Vietnam is blasphemous'" (Heschel 1996: vii–viii).

Abraham Joshua Heschel was well named, for he embodied the passion for holiness and justice manifested in the capacity for audacity that we have associated with the stories of Abraham – and not only Abraham, but also Jacob, Moses, and Job as well as the rabbis of the Talmudic tradition and the spiritual leaders of the Hasidic movement. Indeed, he was shaped by all their stories and in the process added yet another story to the tradition – the story of his own life of holiness and audacity.

Abraham Joshua Heschel was born in Warsaw, Poland on January 11, 1907. He was the son of a Hasidic rebbe and descended from Hasidic aristocracy – a long line of distinguished rebbes, the most notable of whom were Dov Baer (the Maggid) of Mezhirech and Abraham Joshua Heschel of Apt on his father's side of the family, and from his mother's side, Levi Yitzhak of Berdichev. Even as a child, being the son of a rebbe from a distinguished Hasidic line, he was treated with great respect, viewed as a spiritual genius and called upon to teach others.

Heschel's idyllic childhood was brought to a premature end at age seven with the irruption of World War I in 1914. In 1916, just six weeks before Heschel's tenth birthday, his father died in a typhus epidemic in war-torn Warsaw. This tragic event brought about a rather violent change in his Hasidic education, for he was given into the care of his uncle, who proceeded to have him educated in a rather different strand of Hasidism than that of his father. Heschel's first ten years were rooted in the tradition of joy that goes back to the founder of Hasidism, the Ba'al Shem Tov. Now he was introduced into the harsh demands associated with the Kotzker rebbe (Rabbi Menahem Mendl Morgenstern of Kotzk, 1787–1859).

His teacher, Bezalel Levy, set about to teach him the esoteric truths of Jewish mysticism and at the same time the spiritual importance of humility. Bezalel sought to undermine any illusions of self-importance Heschel might have. It was a severe shock to one who had been treated as royalty. Bezalel's goal was to bring about in Heschel a dissolution of selfhood in surrender to God, reached through contrition, repentance, and solitude. Heschel described the lessons of his youth by saying: "I owe intoxication to the Baal Shem, to the Kotzker the blessings of humiliation" (Kaplan and Dresner 1998: 40). By age 14, he had mastered the Talmud and was himself writing Talmudic commentaries. Shortly thereafter he came under the influence of a physician and psychiatrist, Fishl Schneersohn, from the Lubavitch (Habad) branch of Hasidism. It was he who facilitated Heschel's transition to "secular learning," not as a replacement for Hasidic wisdom, but a supplement to it.

Heschel engaged in secular studies at a gymnasium (high school) in Vilna and eventually went on to university studies in Berlin. At the Friedrich Wilhelm University he studied philosophy, history, and Semitic philology. He also studied modern secular exegetical techniques at the School for the Scientific Study of Judaism in Berlin. In 1933, shortly after Hitler came to power, Heschel passed his oral examinations for his doctorate at the University of Berlin. His dissertation was on prophetic consciousness. Then in 1934 he received a rabbinical degree from the School for the Scientific Study of Judaism. In 1936 his dissertation was published under the title *Die Prophetie*, which permitted him to officially receive his doctoral degree. It was well received in scholarly circles in Germany, despite the growing antisemitism of this period. As his reputation spread, Martin Buber asked Heschel to become Director for the School for Jewish Adult Education in Frankfurt. Now 30 years old, he moved to Frankfurt in 1937. During this period further publications of Heschel's appeared on the medieval Jewish philosophers Maimonides and Abravenal.

Heschel lived and taught in Germany as the Nazi Party was taking over society, including its universities. He was disappointed at the lack of support for Jews among the Christian community. The important exception was the Quaker community in Frankfurt. Then, in October of 1938, the Germans began expelling all Polish Jews living in Germany. The Gestapo gave Heschel one hour to pack and then jailed him until he could be deported the next day. At the Polish border, the Jews were refused entry and were held for several months. However, Heschel's family was able to get him released and he finally made it to Warsaw. Just six weeks before the German invasion of Poland, Abraham Joshua Heschel left Warsaw for London, where his brother served as a rabbi. Some of Heschel's family succeeded in getting to the US, but his mother and two sisters were murdered in the Holocaust. About six months after Heschel arrived in England, Julian Morgenstern, the President of Hebrew Union College in Cincinnati, managed to get a visa for him and offered him a teaching job in America. In March of 1940, he arrived in New York and soon took up his teaching duties at Hebrew Union College in Cincinnati.

In Cincinnati, Heschel met and married Sylvia Straus, a concert pianist, and soon after accepted a position at the Jewish Theological Seminary in New York. In the early 1950s he produced some of his most important books: *Man is Not Alone*, *The Sabbath*, *God in Search of Man*, and *Man's Quest for God*. Throughout his work, Heschel tried to communicate the power of the piety and spirituality of East European Hasidism, a world largely destroyed by the Nazis. He sought to show that Hasidic piety cannot be reduced to psychological terms. For the Hasid: "Awareness of God is as close to him as the throbbing of his own heart, often deep and calm, but at times overwhelming, intoxicating, setting the soul afire" (Heschel 1996: xxi). Such piety perceives the nearness of God in the dignity of every person and in the wonder of all creation. Piety is the human response to an encounter with the dimension of the holy that sanctifies all life. It does not begin with human experience but with the God who seeks out human beings. Hasidism, he insisted, is rooted in personal direct experience of the holiness of God. It can never be fully captured in books and writing. It is to be in love with God, filled with a divine madness, intoxicated with God, God's creation, and the stories of God.

As Abraham Joshua Heschel moved from the 1950s to the 1960s, his writing on Jewish spirituality and ethics turned into action. One of the factors that led him in this direction was the project of revising his doctoral thesis for publication under the title *Prophetic Consciousness*, which led him to see the social unrest of his time as a call to action. During the last decade of his life he was deeply involved in the struggle for civil rights, the protest against the war in Vietnam, and in interreligious dialogue.

In November of 1963, Heschel met Martin Luther King, Jr. at a conference on religion and race sponsored by the National Conference of Christians and Jews. Heschel and King became good friends and Heschel spent much of the remainder of his life speaking out and demonstrating on behalf of the civil rights of African-Americans. As Susanna Heschel recalls: "When the police blocked the entrance to FBI headquarters in Manhattan, it was he who gained entry to present a petition protesting police brutality against civil-rights demonstrators in Alabama." And he went on to march with King in Selma, Alabama where "he was welcomed as one of the leaders in the front row of marchers, with Dr. King, Ralph Bunche, and Ralph Abernathy." At a service prior to the march, Heschel read Psalm 27, which affirms: "The Lord is my light and my salvation; whom shall I fear?" He later reported experiencing a strong "sense of the Holy in what I was doing" (1996: xxiii).

Holiness, compassion and justice were simply different faces of the same reality to Heschel. And his commitment to all three spilled over from racial issues into protesting the Vietnam War. Approximately six months after Selma, Heschel, John Bennett, and Richard Neuhaus founded Clergy and Laymen Concerned about Vietnam. Heschel spoke out on this issue at protest rallies, in churches and synagogues, and so on, as persistently as he did on civil rights. "In a free society," he insisted, "some are guilty, but all are responsible" (1996: xxiv). It was under the auspices of this organization that Martin Luther King, Jr. made his own first public statement against the war in the spring of 1967. Heschel, too, spoke eloquently and passionately that evening.

Throughout this same period he was in dialogue with some of the leading religious and theological figures in both Protestant and Catholic Christianity. He was a close friend and neighbor of the great Protestant theologian and ethicist Reinhold Niebuhr, who delivered the eulogy at Heschel's funeral. He was involved in a consulting capacity at the Second Vatican Council with reference to its statement on the Jews. Later, Pope Paul VI told Heschel he had read his books and that they should be read by all Catholics. Heschel's friendships included anti-Vietnam (Catholic and Protestant) activists Daniel and Philip Berrigan, Thomas Merton (the Trappist monk), and William Sloane Coffin. And his organizational involvements included membership on the board of directors of such organizations as the Center for Nonviolent Social

Change, Operation Breadbasket, The Jewish Peace Fellowship, and Trees for Vietnam.

Abraham Joshua Heschel was clearly an extraordinary man for an extraordinary time. On the Sabbath of December 23, 1972 he died in his sleep. To die on the Sabbath in the Jewish tradition is considered "a kiss from God." "He was . . . 'a brand plucked from the fire of Europe [referring to the Holocaust],' and he became God's gift to us. The soil of Jewish piety in which he was bred was destroyed, but through him that world did not vanish. Like the Ba'al Shem Tov, he brought heaven down to earth, and in his writings we have a revelation of the holiness of Jewish life" (1996: xxix).

The way of audacity

"Prayer," says Heschel, "is a radical commitment, a dangerous involvement in the life of God." It is a direct involvement in the divine pathos, which is nothing less than God's participation in the suffering of humanity. "I pray because God, the *Shekinah*, is an outcast. I pray because God is in exile . . . God is in captivity in this world, in the oblivion of our lives. God is in search of man, in search of a home in the soul and deeds of man. God is not at home in our world. Our task is to hallow time, to enable Him to enter our moments, to be at home in our time, in what we do with time" (1996: 260).

To pray is to know what it is like to be in exile, to be a stranger even as God is in exile and a stranger. It is to be enabled to identify with the suffering of the stranger. To pray is, in a sense, to become the other. Thus in speaking of prayer and the Vietnam War, Heschel asserted that in "praying for peace in Vietnam, we are spiritually Vietnamese. Their agony is our affliction, their hope is our commitment" (1996: 231–2). Most human beings insulate themselves from the suffering of others so as not to go mad. But to do so is to lose a sense of urgency and responsibility – a sense that something must be done. For Heschel, both the prophet and the tzaddik are identified by their participation in the suffering of others through their participation in God's participation in the suffering of others. They feel God's sense of urgency to alleviate the suffering of the poor and the outcast. That is, they experience and communicate the divine compassion and the divine imperative – the demand for justice.

Heschel was a true prophet and a true tzaddik – a true, just, and holy man. Heschel's daughter tells us that he spent many a sleepless night agonizing over the suffering and injustice done to African-Americans and to the Vietnamese as the war raged on. And he himself says that he became involved because of the "onslaughts" on his inner life and coming to realize that "indifference to evil is worse than evil itself" (1996: 224–5). There can be no limits on our concern for the suffering of others, he insisted. Our lives are deeply interdependent. When one person is made to suffer we are all hurt and when one is treated unjustly we are all threatened. True prayer and prejudice cannot coexist in the same heart. Heschel was incensed at the response of white clergy to Martin Luther King, Jr. (referred to in King's "Letter from Birmingham Jail") to the effect that it was not the job of the minister to be involved in "transitory social problems." Such a response, he suggested, reflected the essence of idolatry. An idol is "any god who is mine but not yours, any god concerned with me but not with you" (Heschel 1990: 166). To segregate the races, Heschel insisted, is nothing short of "segregating God." It begins with a segregation of the sacred from the secular that allows persons to indulge in the illusion that they can separate "spiritual concerns" from "transitory social problems." A life of holiness challenges all such sacred dualisms.

For Heschel, a prophet is one who holds God and humanity together in "one thought" at all times. Human dignity and equality are derived not from human consensus but from "God's love and commitment to all men." This divine dignity is found in all persons, "criminal as well as saint." Indeed, "wherever you see a trace of man, there is the presence of God." The symbol of God, says Heschel, is not a tree, or a temple, or a statue – it is a human being, every human being. Moreover, whoever insults the poor man insults God and whoever is kind to such a person is kind to God (Proverbs 14: 31, 17: 15). And "it is the audacity of faith that redeems us." What is called for is a "leap of action" that is persistent in the face of all authority and all obstacles. For justice and righteousness are like a mighty stream (Amos 5: 24) that overcomes all obstacles. "No rock is so hard that water cannot pierce it. 'The mountain falls and crumbles away, the rock is removed from its place – the waters wear away the stones'" (Job 14: 8f.; Heschel 1990: 174–7).

Faith is making the impossible, possible. It can reverse discrimination, it can end wars, provided that persons of faith are willing to acknowledge their "duty to disobey" the laws, the social customs and the government policies that promote injustice. Responding to President Lyndon Johnson's criticism of war protestors, Heschel insisted: "Abraham did not hesitate to challenge the Lord's judgment and to carry on an argument with Him whether His decision was just. Can it be that the Judge of the entire universe would fail to act justly? For all the majesty of the office of the President of the United States, he cannot claim greater majesty than God Himself" (1996: 226). This was spoken by the man who had the audacity to ask in 1944: "Where is God? Why dost Thou not halt the trains loaded with Jews being led to slaughter?" as well as: "Where were we when men learned to hate in the days of starvation? When raving madmen were sowing wrath in the hearts of the unemployed?" (1996: 209–10). When it comes to justice, no one is beyond criticism, not God, not humanity, and certainly not the state. For Heschel, the greatest crime is to know about injustice and do or say nothing. Not all are guilty of creating injustice but all are responsible for righting injustice. The greatest sin is to be indifferent. What is required is "a voice of moral compassion and indignation, the sublime and inspired screaming of a prophet uttered by a whole community" (1996: 215).

Heschel's words bring to mind those of another Hasidic Jew from Eastern Europe who was plucked from the fires of the Holocaust, Elie Wiesel, who could also have provided us with a contemporary life story on spirituality and ethics in the Jewish tradition. Wiesel tells us: "I . . . remember my Master . . . telling me, 'Only the Jew knows that he may oppose God as long as he does so in defense of His creation.' To be a Jew 'means to serve God by espousing man's cause, to plead for man while recognizing his need of God.' Or again, 'Judaism teaches man to overcome despair. What is Jewish history if not an endless quarrel with God?' " (Wiesel 1978: 6, 146).

For Heschel, there is one God, one creation, and one humanity. This means that all things are interdependent. No religion is an island, nor is any person. "We are all involved with one another. Spiritual betrayal on the part of one of us affects the faith of all of us . . . whenever one man is hurt, we are all injured. The human is a disclosure of the divine, and all men are one in God's care for man. Many things on earth are precious, some are holy, humanity is holy of holies. To meet a human being is an opportunity to sense the image of God, the *presence* of God. According to a rabbinical interpretation, the Lord said to Moses: 'wherever you see the trace of man there I stand before you'" (1996: 237–8). The scandal of our age is that in a world in which "even political states . . . maintain diplomatic relations and strive for coexistence. Only religions are not on speaking terms." The solution is not to be found in the dominance of one religion but in realizing that "holiness is not the monopoly of any particular religion or tradition" (1996: 241, 247). Holiness is not to be limited to those of any one religion, not even Judaism. Holiness is defined by the intention of the heart and the righteousness of the deed. To equate God and any one religion is, for Heschel, the essence of idolatry, for God is the all-inclusive reality. The will of God is not to be found, he argues, in uniformity but in diversity. Whenever we meet and welcome each other as human beings, sharing a common humanity despite our differences, we encounter the presence of God.

Comparative Reflections: Heschel, Gandhi, and Thich Nhat Hanh

In this section and the questions which follow we invite you to pass over into the life and thought of both Abraham Joshua Heschel and Thich Nhat Hanh and wrestle with both, as well as our conclusions. We draw comparisons and suggest conclusions for your reflection with the hope that they will provoke discussion and the sharing of insight.

Justice: omnipartiality vs. taking the side of the poor and the oppressed

It is striking that the narrative tradition of chutzpah or audacity shares with the Socratic tradition a commitment to questioning all sacred authority in the pursuit of justice. In the life of someone like Abraham Joshua Heschel we see the convergence of the way of doubt with the way of audacity. Moreover, this way of audacity has much in common with Gandhi's way of asceticism, not in its commitment to self-denial so much as in its practice of civil disobedience. All three prove themselves to be paths of the holy, which call into question the sacred order of the world around them.

This does not mean that all perceive the relation between religion and ethics in the same fashion. Masao Abe argued that there is no continuous path from ethics to religion in Buddhism because ethical judgments are dualistic and therefore lead to judgmentalness (i.e., leading each party to blame the other) which creates disharmony and negative karma. Therefore, he argues, in Buddhism the relation between ethics and religion is one of mutual negation. One has to transcend the ethical to be fully enlightened. Enlightenment takes you beyond all judgments of good and evil, enabling you to "become the other," as Thich Nhat Hanh would suggest, seeing all sides with compassion.

In Judaism, by contrast, Abe observes, there is an open pathway in both directions between ethics and religion. This is what gives rise to the ethics-audacity – the chutzpah to wrestle with both God and human beings over questions of justice. Judgments of good and evil are necessary and not even "the holy" or "the Holy One" is exempt from the demand for justice. This is confirmed in the life of Heschel, for he argues that if God is not beyond questioning in the name of justice, then no one is – no matter how great their political or religious authority. For Buddhism, as Abe conceives it, holiness is beyond justice. Holiness is not answerable to ethical questioning. By contrast, in Judaism, as exemplified in the life of Abraham Joshua Heschel, experiencing the demand for justice is an inherent component of the highest spiritual insight one can have. There is no spiritual escape from the demands of justice.

And yet Heschel's spirituality enables him to "become the other" just as much as Thich Nhat Hanh's does. For, to participate in the holiness of God is to participate in God's participation in the suffering of others. So Heschel can claim that in praying for the Vietnamese he becomes Vietnamese. However, Heschel's "becoming the other" does not seem to share with Thich Nhat Hanh the character of "omnipartiality." For, like King David, in the story of David and Nathan, Heschel identifies with the victim rather than with both victim and perpetrator. Justice in the biblical tradition, as we have argued, sees God as taking the side of the poor and the oppressed, and demanding that those who walk in the way of Torah do likewise.

The story of David and Nathan from Jewish scriptures (recounted in chapter

1), unlike Thich Nhat Hanh's poem, leads to the understanding that the ethical point of view is seeing our actions from the viewpoint of the one who suffers from the effects of our actions. In this perspective, ethics does require "becoming the other," but not all others. Ethical consciousness is not "omnipartiality" but rather taking the part of the one who is injured. This, we said, is consistent with the position of contemporary Latin American liberation theologians who argue that justice requires giving a "preferential option" to the poor. It requires taking the side of the poor and the oppressed. And we pointed out in chapter 1 that the "veil of ignorance" proposed as a measure of justice by the contemporary philosopher John Rawls provided a convincing argument why this must be so. In his view, if you are asked to plan a society from behind a "veil of ignorance" you will be motivated to see justice from the point of view of the least member of that society, since you might have to assume the role of that person.

On this issue, Thich Nhat Hanh disagrees radically and he argues, "in Latin America, liberation theologians speak of God's preference, or 'option' for the poor, the oppressed, and the marginalized. But I do not think God wants us to take sides, even with the poor" (1995: 79), for even the rich suffer. Moreover, blaming someone creates a dualism (i.e., the innocent vs. the guilty) and "any dualistic response, any response motivated by anger, will only make the situation worse" (80). We think that the teachings of Gandhi, Heschel, and King offer another perspective. Anger at injustice should not (and need not) be confused with hatred. Anger can be rooted in our compassion for the other who has been wronged, as the story of David and Nathan illustrates. And unlike hatred, anger can be channeled into non-violent actions on behalf of the oppressed, which can heal and transform a social situation.

"Kenosis" or self-annihilation in Judaism

As we noted in the Introduction to Part II, Abe claims that the equation of justice with God "means that in Judaism the realization of spiritual death . . . and great death are absent." In his view, if there is a covenantal path between ethics and religion (the highest spiritual insight) in both directions, then there can be no "kenosis" or "emptying" of the self. To have the chutzpah to call God into question in the name of justice, as Abraham does, apparently would seem to require not a death of the self in total self-surrender but rather an assertion of the self in challenging God. And yet Abe's assumption about Judaism in this regard is not really accurate. Self-annihilation may not be as central in the public presentation of Judaism as it is in Buddhism but it plays an important role in some forms of Judaism, especially in Jewish mysticism and Hasidism. Moreover, not every challenge to authority is rooted in self-assertion. Indeed, we would argue that, rather than "self-assertion," it is selfless compassion and the demand for justice that arises from it that leads to spiritual audacity in Judaism.

That, for example, is the root of Abraham's challenge to God at Sodom. His selfless compassion for the stranger leads him to demand justice from God.

In his book *The Kiss of God: Spiritual and Mystical Death in Judaism* (1994), Michael Fishbane traces the history of "kenosis," or self-annihilation, as a spiritual and mystical doctrine in Judaism. Mystical experience, he notes, is often described as a death of the self experienced as "the kiss of God" – a kind of spiritual ecstasy that comes with cleaving to God. It is said to be the "pinnacle of a saintly life" (1994: 18). By the thirteenth century, "killing one's desires and dying by divine kiss are fixed topics of philosophical and ethical discourse" in Judaism (1994: 26). Maimonides, for instance, advocates recitation of the Shema ("Hear O Israel, the Lord Your God Alone is Lord") with all one's heart, mind, and soul as a lifetime spiritual discipline that can lead to "kenosis" or "emptying" the self in a spiritual death that results in "the kiss of God."

In the Kabbalistic tradition, the paradox is that the practice of dying is viewed as the act of "choosing life" – an act that leads to repairing the universe (*tikkun olam*). The founder of Hasidism, the Ba'al Shem Tov, said that spiritual realization requires killing oneself in order to give oneself totally to God. And the great Hasidic Rabbi Levi Yitzhak of Berdichev, whom we have already cited as a powerful spiritual example of chutzpah or audacity, himself fully subscribed to this spirituality, saying "whoever wants to live should kill himself" (Fishbane 1994: 46). Such a person cleaves to the source of all life, and having died in this life is released from the sting of mortality. So we see that the myth of "life through death" finds a place in Judaism as well as the other religions we have criticized for this doctrine. We criticized it because of its close association with unquestioning obedience. And yet in Levi Yitzhak, this spiritual death does not lead to unquestioning obedience, for it is rooted in a selfless compassion for God's creation, which demands justice – even from God. For, as Emil Fackenheim reminds us, "He once interrupted the sacred Yom Kippur service in order to protest that, whereas kings of flesh and blood protected their peoples, Israel was unprotected by her King in heaven. Yet having made his protest, he recited the Kaddish, which begins with these words: 'Extolled and hallowed be the name of God throughout the world . . .' " (Fackenheim 1970: 76). This would seem to suggest that, counter to Abe's intuition, kenosis and justice can go together, and do in at least some forms of Judaism. The mystery is how. Perhaps when God is understood as also having to answer to justice in order to be God, then surrender to God coincides with a spirituality and ethic of audacity.

Questions for Discussion

1   Compare and contrast the themes of wrestling with the stranger in Gilgamesh, the life of the Buddha, the story of Arjuna and Krishna, the story of Jacob wrestling with the stranger, and the story of Job wrestling

with God. What is the ethical significance of this theme in each story?

2   How does Abraham Joshua Heschel's ethic relate to the modernist paradigm of the privatization of religion?

3   How does the contrast between the sacred and the holy, or morality and ethics, appear in Abraham Joshua Heschel's ethic?

4   Compare and contrast Thich Nhat Hanh's and Abraham Joshua Heschel's understandings of ethical consciousness with respect to the issue of "omnipartiality."

5   Compare and contrast Thich Nhat Hanh's and Abraham Joshua Heschel's understandings of self as found in Zen Buddhism and Hasidism. What ethical implications flow from these understandings?

6   Describe Abraham Joshua Heschel's spirituality and explain how it functions in relation to his ethic.

7   How does Abraham Joshua Heschel's ethic address the ethical challenges of a techno-bureaucratic society?

8   Does the concept of human dignity play a role in Abraham Joshua Heschel's ethic? If so, how does his treatment compare with that of Gandhi and Thich Nhat Hanh?

9   Compare and contrast Abraham Joshua Heschel's ethic with Thich Nhat Hanh's ethic in terms of Masao Abe's models of religion and ethics (see figure 3.1). Do you think Abe's models of Buddhism and Judaism are accurate in these cases?

10 Compare and contrast Abraham Joshua Heschel's and Thich Nhat Hanh's ethics of non-violence.

11 What is the key spiritual practice in Abraham Joshua Heschel's ethic, and how does it function ethically in his life?

12 How is the post/modern spirituality of "passing over" and "coming back" illustrated in Heschel's life story, and what is its ethical significance?

13 How are the Hasidic practices of self-annihilation and audacity reconciled and expressed in Heschel's life?

References

Abe, Masao. 1990. "Kenotic God and Dynamic Sunyata," and "A Rejoinder". In John B Cobb, Jr. and Christopher Ives (eds.), *The Emptying God: A Buddhist–Jewish–Christian Conversation*. Maryknoll, NY: Orbis Books, 3–68, 157–202.

Fackenheim, Emil. 1970. *God's Presence in History*. New York: Harper & Row.

Fishbane, Michael. 1994. *The Kiss of God: Spiritual and Mystical Death in Judaism*. Seattle and London: University of Washington Press.

Heschel, Abraham Joshua. 1990. *To Grow in Wisdom: An Anthology of Abraham Joshua Heschel* (ed. Jacob and Noam Neusner). Lanham, MD: Madison Books.

——. 1996. *Moral Grandeur and Spiritual Audacity: Essays [of] Abraham Joshua Heschel* (ed. Susannah Heschel). New York: Farrar, Straus, & Giroux.

Kaplan, Edward K. and Dresner, Samuel H. 1998. *Abraham Joshua Heschel: Prophetic*

Witness. New Haven, CT: Yale University Press.

Lane, Belden. 1986. "Hutzpa K'Lapei Shamaya: A Christian Response to the Jewish Tradition of Arguing with God." *Journal of Ecumenical Studies* 23, 4, 567–8.

Neusner, Jacob. 1973. *Invitation to the Talmud.* New York: Harper & Row.

Nhat Hanh, Thich. 1995. *Living Buddha, Living Christ.* New York: G. P. Putnam & Sons, Riverhead Books.

Patai, Raphael. 1980. *Gates to the Old City.* New York: Avon Books, 244–5.

Pope, Marvin (trans.). 1965. *Job.* Anchor Bible. New York: Doubleday & Co.

Wiesel, Elie. 1978. *A Jew Today.* New York: Random House.

7

CHRISTIAN STORIES – ANCIENT AND POST/MODERN

We begin this chapter with the formative story of Jesus of Nazareth, because that story led to a transformation in the way the Jewish story of cosmic history was told among his followers. Then in the section on "The Cosmic Story Revised," we explain in what ways the cosmic story was changed in the light of the story of Jesus. Finally, we turn to the life story of Martin Luther King, Jr. to illustrate how a contemporary social activist drew upon these ancient stories to bring about greater social justice in contemporary society. It is the story of the Sermon on the Mount in the Gospel of Matthew that inspired both Gandhi and King to seek a path of non-violence. This message of loving your enemy and doing good to those who persecute you continues the Jewish ethic of audacity on behalf of the stranger. In the revision of the cosmic story, Jesus is viewed as the incarnation of the word and wisdom of God through which all things in the cosmos are created, held together, and brought to fulfillment. The story of the fall of Adam (or original sin), we suggest, brings about a different understanding of human nature, one closer to the Buddhist understanding than to the Jewish in some respects. This view led, in the writings of Paul (for instance), to the need for God to enter into the cosmos and human nature and heal it. To participate in this healing requires "dying and rising with Christ" – a spiritual experience of transformation in which the old self (born of Adam) dies in order to be replaced by a new self (born of Christ). This in turn gives rise to an ethic of interdependence in which one can no longer talk of self in individual terms but only by saying "we are members of one another," sharing each other's joys and sorrows. In this context Paul repeats the injunctions of the Sermon on the Mount to love one's enemy and overcome evil with good. The life story of Martin Luther King, Jr. is then shown to be an embodiment of both the Jewish story of exile (as expressed in the life and death of Moses) and the Christian story of crucifixion (expressed in the life of Jesus), giving birth to an ethic "redemptive suffering" or crucified love for one's enemies. And we show how King's passing over into the life of Gandhi (and Gandhi's reading of the *Gita*) gave social and political power to this ethic through the expression of civil disobedience. Finally, in our comparative reflections, we raise a question about the relationship between love and justice in Buddhism and Christianity that suggests that King would side with Heschel in disagreement with Thich Nhat Hanh concerning "omnipartiality."

Formative Story: Jesus of Nazareth

The stories of Jesus

We have already noted that by the first century tremendous diversity had grown up in ancient Judaism. There were the Sadducees and the Pharisees, the Hellenists, and a variety of sectarian movements like the Samaritans, Essenes, Zealots, and Nazarenes. These sectarian movements believed that God was bringing the world to an end in a final judgment that would be followed by a new creation. One of them, the Zealots, expected a messiah to come and restore the kingdom of God, the kingdom of Israel, through political insurrection. In fact, there was no common agreement among such groups as to who the messiah would be, and others expected a religious reformer, a kind of new Moses, or perhaps a prophet like Jeremiah. However, because the Zealots organized repeated guerrilla attacks on Roman legions, the Romans equated the term "messiah" with Zealot rebellion. This created the context in which the Romans executed Jesus of Nazareth somewhere around 31 CE in the mistaken fear that when some of his Nazarene followers referred to him as "messiah" this meant he was a military threat to the empire.

The teachings of Jesus, however, were anything but militaristic. In his Sermon on the Mount he taught precisely the opposite, that one ought to return love for hate, and do good to those who persecute you. In fact, Jesus lived and died a Jew, teaching much the same teachings as his great contemporary in the Pharisaic movement, Hillel – namely, love God above all and one's neighbor as oneself. And yet the message of Jesus achieved its greatest success not among the Jews but among gentiles, so that by the second century the Nazarenes (followers of Jesus of Nazareth) began to be seen as a separate religious tradition – no longer Jews but "Christians." It was not until the fourth century, however, that Christians developed a new body of sacred writings to add to the Tanak or Jewish Bible, which they called the "New Testament," and came to call the Tanak the "Old Testament." In the fourth century Christianity became the official religion of the Roman empire.

What is interesting about the New Testament is that it provides not one story of Jesus but four: the "Gospels" (meaning "Good News") of Matthew, Mark, Luke, and John. Scholars generally believe that Mark was written first, around the year 70 CE; Matthew and Luke retold his stories with new additions in the 80s, and the last to be written was the Gospel of John in the 90s.

As we have noted in the previous chapter, Jews say that if you want to understand who God is you must tell the story of the people-Israel; Christians add – and you must also tell the story of Jesus. Because of the parallel between the stories of Jesus and of Israel, embracing the story of Jesus is, for Christians, a way of embracing the whole story of the people-Israel with their God. To have faith in Jesus is a way of expressing one's faith in the God of Abraham and Sarah, the God of Moses, David, and the Prophets. Matthew's story indicates this in several ways. First, Jesus is tied into the history of Israel by a genealogy that declares Jesus to be a son of David and of Abraham through whom Israel came into existence (Matthew 1: 1–17). Then Matthew goes to great lengths to show that, like Israel in Egypt, Jesus was "passed over" in the slaying of the firstborn (in this case Herod becomes the new Pharaoh), and that Jesus was taken down into Egypt so that his return to the land of promise would, like Israel's, be the result of being called out of Egypt (Matthew 2: 13–15). Jesus' transfiguration on the mountaintop (Matthew 17: 1–8) is also told as a deliberate parallel to Moses' descent from Mount Sinai with the tablets containing the Ten Commandments. In both cases their faces glow too brightly for humans to look upon. Some scholars have even argued that Matthew's Gospel is divided into five books to parallel the Pentateuch, the five books attributed to Moses.

But that is not the only function of the story. If the story of Jesus is understood by Matthew as the story of the people-Israel writ small, for the apostle Paul the story of Jesus is understood as the story of the individual's own journey of spiritual transformation writ large. If all we had were the letters of Paul we would know very little about the life of Jesus. Paul showed little interest in the details of Jesus' life other than his suffering, death, and resurrection. For Paul, the events of Jesus' death and resurrection become a language for the inner transformation of the self. Through baptism and in faith, the Christian dies to his old self and rises with Christ as a new creature. The old self, born of Adam, dies, and a new self, born of Christ, is raised up. The ethical life consists in learning to die to one's self as a selfish being in order to be born again as a person capable of a love as all-embracing as that of God.

The story of Jesus then intersects with both the story of the people-Israel and the individual's life story, tying and binding the individual's life story into the great historical drama of God's presence in history. In this way the story of Jesus becomes the key to understanding the individual's own life story within the drama of history. It becomes a powerfully intimate way of coming to understand who God is. The God who acts in the history of Israel is the same God who acts in the life story of Jesus and in the Christian's own life story as well. And just as, for Jews, the ethical life consists in being holy, as God is holy, for Christians, it is to be holy as Jesus Christ is holy – a visible image of the invisible God.

We turn now to a retelling of the story of Jesus according to the Gospel of

Matthew. We chose this Gospel because of the central role the Sermon on the Mount from Matthew played in the lives of Tolstoy, Gandhi, and King – and the tradition of religious non-violence they inaugurated.

The story of Jesus according to Matthew

[A retelling of the story of Jesus according to the Gospel of Matthew.]

"An account of the genealogy of Jesus the Messiah, the son of David, the son of Abraham" (1: 1). There was a young woman in the town of Bethlehem named "Mary" who was engaged to a man named Joseph. However, before the wedding, Joseph discovered that Mary was already with child and so he resolved to break off the wedding. But then an angel of God appeared to him in a dream and revealed to him that Mary had conceived not by any man but by the Holy Spirit of God. The angel told him that she would have a male child and that his name was to be "Jesus" which means "God saves." This was done to fulfill the prophecy that a virgin would conceive and the child would be called "Emmanuel," that is, "God with us."

The child was born, as prophesied, in Bethlehem, the city of David during the reign of King Herod, who ruled over the Jews under the authority of the Roman governor. And wise men from the East came to Herod saying that they had seen a star in the sky, which foretold the birth of the King of the Jews. This news alarmed Herod, who saw such a birth as a threat to his own position, so he made inquiries and discovered that prophets had foretold such a birth in Bethlehem. So Herod sent the wise men to Bethlehem with instructions to let him know when they found the child. And they found the child and offered him gifts of gold, frankincense and myrrh. But, being warned in a dream, they did not return to tell Herod.

No sooner had they departed than an angel appeared to Joseph in a dream and urged him to escape with Mary and Jesus into Egypt, for Herod intended to find and kill the child. And indeed, Herod, in a rage, had all male children in Bethlehem under the age of two slaughtered, just as Jeremiah had prophesied. So the family remained in Egypt until Herod died, and then an angel appeared to Joseph once more in a dream and commanded him to take his family back to the land of Israel, where they settled in the town of Nazareth, for it was prophesied that Jesus would be called a Nazarene.

As Jesus grew to be a young man, dramatic changes were occurring around him. John the Baptist, who wore wild animal skins and ate wild locusts and honey, was stirring up the people by spreading the message: Repent, for the kingdom of God is at hand. And people were flocking to him to be baptized in the River Jordan. And he told those who came to him: "I baptize you with water for repentance, but one who is more powerful than I is coming after me; I am not worthy to carry his sandals. He will baptize you with the Holy Spirit and fire" (3: 11). And soon Jesus came to John, moved by his message and seeking baptism. John recognized him as the one prophesied and argued that Jesus ought to baptize him instead. But Jesus insisted, and John relented and baptized him. And as Jesus came out of the water, the Spirit of God descended upon him in the form of a dove and a voice from heaven declared: "This is my Son, the Beloved, with whom I am well pleased" (3: 17).

Then Jesus was led by the Spirit into the desert to be tempted by the devil. There he fasted for forty days and nights. And the tempter came taunting him, saying that if he was really the son of God then he could turn stones into bread. But Jesus rebuffed him, saying that a man does not live by bread alone, but more so by the word of God. Then, like the Buddha six centuries earlier, Jesus was offered the destiny of a great world ruler, and like the Buddha, he declined. For the devil took him to a high mountain and offered him all the kingdoms of the world if Jesus would only worship him. Jesus replied, "Away with you, Satan! for it is written, 'Worship the Lord your God, and serve only him' " (4: 10). With this the devil left him and angels came to care for him.

When he returned from the desert, Jesus heard that John had been arrested. Despite the obvious danger, he immediately took up where John had left off, preaching, "Repent, for the kingdom of heaven has come near." Soon, Jesus had drawn a band of disciples to him, inviting them to leave their professions and become "fishers of men." This group eventually numbered twelve who were called apostles. The leader among them was Simon Peter.

Jesus went with them around Galilee, teaching in synagogues, healing the sick and proclaiming the good news of the kingdom. And he told those who listened that he had not come to abolish the law and the prophets but to complete them. Then Jesus went up a hill so that he could better address all those following him, and he taught them what has come to be known as the Sermon on the Mount, saying to them:

> Blessed are the poor in spirit, for theirs is the kingdom of heaven. Blessed are those who mourn, for they will be comforted. Blessed are the meek, for they will inherit the earth. Blessed are those who hunger and thirst for righteousness, for they will be filled. Blessed are the merciful, for they will receive mercy. Blessed are the pure in heart, for they will see God. Blessed are the peacemakers, for they will be called children of God. Blessed are those who are persecuted for righteousness' sake, for theirs is the kingdom of heaven. Blessed are you when people revile you and persecute you and utter all kinds of evil against you falsely on my account. Rejoice and be glad, for your reward is great in heaven, for in the same way they persecuted the prophets who were before you. (5: 1–12)

He told them they were the salt of the earth and the light of the world, and they must set an example for others by their love. And he went on to say:

> You have heard that it was said, "An eye for an eye and a tooth for a tooth." But I say to you, Do not resist an evildoer. But if anyone strikes you on the right cheek, turn the other also; and if anyone wants to sue you and take your coat, give your

cloak as well; and if anyone forces you to go one mile, go also the second mile. Give to everyone who begs from you, and do not refuse anyone who wants to borrow from you. You have heard that it was said, "You shall love your neighbor and hate your enemy." But I say to you, Love your enemies and pray for those who persecute you, so that you may be children of your Father in heaven; for he makes his sun rise on the evil and on the good, and sends rain on the righteous and on the unrighteous. For if you love those who love you, what reward do you have? Do not even the tax collectors do the same? And if you greet only your brothers and sisters, what more are you doing than others? Do not even the Gentiles do the same? Be perfect, therefore, as your heavenly Father is perfect. (5: 38–48)

He admonished them not to be hypocrites, parading their good deeds and their pious prayers for others to see and praise, for all things should be done only for the eyes of their father in heaven. And he urged them not to be judgmental of others and encouraged them to look to their own faults instead. He reminded them that "not everyone who says to me, 'Lord, Lord,' will enter the kingdom of heaven, but only the one who does the will of my Father in heaven" (7: 21). And Jesus taught them many other things as well, before he descended the mount.

After this he went around the countryside curing the sick and casting out devils. In one case he came across a leper, he stretched out his hand and touched him, commanding "be cured" and it was done. In another case he cured a man who was paralyzed. And at Gadara, he cast the demons out of two men who were possessed and sent them into a herd of pigs that charged off a cliff and perished in the lake below. And everywhere, Jesus taught the crowds using parables. For instance, once he said to them: "The kingdom of heaven is like treasure hidden in a field, which someone found and hid; then in his joy he goes and sells all that he has and buys that field. Again, the kingdom of heaven is like a merchant in search of fine pearls; on finding one pearl of great value, he went and sold all that he had and bought it" (13: 44–6). In this way he made them understand that the kingdom was not far from them, it was not just a goal, for it was already present in the merchant's seeking. He also compared the kingdom to a mustard seed that starts small and grows into a large sheltering tree. And he used many other parables as well.

In the meantime, Herod had John the Baptist beheaded and when he heard stories about Jesus preaching the kingdom, he feared that he was John the Baptist come back from the dead. Jesus was deeply saddened by the news of John's death and sought solitude. However, the crowds followed him, and out of compassion, he healed their sick. Then, seeing the crowd had nothing to eat, he blessed the five loaves of bread and two fish the disciples had with them. They passed these out among the crowd, and miraculously there was enough to feed everyone to their satisfaction.

One day he took Peter, James and John with him to the top of a mountain. And there he was transfigured. His face was like the sun and his clothes like a brilliant light, and Moses and Elijah appeared with him. And the disciples heard a voice say, "This is my Son, the Beloved; with him I am well pleased; listen to him!" (17: 5). And the disciples fell to the ground in fear. Shortly, Jesus tapped them on the shoulders and having returned to his usual appearance, invited them to return down the mountain with him.

On one occasion a young man came to him and wanted to know what he must do to enter eternal life. Jesus responded that he must keep the commandments. The young man replied that he had done so since his youth. Well then, said Jesus, if you want to be perfect, sell all you have, give it to the poor and come follow me. The man, who was very rich, departed in sadness. On another occasion, a Pharisee asked Jesus, which is the greatest of the commandments? Jesus responded in a manner similar to the teaching of the great Pharisee Hillel, saying: "You shall love the Lord your God with all your heart, and with all your soul, and with all your mind. This is the greatest and first commandment. And a second is like it: You shall love your neighbor as yourself" (22: 37–9). On several occasions Jesus got into arguments with some of the Pharisees. He respected and shared the teachings of the Pharisees on most matters but he hated the hypocrisy he saw in some of them. Of those who were hypocrites he said: "The scribes and the Pharisees sit on Moses' seat; therefore, do whatever they teach you and follow it; but do not do as they do, for they do not practice what they teach" (23: 2–3).

Like John the Baptist before him, Jesus' preaching of the message of the kingdom of God drew crowds. On one occasion, as he and his disciples neared Jerusalem, he sent two of them to get him a donkey to ride. And as he rode the donkey into Jerusalem, crowds gathered waving palms and strewing them before him, shouting: "Hosanna to the Son of David! Blessed is the one who comes in the name of the Lord! Hosanna in the highest heaven!" (21: 9). And when he came to the Temple, he overturned the tables of the moneychangers and drove them out. Then he cured the blind and the lame who gathered about him. All of this angered the chief priests in the temple.

As the time grew near for him to suffer and die, he spoke often of the coming of the Son of Man at the end of time to judge the heavens and the earth. But he warned that no one knew the day or the hour, except his father in heaven. Therefore, he urged them to be prepared by a life of righteous deeds. And he told them a parable about final judgment – the parable of the sheep and the goats. On the last day, he said, all nations will be assembled before the Son of Man, who will, like a shepherd, separate the sheep from the goats – the faithful from the faithless. And as king, he will judge them saying to those on his right, come enter the kingdom. And those on his left, he will send to the fires of hell. And on both sides they will ask why he judged them as he had. He will respond to the sheep on his right by saying:

"I was hungry and you gave me food, I was thirsty and you gave me something to drink, I was a stranger and you welcomed me, I was naked and you gave me clothing, I was sick and you took care of me, I was in prison and you visited me." Then the righteous will answer him, "Lord, when was it that we saw you hungry and gave you food, or thirsty and gave you something to drink? And when was it that we saw you a stranger and welcomed you, or naked and gave you clothing? And when was it that we saw you sick or in prison and visited you?" And the king will answer them, "Truly I tell you, just as you did it to one of the least of these who are members of my family, you did it to me." (25: 35–40)

And to the goats on his left, he reminded them that they had neglected to do these things for the least among them and therefore had neglected him.

Now Jesus' popularity had caused jealousy among some priests in the Temple who plotted to have him arrested. Jesus, seeing what had happened to John, anticipated this and predicted his own arrest, death and resurrection on three occasions. However, even his own disciples did not understand these predictions. Then, one of his followers, the apostle Judas Iscariot, met with the chief priests and plotted to betray him for thirty pieces of silver. On the evening of Passover, Jesus dined with his apostles and warned them that one among them would betray him. At that meal he broke and blessed the bread and the wine and declared to his disciples that these were his body and blood given as a new covenant for the forgiveness of sins. The next time he would drink wine with them, he said, would be in the coming kingdom.

Then Jesus and his apostles went to the Mount of Olives to pray. There, he warned Peter that that very night Peter would deny him three times. In the garden of Gethsemane, he prayed: "My Father, if it is possible, let this cup pass from me; yet not what I want but what you want" (26: 39). Shortly thereafter, Judas arrived with a large number of men with swords and clubs. He went up and kissed Jesus in greeting as a prearranged sign to let them know which man to arrest. One of Jesus' followers drew a sword and cut off the ear of one of the High Priest's men. But Jesus commanded him to put away his sword, saying that if he wanted he could have called legions of angels to his defense but then the scriptures would not be fulfilled. After this, Jesus was arrested and his disciples fled in fear.

Jesus was then brought before the high priest, Caiaphas, who demanded to know from him whether he thought he was the messiah. Jesus did not respond directly, but he did predict that the Son of Man would come to judge the heavens and the earth. Caiaphas took this as an affirmative answer and accused him of blasphemy and declared that he deserved to die. That very night, Peter was asked three times if he knew Jesus and all three times, out of fear, he denied it. In the morning, they brought Jesus to Pilate, the Roman governor for the region, who alone could determine the fate of Jesus. Jesus refused to answer any of Pilate's questions, including whether he was "King of the Jews." Pilate's wife had a disturbing dream about Jesus and she urged Pilate to let him go. Pilate then offered the crowd a choice, to release the criminal Barabbas or Jesus, but the crowd chose Barabbas, and Pilate commanded Jesus be put to death.

Pilate's soldiers then stripped Jesus naked and put a crown of thorns on his head, making fun of him as the "King of the Jews." Then they led Jesus to the place of execution, called Golgotha – the place of the skull. There they nailed him to a cross as a common criminal and passers-by jeered, saying that he saved others but could not save himself. From noon until three the sky became very dark. And then at the end, Jesus cried out:

> "Eli, Eli, lema sabachthani?" that is, "My God, my God, why have you forsaken me?" When some of the bystanders heard it, they said, "This man is calling for Elijah." At once one of them ran and got a sponge, filled it with sour wine, put it on a stick, and gave it to him to drink. But the others said, "Wait, let us see whether Elijah will come to save him." Then Jesus cried again with a loud voice and breathed his last. At that moment the curtain of the temple was torn in two, from top to bottom. The earth shook, and the rocks were split. The tombs also were opened, and many bodies of the saints who had fallen asleep were raised. (27: 46–52)

One soldier was moved by Jesus' death to declare: "Truly this man was God's Son!" Afterwards, a man named Joseph of Arimathaea went to Pilate and received permission to bury Jesus. He took his body and placed it in his own burial tomb and rolled a large rock over the entrance.

The chief priests asked Pilate to place a guard so no one could come and steal the body and claim that Jesus had risen. Pilate consented. After the Sabbath, on the third day of burial, Mary of Magdala and another Mary came to the tomb at dawn. As they approached there was a violent earthquake and an angel came and rolled away the stone. The guards fainted in shock. The angel said: "Do not be afraid; I know that you are looking for Jesus who was crucified. He is not here; for he has been raised, as he said. Come, see the place where he lay. Then go quickly and tell his disciples, 'He has been raised from the dead, and indeed he is going ahead of you to Galilee; there you will see him.' This is my message for you" (28: 5–7). Excited and overjoyed, the women set out to tell the disciples. But Jesus himself approached them on the way, telling them not to be afraid and to tell the disciples to meet him in Galilee. There on a mountaintop, the eleven apostles met with the risen Jesus. And there he gave them a final command: "All authority in heaven and on earth has been given to me. Go therefore and make disciples of all nations, baptizing them in the name of the Father and of the Son and of the Holy Spirit, and teaching them to obey everything that I have commanded you. And remember, I am with you always, to the end of the age" (28: 18–20).

The Cosmic Story Revised: The Incarnation of the Word

The Word made flesh

Christians share with Jews the cosmic vision of the myth of history, which sees both the natural order and human life as an unfolding cosmic story being told by God – a story that has a beginning, a middle, and an end. What Christians added to the story was the centrality of Christ to the very act of creation that started the whole story. We can see how this occurred by comparing the story of creation in Genesis with a parallel from the Gospel of John.

According to the Book of Genesis: "In the beginning when God created the heavens and the earth, the earth was a formless void and darkness covered the face of the deep, while a wind from God swept over the face of the waters. Then God said, 'Let there be light;' and there was light. And God saw that the light was good; and God separated the light from the darkness. God called the light Day, and the darkness he called Night. And there was evening and there was morning, the first day" (Genesis 1: 1–5). And so over a period of five days he created the heavens and the earth. Then, on the sixth day: "God said, 'Let us make humankind in our image, according to our likeness; and let them have dominion over the fish of the sea, and over the birds of the air, and over the cattle, and over all the wild animals of the earth, and over every creeping thing that creeps upon the earth.' So God created humankind in his image, in the image of God he created them; male and female he created them" (1: 26–7). Then God saw that creation was good, and rested on the seventh day.

When we compare this cosmic story with the opening of the Gospel of John, we can see both the similarities and the differences between the Jewish and Christian cosmic visions. For John's Gospel begins: "In the beginning was the Word, and the Word was with God, and the Word was God. He was in the beginning with God. All things came into being through him, and without him not one thing came into being. . . . And the Word became flesh and lived among us, and we have seen his glory, the glory as of a father's only son, full of grace and truth" (1: 1–14).

A similar cosmic vision can be found in the letters of Paul, the apostle to the gentiles. Paul, however, refers to Christ not as the word (*logos*) but rather the wisdom (*sophia*) of God through whom all things were created. The Pauline letter to the Colossians says that the Son of God "is the image of the invisible God, the firstborn of all creation; for in him all things in heaven and on earth were created, things visible and invisible, whether thrones or dominions or rulers or powers – all things have been created through him and for him. He himself is before all things, and in him all things hold together. He is the head of the body, the church; he is the beginning, the firstborn from the dead, so that he might come to have first place in everything. For in him [Jesus of Nazareth] all the fullness of God was pleased to dwell, and through him God was pleased to reconcile to himself all things, whether on earth or in heaven, by making peace through the blood of his cross" (Colossians 1: 15–20). For Paul, too, Christ is the cosmic reality (God's preexistent wisdom) through which God not only created the world, but holds it together and brings it to fulfillment.

What these two cosmic visions of Christ share in common with the Jewish understanding is the belief that the world was created by the one and only God of biblical monotheism and that this was done through the divine speech – the Word of God. Christianity separated itself from Judaism, however, by transforming the meaning of the term "Messiah" or "Christ." This was done by identifying "Christ" with the Word. The Messiah is no longer simply an "anointed one" who restores the kingdom of God and brings the end of time (as the apocalyptic Son of Man who comes upon the clouds to judge the heaven and the earth). Now he is also understood as the one who brought the beginning of time as well. This is possible only because the Messiah or Christ preexists all things. All things are created through this Christ and then this Christ becomes united with one particular man – Jesus of Nazareth – in a unique way. The Church Council of Chalcedon (c.450 CE) said that two natures were in the one person of Jesus without confusion or mixture. Jesus was a human being like all others in body and mind, except for sin – and God was wholly present in Jesus.

Ethics, spirituality, and original sin

In Judaism the ethical reflection of experts is dominated by Talmudic dialogue and debate concerning the commandments of Torah. In Christianity the theological experts turned to Greek philosophy as the medium of debate. If we were dealing with "technical ethics" in Christianity we would need to discuss the role of philosophy in ethics and especially the influence of Plato, Aristotle, and Kant. But in this text we are seeking the narratives and forms of spirituality that even the experts presuppose (and share in common with the rest of the community) as the key to understanding ethics. And the narratives of Creation and Fall (original Sin) are formative for the entire tradition.

Christianity needs a savior to make the ethical life possible in a way that Judaism does not. The real issue that separates Christianity from Judaism (and also from Islam) is its understanding of human nature. Western Christianity (Catholic and Protestant) posits a serious flaw in human nature, "original sin," which prevents human beings from heeding the prophetic call for obedience without the intervention of a savior who restores human nature so that obedience is once more possible. The Messiah or Christ has to be a human being in whom human nature is healed – the firstborn of a new creation which through faith can heal the whole human race.

The doctrine of "original sin," formulated by St. Augustine (354–430 CE), has its roots in the letters of Paul; for Paul is puzzled as to why, even though he loves the law given in Torah, still he is unable to obey it. Paul explains:

> We know that the law is spiritual; but I am of the flesh, sold into slavery under sin. I do not understand my own actions. For I do not do what I want, but I do the very thing I hate. Now if I do what I do not want, I agree that the law is good. But in fact it is no longer I that do it, but sin that dwells within me . . . Who will rescue me from this body of death? Thanks be to God through Jesus Christ our Lord! (Romans 7: 14–17, 24–5)

Paul sees sin as a power that renders human beings incapable of obeying the commandments, even when they want to. This is a fundamental flaw in human nature. But it is not inherent in their created nature. Rather, it represents the distortion of human freedom by evil spiritual powers that hold the cosmos enslaved. Augustine called this "bondage of the will." Thus in order for human beings to do the good, they require a redeemer, none other than Christ, the Wisdom of God, to take on human flesh and restore the human condition to the freedom of the children of God.

When Augustine read this in Paul, he thought of the second creation story in Genesis (Genesis 2: 4–3: 24), which tells how God created Eve from the rib of Adam and how a snake (the devil in disguise) then tempted Eve to lure Adam into sin by eating from the forbidden tree of knowledge of Good and Evil. As punishment for this sin of disobedience, they were expelled from the garden of Eden and forced to live by the sweat of their brows, grow old, and die. Augustine interpreted this story as the fall of human nature under the power of sin – a condition that was inherited by all future generations. With the sin of Adam and Eve, the human will was corrupted by slavery to sin and could no longer do the good it desired. Only with the coming of Christ could the human will be restored, and with it, eternal life. For in Jesus Christ God united himself with human nature and transformed it.

Conversion, for Augustine, then (following Paul), was a dying of the old self (inherited from Adam after the fall into original sin) in order to be resurrected as a new self in Christ, a self that was now able to obey the law of God. Hence the paradox – the old self that clung to life was doomed to sin and death, but dying to self in Christ restored this self to freedom and eternal life. Therefore one had to die in order to live – one had to be killed, spiritually speaking, in order to be healed. In this model sin is equated with disobedience, and faith with the total surrender of self in unquestioning obedience.

This set Christianity apart from Judaism, for the rabbis interpreted the sin of Adam and Eve in a less cosmic fashion. They saw the story as about the struggle between good and evil impulses, but they did not believe Adam and Eve's sin corrupted the wills of all future generations. On the contrary, every person faces the same choice between good and evil that they did. And every person has the same freedom as Adam and Eve. Moreover, they believed that God gave the Torah to tip the balance in favor of good and away from evil. Therefore everyone who turns to the Torah is free to obey its commands and no savior, other than the Torah, is needed. Moreover, its notion of the covenant as a two-way street in which God and human beings are both answerable to the demands of justice, while affirming obedience to the demands of a just God, enables the capacity for audacity – the capacity to question all authority in the name of dignity and justice.

For Paul, the first human, Adam, is the model of disobedience and Jesus Christ is the model of obedience who reverses Adam's sin and therefore restores creation – making it a new creation. This leads Paul to formulate the idea of "kenosis," or "self-emptying," that Masao Abe refers to in his comparison with Buddhist "emptiness" in relation to ethics. This is found in the Pauline letter to the Philippians:

> Let the same mind be in you that was in Christ Jesus, who, though he was in the form of God, did not regard equality with God as something to be exploited, but emptied himself, taking the form of a slave, being born in human likeness. And being found in human form, he humbled himself and became obedient to the point of death – even death on a cross. Therefore God also highly exalted him and gave him the name that is above every name, so that at the name of Jesus every knee should bend, in heaven and on earth and under the earth, and every tongue should confess that Jesus Christ is Lord, to the glory of God the Father. (Philippians 2: 5–11)

Here is the core of spirituality that underlies much of Christian ethics – the practice of humility and obedience; a dying to self in order to live for others. One must die to the Old Adam or old self in order to become a new self in Christ.

Interestingly, the ethic that emerges from this "self-emptying" is very similar to the Buddhist ethic of interdependence. For when one dies to self and rises with Christ, Paul says, the only way one can talk of self is to say "we are members of one another."

> Do not be conformed to this world, but be transformed by the renewing of your minds, so that you may discern what is the will of God – what is good and acceptable and perfect. For by the grace given to me I say to everyone among you not to think of yourself more highly than you ought to think, but to think with sober judgment, each according to the measure of faith that God has assigned. For as in one body we have many members, and not all the members have the same function, so we, who are many, are one body in Christ, and individually we are members one of another. (Romans 12: 2–5)

This spiritual transformation of self gives birth to love and compassion, such that "if one member suffers, all suffer together with it; if one member is honored, all rejoice together with it" (I Corinthians 12: 26). Since all things are created and held together in Christ, this compassion embraces the whole of creation which, in its interdependence, forms the body of Christ. The body of Christ is the place where each individual self is healed and transformed to embrace its interdependence with all creation, through the imitation of Christ in "kenosis," or self-emptying.

The goal of this Pauline spirituality is to live the life of the Sermon on the Mount:

> Contribute to the needs of the saints; extend hospitality to strangers. Bless those who persecute you; bless and do not curse them. Rejoice with those who rejoice,

weep with those who weep. Live in harmony with one another; . . . Do not repay anyone evil for evil . . . No, "if your enemies are hungry, feed them; if they are thirsty, give them something to drink; for by doing this you will heap burning coals on their heads." Do not be overcome by evil, but overcome evil with good. (Romans 12: 13–21)

Christianity shares with Judaism a morality and an ethic based on the Ten Commandments revealed at Sinai. These in turn are thought by both Hillel (and other Pharisees) and Jesus to be summarized in two great commandments – to love God above all and one's neighbor as one's self. Both traditions are deeply rooted in the ethics of hospitality to the stranger – an ethic expressed in Jesus' teaching about loving even one's enemy.

The teachings of Jesus and Paul embody the ethic of the holy in a dramatic fashion. And yet we would be remiss if we left the impression that Christianity had not also fostered an ethic of the sacred. For once Christianity separated itself from Judaism and came to be dominated by gentile converts, it no longer thought of itself as a Jewish movement but as a separate and superior religion. In the first four centuries it developed a story of supersession which said that God had rejected the Jews because they had failed to recognize Jesus as the Messiah (and brought about his death) and chose gentile Christians to replace them. By the end of the fourth century Christianity became the official religion of the Roman empire and Christians interpreted their success as a sign from God that they were right. From that time forward hospitality to the stranger was replaced with hostility and mistrust of the stranger, who was no longer welcome in "Christendom." All pagan religions were then outlawed and severe legal restrictions were placed on Jews. As a result, the prejudice against Jews (and others) grew, resulting in synagogue burnings, forced baptisms, and mob violence (pogroms) throughout the Middle Ages and right into the twentieth century. Along the way Jews were forced to live in ghettos and wear yellow badges, and finally expelled from country after country in Western Europe. No wonder that Hitler could say that by ridding the world of Jews he was just finishing what the Church had started and doing the work of the Lord.

What was strikingly absent from Christian ethics during the Holocaust was the chutzpah or audacity to protect the Jews from the Nazi attempt at genocide. Christians for the most part were "unquestioningly obedient" to Nazi policies. Indeed, more Christian clergy died serving in Hitler's armies than in the concentration camps. (For a fuller discussion see Fasching 1992.) Negative teachings about the Jews go a long way toward explaining this. Nevertheless, a complete explanation would also have to take into account the dominant role of "obedience" in Christian ethics. The narrative of Christ as the model of humility, obedient even unto death on the cross, has been, with some exceptions, central to the Christian tradition. And this emphasis on obedience is perhaps a major reason why we see very little discussion of chutzpah or audacity in Christian spirituality and ethics, even though Christians share the very same stories through the adoption of the Jewish Bible, or Tanak, as its own "Old Testament." And yet in a man like Martin Luther King, Jr. we find a contemporary life story that shows that the spirit of audacity can play an important role in Christian spirituality and ethics.

Life Story: Martin Luther King, Jr. and the Way of the Cross

A journey of exodus and crucifixion

On December 1, 1955 a 42-year-old black woman, Rosa Parks, refused to give up her seat to a white man on a Montgomery, Alabama bus. Under the system of segregation that then existed everywhere in the South, American Negroes, as African-Americans were called in the 1950s, were required to sit at the back of the bus, and even there they could be forced to give up their seat to any white person who requested it. The bus regulation was part of an extended pattern of segregation that kept the races apart – separate bathrooms, separate schools, separate entrances to buildings, and so on. Every black person was seen as an alien and a stranger whose presence was both economically necessary and socially threatening. The Southern way of life divided the world into white and black – sacred and profane. In this sacred way of life, all who were white were viewed as fully human and all who were black as less than human. Therefore Southern white morality did not require whites to treat blacks with the same dignity that they treated each other. For a black person to enter the sacred space of white society, except under strictly controlled conditions, was to pollute that space. Therefore, it was strictly taboo for a black person to intrude into such spaces – a violation of sacred order.

Because this Southern way of life was considered sacred, it was unimaginable to most whites that anyone would dare to question it. To do so would be to invite the chaos that comes from mixing races – a chaos that would undermine the sacred order that made the Southern way of life possible. And yet the arrest of Rosa Parks sparked a movement among the black churches that set out not only to question segregation but to bring it to an end. The arrest of Rosa Parks aroused the black churches of Montgomery to organize a boycott of the buses with a demand that the law segregating buses be abolished. A young minister, relatively new to Montgomery, the Reverend Martin Luther King, Jr., pastor of the Dexter Avenue Baptist Church, was elected to lead the boycott. The protestors had legal precedent for their demands to end segregation since the Supreme Court had just recently ruled that the segregation of public schools was unconstitutional (*Brown v. the Board of Education*, May 17, 1954).

This boycott marked the beginning of a long struggle to end all segregation under the leadership of Rev. Dr. Martin Luther King, Jr. and the Southern

Christian Leadership Conference (founded in 1957). As the movement got under way and its actions were visually reported on national television news every evening, the conscience of much of white America was aroused, and many from liberal white congregations in the North (both Christians and Jews) came South to participate with blacks in public marches, engage in civil disobedience, and work for social change. King led important boycotts in Birmingham, St. Augustine, and Selma between 1963 and 1965. The movement escalated from a local to a national one and a major turning point was the passage of the Civil Rights Act in 1964. What was extraordinary about the movement under the leadership of Martin Luther King, Jr. was that it was organized using the principles of non-violence and civil disobedience first perfected by Mahatma Gandhi. The non-violent actions of the black churches, led by King, became a challenge to the sacred way of life of white Americans, first in the South but then also in the North – where discrimination was just as real although less blatant. Before his assassination on April 4, 1968, King had come to challenge not only segregation but also discrimination against the poor of all races, and US involvement in the Vietnam War. He saw them all as part of one pattern – a sacred way of life that violated justice and human dignity.

King grew up in the segregated South, experiencing the restrictions that kept him out of swimming pools, public parks, white schools, theatres, restaurants, and so on. He witnessed the active presence of the Ku Klux Klan and violence against blacks, including violence against his own father. An event at age 14 had a profound effect on him. He had just won a high-school student oratory contest on "The Negro and the Constitution" and was returning to Atlanta by bus. On the trip back he was forced to surrender his seat to a white passenger while he stood for the ninety-mile trip. Like Gandhi's expulsion from the train in South Africa, it was for King a defining moment. He never forgot the anger he felt, but like Gandhi he struggled to turn that emotion into a constructive force for social change. Throughout his early years his parents successfully countered such painful experiences by reinforcing his sense of his God-given dignity and worth as a human being, which not even white society could take from him.

King entered Booker T. Washington high school at age 13 and, after skipping two grades, found himself at Atlanta's all-black institution of higher education, Morehouse College, in 1944, at age 15. He majored in sociology and

Martin Luther King, Jr. was born on January 15, 1929 in Atlanta to Alberta and Martin Luther King, Sr. His father was the pastor of Ebenezer Baptist Church in Atlanta, a leader in the black community there, and a social activist who once served as President of the National Association for the Advancement of Colored People (NAACP) and fought hard for the rights of blacks. Both he and his wife were college educated and raised their three children to value education, social justice, and their own human dignity. While his father undoubtedly instilled in him the passion of social justice, it was his mother, an accomplished pianist, who probably first instilled in Martin an attraction to pacifism.

minored in English. It was there that he refined his superior oratorical skills, and there too that he became inspired to recognize the ministry as his vocation. During his college years he spent a summer working in Connecticut and was astounded to experience living in a community free from overt segregation. Returning to the segregated South was all the more painful after that.

King entered Crozer Seminary in Chester, Pennsylvania in 1948. He was ordained into the Baptist ministry at age 19. Crozer was his first experience with integrated education and he worked diligently to prove himself as good a student as any white seminarian. He more than succeeded, finishing first in his class as well as being elected student body president. It was during his seminary days that King's attention was first seriously drawn to the life and teachings of Gandhi. After hearing lectures on Gandhi by A. J. Muste and Mordecai Johnson, King began to study Gandhi in earnest. Upon completion of his seminary degree in 1951, King went on to do doctoral work at Boston University (BU). His positive experience with integrated education in the seminary and at BU did much to reinforce his hopes for an integrated society.

During his college years, in June of 1953, Martin married Coretta Scott in Marion, Alabama. Upon completion of his coursework he weighed his options for the future; he was strongly attracted to the academic life but he felt the need to make a difference in the Southern black church, and he took a job as pastor of Dexter Avenue Baptist Church in Montgomery, Alabama. This was in October of 1954, just months after the Supreme Court had declared segregation in public schools unconstitutional. Like a prophet called out of the wilderness, he was a man headed for his destiny. In June of 1955 he received his Ph.D. degree from BU and on November 17 his first child was born. Two weeks later, on December 1, Rosa Parks refused to give up her seat on the bus and Martin Luther King, Jr.'s life changed forever.

In response to Rosa Parks' arrest, King organized the Montgomery Improvement Association, which in turn organized the bus boycott. On December 5, the first day of the boycott, he laid out the issues before his church and the whole black community. It was time, he said, to call a halt to the humiliation and despair heaped upon the Negro community. It was not wrong to want to be treated with dignity, in a manner equal with whites. "If we are wrong, then the Supreme Court of this Nation is wrong. If we are wrong the Constitution of the United States is wrong. If we are wrong God Almighty is wrong. If we are wrong Jesus of Nazareth was merely a utopian dreamer" (Cone 1991: 62).

The Montgomery Improvement Association made the bus boycott a frontier for an assault on the racial injustice of the social order. From the beginning King knew that the white population of Montgomery would not respond to appeals to conscience. While love and respect between the races might be the goal, justice had to come first. One might not be able to legislate love but justice could be legislated. The whites of Montgomery may not have been moved to love their black neighbors, but by the end of the boycott, they were prepared to see that they were treated with increased justice.

However, for that to happen unjust laws had to be changed, and only political and economic pressure could make that happen. So King drew immediately
on the techniques of Gandhi, the techniques of non-violent protest and non-
violent civil disobedience. At first this commitment was tactical, but as his spiritual leadership matured non-violence became for him a deep religious conviction.
With over 75 percent of its bus passengers coming from the black community,
a boycott had a powerful economic impact – an impact that forced the need for
political accommodation on the part of the white community. Despite threats
of violence, the bombing of King's home, police harassment, and the loss of
public transport, the movement remained resolute both in its intention to continue the boycott until its demands were met, and to continue to do so non-
violently. After 381 days the boycott ended and the buses were integrated,
backed by a Supreme Court decision (November 13, 1956) declaring state and
local laws requiring segregation of the buses unconstitutional.

The boycott was conducted at a time when television was just beginning to
make itself felt as the new medium of national consciousness and international
awareness. The televising of the civil rights struggle made King a national and
international figure with immense public stature and influence. People were
referring to him as the "American Gandhi" and the news coverage aroused the
support of liberal whites from the North, creating a national public movement.
More importantly, these events thrust King into the leadership role in the black
churches and in the black community. In January of 1957 King met with black
church leaders in Atlanta to form the Southern Christian Leadership Conference (SCLC), of which he was named president.

Given his new stature, leadership role, and national visibility, it was almost
inevitable that King would be asked to spearhead the efforts at gaining civil
rights for blacks throughout the South, and eventually the North as well. After
an unsuccessful attempt to win concessions for blacks in Albany, Georgia in
1961, King went on to Birmingham in the spring of 1963 to lead a protest to
integrate eating establishments, with dramatic results. There King himself was
arrested and wrote his famous "Letter from Birmingham Jail" (Washington
1986b, 1992: 83–100). We shall examine it shortly as perhaps the single most
powerful expression of his ethic. President John F. Kennedy went on national
television in June of 1963, just months before his assassination, to declare civil
rights a national moral issue and ask Congress to commit to eradicating racism
in American society. Before the end of June, Kennedy had submitted a Civil
Rights Bill to Congress. With Birmingham, King succeeded in moving not just
the South but the whole nation to acknowledge the goal of equality and integration, a dramatic step in the direction of his vision of the "beloved community."

Birmingham was then followed by a planned march on Washington to promote the passage of the Civil Rights Bill. When the day arrived (March 28,
1963), the expected 100,000 marchers turned into 250,000, black and white,
from all over the nation, gathered at the Lincoln Memorial where King gave

one of his most famous speeches: "I Have a Dream." He reminded America that it had issued American Negroes a bad check with insufficient funds and now it was time to pay up and include them in the promises of the Constitution for freedom and justice for all, not just for whites. And he reminded Americans that the time to pay up was now. He went on:

> I still have a dream. It is a dream deeply rooted in the American dream that one day this nation will rise up and live out the true meaning of its creed – we hold these truths to be self-evident, that all men are created equal. I have a dream that one day on the red hills of Georgia, sons of former slaves and sons of former slave-owners will be able to sit down together at the table of brotherhood. I have a dream that one day, even the state of Mississippi, a state sweltering with the heat of injustice, sweltering with the heat of oppression, will be transformed into an oasis of freedom and justice. I have a dream my four little children will one day live in a nation where they will not be judged by the color of their skin but by the content of their character. I have a dream today! I have a dream that one day, down in Alabama, with its vicious racists, with its governor having his lips dripping with the words of interposition and nullification, that one day, right here in Alabama, little black boys and black girls will be able to join hands with little white boys and white girls as sisters and brothers. I have a dream today! I have a dream that one day every valley shall be exalted, every hill and mountain shall be made low, the rough places shall be made plain, and the crooked places shall be made straight and the glory of the Lord will be revealed and all flesh shall see it together. This is our hope. This is the faith that I go back to the South with. With this faith we will be able to hew out of the mountain of despair a stone of hope. With this faith we will be able to transform the jangling discords of our nation into a beautiful symphony of brotherhood. (Washington 1986b, 1992: 104–5)

And so King ended that dramatic oration with the resounding cry: "Let freedom ring" in a series of escalating crescendos that looked forward to the day when all can say, "thank God Almighty, we are free at last."

It was an ecstatic moment of vision and hope for the redemption of America, a vision of the "beloved community" that, he insisted, America was called to be. But there would be much struggle and suffering ahead. Two weeks later, four young black girls were killed when a Baptist church was bombed by racists in Birmingham. And yet King refused to see defeat in such tragedy. He read the event through the sign of the cross, as an example of redemptive suffering. The tragic deaths of these innocents might yet redeem the South and the nation, calling it to awaken its conscience. There were more tragic deaths, but King remained steadfast in his commitment to non-violence.

In 1963, *Time* magazine named King "Man of the Year" – the first black American ever so designated. In June of 1964 the Civil Rights Act was passed, and in December King was the youngest person ever to win the Nobel Peace Prize. Then, in the spring of 1965, King, accompanied by Abraham Joshua Heschel and others, led a successful march from Selma to Montgomery, Alabama to emphasize the need for laws to protect the right to vote for all blacks.

He compared it to Gandhi's march to the sea to protest the Salt Act. It was, indeed, a turning point, for on August 6, 1965 the Voter Rights Act was signed by President Lyndon Johnson.

Five days after the Voter Rights Act was signed, a major riot broke out in the Watts ghetto of Los Angeles. With whole blocks burned down and widespread looting and rioting, it took a police action of almost sixteen thousand men to restore order, leaving some thirty-four dead and four thousand arrested (Cone 1991: 221). In his visit to Watts, King discovered that blacks outside the South did not perceive themselves as greatly benefited by the strides toward freedom accomplished in the South. Northern blacks already had the right to eat in white restaurants, but they couldn't afford the price of a meal. They suffered from poverty and from a more subtle racism that in some ways was harder to confront and combat. And many Northern blacks found Malcolm X's appeal to violence made more sense than King's seemingly naïve appeal to non-violence.

With this experience, King began to turn his attention from South to North and from racism to the link between racism and poverty. He chose Chicago as the frontier for this new assault and in January of 1966 rented a slum apartment on the South Side. There he exposed the structural (and therefore often hidden) prejudice that virtually made it impossible for blacks to rent or buy outside the ghetto. It was, he argued, evidence that America was a sick society – a land of wealth where forty to fifty million people cannot afford proper housing, food and health care. And his consciousness expanded beyond the borders of the US, as he began to identify the global nature of the political and economic forces that created bonds of affinity in oppression between American blacks and the poverty-stricken populations of the Third World.

As King moved to challenge the prejudices of the North he began to lose some of the popular white liberal support he had experienced in the South. And the failure of white support for his Northern initiatives only more deeply fed the Black Power movement that had been gaining ascendancy since Watts, giving new power to voices like those of Stokely Carmichael and Malcolm X. Responding to such voices, his own language more and more shifted from talk of "Negroes" to "blacks." There was more emphasis on black history and black pride and the need for blacks to gain political power. And while he would not condone the separatism advocated by Malcolm X, he did begin to speak of the necessity for temporary self-segregation, initiated by blacks, in order to protect their dignity as blacks and to develop their own leadership and goals. That, he argued, was preferable to being co-opted out of power by white strategies of token integration.

As King entered what was to be the last year of his life, he began to speak out not only on racism and economic injustice but the war in Vietnam. In the previous two years he had lost significant support among both whites who feared sharing power with blacks, and blacks who were gravitating toward black separatism. His decision to speak out against the war in Vietnam still further eroded his support both in the white community, among those who considered it unpatriotic, and in the black community, among those who feared diluting the civil rights focus of his work. King was beginning to experience the loneliness of the long-distance runner, the prophet in the wilderness whose only source of courage remains his deep abiding faith in the presence of God despite the power of evil.

As early as 1965 he began to make tentative criticisms of the war, but it was not until 1967 that it became clear to him that he must, in conscience, speak out forcefully against the Vietnam War and American foreign policy. Influenced by his meeting with Thich Nhat Hanh the year before and accompanied by Abraham Joshua Heschel and others, he spoke his conscience in a speech at Riverside Church in New York in the spring of 1967. His critique linked racism, poverty, and militarism. He came to see American foreign policy in Vietnam as a racist policy made by white men with a colonialist mentality, who had no respect for the struggles for freedom of persons of color in Vietnam or elsewhere. In that speech and elsewhere, King decried the violence at the heart of the American way of life and concluded: "There is something strangely inconsistent about a nation and a press that would praise you when you say, 'Be nonviolent toward Jim Clark,' [the Sheriff who violently enforced segregation laws in Selma] but will curse and damn you when you say, 'Be nonviolent toward little brown Vietnamese children!'" (Cone 1991: 239). There is something wrong with a nation, he argued, that spends half a million dollars to kill a North Vietnamese soldier but only fifty to lift one of its own out of poverty.

Although his advisors tried to persuade him to tone down his criticism, King would not be deterred. He told his followers that his calling came from God and not men. "The word of God is upon me like a fire shut up in my bones . . . And God has called me to deliver those in captivity. . . I'm going to fight for them. I'll die for them if necessary, because . . . the God that called me to preach told me that every now and then . . . I'll have to agonize and suffer for the freedom of his children. I may even have to die for it. But if that's necessary I'd rather follow the guidelines of God than to follow the guidelines of men" (Cone 1991: 242). These words were prophetic in two senses. They were a genuine prophetic word about justice addressed to the American people and they were prophetic of the price King would pay for his life of protest on behalf of others. Called to Memphis to play a role in a black sanitation workers' strike, he spoke eloquently of the risks he knowingly took on behalf of God's call to be a voice for justice. On the night before his assassination at the Bishop Charles Mason Temple in Memphis, he concluded his speech by saying:

> And then I got into Memphis. And some began to say the threats, or talk about the threats that were out. What would happen to me from some of our sick white brothers? Well, I don't know what will happen now. We've got some difficult days ahead. But it doesn't matter with me now. Because I've been to the mountaintop. And I don't mind. Like anybody, I would like to live a long life. Longevity has its place. But I'm not concerned about that now. I just want to do God's will. And

He's allowed me to go up to the mountain. And I've looked over. And I've seen the promised land. I may not get there with you. But I want you to know tonight, that we, as a people will get to the promised land. And I'm happy, tonight. I'm not worried about anything. I'm not fearing any man. Mine eyes have seen the glory of the coming of the Lord. (Washington 1986a: 286)

The next day Martin Luther King, Jr. was struck down by an assassin's bullet on the balcony of his second-floor room at the Lorraine Motel in Memphis, Tennessee.

King's spirituality and ethics: the way of the cross

Martin Luther King, Jr.'s life and its ethical significance would not be under-standable apart from his religious faith and experience. Like Socrates, one of his heroes in the tradition of civil disobedience, he understood that in order to do the good one must overcome the fear of death. Like Moses, he saw himself as a prophet who would help his people enter the promised land even if he would not enter it himself. And like Jesus, he embraced the way of the cross, the way of redemptive suffering that proves love is stronger than death.

At the very beginning of his public career, in the early days of the Montgomery bus strike, King had a profound religious experience that permeated everything he did from that day forward. As James Cone retells it, King came home late from a boycott meeting only to get a phone call: "Nigger . . . we are tired of you and your mess now, and if you are not out of this town in three days, we're going to blow your brains out and blow up your house." Although he had received dozens of such calls before, this one got to him. He thought of losing his family or of them losing him. It was unbearable and he could not sleep. He went to the kitchen for a cup of coffee. Rationality left him and none of his philosophy or theology seemed of any help.

Something said to me, you can't call on daddy now; he's in Atlanta, a hundred seventy-five miles away. . . . You've got to call on that something, on that person that your daddy used to tell you about, that power that can make a way out of no way. And I discovered then that religion had to become real to me and I had to know God for myself. And I bowed down over that cup of coffee. I never will forget it. Oh yes, I prayed a prayer. And I prayed out loud that night. I said, "Lord, I'm down here trying to do what's right. I think I'm right. I think the cause that we represent is right. But Lord, I must confess that I'm faltering, I'm losing my courage and I can't let the people see me like this because if they see me weak and losing my courage they will begin to get weak." . . . Almost out of nowhere I heard a voice . . . "Martin Luther, stand up for righteousness. Stand up for justice. Stand up for truth. And lo, I will be with you, even until the end of the world." After that experience . . . I was ready to face anything. (Cone 1991: 124–5)

As indeed he did, for three days later King's home was bombed. His wife and child, fortunately, were not hurt. While a crowd with weapons gathered protectively around him, King urged them to remain non-violent, and he reminded them that no matter what happened to him, God would be with them in their struggle. King's experience was in direct continuity with the myth of history. He encountered the God who acts in time and leads his people through time – the God who promises to be with him until the end of time. He was claimed by the Holy One whose covenantal demand is justice and mercy. King found the path that moves from religion to ethics – the way that is no way. It was, he discovered, the way of the cross, the way of redemptive suffering.

As James Cone has eloquently shown in his book *Martin & Malcolm & America*, Martin Luther King, Jr.'s ethic was deeply rooted in his spiritual life – a life that, from the day of his "kitchen experience" forward, was grounded in an experience of the immediacy of God in his life. This God who made his presence known to him, however, was a God he had heard about all his life within the Black Baptist tradition. King's spirituality was deeply rooted in Israel's story, the Exodus tradition of the God of the covenant who demands justice and inspires hope for liberation from slavery. And it was just as deeply rooted in the story of the cross, the story of Jesus. The cross, said King, was "God's way of saying no to segregation and yes to integration" – it expressed "the length to which God is willing to go to restore broken communities" (Cone 1991: 127). And it was a length Christians were asked to go, as well.

King enriched the black church tradition on the way of the cross with his commitment to non-violence – a commitment grounded in his trust in the God who revealed himself not only in the cross of Jesus but in the cross of his own life. One cannot build the kingdom of God, one cannot build the beloved community, on violence. The means and the ends of one's actions must be commensurate. Therefore, one cannot create a community of reconciliation through coercion; one must rather win hearts and minds through a willingness to turn the other cheek while never backing away from the demands for justice. The way to the resurrection is through the crucifixion. Unmerited suffering, King said repeatedly, is redemptive. The God of the resurrection is at work in our crucifixions. Thus, for King, non-violence was not just a strategy, it was a way of life – the way of the cross.

It is at this point that Gandhi played a critical role in King's spirituality, for Gandhi's contribution to the understanding of the Sermon on the Mount was to read it through the eyes of a Hindu shaped by the story of Arjuna and Krishna in the *Bhagavad Gita*. Before Gandhi, the admonition to love your enemies and do good to those who persecute you were seen as lofty ideals, but ones that could only invite evil and injustice to reign unresisted in the world. Before Gandhi, it was thought that only violence could restrain evil. Gandhi brought a new dimension of understanding to the Sermon on the Mount. For, as he interpreted the *Gita,* we must really be prepared to go to war in the pursuit of justice, but this warfare must be non-violent. For to engage in violence is to become like our enemy and only increase the sum total of violence in the world. But Gandhi showed that non-violent warfare, in the form of civil disobedience, can restrain evil and transform the evildoer. The tactics of organized non-violent civil disobedience put the teeth of justice into "love of enemies." It transformed the Sermon on the Mount into an effective political strategy for paradoxically bringing about justice with love. Moreover, even when non-violence failed to change the enemy, it succeeded in limiting the power of evil and violence in the world by refusing to add to it. The cost, in that case, could be high, as the assassinations of both Gandhi and King demonstrate. But the effects were equally as profound.

When King found that leadership of the Montgomery bus boycott had been thrust upon him, he spontaneously found himself turning to "the Sermon on the Mount and the Gandhian method of non-violent resistance. This principle became the guiding light of our movement. Christ furnished the spirit and motivation while Gandhi furnished the method" (Washington 1986b, 1992: 59). King used this formula frequently. It was certainly true as a personal expression of his own spirituality. And yet we know the relation of the *Gita* and the Sermon on the Mount, from Tolstoy, through Gandhi, to King, was more complicated than that. For, in his own interpretation of the *Gita*, Gandhi was deeply moved and inspired by the Sermon on the Mount as interpreted by Tolstoy. And his spiritual insight, as a Hindu, into the meaning of the *Gita* then added something new to his understanding of the Sermon on the Mount – the notion of spiritual warfare conducted through non-violent civil disobedience. And that new complex of spiritual insights then, in turn, inspired King's understanding of how to apply the Sermon on the Mount to the question of racial justice in America. King's spirituality and ethics could not have been what it was without the influence of not just Gandhi's techniques but Gandhi's spiritual insight as a Hindu, even as Gandhi's Hinduism would not have been what it was but for Tolstoy.

The goal, he insisted, is not to humiliate and defeat your enemy but to win him or her over and bring about not only justice but reconciliation. The goal, he said, was to attack the evil in systems, not to attack persons. The goal was to love one's enemy, not in the sentimental sense of affection (*eros*), nor in the reciprocal sense of friendship (*philia*), but in the constructive sense of seeking their well-being (*agape*). Non-violence, he argued, is more than just a remedy for racism. It is, he became convinced, essential to the future survival of humanity in an age of nuclear weapons. "The choice today is no longer between violence and nonviolence. It is either nonviolence or nonexistence." Finally, King insisted (perhaps recalling his "kitchen experience" and other such moments), his commitment to non-violence was deeply rooted in his experiences of God as a personal God, a God to whom he prayed in personal dialogue and who was with him and guided him. "In him there is feeling and will, responsive to the deepest yearnings of the human heart: thus God both evokes and answers prayers"

(Washington 1986b, 1992: 61). It was, he said, his source of inner calm and strength in the midst of danger.

King's spirituality was the deeply prayerful spirituality of one called to make a journey with God through time in the name of justice and human liberation. His was the journey of one who had been to the mountaintop of unfulfilled aspiration with Moses and the mountaintop of crucifixion with Jesus – both of whom gave their lives for the salvation of others. Like Abraham before him, for King, faith was a willingness to set out on a journey without knowing where he was going, trusting the God who was a stranger (the one who cannot be named) to lead the way – a God whose deepest yearnings coincided with the human yearnings for justice, love, and hope.

King's spirituality can be summed up in a trust that God can make "a way out of no way." It was a spirituality that gave him tremendous ethical courage in the face of overwhelming odds. One of the most eloquent statements of King's ethic comes out of his "Letter from Birmingham Jail" (Washington 1986b, 1992: 83–100), written after his arrest for leading the sit-ins to integrate the lunch counters of Birmingham. It was a masterful statement in the Socratic as well as prophetic traditions of calling the sacred order of society into question in the name of the holy. In his letter, he responded to a letter from the white clergy who called the civil rights movement "unwise and untimely." Why, they asked, had he not remained in Montgomery but insisted on coming to Birmingham? King's response was rooted in his deep sense of the interdependence of all life before its Creator. "Injustice anywhere is a threat to justice everywhere. We are caught in an inescapable network of mutuality, tied in a single garment of destiny. Whatever affects one directly affects all indirectly."

King went on to outline the strategy of non-violence: collect the facts to determine if injustices exist; negotiate to correct them; if that fails, purify yourself through prayer and self-examination and workshops on non-violence; and then take direct non-violent action. He reminded his white colleagues that the movement only proceeded to sit-ins when the city refused to act justly and refused to negotiate. Like Socrates, he said, they were sent as gadflies to create a little tension in society in order to bring its citizens to reconsider their behavior. Human beings can only endure so much oppression and despair. To ask blacks for patience after so much suffering at the hands of segregation is to commit only a further act of violence upon them. The goal is to create a crisis sufficient to motivate people to negotiate, for history teaches us that freedom is never given by those who hold the power.

In such a situation, those oppressed have no choice but to break the laws. This is legitimate because not all laws are just and unjust laws must be disobeyed in order to call them into question and reestablish justice. In such cases, one has an ethical responsibility to break the law. An unjust law is any law that violates the eternal law of God. "Any law that uplifts human personality is just. Any law that degrades human personality is unjust." Segregation laws are just such laws that violate and degrade the humanity of blacks. King went on to put it another way: "An unjust law is a code that a majority inflicts on a minority that is not binding on itself."

The heart of civil disobedience in refusing to honor an unjust law is to do as Socrates did: openly disobey the unjust law while willingly accepting the penalty so as to arouse the conscience of the public and bring about a change in the law. Such an act is one of respect, not disrespect, for the law as the guarantor of justice. And then King reminded his readers that everything that Hitler did in Germany was legal. But the obligation of the Christian was to comfort and aid his Jewish brothers and sisters, even if it was illegal. In his own way, King was articulating an ethic of audacity. He refused to allow his enemies to define his actions as extremism in the negative sense: "Was not Jesus an extremist in love – 'Love your enemies . . .' Was not Amos an extremist for justice – 'Let justice roll down like waters and righteousness like a mighty stream'" (ibid.: 94). Is it not, he asked, better to be an extremist for love rather than hate?

King went on to express his disappointment with the white churches that had spiritualized the Gospel message and turned their backs on questions of law and social justice, being committed to "a completely otherworldly religion which made a strange distinction between body and soul, the sacred and the secular." To King, this made no sense at all, for the holiness of God and justice in the secular world were mutually implied. King went on to take exception to the ministers who praised the non-violence of those upholding unjust laws while ignoring the non-violence of those who sought to reestablish justice. Just as it is immoral to use violence to establish justice, so it is immoral to use peaceful means to preserve injustice. It was time, he suggested, for the churches to stop being conformed to the world and to set out to transform it. In our terms, King was calling the sacred order of society into question in the name of the holy. He was calling the church back to its vocation to be a holy community committed to audacity on behalf of the stranger rather than the mirror of a sacred society. And he did it by following the way of the cross.

Comparative Reflections: King, Heschel, Gandhi, and Nhat Hanh

In this section and the questions which follow we invite you to pass over into the life and thought of Martin Luther King, Jr., and imagine where he would stand in the disagreement about justice we highlighted between Abraham Joshua Heschel and Thich Nhat Hanh in the previous chapters. We invite you to wrestle with both, as well as our conclusions, and arrive at your own. We draw comparisons and suggest conclusions for your reflection with the hope that they will provoke discussion and the sharing of insights.

What is distinctive about Martin Luther King, Jr.'s spirituality is that it managed to recover the spirit of audacity found in the Jewish roots of the Christian tradition. Like Job's argument with his comforters, King's "Letter from Birmingham Jail" called into question the God presented to him by conservative white ministers (his "comforters"), a God who is more interested in saccharine piety and sacred order than in justice. Many scholars have attributed this solely to King's exposure to liberal theology in his graduate education. But they fail to take into account the fact that the Baptist tradition in its historical origins took exception to the doctrine of original sin and affirmed the freedom of the will – hence it asserts that only adults who freely choose Christ should be baptized. King had no illusions about human evil, but he was also more optimistic about the human capacity for conversion and goodness than many traditional theological children of Augustine and his views on "original sin."

In his view of human nature, King was more the exception than the rule in Christianity. Although Christianity has deep roots in the prophetic religion of Judaism, its doctrine of original sin leads it to function spiritually in a way more analogous to the religions of India, Hinduism and Buddhism. For the notion of "illusion" in these religions functions in a way parallel to the idea of "original sin" in Christianity. For illusion, too, is seen as a corruption of human consciousness that renders the self unable to see and do the good. Hence in Hinduism and Buddhism, as in Christianity, we find parallel notions of the self having to die in order to live – of having to be killed, spiritually speaking, in order to be healed.

These distinctions help to explain the similarities and differences Masao Abe saw between Jewish, Christian, and Buddhist ethics. While Abe's models do not fit all variations in any of the three religious traditions, they do provide a helpful set of questions for making comparisons and contrasts. As you will recall (see figure 2.1 and the discussion in the Introduction to Part II), Abe saw a similarity between Buddhism and Christianity in that they both called for the death of the self, while he did not see such a requirement in Judaism. The parallel here is really between the Buddhist doctrine of slavery to illusion, and the Christian doctrine of slavery to sin, as a fundamental flaw in human consciousness from which humans must be liberated through the death of self. Judaism, he suggested, not seeing such a flaw (at least in the same way), sees no need for self-annihilation, only for sanctification. However, we noted in chapter 6 that an understanding of self-annihilation, or "kenosis," can be found in Judaism, especially in Hasidism.

As we have said, Abe argued that there is no continuous path from ethics to religion in Buddhism, because ethical judgments are dualistic and therefore lead to judgmentalness (leading each party to blame the other), which creates disharmony and negative karma. The only relation between religion and ethics is one of mutual negation. Enlightenment takes you beyond all judgments of good and evil, enabling you to "become the other," as Thich Nhat Hanh would suggest, seeing all sides with compassion.

In Judaism, by contrast, there is an open covenantal pathway in both directions between ethics and religion. This is what gives rise to the ethic of audacity – the chutzpah to wrestle with both God and human beings over questions of justice, even in its Hasidic forms, where chutzpah and self-annihilation co-exist. Judgments of good and evil are necessary and not even "The Holy One" (i.e., God) is exempt from the demand for justice. Finally, Christianity offers an intermediate position in which there is a continuous path from religion to ethics but not from ethics to religion. This is because "original sin" prevents one from doing the good, so that only after religious conversion and the transformation of the self that dies and rises with Christ (kenosis) can the self restored by religion then proceed to ethics. Hence, what Buddhism and Christianity share that separates them from Judaism, from Abe's perspective, is the spirituality of the "death of the self." What Judaism and Christianity share with each other that separates them from Buddhism, Abe suggests, is making justice the highest ideal of spiritual insight. For Buddhism, as Abe conceives it, holiness is beyond justice, while for the other two, holiness must include justice.

It may be that we have stumbled upon a significant difference between Eastern and Western ethics here. As we suggested in chapter 1, in some ways a karmic worldview makes it more difficult to perceive injustice. Buddhist ethics places great emphasis on compassion but does not really have a language for justice. As Masao Abe has noted, "love and justice" go together in Judaism and Christianity, and cannot be separated. In Buddhism there is an equivalent of love, "compassion," but "there is no Buddhist equivalent to the [Jewish and] Christian notion of justice. Overall, Buddhist history shows indifference to social evil. . . . It is important for Buddhists to grapple with the question of how to incorporate the notion of justice into the traditional context of wisdom and compassion" (Abe 1990: 179–80).

We would argue that compassion and justice need to temper each other. We should try to understand our enemies and have compassion for them, appreciating the "mitigating circumstances" that may have led them to violence and oppression. Indeed, we need to recognize that same capacity in ourselves and so avoid a self-righteous dualism in which we see ourselves as totally good and the other as totally evil. As Thich Nhat Hanh, quoting the Gospel of Matthew, reminds us: God's love falls like the rain on the just and the unjust alike. But this does not mean that there are no unjust persons, any more than loving your enemies means you have no enemies. Loving one's enemies, and all who are unjust, does not exempt us from the demands of justice – for no matter what the reasons for the action of the victimizer, still the possible violation of the dignity of another requires one to take the side of those unjustly threatened or injured. Gandhi may be our bridge between Eastern and Western views, for he shows how we can make such ethical judgments without falling into the trap of the self-righteous dualism of hatred and violence. So we have a difference of perspective here on what spirituality and ethics require. However, it may be that the disagreement is largely verbal, for although Thich Nhat Hanh says one must not take sides, his own actions (e.g., with the boat people) have been to take the side of those whose dignity is being violated. In the remaining chapters we will ask whether we have to choose between these views or whether these differences can be reconciled.

Questions for Discussion

1   Compare and contrast the story of Jesus with that of Arjuna with respect to the use of violence. Do you think Gandhi was right to find the message of non-violence in both? Why or why not?
2   How does Martin Luther King, Jr.'s ethic relate to the modernist paradigm of the privatization of religion?
3   How does the contrast between the sacred and the holy, or morality and ethics, appear in Martin Luther King, Jr.'s ethic as expressed in his "Letter from Birmingham Jail"?
4   Describe Martin Luther King, Jr.'s spirituality and explain how it functions in relation to his ethic.
5   How does Martin Luther King, Jr.'s ethic address the ethical challenges of a techno-bureaucratic society?
6   Compare and contrast Martin Luther King, Jr.'s ethic in comparison to Abraham Joshua Heschel's and Thich Nhat Hanh's ethics in terms of Masao Abe's models of religion and ethics (see figure 3.1). Do you think Abe's models of Judaism, Christianity, and Buddhism are correct in these cases?
7   What makes it possible for Gandhi, Thich Nhat Hanh, Heschel, and King to share a common ethic of non-violence despite being shaped by largely different narrative histories? Are there any significant differences among them concerning this ethic?
8   Describe Martin Luther King, Jr.'s "kitchen experience" and explain its significance for his spirituality and ethics.
9   Compare and contrast Martin Luther King, Jr.'s bus experience (returning from a high-school debate) with Gandhi's train experience in South Africa. How did each influence his respective spirituality and ethic?
10   How is the post/modern spirituality of "passing over" and "coming back" illustrated in King's life story, and what is its ethical significance?

References

Abe, Masao. 1990. "Kenotic God and Dynamic Sunyata," and "A Rejoinder." In John B. Cobb, Jr. and Christopher Ives (eds.), *The Emptying God: A Buddhist–Jewish–Christian Conversation*. Maryknoll, NY: Orbis Books, 3–68, 157–202.
Baldwin, Lewis V. 1991. *There is a Balm in Gilead: The Cultural Roots of Martin Luther*

King, Jr. Minneapolis: Fortress Press.

Cone, James. 1991. *Martin & Malcolm & America: A Dream or a Nightmare.* Maryknoll, NY: Orbis Books.

Fasching, Darrell J. 1992. *After Auschwitz: From Alienation to Ethics.* Minneapolis: Fortress Press).

Washington, James M. (ed.). 1986a. *A Testament of Hope: The Essential Writings and Speeches of Martin Luther King, Jr.* San Francisco: HarperSanFrancisco.

——. 1986b, 1992. *I Have a Dream: Writings and Speeches that Changed the World,* by Martin Luther King, Jr. San Francisco: HarperSanFrancisco.

8

ISLAMIC STORIES –
ANCIENT AND
POST/MODERN

As the Jewish story of cosmic history was reinterpreted among Christians to accommodate the story of Jesus, so both the Jewish and Christian versions were reinterpreted yet again by Islam – this time to accommodate the story of Muhammad. Consequently, as with the Christian chapter, we start here with the formative story and proceed to the revision of the cosmic story that followed from it. To gain some sense of why and how Islam reinterpreted the story, this section focuses on elements in the Muslim story that reveal both its continuity with and distinction from the cosmic stories of Judaism and Christianity. Specifically, we review the Quran's reinterpretation of the story of creation and its implications for Islamic law and ethics; the story of Abraham and his sons, including the Muslim version of Abraham's testing; and finally the Muslim understanding of Jesus as prophet and messenger of God. For this chapter's contemporary life story, we turn to Malcolm X. Unlike the other contemporary figures we have studied thus far, Malcolm X was a convert to his faith – Islam. In fact, as you will see, Malcolm's life can be understood as a journey of continuous transformation leading to two profound religious conversions – the first to the Black Muslim movement as a sacred society and then to Sunni Islam and a vision of the holy community. This second conversion was the result of a pilgrimage to Mecca, where he experienced persons of all races living in harmony. In our comparative reflections section we consider the challenge Malcolm X represents to the Gandhian tradition of the ethics of non-violence and his possible relation to the alternative "just-war" tradition, where violence is understood to be legitimate in defense of the weak and the innocent.

Formative Story: Muhammad

Introduction

The story of Islam begins and ends with God (*Allah* in Arabic). As the first "pillar" of Islamic faith proclaims: "There is no god but God." For Muslims, this is the first and most important religious assertion. It is part of their *shahada* (confession), which all Muslims are called upon to believe in the heart, understand perfectly, and profess until death. It is a statement about the foundation of the universe and the formal expression of the most fundamental understanding of life that human beings can have. There is one and only one God. There are no Avatars or incarnations, no divine progeny, and no material representations of this one God.

The uncompromising monotheism of Islam is rivaled only by Judaism, and yet the selection from the shahada given above is not complete, for there is a second phrase in the confession, a second phrase that tells us much about Islam as a world religion. This second part of the shahada affirms: "and Muhammad is the messenger of God." As a prophet, Muhammad is similar to other prophets before him. Some of these previous prophets of Islam are well known to Jews and Christians, including Adam, Abraham, Moses, and Jesus. These and more than twenty other notable figures are recognized as prophets in Islam.

What separates Muhammad from the others and what makes the story of his life and the divine revelation he received unique is that for Muslims he is the "seal of the prophets" – the one who brings the final and definitive message from God and whose life serves as the ideal for all believers. Unlike the stories of the Patriarchs in the Jewish (Tanak) and Christian (Gospel) scriptures, the revelation given to Muslims (the Quran) does not contain a biography of Muhammad; it is, rather, a book of God's messages to humanity. What we know of his life is derived from later biographies (called *siras*), reports of his actions and teachings (called *hadith*), and some material found in the Quran itself.

Like the stories of Gilgamesh and Siddhartha, Muhammad's story is about a man who withdraws from his community to seek the meaning of life and find answers to the problems plaguing society. As with Gilgamesh and Siddhartha, the context for Muhammad's quest was the urbanization process, which in the sixth century was intensifying in Arabia, and especially in the city of his birth, Mecca. Like Siddhartha, Muhammad received an answer to his questions and shared this answer with the world. For him the answer was submission to God and the recognition of equality among believers.

The life of Muhammad

[A retelling of the life of Muhammad, based on the *Sirat Rasul Allah* of Ibn Ishaq and other biographies of Muhammad, especially those cited in *Muhammad:*

His Life Based on the Earliest Sources by Martin Lings (Rochester, VT: Inner Traditions International, 1983). Quotes from Ishaq's *Sirat* (cited by page) are from Alfred Guillaume's translation, *The Life of Muhammad: A Translation of Ishaq's "Sirat Rasul Allah"* (Oxford: Oxford University Press, 1955). All quotes from the Quran (cited by surah and verse) are from T. B. Irving's translation, *The Quran: The First American Version* (Brattleboro, VT: Amana Books, 1985), unless otherwise noted.]

The year of Muhammad's birth, 570 CE, was known as the Year of the Elephant in commemoration of the role of an elephant in a divine intervention, which saved Mecca's sacred shrine, the Kaba, from an Abyssinian army bent on its destruction. The elephant, which the Abyssinians had placed at the head of their troops, mysteriously knelt on the ground as the army neared the city. Although beaten and goaded with iron hooks, the animal would not move. Then a great flock of birds swept out of the west, darkening the skies above the Abyssinians. Each bird carried three pebbles, one in each claw and one in its beak. Before the Abyssinians knew what was happening, the birds began hurling the pebbles into their ranks. The army was decimated, for every stone wounded a soldier and every wound was fatal. The few who escaped death fled in terror. The elephant was spared and the Kaba was saved.

While all of Mecca celebrated the miraculous victory, a young woman, soon to give birth, was grieving over a terrible loss. The woman, Amina, had just received news that her husband had died while away on a trading expedition to Syria and Palestine. They had been married only the year before and his death was heartbreaking. Amina found relief from her sorrow in contemplating the birth of her child, for shortly before learning of her husband's death she experienced a miracle of her own. She had noticed a supernatural light shining forth from within her body and heard a voice that told her: "You are pregnant with the lord of this people, and when he is born, say, 'I put him in the care of the One from the evil of every envier, then call him Muhammad' " (69). When he was born he put his hands on the ground and lifted his head toward the heavens (106).

Although Muhammad entered the world without a father, he had been born into a prominent family. And when her son was born, Amina immediately sent word to her husband's father, the venerable Abd al-Muttalib. Abd al-Muttalib was famous for having been guided in a vision to the location of the long-lost well of Zamzam, which God had created for Abraham's son Ishmael and his mother Hagar. He became the official host to pilgrims from all parts of Arabia who came to the Kaba. It was to the Kaba that al-Muttalib took the infant child on his first journey away from home. Once there, al-Muttalib offered a prayer of thanksgiving to God.

Soon, however, more tragedy entered Muhammad's life. His mother died when he was only six, making him an orphan, which was a perilous state in the society of his day. Fortunately, his grandfather, Abd al-Muttalib, immediately stepped in and adopted him. However, Muhammad spent only two years in the care of his grandfather before he, too, died. Still only a boy, Muhammad had lost the two people who loved him most in all the world. Even at the point of his own death, however, al-Muttalib sought to safeguard the welfare of his grandson by entrusting the youth to his own son, Abu Talib.

Abu Talib was not wealthy and Muhammad did what he could to support himself. His first occupation was as a shepherd but soon he became involved in the lucrative caravan trade. His good character and responsibility were noticed early on and he was given the nickname "al-Amin" (the trusted one). His work as a successful caravan leader led Muhammad into the service of Khadija, a wealthy widow. In a short time Muhammad became the business manager of Khadija's trading operations and soon thereafter her husband. He was 25 at the time and she was 40. They lived together happily for fifteen years, until Khadija's death.

During his early life, Muhammad was exposed to the indigenous religion of the Arabian peninsula. Soon after his marriage to Khadija he became involved with his community and its social and political issues. He was a member of the Hashimite clan, which was one of the smaller clan communities of the Quraysh tribe that ruled Mecca. His nickname, "al-Amin," stayed with him and in a short time he came to be recognized as an emerging leader. Everything seemed to be indicating that Muhammad was on his way to social success and political power in Mecca.

In addition to his community involvements, Muhammad also had an interest in religion, which was not surprising, since religion was a chief concern of the Quraysh leaders. The focal point of religious activity in Mecca was, of course, the Kaba, which Abraham and Ishmael had built to house the "Black Stone." This stone, still residing in the Kaba, had been brought to earth from paradise by an angel; originally pure white, it had been turned black by human sin.

Although built by Abraham and Ishmael at a location God had given to Adam long before, the Kaba had, over time, come to be occupied by sacred statues, which represented local deities – 360 in all. It also had fallen into disrepair. Muhammad's interest in the Kaba led him to assist in its renovation. Not long after this, Muhammad's life would be changed drastically; so too would the city of Mecca, and soon enough the entire world.

Muhammad's practice was to take a month-long retreat each year, which took him to a cave on Mount Hira, near Mecca. During this time he meditated in solitude, seeking answers to the meaning of life. While on his annual retreat, in 610, when he was 40 years old, he realized that he was not alone in this cave. "The Night of Power and Glory" had begun, but for Muhammad it was more of an experience of powerlessness and fear, for God sent the angel Gabriel, who commanded him to recite an inscription written on a piece of fabric. Muhammad was terrified, not only because of the presence of the supernatural being, but because he was illiterate and could not read the inscription. Muhammad resisted, fearfully telling the angel he could not recite. Gabriel then told Muhammad even more emphatically that he was to recite. The panic-stricken Muhammad again told the angel he was incapable of doing what he was told. Then, in a tone so terrifying that Muhammad feared for his life, Gabriel demanded that he recite. Finally, feeling himself in mortal danger, Muhammad asked what he should recite. The angel told him:

> In the Name of God, the Mercy-giving, the Merciful!: Read in the name of your Lord Who creates – created man from a clot! Read, for your Lord is most Generous; [it is He] Who teaches by means of the pen, teaches man what he does not know. (96: 1–5)

Muhammad repeated the message given by Gabriel and the angel left him, but he felt the words had been written in his heart. After the encounter, Muhammad was greatly distressed and fled from the cave and down the slope of the mountain. He then heard the voice again, saying: "O, Muhammad, You are the messenger, the messenger of Allah, and I am Gabriel." He then raised his eyes and saw the angel, standing in the sky above the horizon; and the same direction was given again: "You are the messenger!" He tried to turn away from the angel because he was so brilliant and terrifying – but everywhere he turned the angel appeared. Finally, only after Khadija had sent out a search party to find Muhammad did the angel depart, and Muhammad returned home. With this, Muhammad's revelations had begun and with it the miracle of the illiterate messenger's recitation of God's words (Quran).

Muhammad was stunned by the experience and thought himself delusional. He rushed home to tell Khadija and seek her comfort. He feared that he might be crazy or tricked by jinns (nature spirits) that lived in the desert. His wife sought to console and support him. Out of concern for Muhammad, Khadija visited her cousin (Waraqa), who was a Christian. It was Waraqa who affirmed that the angel who had visited Muhammad had also visited Moses, that the visit was the beginning of a great revelation, and Muhammad was the chosen one who would renew the faith in Allah. Having received Waraqa's comforting message from Khadija, Muhammad returned to his retreat and when it was over he went to the Kaba, where he encountered Waraqa himself. Waraqa reaffirmed the message he had given Khadija and added a warning that Muhammad would be persecuted because of his revelations.

Muhammad soon received a second message but then the communications ceased for a time. The sudden cessation caused Muhammad to believe that he might have displeased God in some way. Soon, however, additional commands, with a powerful ethical message, were received:

> Did He not find you an orphan and sheltered [you]? He found you lost and guided [you]. He found you destitute and made you rich! Thus the orphan must not be exploited and the beggar should not be brushed aside. Still tell about your Lord's favor. (93)

Muhammad soon began proclaiming the message he was receiving: telling all who would listen of the Lord's favor. He first told only his family and closest friends. Included in the first messages were directions for proper prayer and concern for others, as well as warnings about the final judgment of the world.

> When the bugle is sounded on that day, it will be such a harsh day, anything but easy on disbelievers! . . . I shall weigh him down with mounting trouble. Let him think things over and measure them out. Yet he still will be damned just as he has measured; . . . I'll roast him by scorching! What will make you realize what scorching is? It spares nothing nor leaves anything over as it shrivels human [flesh]. (74: 9–10, 17–19, 26–9)

At first Muhammad's followers were few, very few, only family members and his friend Abu Bekr. The people of Mecca mocked him and thought he was insane. Soon enough, however, the leaders of Mecca came to see Muhammad as a serious threat to their power, for not only did he challenge the indigenous animism of their primal culture with his proclamation of God's omnipotence, he also called into question the status quo of Meccan society. They had good reason for concern, for even if Muhammad lacked many followers, his very intensity disturbed the order of the city. People from all over Arabia made pilgrimages to Mecca and the Kaba with its statues of various deities. Muhammad's message threatened this activity and with it a major part of the commerce related to it. Additionally, and perhaps even more importantly, the revelations from God he proclaimed included ethical directions, which demanded support for the less fortunate, assistance to orphans, and improved conditions for women. For the elite of Mecca, Muhammad's message could not be tolerated and their opposition quickly became severe and direct.

Threats were made against the Prophet and his few followers, and his gatherings were broken up, often violently. Members of Muhammad's clan were forcibly confined to a single sector of the city. But the revelations did not cease, and he continued to call upon the city to recognize the supremacy of God, correct the social and economic inequalities, and to do so quickly because of God's impending judgment.

In 619 Muhammad's wife and his beloved uncle (Abu Talib) died, but in this same year he was invited to Yathrib, a city 200 miles north of Mecca. Ironically, it was just when the situation in Mecca was at its worst that a delegation from Yathrib asked Muhammad to come to their city and end the civil discord there. Muhammad's vision and mission appealed to them and certainly his reputation as "al-Amin" (the trusted one) was well known, in spite of his troubles with the authorities in Mecca. Muhammad demanded that the people of Yathrib follow his teachings. The following year twelve people came from Yathrib and affirmed their commitment to Muhammad's teaching. The year after, seventy-five came from Yathrib, also affirmed commitment, and asked the Prophet again to come to their city. He declined both invitations.

During this time, Muhammad continued to receive revelations and he continued to preach them to all who would listen, just as he had for the previous ten years. The message of God he brought integrated demands for justice with warnings of the coming day of judgment. He also received a message that would change the character of the religion and possibly save it from destruction at the hands of Muhammad's adversaries. Until this time Muhammad and his followers had been directed not to resist their persecutors or to do so passively, but with the revelation of Surah 22 this would change.

> God defends those who believe; God does not love every thankless traitor. Those who have been wronged are permitted to fight [back] – since God is able to support them – any who have been driven from their homes unjustly, merely because they say: "Our Lord is God [Alone]." If it were not because God repels some men by means of others, cloisters, churches, synagogues and mosques where God's name is mentioned frequently would have been demolished. (22: 38–41)

Muhammad had received a divine blessing on the just use of violence in defense of religious freedom. Rather than stay in Mecca and resist his adversaries with force, however, Muhammad was guided to leave the city and accept the longstanding invitation from the people of Yathrib. And so Muhammad, Abu Bekr, and a small handful of Muslims left Mecca for Yathrib. The *hijra* (migration) would mark yet another decisive change in the Prophet's life. Miraculously, the journey of 300 miles took only eight days, three less than usual.

Once in Yathrib, Muhammad became the recognized leader, just as the delegates who had contacted him earlier desired. Muhammad quickly revealed himself to be not only the messenger of God but also, as "al-Amin," a gifted political leader, forming the first Muslim *ummah* or community. Not only was the name of the city changed from Yathrib to Medina (the city), the entire social structure was transformed. Muhammad was an extraordinary leader who skillfully combined religious authority with ethical direction. He always acted in careful consultation with others, which led to the development of a strong sense of community. In Medina he built a house of worship – the first mosque – and developed an institutional structure to give order and stability to religious and social life. Religious services were held on Fridays, daily prayers were offered, and alms-giving was advocated. Prayers were to be offered in the prostrate position, at first facing Jerusalem, but soon the direction was changed to Mecca, which was also reaffirmed as the center of religious pilgrimage. The Jewish community in Medina was given religious autonomy.

Politically, Muhammad quickly consolidated power, established a constitution on the basis of the revelations he continued to receive, and unified the city's heretofore rival clans. In short order, Medina became the first Muslim community and the model of an Islamic society. Muhammad made alliances with other tribes and converts throughout the area. He began raiding caravans headed to Mecca, and in 624, at the famous Battle of Badr, his forces defeated a superior army from Mecca, which had been sent to put an end to Muhammad and his message. Finally, in 630, after other diplomatic and military engagements with the Meccans, Muhammad entered the city in triumph.

As had been the case with his arrival in Medina, Muhammad moved immediately to establish a new society and a new way of life. Among his first actions was the pardoning of his adversaries. No longer was vengeance to be the norm; now justice and mercy would form the foundations of society and guide leaders in their rule. This was, after all, the way God governed the universe. Muhammad also performed the proper rituals at the Kaba, and then destroyed the sacred images and statues there. It was the Kaba that was sacred to Muhammad, not the images and statues, for only God was worthy of worship and God had no image. Muhammad's pardon of his enemies was conditional on their rejection of polytheism and acceptance of Islam. Jews and Christians were recognized as fellow "people of the book" and given special exemption from the requirement for conversion, although they were obliged to pay a special tax.

The Prophet's death

From the capture of Mecca in 630, until Muhammad's death in 632, Islam became the dominant religion in Arabia, in part due to military conquest by Muhammad's armies (he was a brilliant general), but largely due to conversions. His revelations continued until his death, and these revelations, of the "seal" (last) of the prophets and final messenger of Allah, became the Holy Quran.

When Muhammad died in 632, one of his followers, Umar, addressed the community and said: "Some of the disaffected will allege that the Messenger is dead, but by God, he is not dead: he has gone to his Lord as Moses son of Imran went and was hidden [on Sinai] from his people for forty days. By God, the Messenger will return as Moses returned and will cut off the hands and feet of men who allege that the Messenger is dead" (682–3). For many this was surely a great hope, but it would be short-lived.

Upon hearing of Umar's speech, Muhammad's eventual successor, Abu Bekr, went to the dead body of the Prophet, kissed him and said: "You are dearer than my father and mother. You have tasted the death that God had decreed; a second death will never overtake you" (683). Abu Bekr then went into the Mosque, where Umar was still speaking, and said to him, " 'Gently, Umar, be quiet.' But Umar refused and went on talking" (683). Seeing Abu Bekr, the congregation immediately turned from Umar and directed their attention to him. Clearly and directly, Bekr declared: "O men, if anyone worships Muhammad, Muhammad is dead; if anyone worships God, God is alive, immortal" (683). In Abu Bekr's memorial address, the true essence of Islam was reaffirmed, the very core of the first pillar, the shahada (confession) – there is no God but God. Muhammad would have been in total agreement. The religion had not been about God's messenger, Muhammad, but about God. There would be no resurrection, no deification of Muhammad. God was without equal and utterly supreme. The congregation had stopped listening to Umar; Abu Bekr had carried the day and his words are those that are remembered. But even more so are the words of Muhammad remembered in his farewell sermon, three months prior to his death:

> Know ye that every Moslem is a brother unto every other Moslem, and that ye are now one brotherhood. It is not legitimate for any one of you, therefore, to appropriate unto himself anything that belongs to his brother unless it is willingly given him by that brother. (Ibn Hishmam/Philip Hitti, quoted in Esposito 1998: 11)

God (Allah) is the one and only God, and all are to make *submission* to him (*Islam* means surrender or submission), but with this submission comes the obligation of *peace* (which *Islam* also means), justice, and dignity for all people. *Assalam wa alaykum* (peace be with you) is a familiar greeting among Muslims.

Cosmic Story: Further Revisions of the Myth of History

Creation, submission, and Sharia

Even as Christianity modified and added to the Jewish story, so Islam added to and modified the stories of both of its precursors. Islam remains closest to Judaism and farthest from Christianity.

According to Muslims, God's will for humanity is found first and foremost in the Quran. The Quran is the collection of revelations in Arabic, given to Muhammad by God over a period of twenty-three years, as collected in 114 *surahs* or chapters organized by length, from longest to shortest. Of these, ninety are said to have occurred in the early years at Mecca and the remaining twenty-four at Medina. According to the Quran, all of creation is Muslim; that is, all creation submits to God's will, and only humans and the angels are capable of deviating and introducing disharmony into the created order. Because God is patient and merciful, he gives humans the Quran to show them how to submit and return to the straight path. For this he sent his messenger Muhammad, the seal of the prophets, to remind humans that God alone is God. God has no associates or equals. Moreover, he rules with justice and mercy and demands such from his creatures: woe on the day of judgment to those who make a great display of their piety while turning away the needy and the orphan (107).

The Quran offers several stories of creation. The following suggests both the similarities and the differences between the Islamic stories and those of the two prior monotheistic traditions:

We have decked the heavens with constellations and made them lovely to behold. We have guarded them from every cursed devil. Eavesdroppers are pursued by fiery comets.

We have spread out the earth and set upon it immovable mountains. We have planted it with every seasonable fruit, providing sustenance for yourselves and for those whom you do not provide for. We hold the store of every blessing and send it down in appropriate measure. We let loose the fertilizing winds and bring down water from the sky for you to drink; its stores are beyond your reach.

We ordain life and death. We are the Heir of all things. We know those who have gone before you, and those who will come hereafter. Your Lord will gather them all before Him. He is wise and all-knowing.

We created man from dry clay, from black moulded loam, and before him Satan from smokeless fire. Your Lord said to the angels: "I am creating man from dry clay, from black moulded loam. When I have fashioned him and breathed of My spirit into him, kneel down and prostrate yourselves before him."

The angels, one and all, prostrated themselves, except Satan. He refused to prostrate himself with the others.

"Satan," said God, "why do you not prostrate yourself?"

He replied, "I will not bow to a mortal who You created from dry clay, of black moulded clay."

"Begone," said God, "you are accursed. My curse shall be on you till Judgment-day."

"Lord," said Satan, "reprieve me till the Day of Resurrection."

He answered: "You are reprieved till the Appointed Day."

"Lord," said Satan, "since You have thus seduced me, I will tempt mankind on earth. I will seduce them all, except those of them who are your faithful servants."

He replied: "This is the right course for Me. You shall have no power over My servants, only the sinners who follow you. They are all destined for Hell." (Quran 15: 16–44, VanVoorst 1996: 300–1)

From the outset of creation, the cosmic struggle is established. God and Satan are at odds with one another, the day of judgment, which brings the end of the world, is already a consideration, and human beings are involved in the cosmic struggle. In Islam, Satan is an angel who opposed God, but the original error of Satan is not his desire to usurp God's power, but rather his refusal to recognize human beings as God's agents on earth, created as superior to all else in creation, including Satan. Satan is the tempter, by God's decision (as in the case of the book of Job), and he is successful in getting human beings to turn away from their creator. Here the Islamic story and the Christian story begin to differ significantly and Islam draws closer to Judaism.

Like Judaism, Islam does not interpret the sin of Adam as cosmic in scope. Human beings are not by nature sinful, only weak, and the errors of Adam are not passed on to the rest of humanity. There is no original sin and therefore there is no need for the incarnation of God to heal human nature and restore human freedom. The explanation for Adam's error is the same as any other person's. Human beings are shortsighted, weak, and vulnerable to the seductions of Satan. Such shortcomings are not cause for God's cosmic condemnation of humanity, rather each is answerable to God for his/her own conduct. God has absolute sovereignty over the universe and delivers the final judgment. The result is paradise for those who submit or hell for those who do not. This is a cause not for despair but for hope. Hence Adam, rather than being the paradigm of human failure, becomes in Islam, the first Muslim (one who submits), and the first prophet of God.

Adam is a model of the true Muslim. He failed, yes, but he also repented and turned back to God; not out of guilt but out of fear (*taqwaa*). He feared God, as all true Muslims should. And God forgave Adam. It is the quality of mercy found in God that is central to Islam. So central is God's compassion and mercy that every surah of the Quran begins with the preamble: "In the name of Allah, the compassionate, the merciful."

After Adam, God continuously sent his messengers to guide humanity on the straight path. According to the Quran: "Surely We sent down the Torah, wherein is guidance and light. . . . And We sent . . . Jesus son of Mary, confirming the Torah before him; and We gave to him the Gospel, wherein is guidance and light, and confirming the Torah before it, as a guidance and an admonition unto the godfearing" (5: 45–51, Arberry 1955: 134, 135). Thus both Jews and Christians were sent guidance but they deviated from the straight path offered to them. "Had the People of the Book believed and been godfearing, We would have acquitted them of their evil deeds, and admitted them to Gardens of Bliss" (5: 70, Arberry 1955: 138). But God is patient and merciful, so he sent one final messenger, Muhammad, the seal of the prophets, to rightly guide humanity on the straight path of God's will.

The outlines of this path are expressed in the Muslim way of life that is summarized in the five pillars of Islam: (1) The shahada. There is but one God and Muhammad is his prophet. (2) Prayer (*salat*). The Quran mentions prayer three times a day, but later this was increased to five times, at first facing Jerusalem, but then changed to facing Mecca. (3) Fasting (*saum*). To fast from sunrise to sunset during the month of Ramadan, which recalls the hijra of Muhammad. (4) Alms-giving (*zakat*). Giving financial aid to the poor; a tax of 2.5 percent of one's wealth. (5) A pilgrimage to Mecca (*hajj*) at least once in one's lifetime, if at all possible.

Islam divided into two branches shortly after Muhammad's death; the majority *Sunni* tradition and the minority *Shi'ite* tradition. The key issue between the two traditions was the succession of leadership and spiritual authority after the time of Muhammad. The Shi'ites trace themselves back to Ali, a cousin and son-in-law of Muhammad, who was assassinated (they would say "martyred") in the struggle for leadership. They believed that both political and spiritual leadership should remain with the family of the Prophet, and Ali was Muhammad's rightful successor. They came to believe that God would always provide them with a charismatic, divinely inspired leader, or imam, who would rule with absolute political and religious authority. The Sunnis separated the leadership of the Muslim community into the political (caliphs) and the religious (*ulama*). Caliphs were elected, and the ulama achieved spiritual leadership through their learning.

Shi'ites, therefore, came to believe the surest way to follow God's will was to follow the teachings of a divinely inspired religious leader, or imam. But the majority Sunni tradition turned to the guidance of the ulama, or learned scholars, who discovered God's will by studying (1) the Quran (the revelation of God) and (2) the hadith, or stories of the Prophet and his interactions with his first followers, which provided an example (*sunna*) for following the straight path. It was the (3) consensus (*ijma*) interpretation of these sources arrived at by the ulama that provided Muslims with ethical guidance expressed in particular laws (*fiqh*). Finally, in situations where ethical issues are not directly addressed by the Quran and hadith, the ulama sought (4) analogies (*qiyas*) between such situations and those contained in the Quran and the sunna. Together these four elements form the basis for *Sharia*, which is understood to be "God's law for the entire Islamic community, indeed for all humanity . . . [and] . . . as much a system of ethics as it is law" (Esposito 1998: 87). Eventually, four major schools of Islamic law, whose leaders were the ulama, emerged to provide right guidance: the Hanafi, Maliki, Shafii, and Hanabali schools. Rather than force a choice among these, Muslims recognized that even among learned scholars legitimate differences can occur and so declared all four schools to be orthodox. If our purpose in this text was to survey the thought of ethical experts of Islam, it is to these schools and Islamic jurisprudence that we would turn. But the task we have set ourselves is to understand the ethical power of some of the stories and spiritual practices that have shaped the ethical imagination of Muslims, stories that have the power to grab those who are wandering far from the straight path, turn them around, and set them on the path of God's justice and compassion – the way of Sharia.

Abraham, Ishmael, and Isaac

Islam's understanding of its uniqueness is emphasized by contrasting accounts of Abraham and Jesus, both of whom are not only recognized as prophets in Islam, but accorded the even more prestigious title of messengers – those prophets whose message from God was recorded in a book and whose "success was assured by God" (Esposito 1998: 20). Like Jews and Christians, Muslims venerate Abraham as a patriarch. Unlike their precursors, however, Muslims trace their lineage through Abraham's first son, Ishmael, born to his wife's Egyptian slave, Hagar. The biblical tradition traces the Abrahamic line and its divine inheritance and responsibility through the second son, Isaac, the child of "divine promise." But Muslims point out that God's covenant and God's promise to Abraham occurred before the birth of Ishmael and includes both sons. While the Torah tells of Ishmael and Hagar being banished to the desert, the Quran supplies information left out of the Torah: Abraham continues to have an interest in Ishmael, and accompanies his banished son and Hagar to Mecca. Their journey is guided by Gabriel, who leads them to the site of the original house (the Kaba) constructed by Adam. Gabriel then leaves the family in God's protection and God directs Abraham and his son to rebuild the Kaba.

The testing of Abraham: Jewish, Muslim, and Christian interpretations

Notably, both the Quran and the Torah contain a story about God testing Abraham's faith by directing him to sacrifice his son. The Torah's version is found in Genesis 22 and the Quran's in "As-Saffat" ("Those Who Set the Ranks," Surah 37). Although the son is unnamed in the Quran, the text clearly suggests it was Ishmael (not Isaac) whom Abraham was called upon to sacrifice. The Quranic narrative unfolds in the context of Abraham's hijra, when he left his homeland (just like Muhammad) due to intense opposition from polytheists. When Abraham prays to God for a son, God answers the prayer with the birth of Ishmael. When Ishmael is old enough to be of assistance to his father, Abraham receives a revelation that the youth is to be sacrificed. Until this point, the story in the Torah and in the Quran are similar – except for the identity of the son. After this point they differ dramatically.

As in Genesis 22 (see chapter 6), "As-Saffat" tells us that Abraham is told to sacrifice his son, but unlike the biblical narrative, the Quran says that Abraham shares this with his son immediately (37: 102). Here there is no guile, no ambiguity, and indeed, no hope. Abraham is clear and direct with Ishmael. He tells his son that he has been directed to sacrifice him. It is God's will and Abraham is committed to the divine command; but he is also committed to sharing the command with his son. In the Torah Abraham avoids telling Isaac of God's command and instead says that that God will supply a lamb; the Quran's story has Abraham forthrightly asking Ishmael what he thinks of the divine command that he be sacrificed! Ishmael responds that Muhammad should do as God commands – his only hope is that he be found steadfast and worthy of the sacrifice. Ishmael thus reveals himself to be the perfect Muslim – one who submits, even unto death. And yet, in the Quran, Abraham seems willing to leave the matter up to Ishmael. There seems to be a slight element of hesitation – for Abraham doesn't just act, he seeks Ishmael's consent. In the end, in both versions of the story (Torah and Quran), there is a divine intervention and the sacrifice does not occur.

The two stories are significant in their similarities and differences. Both stories celebrate Abraham for his obedience. However, in the Quran, Ishmael is revealed as a hero and a prophet because he does not resist, while Abraham is revealed as a hero and a prophet because he does not let his human nature compromise the divine command. Ishmael is the primary hero of the Muslim story, for it is he who keeps his father obedient even though he may have reservations. In this way, both Abraham and Ishmael are revealed to be true Muslims, and perhaps Ishmael the greater of the two, since he had the most to lose! What is missing from the Quranic narrative is the other side of Abraham, so to speak. Nowhere does Abraham have the chutzpah to say, "Shall not the judge of all also be just?" as he did in defending the strangers of Sodom. And yet we might ask of the biblical stories – why does Abraham not protest in this fashion to save his son Isaac from sacrifice and his son Ishmael from banishment into the desert?

Finally, in the Quran, neither God nor Abraham choose one son over the other. Although the God of the biblical narrative does not curse Ishmael, and in fact cares for him and promises him and his descendants success, he clearly has chosen Isaac and Isaac's descendants as the inheritors of the covenant he made with Abraham (see Genesis 17: 19). In Islam, God affirms the legitimacy of both sons and calls on both, and their descendants, to submit.

Christianity retains the Jewish version of Abraham's testing in the Old Testament of its Bible. However, there are only two very brief comments on the story in the New Testament: James 2: 21–3 and Hebrews 11: 17–19. Neither questions God's justice in asking Abraham to sacrifice his son. The letter of James suggests that Abraham proved his faith by his works, namely by his willingness to sacrifice his son at the command of God. The letter to the Hebrews sees what almost happened to Isaac as a prophetic foreshadowing of what did happen to Jesus. Abraham's willingness to sacrifice "his only son" serves to bring to mind God's sacrifice of his only son on the cross to save all humanity. Therefore Abraham's action, it is suggested, was an expression of his faith that God would give him his son back in the final resurrection of the dead assured by Christ's resurrection. As to the two sons of Abraham, Ishmael and Isaac, Christians turned to the writings of Paul in the New Testament (especially Romans 9) and interpreted him to be saying that the promises made to Abraham belong to the line of Isaac rather than Ishmael, and that the true children of Abraham are not those of the flesh (the Jews) but those who are children of the spirit (Christians). God's promises are for all humanity, just as all humanity is called to be Christian.

In a parallel fashion, for Islam, all humanity receives the same command; it was the command given by God first to Adam but then to Abraham and his two sons. This command was not just for Abraham, Ishmael, Isaac, and their descendants, it was for all the world – it was the message of Islam (surrender to the will of God) and all the world is called to be Muslim. Both rejected the Jewish belief that some were given special obligations (the covenant of Moses) that are not binding on others who may be acceptable to God in their gentile status, provided they worship the one true God and live good lives (sometimes called the Noachite covenant).

Jesus as a messenger of the straight path

As we have suggested, Islam recognizes its kinship with Christianity just as with Judaism. They share, for example, expectations of a final judgment and resurrection of the dead, and a recognition of the unique significance of Jesus. Both traditions are people of the book, and both traditions are based in divine commandments received by prophets of God. The problem with Christianity, as Muslims see it, is similar to the problem Christianity had with Judaism. In both cases they argue that those who preceded them did not understand the message correctly and had to be replaced by a more faithful community. In both traditions God sent genuine prophets who revealed true faith or the "straight path" and in both cases the followers "deviated" from this path with their own erroneous interpretations, which corrupted the message of true faith or submission.

According to Islam, the misunderstanding in Judaism is rooted in the tendency toward exclusivity; the misunderstanding in Christianity is tied to both exclusivity and the great sin of *shirk* (association of anything mortal/material with God). This is how the Christian belief in the incarnation of God in the person of Jesus is viewed within Islam. The sin of *shirk* is far-reaching and its implications significant indeed. Like Abraham, Isaac, and Moses, Jesus is not understood as the problem – the problem is with those who come later.

Islam grants and celebrates the importance of the work of the prophet Jesus. It affirms his virgin birth (and devotes an entire surah to Mary [19]), refers to him as messiah, and acknowledges his miracles. It was he who, like Muhammad, received God's divine guidance. Again, like Muhammad, he sought to impart this guidance to the world. It was his virtue that he preached a universalist message, that all persons were equal before God, and all are called to submit. Yet, for Muslims, Jesus is not God but God's messenger. He is the Messiah sent by God and celebrated son of Mary but not the Son of God. Jesus brings the message of Islam, the message of following the straight path in submission to God's will, but he does not save anyone, nor does he transform human nature, for there is no original sin that corrupts human nature. Hardly the triumphant savior of the world and second person of the Trinity, the Quran's Jesus is only human. In the Quran, Jesus himself is portrayed as confirming his subordinate relationship with God and reaffirming the truth of the Muslim message. It is God who is the Lord, the one and only; it is he and he alone who judges, punishes, and forgives; and Jesus, for his part, says only what God commands him to say– worship God alone!

Life Story: Malcolm X and the Way of Pilgrimage

Malcolm's life in context

At first glance the life of Malcolm X does not seem to be a good choice as an example of a social activist from the tradition of Islam. For much of his life, Malcolm knew virtually nothing of Islam, then, while in prison (as we shall see), he underwent the first of two major conversions – to the Nation of Islam, a black religious movement that had very little to do with traditional Islam. Most of Malcolm's public life as a social activist for racial justice for African-Americans belongs to this period. Only in the last year of his life, after breaking with the Black Muslim movement, did he experience a second conversion, largely as a result of his pilgrimage to Mecca – a conversion to traditional Sunni Islam. And yet, Malcolm X is the appropriate example for this book for two reasons. First, although Malcolm does not provide us with a life shaped from cradle to grave by Islam (the way Martin Luther King, Jr. was shaped by Christianity, for example), he does exemplify the power of Islam and of its practice of pilgrimage (the hajj), to bring about a profound spiritual and ethical transformation in even the most unlikely candidate. What Malcolm X came to appreciate is what lies at the heart of Islamic ethics: "Islamic law is . . . egalitarian; it transcends regional, family, tribal, and ethnic boundaries. It does not recognize social class or caste differences. All Muslims, Arab and non-Arab, rich and poor, black and white, caliph and craftsman, male and female, are bound by Islamic law as members of a single, transnational community or brotherhood of believers" (Esposito 1998: 88). Second, as a contemporary of King, Heschel, and Nhat Hanh, who openly challenged their Gandhian ethic of non-violence, Malcolm X provides an important voice for an alternative view of the relation between violence and social justice.

Islam dates its beginnings to Muhammad's journey or flight (hijra) from Mecca to Medina (Yathrib). And Muslims confirm their own religious commitments by making a journey or pilgrimage (hajj) to Mecca. Stories of journeys or pilgrimages play an important role in the history of religions – Gilgamesh's journey to the land of the rising sun; Siddhartha's journey into the forest; the journey of Moses and the people Israel from Egypt to the land of promise; the journey of Jesus into the desert, and then to Jerusalem and crucifixion. The journey is about the hero who leaves familiar territory to discover a new truth to guide humanity on its journey through time. Typically, the hero sets out on a journey trusting that guidance will be provided and returns to society to share the guidance he has been given. On such journeys the hero discovers not just new places but, more importantly, new identities that transcend previous identities so completely that names are changed and vocations radically altered. Abram becomes Abraham; Jacob becomes Israel; Saul becomes Paul; Jesus becomes the Christ; Siddhartha becomes the Buddha, and so on. Joining these others, and providing a dramatic example of the power of pilgrimage to transform one's ethical orientation, is an American whose given name was Malcolm Little, but who was and is known to the world as Malcolm X (1925–65).

In 1952, less than a year after Martin Luther King, Jr. graduated from the seminary and began his doctoral studies at Boston University, another African-American graduated from a Massachusetts institution of "higher" education. The man was Malcolm Little, and the "school" (not far from King at BU) was Charlestown Prison. Malcolm Little had received parole. At this point both men's life journeys came very close to intersecting but they did not, for Malcolm Little and Martin Luther King, Jr. were following strikingly different paths. Only much later would they finally meet face to face, once, for a brief moment.

Yet in death they would again be joined, for both died as martyrs at assassins' hands, Malcolm on February 21, 1965, and Martin three years later on April 4, 1968; both were 39 years old when they were killed.

The story of Malcolm's life is found in *The Autobiography of Malcolm X* (X 1973). It is one of the great religious narratives of all time – it is not a happy tale, but it is a moving one. It tells us about the power of religious conversion, and is a story of a pilgrimage that led Malcolm out of the sacred and into the holy. It is the story of a man on a journey of self-discovery, whose perpetually changing identity enabled him to break decisively with the sacred worldview of the Nation of Islam and embrace a vision of the holy during his pilgrimage to Mecca.

The journey of Malcolm X

Malcolm Little was born on May 19, 1925, in Omaha, Nebraska, the ninth of the Reverend Earl Little's eleven children. His mother was Louise, his father's second wife. She was born in Grenada and her father was white. She herself was fair-skinned, as was Malcolm. Later in life, Malcolm would reflect that he was treated well by his father and other blacks because of the light complexion and reddish-brown hair he had inherited from his white grandfather, a man he knew to have raped his grandmother. Blacks with lighter skin color, he recalled, were given a higher status by other blacks who had accepted the racial structuring of society established by whites. Tormented by the ignominy of his grandmother's rape, reflected in his very complexion, Malcolm said that he "learned to hate every drop of that white rapist's blood that is in me" (X 1973: 2).

Malcolm's early life was filled with fear, terror, and heartbreak. His father was a Baptist minister and a supporter of Marcus Garvey, which cast him as a radical in the Nebraska of his day. The Ku Klux Klan threatened him and his family, once storming up to their home while his father was away doing religious work and his mother was pregnant with him. The Klan broke every window in the house but spared the family.

The event set the stage for Malcolm's ongoing journey through life, for soon after Malcolm's birth his father moved the family to Lansing, Michigan. There the family and young Malcolm again encountered racial violence, this time from the Black Legion – a northern equivalent of the Ku Klux Klan (they wore black robes, not white). The Legion called the Reverend Little an "uppity nigger" and set fire to his home. One of his parishioners observed he scared "these white folks to death!"(6). The Reverend Little was challenging the sacred order of society. He dared to step out of his place and this scared "white folks." His son would come to scare them even more.

On the night the Black Legion attacked the Littles' home, Malcolm's father fired his pistol at the Legionnaires and drove them off. The house still burned to the ground as firemen and police watched. Like five of his six brothers, Earl died violently, and like four of the others he was killed by whites; one brother had been lynched, and he himself had his skull crushed and was then put on a streetcar track, where he was run over. With his father's death young Malcolm received his introduction to the viciousness and brutality of racism in America. What Malcolm confronted as a youth, less than ten years old, would leave a permanent mark on his consciousness. He had learned that America was a violent culture and, for blacks especially, a murderous one.

The early years

After his family's move north, and after the death of his father, Malcolm entered junior high school. There he had what he described as "the first major turning point of my life" (35). It was a discussion he had with his junior high school English teacher, Mr. Ostrowski, who told Malcolm that his dream of being a lawyer was inappropriate for a black person. As Ostrowski told the young man: "You've got to be realistic about being a nigger. A lawyer – that's no realistic goal for a nigger. . . . Everybody admires your carpentry work. Why don't you plan on carpentry? People like you as a person – you'd get all kinds of work" (36). This moment shaped the rest of his life. "Whatever I have done since then, I have driven myself to become a success at it"(38).

This first turning point led him to doubt and question the sacred order of society. Quite literally, his consciousness was raised by his self-image being radically lowered. He had learned that to whites, even those who "probably meant well"(36), blacks were inferior beings, persons perhaps, but persons who should have limited dreams and narrow hopes; even the best and brightest should have no greater expectations than to be a carpenter. Thus, at the age of 16, Malcolm's worldview was transformed and he was changed forever – from a person complacently accepting his inferior cultural status to an individual who was conscious of his oppression and the efforts of white society to keep him and his race in their place.

Ghetto life

Malcolm moved on to Boston, then to New York City, and finally back to Boston again. In Boston he lived in the ghetto of Roxbury and in New York he lived in the ghetto of Harlem. His stay in those communities exposed the young Malcolm to both the vitality and degradation of inner-city urban life in the 1940s, and he embraced the morality of the streets. Unlike Martin Luther King, Jr., whose summer working in Connecticut in the 1940s led him to marvel at the lack of overt segregation in the North, Malcolm was amazed by the insidious evil of superficial integration.

At the Roseland and other locales in Roxbury and later in Harlem, Malcolm did find integration of a sort; whites and blacks did mix socially, engage in commerce, and share sexual intimacies. Whites would come to the inner city for a "good time" and blacks would facilitate it. Often white men came surreptitiously to listen to the big bands or to dance, while actually looking for "dates" with black women. White women, on the other hand, came to the inner city openly and enthusiastically looking for dates with black men. Masochistic interludes were not uncommon. Whites of both genders would often demand the "blackest" partner available. White men paid black pimps for their dates in cash; white women paid the black men with their company and the status the men derived from it.

Whites visited this integrated abyss when interest or need compelled them. Blacks lived there. And although many blacks profited from this degrading sort of integration, Malcolm came to realize that all who did lost their souls. Moreover, the system itself promoted the dehumanization of blacks. Malcolm knew this from first-hand experience, for he himself was sucked down into that abyss. This was the context of his second turning point as he transformed himself into "Detroit Red," a streetwise "predatory animal" (134). His brilliant mind and remarkable social skills allowed him to successfully learn the logic of the inner city and the morality of its culture. He became a gambler, a lover of white women, a drug dealer and addict, a hustler and burglar.

Eventually he was arrested, along with his friend, Shorty, and two white women. The women got a low bail and were sentenced to from one to five years in the Massachusetts Women's Reformatory. Malcolm and his friend had bail set at $10,000 and were sentenced to ten years in prison. The disparity in the bail and sentences was not lost on Malcolm: "Even the court clerks and the bailiffs [observed]: 'Nice white girls . . . goddam niggers–' It was the same even from our court-appointed lawyers . . . 'You had no business with white girls!' . . . We weren't going to get the average [about two years] – not for *our* crime" (149–50). Sentenced to ten years, Malcolm was released on parole after six. Prison brought Malcolm to another decisive moment in his life. Just as Muhammad was called by God in the isolation of the cave on Mount Hira, so Malcolm believed he was called from the isolation of a Massachusetts prison cell. During this time in prison he experienced the first of two decisive religious conversions that shaped his life.

Prison and the first conversion

Malcolm entered prison in 1946 when he was 20 years old. In 1948 he was transferred to Norfolk Prison Colony, a progressive institution that stressed rehabilitation of its inmates. Malcolm thrived at Norfolk, utilizing its library to educate himself. He began by reading the dictionary from A to Z and then went on to study the history of slavery and colonialism. He also became a member of the Nation of Islam – a Black Muslim. This was a major turning point in his life.

At the time of Malcolm's conversion, the Nation of Islam was led by Elijah Muhammad, the successor to the movement's mysterious founder, and the Messiah, Wallace D. Fard. Malcolm had been introduced to the Nation of

Islam by his brothers and sisters, most notably his brother, Reginald, and sisters, Ella and Hilda, who had converted earlier. Through letters and discussions during their visits, Malcolm's siblings educated him in the doctrines of the "natural religion for the black man." Years later Malcolm discovered that many of the teachings of Elijah Muhammad departed from traditional Islam, but in the early days they were his inspiration and salvation. He became a devout follower, writing letters to Elijah Muhammad every day and meditating on his photographs. In prison Malcolm also began to pray and follow the health and dietary rules of the Nation of Islam. His full conversion to the Nation of Islam was precipitated by a remarkable experience he had after composing a letter to Elijah Muhammad in defense of Reginald, who had been suspended from the community for "not practicing moral restraint" (186). After laying the letter in the box for the prison censor's review, Malcolm prayed the rest of the night. The following night, Malcolm awoke suddenly and discovered a man in a dark suit sitting in the chair next to his bed. He described his visitor as neither black nor white, but "light-brown-skinned, an Asiatic cast of countenance, and he had oily black hair" (186). Although he was not afraid of the visitor, Malcolm was rendered immobile by the presence of the mysterious stranger. The two men sat together in silence for a time and then "suddenly as he had come, he was gone" (187). Shortly thereafter, Malcolm came to believe that his mysterious visitor had been none other than W. D. Fard, the man who had appointed Elijah Muhammad as the "last Messenger to the black people of North America" (189). Although Malcolm's vision solidified his commitment to Elijah Muhammad, he had already been talking to other prisoners about his newfound faith; seeking "to catch every chance I could to recruit for Mr. Muhammad" (182). His missionary work focused on reeducation, rather than mere proclamation. As he explains:

> I began first telling my black brother inmates about the glorious history of the black man – things they never had dreamed. I told them the horrible slavery-trade truths that they never knew. . . . I told them that some slaves brought from Africa spoke Arabic, and were Islamic in their religion. . . . I'd explain to them that the real truth was known to some white men, the scholars; but there had been a conspiracy down through the generations to keep the truth from black men. I would keep close watch on how each one reacted. I always had to be careful. I never knew when some brainwashed black imp, some dyed-in-the-wool Uncle Tom, would nod at me and then go running to tell the white man. When one was ripe – and I could tell – then away from the rest, I'd drop it on him, what Mr. Muhammad taught: "The white man is the devil." (182–3)

Unlike traditional Islam, the Nation of Islam taught that God was a black man, whites were devils and would soon be punished by God, and the races should be kept separate. Its worldview was an inversion of the sacred society constructed by white segregationists. Everything Malcolm Little had experienced in his life prepared him to accept these teachings as the absolute truth. His conversion was profound and profoundly religious. It ended forever his life as a criminal and his identity as "Detroit Red," and the atheist other convicts had once called "Satan." Upon his release from prison he gave up the last vestige of his past – his last name. No longer would Malcolm use the "slave name" Little; after his release from prison he became Malcolm X – the brilliant charismatic minister of the Nation of Islam and loyal lieutenant of the movement's leader, Elijah Muhammad. His ministry would change the movement, the country, and eventually, himself.

Malcolm's prison conversion to the Nation of Islam liberated him from his past and the powerlessness he had felt throughout his life. He emerged from prison a proud and articulate defender of his religion and his race. He requested and received the name "Malcolm X" from the Nation of Islam. It replaced, he said, his slave name "Malcolm Little." The "X" stood for that which is unknown, his true and holy name, known only to God (199). It was Malcolm's way of rejecting the sacred order of white racist society and affirming his dignity as a human being.

Elijah Muhammad took immediate interest in Malcolm and personally directed his ministerial education. Malcolm "adored" Muhammad and "believed he had been divinely sent . . . by Allah Himself" (214). In less than a year Elijah Muhammad sent Malcolm to his first ministry and with breathtaking speed Malcolm became a major leader in the Nation of Islam. Wherever Malcolm was sent he was successful, first in Boston, then in Philadelphia. By 1954, two years after being released from prison, Malcolm was appointed minister of the Nation's Temple Seven, in New York City. Malcolm was back in Harlem. Still, he was not entirely free and in some ways he was in greater bondage after his release than he had been while in prison. Ironically, the very force that had freed his thought and imagination also confined them, for the vision of Islam presented by Elijah Muhammad rejected white sacred society only to replace it with a vision of a black one.

In 1959 Malcolm and the Nation of Islam gained large-scale national notoriety for the first time, when a television program portrayed the Nation of Islam as a racist organization that preached hatred of whites. The program, "The Hate that Hate Produced," unleashed a flood of negative publicity. A short time before the program aired and his rise to national and international fame began, Malcolm's personal power and the success of the Nation of Islam were revealed to the people of Harlem. The event grew out of an incident in which the New York police brutally attacked Johnson Hinton when he did not move quickly enough after they told him to. The injured man was taken to a local police station where he received no medical attention. Hinton was a member of Malcolm's temple and when Malcolm received news of the attack he, and a contingent of his well-disciplined followers (the Fruit of Islam), marched to the station. Malcolm demanded to see the injured man. A crowd gathered outside the station. Neither the police nor residents of Harlem had ever witnessed anything like the Fruit of Islam, who stood at attention outside the police station while their religious leader confronted the police. They had never seen anything like Malcolm X, either. Upon finding Hinton severely beaten, semiconscious, and covered in blood, Malcolm told the police to call an ambulance, which they did immediately. The Muslims followed the ambulance along Lenox Avenue, a major street in Harlem, and as they marched, persons came out of restaurants and stores to join them. The crowd grew angry as word of the beating spread. Finally, a police official told Malcolm to direct the crowd to disperse. Malcolm's response to the official and the evening's subsequent events are telling: "I told him that our brothers were standing peacefully, disciplined perfectly, and harming no one. He told me those others, behind them, weren't disciplined. I politely told him those others were his problem" (234).

Malcolm had the audacity to debate college professors, directly challenge law-enforcement officials, and turn to his advantage the very media that often sought to caricature or stereotype him. Although he did not advocate the aggressive use of force, he adamantly affirmed that violence was entirely justified in self-defense: "Never be the aggressor," he told his listeners, "but if anyone attacks you, we do not teach you to turn the other cheek. May Allah bless you to be successful and victorious in all that you do" (214). On the other hand, his resistance to integration on the basis of the Nation's doctrine of racial separation was inconsistent with traditional Islam, which teaches the unity of all humanity in submission to Allah. In all the world, there was only one person who had authority over Malcolm and that was Elijah Muhammad, the man who had been his mentor, inspiration, and savior. Malcolm's life centered on Elijah Muhammad and the religion whose doctrines he defined. For Malcolm, Muhammad was beyond questioning and his teachings were sacred truths. To question the authority of his master would call his entire world into question, yet, as if responding to the inner promptings of the holy, this is exactly what Malcolm did. As with Job, it was a matter of integrity. As he tells it: "my faith had been shaken in a way that I can never fully describe. For I had discovered Muslims had been betrayed by Elijah Muhammad himself" (294). Elijah Muhammad had committed adultery, one of the most grievous of sins in the Nation of Islam. Malcolm's life and world were torn asunder.

Disillusionment and the second conversion

The final turning point of Malcolm's journey through life began with his rejection of teachings of the Nation of Islam and the person of Elijah Muhammad. To understand the enormity of this act, we need to consider his relationship to the "Master" of the Nation of Islam, The Honorable Elijah Muhammad. As Alex Haley notes in the "Epilogue" of the *Autobiography*, Malcolm had originally planned to dedicate his autobiography to Elijah Muhammad (387). Malcolm's relationship with him went beyond professional respect and admiration; it went even beyond love, for Malcolm X saw Elijah Muhammad as a divine figure, and if not a god, certainly a new messiah. His was a relationship of the disciple to the divine master. Malcolm tells us, without qualification: "I worshiped him" (199). For Malcolm, Elijah Muhammad had been a "divine leader" (365).

The crisis that forced Malcolm out of the Nation of Islam soon led him to make a pilgrimage to Saudi Arabia and the holy city of Mecca, where the power of the experience led him to his second great religious conversion – to traditional Sunni Islam. Malcolm decided to go on the hajj – the religious pilgrimage that all Muslims are required to make, if at all possible, once in their life. It was, for Malcolm, his own flight (hijra) from the sacred society of the Nation of Islam to the traditional Islam and a new vision of a holy community, open to all races and religions.

Before his pilgrimage to Mecca, Malcolm's understanding of Islam had been restricted to the teachings of Elijah Muhammad on black separatism. When the Master lost his honor, the religion lost its meaning for Malcolm. The fall from faith in Elijah Muhammad revealed the tenuousness of his own belief. Malcolm found himself wrestling with his own identity, that of Elijah Muhammad, and that of his God. He emerged from this wrestling match with a new identity – that of a religious and political leader in a world of conflicting values and claims, who sought justice for all races and peoples throughout the world.

Within a few months of his break with the Nation of Islam, on March 12, 1965, Malcolm called a news conference to announce his formation of a new organization, the Muslim Mosque, Inc. He called the announcement his "declaration of independence." The Muslim Mosque "would embrace all faiths of black men, and it would carry into practice what the Nation of Islam had only preached" (315). To prepare himself for his new mission, Malcolm knew he needed "one further major preparation" – the pilgrimage to Mecca (317). On March 26, 1964, he attended the Senate debate on the Civil Rights Bill and there, he and Martin Luther King, Jr. met for the first and only time. Despite years of intense debate there was a genuine element of respect between them and a photograph of their meeting shows both men smiling. In April, Malcolm began his life-transforming pilgrimage. The journey would take him to Mecca, the very heart of the Muslim world. It would also take him to Africa. In Mecca he learned that what it meant to be a Muslim was something quite different from what he had been taught in the Nation of Islam. This discovery led to the most radical conversion of his life, for in Mecca, Malcolm found that Islam means submission, peace, and the unity of all the peoples of the world. In Africa, this conversion was reinforced through the unity he felt with persons struggling against Euro-American economic and political oppression.

In Mecca and throughout his journey, Malcolm witnessed the universality of Islam and glimpsed the vision of a holy community. He met Muslims of all races and ethnicities praying and eating together. The entire adventure was thrilling to him; after years of being a minister and the great spokesperson of the Nation of Islam, he now was becoming a Muslim! Of all the many experiences that impressed him on the hajj, what impressed him most of all was the unity among Muslims of all races. This would change him forever and stand as the foundational experience of his last conversion – the conversion to orthodox Sunni Islam. Indeed, on the pilgrimage he learned how to pray. In the Nation of Islam he had never prayed in the universal language of Islam, Arabic, and never learned the proper posture for prayer.

Malcolm's conversion was both religious and ethical. Malcolm captured the essence of his conversion in a letter he sent to his friends in America. This letter from Mecca is as powerful a witness to his mature faith as is King's "Letter from Birmingham Jail."

Never have I witnessed such sincere hospitality and the overwhelming spirit of true brotherhood as is practiced by people of all colors and races here in this Ancient Holy Land, the home of Abraham, Muhammad, and all the other proph- ets of the Holy Scriptures. . . . I have been blessed to visit the Holy City of Mecca. I have made my seven circuits around the Ka'ba, led by a young *Mutawaf* named Muhammad. I drank water from the well of Zem Zem. I ran seven times back and forth between the hills of Mt. Al-Safa and Al Marwah. I have prayed in the ancient city of Mina, and I have prayed on Mt. Arafat.

There were tens of thousands of pilgrims, from all over the world. They were of all colors, from blue-eyed blonds to black-skinned Africans. But we were all par- ticipating in the same ritual, displaying a spirit of unity and brotherhood that my experiences in America had led me to believe never could exist between the white and the non-white. . . .

Throughout my travels in the Muslim world, I have met, talked to, and even eaten with people who in America would have been considered "white"– but the "white" attitude was removed from their minds by the religion of Islam. I have never before seen *sincere* and *true* brotherhood practiced by all colors together, irrespective of their color.

You may be shocked by these words coming from me. But on this pilgrimage, what I have seen, and experienced, has forced me to *re-arrange* much of my thought-patterns previously held, and to *toss aside* some of my previous conclu- sions. This was not too difficult for me. Despite my firm convictions, I have been always a man who tries to face facts, and to accept the reality of life as new experi- ence and new knowledge unfolds it. I have always kept an open mind, which is necessary to the flexibility that must go hand in hand with every form of intelli- gent search for truth.

During the past eleven days here in the Muslim world, I have eaten from the same plate, drunk from the same glass . . . while praying to the *same* God – with fellow Muslims, whose eyes were the bluest of blue, whose hair was the blondest of blond, and whose skin was the whitest of white. . . . We were *truly* all the same (brothers) – because their belief in one God had removed the "white" from their *minds*, the "white" from their *behavior* and the "white" from their *attitude*. I could see from this, that perhaps if white Americans could accept the Oneness of God, then perhaps, too, they could accept *in reality* the oneness of Man . . .

Each hour here in the Holy Land enables me to have greater spiritual insights into what is happening in America between black and white. . . . As racism leads

America up the suicide path, I do believe, from the experiences that I have had with them, that the whites of the younger generation, in the colleges and universities, will see the handwriting on the wall and many of them will turn to the *spiritual path* of truth – the *only* way left to America to ward off the disaster that racism inevitably must lead to . . .

All praise is due to Allah, the Lord of all the Worlds.

Sincerely,
El-Hajj Malik El-Shabazz
(Malcolm X) (339–42)

In Mecca, Malcolm had discovered the essence of Islam and experienced the living reality that Muhammad himself articulated in his farewell sermon thirteen centuries earlier: "Know ye that every Moslem is a brother unto every other Moslem, and that ye are now one brotherhood. It is not legitimate for any one of you, therefore, to appropriate unto himself anything that belongs to his brother unless it is willingly given him by that brother."

On his way back to America, Malcolm visited several African nations, where he was welcomed enthusiastically by government officials and the general population. As with his hajj, Malcolm's visits to the African states dramatically broadened his horizons. In Mecca he found affinities with Muslims worldwide, regardless of race; in Africa he found solidarity with oppressed people in every nation that he visited – from Nigeria to Ghana and from Senegal to Algeria. In Nigeria he received yet another new name, Omowale, which means "the son who has come home"(351). But the son who had come home to Africa had done so by way of Mecca.

He returned to America in late May of 1964, on the eve of the "long hot summer," when riots erupted in many American cities. To the press and the public at large, he was once again typecast as Malcolm X, the radical advocate of violence who had helped to inspire the violence that was engulfing the nation's inner cities. Soon enough, however, the country and the world heard a new message from the man who had once so terrified white America. It was the message of El-Hajj Malik El-Shabazz, the pilgrim who had returned from Mecca, and Omowale, the son who had come home.

In the nine remaining months of his life Malcolm combined the insights of his final pilgrimage in forming the Organization of Afro-American Unity (OAAU), which he saw as complementing Muslim Mosque, Inc., inviting both Muslims and non-Muslims to work together in the struggle for racial justice. The OAAU was an umbrella organization that sought to promote unity among black Americans and link their struggles with those of the nations of Africa. Central to its mission was the achievement of basic human rights for African-Americans. Malcolm's vision more and more approximated that of a holy community with justice for persons of every color and religion. He cited the United Nations, its Charter and its Universal Declaration of Human Rights; he also cited the American Constitution and Bill of Rights. It is notable, however, that in the organizational documents of the OAAU, there is no mention of Islam.

The absence of religious particularity was strategic and the flowering of Malcolm's final conversion in Mecca *and* Africa. By removing direct reference to any religion and in fact establishing the OAAU as explicitly non-religious and non-sectarian, Malcolm made explicit the ideal behind the Muslim Mosque, Inc. Where the Muslim orientation of that group was self-evident in its name and Malcolm's own religious orientation, the new organization was clearly and emphatically open to blacks of all faiths. It expressed his new sense of the inter-dependence of all persons. Moreover, the *spiritual* force he had sought initially was hardly compromised by the OAAU's non-religious position, for now the one element that had served to divide blacks (especially the separatist Black Muslims), religion, was deemphasized in favor of the broader *spiritual* ideals of universal human rights. In forming the OAAU Malcolm had transcended any limitations that might have been imposed by religion, even his newfound religion of orthodox Islam; he no longer saw the issues as exclusively Muslim issues or the problems as ones that Islam alone could eliminate. Malcolm never ceased being a Muslim but in the wake of his discovery of traditional Islam, he also discovered that the pursuit of human rights was found not through the establishment of a sacred uniformity but rather in an audacious commitment to unity-in-diversity.

The OAAU was an organization meant to bring African-Americans together across religions and cultures in a common struggle for racial justice in which blacks were to assume responsibility for their own destiny. Given this task, it could not include whites. However, its goal was not that of Malcolm's earlier vision of black separatism but his new vision in which whites and blacks might live together in a single society with justice for all. By the end of his life, he envisioned the outcome of their work to be inclusive of all people and his mission to rid America of oppression and racism had become an inspiration whose goal was to transcend racial divisions.

Malcolm's death

On Sunday February 21, 1965, Malcolm X was assassinated – some say by the Nation of Islam, others by US government agents, still others both. The last words he spoke that day were words of peace. Sundays were days when Malcolm often made public addresses and this Sunday was no different. As he stood to speak to a large audience at the Audubon Ballroom in Harlem, he greeted them with the familiar *Assalam wa alaykum* (peace be with you). Then a scuffle broke out among some members of the audience. Addressing the people tussling, Malcolm said, "Let's cool it, brothers – "(434). Moments later he was shot to death. In the end, these last statements summarize the legacy of Malcolm X – first the traditional Muslim greeting of peace, then its contemporary translation.

As we have seen in the stories of Gandhi and King, Malcolm X also died before his goals were achieved. What he would have done had he lived we can only speculate; but one thing that seems certain is that Malcolm would have changed, there would have been further journeys and new turning points. Indeed! Malcolm's life is nothing if not a story of drastic changes. In the last year of his life he said: "Anything that I do today, I regard as urgent. No man is given but so much time to accomplish whatever is his life's work. My life in particular never has stayed fixed in one position for very long. You have seen how throughout my life, I have often known unexpected drastic changes" (378). On the Thursday before his death he told a reporter, "I'm man enough to tell you that I can't put my finger on exactly what my philosophy is now, but I'm flexible" (428). Malcolm's life had taught him that his identity was not predicated on completion but rather on change, on advance, on the transcendence of states of seeming completion through a willingness to continue the journey. The single great constant in Malcolm's life was his openness to the journey. For him, as for Abraham and Muhammad before him, faith truly was setting out on a journey without knowing where one is going, trusting God to lead the way. That this was his spiritual path, he seems to have recognized fully only late in his life.

Malcolm was a man of many names. Because of his provincial ways he was called "homeboy" in Roxbury, but he moved to Harlem and became "Detroit Red," a force to be reckoned with in the inner-city underworld. He was so atheistic that he was known as "Satan" but he ended up as the greatest spokesperson for the Nation of Islam, and as "minister Malcolm X" converted thousands, perhaps tens of thousands, to the "true religion of black people." Then he became El-Hajj Malik El-Shabazz, the orthodox Muslim whose pilgrimage to Mecca severed his last ties with the Nation of Islam; and El-Shabazz also became "Alhadji," the man who received the robe of kinship from the Nigerian High Commissioner, Alhadji Isa Wali. Finally, he was "Omowale," which in the Yoruba language means the "son who has come home." Yet Malcolm's identity was never permanently defined by any of these names. He was known by many names during his life, but no one name entirely captured his essence. He remained undefined. He remained Malcolm X.

Rather than allowing his identity to be defined by any of the sacred societies in which he participated, Malcolm constantly and consistently said, I am more than this, whatever *this* may be. I shall not be what society tells me I must be because I am black; I shall not conform to your sacred stereotype of my race; and I shall not allow myself to be limited by lack of formal education, lack of exposure to bourgeois culture, or my years in prison. I shall not be merely a Black Muslim, I will become a Muslim who will be a leader of oppressed people from all religions, races, and nations. In dramatic fashion, Malcolm's openness to the infinite, his refusal to allow his identity to become finalized, allowed him to exemplify the way of pilgrimage in a post/modern world – a pilgrimage beyond every sacred order and toward that holy city where unity will be found in the midst of diversity.

Comparative Reflections: Just War or Non-Violence? – Malcolm X's Argument with the Gandhian Tradition

In this section, and the questions that follow, we invite you to wrestle with Malcolm X and his advocacy of the right of self-defense to establish racial justice "by any means necessary." And we invite you to pass over into Malcolm's life, and his wrestling with King's views on non-violence, and see Malcolm X as standing in the "just-war" tradition which allows violence in order to protect the weak and the innocent. We draw comparisons and suggest conclusions for your reflection with the hope that they will provoke discussion and the sharing of insight.

Sin and human nature

As we have noted, Christianity set itself apart from Judaism because of its view of "original sin." The rabbis did not interpret the sin of Adam and Eve as causing the cosmic order of creation to fall, corrupting human nature – nor did their Muslim counterparts, the ulama. Both would agree that there is no corporate sin corrupting human nature, no incarnation needed to mend human nature, and no vicarious atonement required. That is, no one need die for the sins of another. Rather, sin is the misuse of human freedom in response to God's commands. Every person remains in the situation of Adam, free to do either good or evil. However, unlike both Judaism and Christianity, Islam does not consider the first act of disobedience to be shared by both Adam and Eve. Eve does not tempt Adam to sin. Adam is responsible for his own sins.

For Muslims, human beings are not by nature sinful, only weak. The explanation for Adam's sins is the same as any other person's, simply human weakness before the temptations of Satan. Human beings are weak but responsible for their actions. They are called to submit through total surrender of their will to God, who will be their final judge. Those who surrender will be rewarded in paradise; those who do not will be consigned to hell. Adam's archetypal act is not his sin but his repentance. He failed, yes, but he also repented and turned back to God; not out of guilt but out of fear (taqwaa). He feared God, as all true Muslims should. God's action in the story is also representative, for God forgave Adam. Adam realized his error, feared God, and repented.

According to Islam, humans are to submit to the will of God, who stands as the guide and the judge of humans; human failing is not met with immediate or lasting punishment, for that is not God's way. Instead, God meets the honest repentance of the sinner with compassion and mercy. It is the quality of God's mercy that is central to Islam. So central is the compassion and mercy of God that every surah of the Quran begins with the preamble: "In the name of Allah, the compassionate, the merciful." The root of Islamic ethics, says John Esposito, is found in Surah 6: "It is He who had made you [His] agents, inheritors of the earth. He hath raised you in ranks, some above others that He may try you. For thy Lord is quick in punishment, yet He is indeed Oft Forgiving, Most Merciful" (Quran 6: 165, cited with comment in Esposito 1998: 26).

Abe's typology of religion and ethics

As we have noted, Masao Abe established a typology for ethics based on his comparisons of Jewish, Christian, and Buddhist ethics. Abe, however, is silent on Islamic ethics. Nevertheless, this does not mean that his typology cannot be applied to Islam. As you will recall, Abe saw no path at all between ethics and religion in Buddhism, a continuous path from religion to ethics but not from ethics to religion in Christianity, and a path in both directions in Judaism. Islam resembles Abe's Buddhist and Christian models in its recognition that the divine realm transcends the range of human questioning and challenge. On the other hand, like the Christian and Jewish models (in distinction to the Buddhist model), Islam affirms that the passion for justice expresses the highest level of spiritual commitment. Nowhere in Islam would one find (except with some sort of highly qualified nuance) the notion expressed by Abe with regard to Buddhism: "In order to enter the realm of religion, human ethics must die."

In Islam, there is no path in either direction between ethics and religion. Islam lacks a path between ethics and religion not because of the Buddhist problem with dualism or the Christian problem with original sin but rather because of the radicalness of the Islamic virtue of submission. In Islam, there is no movement either way between ethics and religion because there is, in principle and practice, no differentiation between them. Ethics is subsumed in religion and religion is defined in the context of humanity's submission to God's immeasurable glory and unfathomable supremacy. The human world is called to submit to God in *all* things and *all* ways – ethics is part of that submission. And just as the ethical realm is subsumed in the religious, so the religious is infused with the ethical. There is no separation of the religious realm from the non-religious, as one finds in Christianity.

Dar al-islam and dar al-harb: the tension between the sacred and the holy

Like all traditions, Islam embodies the tension between the sacred and the holy. As the Islamic tradition developed, Muslims made a distinction between *dar al-islam* and *dar al-harb*. *Dar al-islam* represents the *ummah*, or Muslim community – all those who have surrendered themselves to God and secondly, all others who are willing to live under Muslim rule according to the demands of the one true God for justice and mercy. Dar al-harb is "the territory of war" where warlike behavior is the norm and God's will for justice and mercy among all people is ignored, so that consequently, disorder, injustice, and conflict reign. This vision required Muslims to struggle (*jihad*) to bring the whole world under the realm of God's rule as revealed to Muhammad. Forced conversion was not acceptable according to Islamic law, as it would be insincere. True struggle or jihad was first and foremost wrestling with oneself in order to surrender to the will of God, and secondly, to struggle to bring about the conversion of unbelievers through education and persuasion, which leads to a free surrender of will to God.

Nevertheless, jihad could also mean armed struggle, or war. This kind of jihad had a legitimate purpose, namely to bring all – both believers and unbelievers – under the rule of dar al-islam. Dar al-islam, therefore, came to mean all territory under Muslim rule with the expectation (in theory if not always in fact) that that rule would be a faithful expression of the justice and mercy of God. It included those who, as Muslims, had made a personal surrender to God but also those who, while not embracing Islam, were willing to accept Muslim rule and live within this order established by God. In this way Islam allowed for religious diversity (non-Muslims, or *dhimmi*) while maintaining Islamic hegemony. Among these, a special place was given to the people of the book, Jews and Christians, who were viewed as set apart from polytheists, who know nothing of the one true God.

In the conception of dar al-islam there is a strong element of the sacred society, in which only those who share Muslim identity have full privileges. Dar al-harb readily appeared to be a profane threat (the realm of chaos) to the sacred order of dar al-islam. And yet within dar al-islam there is an element of the holy – an acknowledgment that even the stranger is a child of God who ought to be welcomed, provided he or she is willing to live under the authority of Muslim rule as established by Sharia. On the whole, in the Middle Ages, Islam offered more hospitality to strangers than European Christendom did. Nevertheless, like Christianity, it also often resorted to war against the stranger, rejecting the stranger as an infidel and a threat to the sacred order of society.

Just war

The beginnings of just-war theory in Christianity go back to the early church fathers, especially Augustine of Hippo. His arguments were further refined by Thomas Aquinas and others, taking definitive shape by the sixteenth century. The distance between those committed to non-violence and the advocates of the just use of violence is not as great as it may seem at first. For, as Augustine argued, Christians are commanded to love their enemies, so individual Christians were not permitted to kill another in defense of themselves. However, the threat of violence against the weak and the innocent presented a powerful ethical dilemma for Christians. Is it ethical to stand by and do nothing while others are unjustly harmed? Augustine resolved this dilemma by allowing a limited use of violence. The only legitimate use of violence, he argued, is to protect the weak and the innocent from serious harm. In that situation to refuse to use violence would be a greater evil than the use of it. Thus while violence cannot be used in personal defense, it can be justifiable in defense of one's community.

In such situations where protection of the innocent is involved, there are a series of conditions that must be met for the use of violence to be considered just:

1 War must always be a last resort, to be used only when all peaceful means have been exhausted.
2 There must always be a just cause. War can only be used in self-defense against an aggressor to protect the innocent who are being violated by an aggressor. It can never be used simply to expand one's wealth, power or territory, etc.
3 War must always be declared by legitimate political authority.
4 The goal of war must always be attainable. It is wrong to risk lives if there is no hope of being successful.
5 The ultimate objective of war must always be a restoration of peace.
6 The means used to conduct the war must always be proportionate to the end sought. That is, the good to be achieved must be greater than the evil that would have to be caused to achieve it.
7 Non-combatants must always be protected in the conduct of war. (This condition tends to disqualify modern atomic warfare, which not only kills non-combatants along with combatants but also risks ecological disaster or "omnicide" – destroying all life on the planet.)

Under these conditions, it is clear that the use of violence is not permitted to individuals or small groups, only to organized political entities – empires or nation-states that are responsible for the protection of their citizens. Moreover, these conditions are usually divided into two categories, *jus ad bellum* or conditions necessary in order to go to war justly (1–5), and *jus in bellum,* or the conditions that must be observed for war to be conducted justly (6, 7).

Islamic theory on war or jihad shares many of these criteria (Kelsay 1993). The cause must be just (2), it must be declared by legitimate authority (3), there must be a reasonable hope of success (4), and its goal must be the reestablishment of peace (5). The proportional use of force (6), while not a formal principle, tends to be present as a form of "prudential reasoning" in military strategy. The two areas where notable differences occur is the declaration of war as a "last resort" (1) and avoiding harm to non-combatants (7). For classical Sunni Islam, a holy war (jihad) was not a war of self-defense but a war to extend the rule of Islam so as to include more and more of humanity under the order of God's justice and mercy (dar al-islam). As such, it was a positive religious obligation rather than a matter of last resort. And yet, even here, opportunity to voluntarily accept Muslim rule must precede the resort to war. The emphasis here was not on making converts (although that was desired) but on expanding the realm of justice under God. Wars fought for any other purpose (power, glory, self-defense) were "harb" and not "jihad," that is; they were not truly holy wars. Finally, there is no precise parallel to non-combatant immunity (7) in Islam. Considerations of proportionality in the use of force would limit the unnecessary use of violence. However, if women and children are killed, the responsibility would fall upon the leaders of the dar al-harb for risking their women and children in order to resist accepting the order of justice and mercy offered by the leaders of dar al-islam (Kelsay 1993: 66–7).

It is unlikely that Malcolm X's stand on violence as a means to secure justice was based on the nuances of the historical development of the Islamic position on just wars. And of course, Malcolm was not the head of an Islamic state that could formally declare such a war. Perhaps Malcolm X should be compared to those Islamic revolutionaries in the contemporary world that have argued that Islam can be understood as justifying guerrilla tactics and terrorism under extreme conditions and have acted on their own initiative. But to engage in such actions, these revolutionaries have had to stretch the just-war tradition of Islam to breaking point. Moreover, Malcolm X advocated not the proactive aggression of guerrilla warfare but aggression in self-defense. In doing so we believe he actually stood closer to the teachings of Muhammad and the classical tradition. We would suggest that there are analogies between classical Islamic just-war thought and his position on the use of violence as a means to bring about racial justice and harmony (the kind he encountered in dar al-islam on the hajj) in an unjust or racist world (the dar al-harb of racist America).

In this book we have focused on Gandhi and the spiritual children of Gandhi (Nhat Hanh, King, and Heschel) – individuals whose lives converged around the non-violent protest of racism, colonialism, and all other forms of human prejudice in a post-Auschwitz and post-Hiroshima age. They protested segregation in America and American involvement in the Vietnam War, mindful of the lessons of Auschwitz and Hiroshima which reveal the ultimate self-destructive MADness of prejudice and hatred. In our account, Malcolm X stands apart as one who advocated the establishment of racial justice "by any means necessary." In a speech he made to domestic Peace Corps volunteers in December of 1964, less than three months before his death, Malcolm made it clear that he did not share Martin Luther King, Jr.'s commitment to non-violence:

> I would like to say this: It concerns my own personal self, whose image they [the white press] have projected in their own light. I am against any form of racism. We are all against racism. The only difference between you and me is that you want to fight racism and racists non-violently and lovingly and I'll fight them the way they fight me. Whatever weapon they use, that's the one I'll use. I go for talking the kind of language he talks. You can't communicate with a person unless you use the language he uses. If a man is speaking French, you can talk German all night long, he won't know what you're talking about. You have to find out what kind of language he understands and then you put it to him in the language he understands.

I'm a Muslim, which means my religion is Islam. I believe in Allah. I believe in all the prophets, whoever represented God on this earth. I believe what Muslims believe: prayer, fasting, charity, and the pilgrimage to the Holy Land, Mecca, which I've been fortunate to have made four or five times. I believe in the brotherhood of man, all men, but I don't believe in brotherhood with anybody who doesn't want brotherhood with me. I believe in treating people right, but I'm not going to waste my time trying to treat somebody right who doesn't know how to return that treatment. This is the only difference between you and me.

You believe in treating everybody right whether they put a rope around your neck or whether they put you in the grave. Well, my belief isn't that strong. I believe in the brotherhood of man, but I think that anybody who wants to lynch a Negro is not qualified for that brotherhood and I don't put forth any effort to get them into that brotherhood. You want to save him and I don't.

Despite the fact that I believe in the brotherhood of man as a Muslim, and in the religion of Islam, there is one fact also that I can't overlook: I'm an Afro-American and Afro-Americans have problems that go well beyond religion. We have problems that our religious organization in itself cannot solve and we have problems that no one organization can solve or no one leader can solve. We have a problem that is going to take the combined efforts of every leader and every organization if we are going to get a solution. For that reason, I don't believe that as a Muslim it is possible for me to bring my religion into any discussion with non-Muslims without causing more division, animosity, and hostility; then we will only be involved in self-defeating action. So based upon that, there is a group of us that have formed an organization. Besides being Muslims, we have gotten together and formed an organization that has nothing to do with religion at all: it is known as the Organization of Afro-American Unity . . .

Those of us in the Organization of Afro-American Unity have adopted as our slogan "by any means necessary" and we feel we are justified. Whenever someone is treating you in a criminal, illegal, or immoral way, why, you are well within your rights to use anything at your disposal to bring an end to that unjust, illegal, and immoral condition. If we do like that, we will find that we will get more respect and will be further down the road toward freedom, toward recognition and respect as human beings. But as long as we dillydally and try to appear that we're more moral by taking a beating without fight back, people will continue to refer to us as very moral and well disciplined persons, but at the same time we will be as far back a hundred years from now as we are today. So I believe that fighting those who fight us is the best course of action in any situation . . .

So I must emphasize, we are dealing with a powerful enemy, and again, I am not anti-American or un-American. I think there are plenty of good people in America, but there are also plenty of bad people in America and the bad ones are the ones who seem to have all the power and be in these positions to block things that you and I need. Because this is the situation, you and I have to preserve the right to do what is necessary to bring an end to that situation, and it doesn't mean that I advocate violence, but at the same time I am not against using violence in self-defense. I don't even call it violence when it's self-defense, I call it intelligence. (Clarke 1969: 311–13)

Two things should be clear from this statement. First, while Malcolm's pilgrimage to Mecca gave him a glimpse of the vision of a holy community that could unite persons of all races within, and even beyond, the Islamic faith, it remains unclear how far he is willing to extend that hospitality. On the one hand, he seems to want to extend it beyond religious differences. On the other hand, it does not include love of one's enemy and so falls short of the full vision. Second, Malcolm was not advocating indiscriminate violence, but rather the right of self-defense in protection of the weak and the innocent and in order to move society toward the justice and mercy commanded by God (dar al-islam).

Narratives of war, we have said, are extraordinarily dangerous because they allow us to invert our normal ethical orientation so that killing becomes good and not killing becomes evil. Both Gandhi and Malcolm X understood the story in which they existed to be one of war. Both believed there really was evil and injustice in this world that must be combated. And yet their paths diverge. Gandhi was committed to "soul force" and Malcolm X to "body force." Malcolm X was convinced that the protection of the weak and the innocent requires a willingness to use violence in self-defense. Gandhi was convinced that when you return evil for evil, you become like your enemy and the sum total of evil and violence in the world is increased. Therefore, the only way to conquer evil is to return good for evil and return non-violent resistance (civil disobedience) for violence. Both were selflessly committed to justice on behalf of those oppressed. Gandhi sought to transform a story of war (the *Gita*) into a story of peace. Malcolm X thought the best way to insure peace was to be prepared to engage in war.

One should not conclude that Malcolm advocated armed self-defense simply because he was a Muslim. Virtually all religions have permitted the use of violence in self-defense and in order to promote justice. That is the literal position taken by Krishna (Vishnu) in his argument with Arjuna in the *Bhagavad Gita* (which Gandhi transformed through an allegorical interpretation). Likewise, Jews, Christians and Muslims, and even Buddhists, have allowed that there is such a thing as the just use of violence. In fact, throughout history, in both Eastern and Western cultures, the idea of "just war" and the just use of violence have been dominant in virtually all religious traditions. The advocacy of non-violence has been the exception, not the rule – the lives and teachings of Jesus and the Buddha notwithstanding. It was only in the twentieth century, in the wake of the lives of Tolstoy, Gandhi, and King, and especially after Auschwitz and Hiroshima, that non-violence began to get a serious hearing,

Malcolm X did not advocate the aggressive use of force, but he did recognize violence to be justified in self-defense. This was a teaching of the Nation of Islam as well as traditional Islam. Malcolm said: "Never be the aggressor, but if anyone attacks you, we do not teach you to turn the other cheek. May Allah bless you to be successful and victorious in all that you do" (X 1973: 214). This does not sound all that different from the message given to Muhammad: "Those who have been wronged are permitted to fight"(Quran 22: 39).

The problem with "just war" and the just use of violence is that even the legitimate use of violence creates a "slippery slope," for as history has revealed, the line between self-defense and aggression is a thin one. Historically, the buildup of weapons in order to be prepared to defend one's people has typically been interpreted by others as an aggressive act requiring a similar response. Self-defense then becomes a provocation for preemptive strikes against the other, which the other interprets as unprovoked and unnecessary aggression. This does not mean that there is no such thing as ethically legitimate self-defense, just that it is difficult to put into practice without provoking unnecessary violence. We would argue that asking whether violence can ever be ethically justified is perhaps asking the wrong question. The real question is whether violence can ever be redemptive. Can violence be used without provoking still further violence, leading to an unending cycle of violence? What makes non-violence redemptive is that it offers the possibility of breaking this cycle.

The Gandhian tradition is aggressive in its pursuit of justice for the oppressed through civil disobedience and other non-violent tactics. By refusing to engage in violence the children of Gandhi seek to awaken the humanity and conscience of the other. And even when they fail to do so, they refuse to add to the sum total of violence in the world. By refusing to resort to violence, they offer the "enemy" no legitimation for the continuance or escalation of violence. They break the cycle of violence (an eye for an eye) through their willingness to suffer rather than be the cause of suffering. However, the practice of non-violent resistance does not occur in a political vaccum. James Cone has suggested that Martin Luther King, Jr.'s message of non-violence would never have achieved the positive reception it did in white America (often a reluctant acceptance) without the threat of violence that Malcolm X's rhetoric created. The threat of the latter, Cone suggests, made the promise of the former the more palatable option.

Although Malcolm X never actually used violence aggressively, his advocacy of violence in self-defense takes us to the very heart of the question of religion and violence. The issue is of critical importance to the world today, for if religion can be seen to legitimate violence, for any reason, it can become yet another motivating factor in the escalation of tensions between peoples and nations. It goes without saying that in a nuclear age the consequences of such escalations may prove fatal to us all.

If religious traditions take a position more in the spirit of Gandhi and his heirs, they can function not only to reduce tensions but also to bring healing and reconciliation between peoples. The challenge, of course, is that all the religions we have studied contain narratives that can be interpreted as not only justifying violence and war, but even giving them divine sanction as a "sacred duty." In this book we have also explored other narratives that advocate a spirituality of holiness; stories of hospitality to the stranger, stories of peace and reconciliation, of equality among people, and of audacity in protecting the poor and oppressed. We have called attention to these narrative traditions, but we would be wrong to summarily dismiss the narratives that have legitimated the just use of violence, for they address a legitimate ethical concern – protection of the weak and the innocent.

Only in the twentieth century did the minority traditions of non-violence achieve significant prominence. Why? Perhaps because, as Martin Luther King, Jr. put it, in a nuclear age our choice is not between violence and non-violence but between non-violence and non-existence. Although it still remains a minority voice, the emergence of an international and interreligious movement for non-violence, deeply indebted to Tolstoy, Gandhi, and King, represents a fundamental change in the ethical climate of our world. We have sketched the human dimensions of this change in our biographical studies and here we can state explicitly that this is really something quite new in the history of the world and its religions.

In spite of this breathtaking change, however, the intimate embrace of violence by religions continues. Whether the change we have recognized continues and expands is an open question, and as much a matter of hope for some as it is a matter for concern for those who would use religion to justify violence. In this regard we may note that when reports of Pakistan's detonation of an atomic bomb reached the streets of Karachi, the crowds affirmed "Allah Akbar." The event was certainly one of significance to people living in Karachi and their response was justifiably religious, but it does suggest something of the relationship between religion and violence. For Pakistanis, the bomb was seen as a defensive weapon, one developed to protect them from India, which had just detonated its own atomic device. Moreover, Pakistanis knew that the Indians also had missiles capable of reaching Karachi and other cities in Pakistan, hence all the more reason to demonstrate their military might. It is a tragic irony that the land that spawned Gandhi created its own atomic bomb and named the missile that would deliver it "Indra," the name of the ancient Vedic god of the heavens and of war. Gandhi's dream of one united India of Hindus and Muslims has become the nightmare of two countries that fear each other as strangers. The escalation between the two countries mimics that of the Cold-War powers, Soviet Russia and the US, and illustrates why self-defense is not redemptive. What one country sees as self-defense, the other interprets as aggression. An "eye for an eye" not only can make everybody blind, it can also make everybody dead.

After Auschwitz and Hiroshima, the ethic of non-violence deserves, and is getting, a serious hearing. In a world of nuclear power, one has to ask if it is realistic to think that human conflicts can be settled with violence without risking omnicide (i.e., the annihilation of all). Some pacifists hold an absolutist position, never allowing violence; still others hold a contextualist position that would allow for exceptions under extreme circumstances. It may not be "realistic" to believe the world will ever be completely non-violent, but that does not mean that it cannot be less violent. But it will only be less violent if people of different religions and cultures find ways to transform the various cultural moralities of self-defense, by passing over into each other's worlds so as to increase understanding and transform stories of war into stories of peace.

Questions for Discussion

1   Comment on the differences between the speeches made by Umar and Abu Bekr when Muhammad died. What makes Bekr's speech the more appropriate Islamic response?

2   Discuss the various transformations of Malcolm X. How do they reveal his capacity for openness to the infinite?

3   Discuss the similarities and differences in the cosmic stories of Judaism, Christianity, and Islam. How do differences in the stories lead to differences in the ethics of the three religions?

4   Compare and contrast the stories of Arjuna and Muhammad with those of Jesus and Siddhartha with respect to the question of the just use of violence. What are the points of agreement and disagreement in these stories, and of what significance are these points?

5   Construct a dialogue between Malcolm X and Muhammad in which they talk about the pivotal experiences in their lives.

6   How would Malcolm X respond to the argument we have constructed between Abraham Joshua Heschel and Thich Nhat Hanh concerning "taking sides" in order to achieve justice?

7   Construct a dialogue between Malcolm X and Martin Luther King, Jr. in which they talk about the ethics of violence and non-violence.

8   What is the hajj, and why was it so important to Malcolm X? What made Malcolm's experience different from that of the Muslims he met during the hajj?

9   To what degree does Malcolm X's advocacy of violence meet the conditions for the just use of violence in the "just-war" tradition as advocated within either Christianity or Islam? Is his position closer to one than the other, and if so, in what ways? Finally, are there ways in which his position is at odds with both?

10   How does the contrast between the sacred and the holy, or morality and ethics, appear in Malcolm X's life and changing ethic?

11   Describe Malcolm X's spirituality and explain how it functions in relation to his ethic.

12   Is the model of holiness as a surrender to the questions and to doubt exemplified in the life and spirituality of Malcolm X?

13   Can elements of both a morality of obedience and an ethic of audacity be found in the stories of Islam and Malcolm X? Compare and contrast to Judaism and Abraham Joshua Heschel.

14   Using Abe's models of religion and ethics as a starting point (figure 3.1), compare the lives of Malcolm X, Gandhi, Nhat Hanh, King, and Heschel.

15   Does the model of "passing over" and "coming back" apply to Malcolm X's life? Explain.

References

Arberry, A. J. (trans.). 1955. *The Koran Interpreted*. New York: Macmillan.

Clarke, John Henrik (ed.). 1969. *Malcolm X: The Man and His Times*. New York: Collier Books.

Cone, James. 1991. *Martin & Malcolm & America: A Dream or a Nightmare*. Maryknoll, NY: Orbis Books.

Dawood, N. J. (trans.). 1990. *The Koran*. London: Penguin Books.

Esposito, John. 1998. *Islam: The Straight Path*. New York: Oxford University Press.

Ferguson, John. 1978. *War and Peace in the World's Religions*. New York: Oxford University Press.

Irving, T. B. (trans.). 1985. *The Quran: The First American Version*. Brattleboro, VT: Amana Books.

Ishaq, Ibn. 1955. *The Life of Muhammad: A Translation of Ishaq's Sirat Rasul Allah*, (trans. A. Guillaume). Oxford: Oxford University Press.

Kelsay, John. 1993. *Islam and War: A Study in Comparative Ethics*. Louisville, KY: John Knox Press.

Lings, Martin. 1983. *Muhammad: His Life Based on the Earliest Sources*. Rochester, VT: Inner Traditions International.

Peters, F. E. 1994. *Muhammad and the Origins of Islam*. Albany: State University of New York Press.

Ramsey, Paul. 1968, 1983. *The Just War: Force and Responsibility*. Savage, MD: Rowman & Littlefield.

VanVoorst, Robert E. 1996. *Anthology of World Scriptures*. 2nd edition. Belmont, CA: Wadsworth.

X, Malcolm. 1973. *The Autobiography of Malcolm X* (as told to Alex Haley). New York: Ballantine.

PART III
THE WAY OF ALL THE EARTH

INTRODUCTION

We are nearing the end of a journey that began with Gilgamesh and Socrates and led us to Mohandas Gandhi, Thich Nhat Hanh, Martin Luther King, Jr., Abraham Joshua Heschel, and Malcolm X. Along the way we have noted similarities and differences in the stories and spiritual practices of these figures. We have also noted similarities and differences among their ethical visions. In particular we have noted differences, East and West, with regard to understanding eco-justice and social justice and with regard to the relation between religion and ethics.

In Part III we bring our journey to a conclusion by looking for ways to reconcile these differences as far as possible. In chapter 9 we explore the ecofeminist critique of the masculine bias in religious ethics and examine Buddhist and Christian ecofeminist alternatives. Then, in chapter 10, we explore the possibility that ecofeminism may provide a reconciling synthesis between East and West, opening up a post/modern spirituality and ethics that could be "the way of all the earth," seeking justice and care not just for human life, but for the total ecology of the web of life in which we live, move and have our being.

9
FEMINIST AUDACITY AND THE ETHICS OF INTERDEPENDENCE

In this chapter we turn to a discussion of the stories of women, the missing voices of women in religious ethics, and how their inclusion can change things. The spirituality of both Buddhists and Christians, says Catherine Keller, has assumed that women's spiritual task was the same as that of men – the heroic task of self-sacrifice on behalf of others (i.e., becoming selfless). But, as both she and Carol Gilligan point out, men are, from early on, raised to develop strong egos that must be tempered by "selflessness," whereas women's spiritual task is the opposite, to develop a sense of self. Because women have typically been raised to sacrifice themselves for the sake of their relationships to others (family, spouse, children), they have not developed a strong sense of self. Both their bodily and social experience, as childbearers and child-rearers, reinforced a sense not of autonomy but of relationality or interdependence within the web of life. Both Buddhist and Christian spiritualities that call for total selflessness or "emptying of self" (sunyata and kenosis) have consistently led to the suppression of the voices of women. Feminist spirituality can bring a mediating voice to the dialogue among religions by balancing interdependence with audacity – the audacity to call into question the spirituality of "life through death" of the self. Carol Gilligan suggests that women need to balance their relational ethic of care with a masculine ethic of justice as two complementary elements of one ethic. In this composite ethic men need to learn to temper their sense of autonomy and affirm their interdependence with all things, and women, already sensitive to interdependence, need to assert their autonomy as selves. Justice requires that the expression of care in relationships be reciprocal. Therefore women need to have the audacity to find their own voice in masculine–feminine relationships. In this context, the life stories and spiritualities of Joanna Macy and Rosemary Ruether offer us feminist models of Buddhist and Christian ethics of eco-justice (combining audacity and interdependence) that integrate the Eastern emphasis on the continuity (relationality) between humanity and nature with the Western emphasis on social justice, helping us to realize that violence against nature is also violence against human nature and human dignity – and vice versa. Their lives and thought offer us the possibility of seeing feminist experience and thought as a bridge between Eastern and Western forms of religious ethics – a bridge that both complements and corrects the legacy of the Gandhian tradition of non-violent civil disobedience. Comparative reflections on all of this are deferred to the next and final chapter which explores the possibilities of an emerging ethic and spirituality we might call "the way of all the earth."

The Feminist Challenge to the Myths of Life through Death

Two women who were prostitutes came to the king [Solomon] and stood before him. The one woman said, "Please, my lord, this woman and I live in the same house; and I gave birth while she was in the house. Then on the third day after I gave birth, this woman also gave birth. We were together; there was no one else with us in the house, only the two of us were in the house. Then this woman's son died in the night, because she lay on him. She got up in the middle of the night and took my son from beside me while your servant slept. She laid him at her breast, and laid her dead son at my breast. When I rose in the morning to nurse my son, I saw that he was dead; but when I looked at him closely in the morning, clearly it was not the son I had borne." But the other woman said, "No, the living son is mine, and the dead son is yours." The first said, "No, the dead son is yours, and the living son is mine." So they argued before the king. Then the king said, "The one says, 'This is my son that is alive, and your son is dead'; while the other says, 'Not so! Your son is dead, and my son is the living one.'" So the king said, "Bring me a sword," and they brought a sword before the king. The king said, "Divide the living boy in two; then give half to the one, and half to the other." But the woman whose son was alive said to the king – because compassion for her son burned within her – "Please, my lord, give her the living boy; certainly do not kill him!" The other said, "It shall be neither mine nor yours; divide it." Then the king responded: "Give the first woman the living boy; do not kill him. She is his mother." (I Kings 3: 16–27)

In the face of life and death decisions, the above story, as Carol Gilligan notes, illustrates an important theme in feminist ethics – a theme that will be made clear in due course. One of the striking things about the religious traditions and their stories, as we have retold them, is the absence of stories about women. There are, of course, stories of women in every religious tradition, and some of them are quite surprising and inspiring. And yet the central figures in every one of the great religions of the world are males – Moses, Jesus, Muhammad, Siddhartha, and so on. In telling the stories of the traditions as we have, therefore, we have not distorted the way these traditions have passed on their own stories. We have simply reflected the actual male bias that exists in the world's major religions. The reasons for this bias are both simple and complex. The simple answer is that the civilizations in which these religions emerged were themselves patriarchal, and so it should be no surprise that their religious leaders and religious interpreters should, by and large, be men who see the world with a male bias.

But why have civilizations been dominated for the most part by men? Speculating on the beginnings of human societies, the answer, it has been suggested, has a lot to do with the superior physical strength of males and the dependency of women as childbearers on men as providers. In addition, the great transition from tribal to urban life brought about a profound devaluation of the feminine. Urban life brought with it an awareness of differences that led to a profound individuation of human identity (i.e., the awareness of self), which, in turn, created the threefold crisis of mortality, morality, and meaning that we outlined in chapter 1.

This transition had a powerful impact on the meaning of "male" and "female." For, in tribal cultures where identity was collective and embedded in the rhythms of nature, death did not create a rupture in the community. It simply marked the elevation of one's status to that of a sacred ancestor who provided guidance and protection to the community as it lived in harmony with the rhythms of nature. In such cultures, religions were oriented to rituals of fertility that affirmed the continuity of life, and women as life-givers were affirmed in the image of the divine goddess as the source of life and fertility in all its goodness.

However, once identity became individuated, as it was for Gilgamesh, death became an immense crisis, threatening the loss of "self." Life, and the giving of life, were no longer seen as unambiguously good, especially in the new cities, where the care of the extended tribal family gave way to anonymity. In the urban environment injustice proliferated and life came to be experienced as a process of suffering which ended in old age, sickness, and death. To have a body was to have a destiny that ended in suffering and death, and since bodily existence came from women, the feminine became identified with death rather than life. The realm of the goddess – feminine sexuality and fertility – was associated with the earth, the body, and rhythms of nature that end in decay and death. In contrast, the masculine became associated with the sky god who lives in the eternal realm of the heavens, free of all change, decay, and death. Women, tied to the rhythms of nature by their menstrual cycle, had experiential knowledge of their interdependence with all things. Men, sharing no such experience, sought autonomy, mastery, and independence.

The masculine worldview became one that divided reality into two realms, the earthly and the heavenly, and the ideal of the holy "man" became the ascetic, the one who denied the desires of the body and renounced feminine contact and all sexual pleasure in order to transcend the body and death. The feminine, erotic desire, ignorance/sin (as selfish desire), and death came to be interlocked in the masculine psyche. Spiritual liberation or salvation was associated with the death of the self, constituted by desire – by the seduction of the earth, the world – the feminine. In the traditions of India (Hinduism and Buddhism), governed by the myth of liberation, it was once thought that you had to live your last incarnation as a man in order to achieve final liberation from all death and rebirth. And if, as we have suggested, the great world religions all emerged to deal with the crisis of identity created by urbanization, then it should be no surprise that similar attitudes prevailed in the other great religions of the world.

With this in mind, we wish to return to the hypothesis put forward by the Buddhist scholar Masao Abe which we discussed in the Introduction to Part II and in each chapter's "comparative reflections." For Abe argues that full spiritual realization requires the death of the self – a phenomenon he found present in different ways in Buddhism and Christianity, but absent in Judaism. In his view, both Buddhism and Christianity express the most profound religious insight – the myth of life through death. The self must be annihilated in order to realize the truth that liberates or saves. In Buddhism, he suggested, this death of the self (the realization of no-self) carries one beyond ethics, while in Christianity it becomes the basis for ethics.

In chapter 2 we suggested that the myth of life through death too often functioned as a rationale for unquestioning obedience to higher authority in promoting mass death in the twentieth century. The total surrender of the self, achieved through the spiritual death of the self, we suggested, is ethically dangerous. As we shall see now, feminist ethicists share this concern and do so eloquently. The feminist scholar Catherine Keller, for instance, has taken deep exception to Masao Abe's position and her objections will help us see the stories we have been exploring in Part II from a new perspective; namely, from the perspective of those who have been largely left out of the storytelling process until now – women. For it is not just the ancient stories that silenced women: even the life stories of the holy "men" we have reviewed in this book (such as Gandhi, King, and Malcolm X) seem to leave women in their traditional subservient roles. In fact, the feminist movement emerged in its strength in the generation *after* Martin Luther King, Jr. and Malcolm X, partly in response to a sense that justice for women was being left out of the struggle for human liberation. If the 1960s were dominated by the racial struggle for liberation, the 1970s were the years in which women's liberation found its voice and women began to tell their own stories. In this chapter we will let Catherine Keller and Carol Gilligan set the agenda and then we will turn to two other women who have their own stories to tell – Joanna Macy and Rosemary Ruether. Macy and Ruether belong to a generation whose lives overlapped with those of King, Heschel, Malcolm X, and Nhat Hanh, giving birth to the ecofeminist movement.

Keller takes issue with Masao Abe by suggesting that a feminist can only enter into a Buddhist–Christian dialogue with a sense of irony, for the most obvious common ground between Buddhism and Christianity is not kenosis and sunyata (the "emptying" or death of the self), as Abe suggests, but patriarchalism. The subordination of women in both traditions, she suggests, is so taken for granted that it tends to be overlooked. Consequently "it simply continues." What she is looking for is some sign of a change of heart – a "post-patriarchal enlightenment." Reminding Masao Abe that he himself calls for "mutual transformation" as a goal of dialogue between religions, Keller has the audacity, or chutzpah, to challenge both religions to abandon their patriarchalism. The goal, she says, is to subvert "masculine socio-cultural dominance" by "unmasking the religious justifications of dominance."

> We recognize in the absence of women among the spiritual leadership of both Christianity and Buddhism a cause of shameful waste and suffering, attributable not to lack of talent but to deprivation of opportunity. And we have come also to realize that the specific oppression of women, as the most universal form of social subjugation, cannot be understood in isolation from the intertwined sufferings imposed by injustice toward all who live in situations of social vulnerability – including not only the poor and those of color, but the earth and all its creatures. Patriarchy, as the original and most pervasive model of systematic exploitation, names the superstructure depending upon all of these sufferings. So any feminist spirituality unfolds in and through an enlarged, politicized, and yet intricately particularized web-consciousness. (Keller 1990: 103)

Keller notes that the story of the self-emptying (kenosis) of Christ to take on the form of a servant, suffer, and die for the sins of others in obedience to the divine will, even unto death on the cross (Philippians 2: 1–11), has deep roots in the Hebrew tradition of the prophets and their call for repentance and justice. In particular, it draws on the suffering servant images of the prophet Isaiah. But she is worried that the spirituality of kenosis (and its Buddhist parallel, sunyata, or emptiness) offers little hope of justice for women in either Christianity or Buddhism.

Even though she finds the Buddhist notion of emptiness as interdependence congenial to a feminist understanding of the interrelatedness of all things, she finds its use in Buddhism problematic for women. On the positive side, there is an affinity between Buddhist emptiness (sunyata) and the notion of *the web of life,* which is fundamental to feminist thought. It is a view "in which selfhood cannot be construed in isolation from its network of relationships." Indeed, "the Chinese Hua-yen Buddhists drew inspiration from the image of Indra's net to express the 'intercausation and interpenetration' of all beings. The realization of such causal interrelatedness, as Abe explains, results in the realization that all things are empty, sunya. For there is no-thing and no-self – if to be a thing or a self means to have a substantial, separate, and self-identically enduring existence" (Keller 1990: 103–4). On the negative side, Abe goes on to interpret sunyata as requiring a state of absolute selflessness, and such a notion, Keller argues, simply reinforces patriarchalism in religion.

"Abe's interpretation of the kenosis passage in Philippians," Keller argues, "brings us (inadvertently) to the very heart of women's disenchantment with traditional religious categories, but also of our hope for certain radical revisions" (1990: 105). For he interprets the passage, as Christians generally have, as advocating absolute selflessness and humility. This requires a total emptying of the self in servanthood to the needs of others and obedience unto death. Historically, such rhetoric has been oppressive, intended to keep women in their place. This kind of spirituality views "prideful self-assertion" as a universal human problem to be cured by achieving selflessness. But that is a misperception, for while such a view is applicable to male identity in most societies, just the opposite is the case for most women. That is, women have typically been raised to accept the subordination of their selves and their desires to those of men, and to the needs of their families. As a result they have never had an opportunity to develop a strong sense of self, a separate and independent identity. The deepest problem of women is not pride but absence of a sense of self and self-worth. Fundamental to feminist thought is the saying of the nineteenth-century feminist Elizabeth Cady Stanton that for women "self-development is a higher duty than self-sacrifice."

The male notion of an independent ego-self, says Keller, is precisely what Buddhism labels as "ignorance" and Christianity as "sin." Feminists concur in this. The goal of feminists is not to develop strong male-type egos in retaliation for male dominance, nor to accept the traditional model of subordination, but rather to develop a new model of self – the relational self. For women are more deeply in touch with the rhythms of nature, and the dependencies of nurture, through their bodies, and experience themselves as embodied in interdependence with all things. The danger of Buddhist–Christian dialogue, as Keller sees it, is that women will get the worst of both worlds. "How can the two patriarchies, with their common problem of the inflationary male ego and their common solution of selflessness, fail to redouble the oppressive irrelevance of the 'world religions' for the liberation of women? Or indeed of any persons already suffering from their internalization of the role of the victim?" (1990: 106).

A feminist ontology will affirm the interdependence of self, argues Keller, without accepting the Buddhist notion that therefore the self is unreal and that the language of "self" must be negated. A feminist notion of self resists both the isolated ego-self, on the one hand, and the mystical "oceanic feeling" which obliterates all awareness of difference, on the other hand. Feminism, rather, affirms otherness as integral to the experience of self. Interrelationality undermines both dualism and monism.

A feminist understanding of relationality, Keller argues, leads to an ethic of responsibility that sees evil as "the effect upon the network of relationships of an individual or systemic denial of interrelatedness itself. In [Rosemary] Ruether's words, 'sin exists precisely in the distortion of relationality, including relation to

oneself'" (1990: 110). In this respect, Abe's suggestion that the religious perspective must transcend the ethical dimension (the "horizontal" dimension of
history) is, for Keller, a violation of the indissoluble relationality of all things.
Our relations, our actions, and our responsibilities are real, particular, and con-
textual, and cannot be absolved by an appeal to universal karma, universal greed
(avidya), or universal emptiness (sunyata), as understood from a "higher" (ver-
tical dimension of transcendence) plane, as Abe wishes to do. When everyone
is declared responsible for suffering (including the victims of Auschwitz and
Hiroshima), then no one feels responsible. And in every major religious tradition responsibility must be accepted for the exclusion of women's voices and
must lead to their inclusion. In Keller's view, the recovery of women's voices
and women's stories could transform and liberate all religious traditions so as to
make them part of the solution rather than part of the problem. What is required is the emptying of each tradition of its patriarchy.

The Feminist Alternative: Interdependence and the Ethics of Care

One of the groundbreaking books on feminist theory in ethics was written by
Carol Gilligan and published under the title *In a Different Voice* in 1982. "I
began writing *In a Different Voice*," she says, "in the early 1970s, at a time of
resurgence in the Women's Movement. College students now are incredulous
when I say that in the spring of 1970, at the height of the demonstrations
against the Vietnam war, after the shooting of students at Kent State University
by members of the National Guard, final exams were canceled at Harvard and
there was no graduation. For a moment, the university came to a stop and the
foundations of knowledge were opened for reexamination" (Gilligan 1982: ix).
Then, in 1973, the US Supreme Court decision *Roe v. Wade* gave women the
right to choose an abortion. Suddenly women were given a voice in their own
destiny.

  The struggle for women to speak in their own voices was a difficult one, for
women were not used to having a voice in their own destiny. Women were
raised to see their role in life as that of serving the needs of others, especially
their spouses and their families. A virtuous woman was a woman who sacrificed
herself for others. And a virtuous woman was not supposed to have any other
desire but this. Thus even an occasional thought concerning what "I want"
would be suppressed in a cascade of self-guilt, if it ever managed to emerge to
the surface of consciousness at all. Women had internalized a masculine ideal of
the feminine and allowed it to smother their own inner voice. It was an ideal
that said that in order to have a husband and a family, in order to have human
relationships, one must be completely selfless. One must suppress one's own
desires and individuality and live only for others.

The feminism of the 1970s and 1980s was about women finding their voice. And this discovery has proved unsettling in virtually every area of human life, including religion and ethics. For to introduce women's voices changes how a story is told, because it changes who tells the story, including the stories of religions and of ethics. Men who have told the story of civilization and spiritual realization tell it as a heroic journey of separation from family and loved ones, an adventure of exploration and conquest in which the hero sacrifices himself in order to save civilization. As a model for men's stories, the heroic journey (such as we find in *The Epic of Gilgamesh*, for example) requires the male to mature through a process of separation (from mother, from family, and eventually, all others). This requires the repression of those emotions that sustain relationships in order to achieve autonomy and the skills needed to conquer the world.

Human development theory in psychology, Gilligan argues, has from the beginning been held captive by the masculine myth of the heroic journey. And she demonstrates this in the work of Freud, Piaget, Erickson, and her own mentor, Lawrence Kohlberg, who developed a model of the progressive stages of moral development. The problem with all their developmental theories, argues Gilligan, is that they were derived from the study of males and take male experience as normative, and so treat female behavior as deviant if it does not conform to the male model. Thus, for example, motivational theories have tended to posit human behavior as shaped by "hope of success" and "fear of failure." But studies of women have shown that they often exhibit "fear of success." From a perspective of male experience, such a fear could only mean there is a failure to develop the appropriate level of psychological maturity. But from the perspective of women's experience, success that is the result of competition leads inevitably to "social rejection and loss of femininity." Women are not supposed to be aggressive and competitive and to be so will lead to their being perceived as less than feminine, and therefore, as not good candidates for marriage and family.

In Kohlberg's theory, moral development proceeds through six stages organized into three progressive levels: pre-conventional, conventional and post-conventional. Children begin at the pre-conventional level where their moral decisions are egocentrically based on self-advantage, especially calculating a fear of punishment and hope for reward. As children mature they begin to develop a social contract that brings them into the conventional level where their goal is to be a good person as that is defined by their community. Here they seek the approval of others and learn to make sacrifices for the good of the group as a whole. Finally, as the children grow into mature persons, they arrive at a level where moral judgments are made through the use of logical and autonomous abstract reasoning, based on universal principles with respect to equality and reciprocity. At this level individuals are capable of asking not only what society approves of, but whether what it approves of is just and fair. When men and women are compared on this scale in their responses as to how they would solve a specific moral problem, men will typically operate at the third level of rational justice. Some women will also respond in rational terms, third-level terms, but women more often seem to be stuck at the second level of social agreement. Hence, on Kohlberg's scale, women are typically judged to be less ethically mature than men.

Gilligan reports that when 11-year-old males and females were asked whether a man could be permitted to steal a drug he cannot afford to buy, in order to save the life of his wife, the answers revealed the different patterns of ethical thought among males and females. For example, one young male's response was yes, "because life is worth more than money, noting that the druggist can always make up the loss with a profit elsewhere while the man's wife is irreplace-able." One young female's response was to suggest that the man should seek other options besides stealing, like telling the full story to the druggist to awaken his compassion, or borrowing the money, or appealing to others for help. And when asked why the man should not steal she responded: "If he stole the drug, he might save his wife then, but if he did, he might have to go to jail, and then his wife might get sicker again, and he couldn't get more of the drug" (Gilligan 1982: 28).

Kohlberg would rate the female's response as less mature and developed than the male's because she seems to be stuck at the conventional level and has not yet arrived at the level of abstract autonomous reasoning based on principles. Gilligan, however, suggests that what is going on in these diverse responses is alternative frames of reference for approaching ethics. Males tend to approach ethical problems as a matter of rational calculus. The young male sees the prob-lem as a matter of calculating the comparative worth of things at a level of philosophical abstraction. When he makes a decision he is assuming his per-sonal autonomy and bases his decision on principle. He sees the world as a world of autonomous, separate individuals who must balance their rights and duties. The young female tends to see the ethical problem as having to do with how to sustain relationships and the responsibilities they entail. She contextualizes the judgment in terms of the concrete ongoing network of human relationships needed to sustain life, instead of abstracting the judgment from the situation as the young man does. He thinks mathematically in terms of exchange value in abstraction from the particulars of the situation. She thinks narratively in terms of the total environment or ecology of relationships. He thinks in terms of justice and fairness, she in terms of relationships and care. He thinks in terms of the hierarchy of principles and of social order, she thinks in terms of the web of life, interdependence, and equality. As a result, he advocates action (i.e., steal-ing the drug) based on principle, while she worries that the act of stealing is a short-term solution that will lead later to the loss of the very relationship it seeks to sustain.

From Gilligan's perspective these two views (the male ethic of justice and human rights and the female ethic of relationality and care) are not contradic-tory, but complementary. Each has something the other needs. The problem is that when developmental theories are posited only on male experience this is not apparent. To the degree that Kohlberg's developmental model is taken as normative, female perspectives can only seem inferior. The problem is the heroic narrative implicit in Kohlberg's theory. It describes the male's journey through life but not the female's. Men start off dependent on their mothers, learn to separate and become autonomous, and go out to conquer the world. Only later, if at all, do they learn intimacy and caring. By the time a man learns these things his children are likely to be grown up. Were it not for the mother, they would not have the experience of intimacy and caring they need for their own growth and maturation. Women, too, start off dependent on their mothers, but are raised to continue rather than break the relationship, so as to develop their skills in intimacy and caring. Only later in life, typically when the family is grown, do they learn to separate and develop autonomy. According to Gilligan, what is needed are complementary theories of male and female moral development that reflect these differences rather than a male-dominated theory that obscures them.

Gilligan is struck by the role of violence in the competitive psyche of males in contrast to the relational psyche of women. She reports contrasting stories used by men and women to interpret a rather peaceful scene, a picture of a couple sitting on a bench, overlooking a river near a bridge. Both men and women were asked to provide a story interpreting what was going on in the scene. In one study, 21 percent of the men told stories that involved violence, such as rape, homicide, suicide, and kidnapping. In contrast, none of the woman's stories had violence in them. Follow-up studies showed that men projected violence into situations depicting intimacy whereas women projected violence into situations suggesting competitive achievement. These findings, she suggests, reflect the differences in life experience between men and women. Men are raised to seek autonomy and find the intimacy of relationships threatening. Women are raised to seek relationships and find competitive achievement threatening. Men are taught to climb the ladder of success to the top of the hierarchy. This requires competition and separation. Women are encouraged to be the center of all connections, holding the family together. This requires eschewal of competition because it brings separation. Each finds identity and security in what the other fears.

These and other findings also suggest why men are more likely to see conflict resolution as a process requiring the use of violence to subdue an opponent, while women are more likely to seek non-violent solutions through communications oriented toward repairing relationships. Men see doing harm as the result of doing something aggressive toward another, while women see harm as failing to meet the needs of another – a failure to relate to the other. Although the difference may be more psychological than substantive, for men, responsibility tends to be interpreted as *not doing* (a restriction on their autonomy) what one desires in order to promote the good of others, while for women, responsibility means *doing* (acknowledging their relationality) what others are counting on them to do, regardless of what one wants.

In Kohlberg's developmental model moral maturity is reached when moral reasoning is based on abstract rational autonomy that champions the heroic task of sacrificing oneself for others – of doing the selfless and responsible thing in protecting the rights of all individuals. Autonomous persons need to sacrifice their egos in seeking justice through securing the rights of others. From Gilligan's perspective this is true for men, but not for women. For women, moral maturity occurs not through sacrificing themselves but through realizing that justice requires the affirmation of a self without which no relationship is possible. She argues that *the ethics of justice and rights* and *the ethics of relationality and care* are complementary and mutually require each other.

For ethical maturity to occur, both men and women need to affirm the truth of interdependence, but in different ways. Men need to discover that their self only occurs in interdependence with other selves and women need to discover that interdependence requires them to have a self. Not all self-regard is selfishness. If justice demands that all selves have dignity and rights, then the moral agent herself must be included in ethical reflection.

In women's development, the absolute of care, defined initially as not hurting others, becomes complicated through a recognition of the need for personal integrity. This recognition gives rise to the claim for equality embodied in the concept of rights, which changes the understanding of relationships and transforms the definition of care. For men, the absolutes of truth and fairness, defined by the concepts of equality and reciprocity, are called into question by experiences that demonstrate the existence of differences between other and self. Then the awareness of multiple truths leads to a relativizing of equality in the direction of equity [i.e., to each according to their individual need] and gives rise to an ethic of generosity and care (Gilligan 1982: 166).

Gilligan envisions a postconventional morality that would call into question and transcend the morality of masculine social convention.

> The moral imperative that emerges repeatedly in interviews with women is an injunction to care, a responsibility to discern and alleviate the "real and recognizable trouble" of this world. For men, the moral imperative appears rather as an injunction to respect the rights of others and thus to protect from interference the rights to life and self-fulfillment. . . . Development for both sexes would therefore seem to entail an integration of rights and responsibilities through the discovery of the complementarity of these disparate views. . . . In the development of a postconventional ethical understanding, women come to see the violence inherent in inequality, while men come to see the limitations of a conception of justice blinded to the differences in human life. (Gilligan 1982: 100)

What a feminist perspective brings to the masculine approach is an emphasis on thinking contextually and narratively rather than emphasizing the logical priority of one principle over another. It encourages a consequential and relational way of thinking rather than the violence of principled thinking. In this respect, Gilligan reflects on the paradoxical violence of Gandhi. Drawing on Erik Erikson's study of Gandhi, she points out that Gandhi's life of non-violence was tainted by the psychological violence he expressed toward his wife and children. Erikson notes that Gandhi describes himself as a "cruelly kind husband" who harassed his wife into seeing the world as he did. Paradoxically, Gilligan argues, Gandhi was willing to "sacrifice people to truth" much the way Abraham was willing to sacrifice his son to prove his faith. "Both men . . . stand in implicit contrast to the woman who comes before Solomon and verifies her motherhood by relinquishing truth in order to save the life of her child" (1982: 104–5). "An ethic of justice proceeds from the premise of equality – that everyone should be treated the same – an ethic of care rests on the premise of nonviolence – that no one should be hurt" (1982: 174). It was an audacious ethical moment when, out of a deeper sense of obligation and responsibility to her son, the mother gave up her claim to her child in order to save his life. The lives of the mother and child were so interdependent that there could be no violence against the one that was not also violence against the other. It is doubtful if there can be an ethic of non-violence without a capacity for intimacy based on mutual respect and equality between men and women that grows out of their personal awareness of interdependence. Thus, Gilligan argues, it is doubtful that there can be an ethic of non-violence without the inclusion of the feminist perspective. There can be no justice without an ethic of care.

Life Story: Joanna Macy and Buddhist Ecofeminism

Life story

Joanna Rogers (Macy) was born in Los Angeles, California on May 2, 1929, and grew up in the greater New York City area. Her father was an investment broker, but his father and grandfather were Presbyterian ministers. Her primary and secondary education had an international flavor, as she was one of the few American students in a French-speaking school in New York City. She does not remember her childhood as a happy one, except for the summers when she was able to escape the concrete jungle of New York's streets to enjoy the rural life on her grandfather's farm. There her best friends were "two trees and a horse" (Ingram 1990: 143). As a child, she had a transforming religious experience in that she recognized the many ways that Jesus was still being crucified in the present day. She came away from this experience seeing the crucifixion in all the suffering and injustice in the world. And from that time on she knew her life was not her own.

Joanna went on to major in biblical history at Wellesley College, with ambitions of becoming a missionary to Africa. During her college years she corresponded with Albert Schweitzer and on one occasion served as his interpreter when he was in New York City. Their paths crossed again, years later in France. However, as she progressed in her college education she began to have doubts about Christianity and its claims to absolute truth. This led to a period of atheism in her life. In her senior year she went to France to study Marxism and the French Communist Party under a Fulbright scholarship. This later led to a job in Washington as an intelligence analyst. About this time, she also became involved in the civil rights movement and worked to have an impact on housing discrimination. In Washington she met her husband, Fran Macy, a Soviet affairs analyst. They married and eventually had three children and his work led them to live in Europe for many years. An important turning point in Joanna's life came when her husband turned down a job in Moscow and accepted a staff position with the Peace Corps in India.

In the mid-1960s they moved to New Delhi, where Joanna began the journey that led her to embrace the teachings of the Buddha. In India she made contact with Tibetan refugees and began to gain insight into the Buddhist path, especially as a result of a meditation retreat in the Himalayas. After India, they took another assignment with the Peace Corps in Africa and then finally returned to Washington, where Joanna became heavily involved in anti-Vietnam War activities and also worked with the National Urban League to improve the legal rights of blacks.

In 1973 Fran and Joanna moved to Syracuse, New York, where Joanna began work on a doctorate in Religious Studies at Syracuse University. It was in the context of her graduate studies in religion that Joanna first encountered general systems theory and began to explore the relationship between it and the Buddhist doctrine of dependent co-arising. This became the topic of her doctoral dissertation, which was eventually published under the title *Mutual Causality in Buddhism and General Systems Theory* (1991b). Then, in 1976, Joanna made a four-month pilgrimage to India and Sri Lanka. In Sri Lanka she met A. T. Ariyaratne, the founder of the Gandhi-influenced Sarvodaya social action movement. She later returned to work with Sarvodaya for a year and wrote a book on the movement entitled *Dharma and Development* (1983a). Back in the US Joanna began her despair and empowerment workshops for people concerned about nuclear and environmental issues. This work is described in *Despair and Personal Power in the Nuclear Age* (1983b). And in 1988 her work on nuclear issues led to the nuclear guardianship project, which proposes mindful, long-term monitoring of the radioactive materials generated in the process of nuclear power and weapons production. She began organizing councils of people to occupy nuclear missile sites with a view to converting them into sacred places of pilgrimage – the monasteries of the future – where citizens keep vigil. They will monitor radioactivity, remind people of the contamination and death caused by our generations' nuclear folly, and transform these sites of continuing peril into places affirming mutual responsibility for sustaining the web of life.

Spirituality and ethics

The third turning of the wheel: from ego-self to eco-self

What is destroying our world, says Joanna Macy, is the illusion that every self is an independent individual with only accidental connections to other persons and other species. The cure for this is the Buddha's enlightenment insight that the self is empty, meaning it has no independent reality (svabhava). Buddhist practice brings the realization that one has no such separate self (anatta). Rather, all things co-arise in interdependence as part of the web of life. To realize anatta is to discover, as Thich Nhat Hanh has said, that the skin of our bodies is not the boundary of the self. Who we are is not defined by independence but by interdependence with all other beings who make up the universe.

To discover our radical interdependence with all things, says Joanna Macy, does not require a loss of our individuality. A body is not an undifferentiated unity but a unity in diversity. It is made up of many unique and different parts which are interdependent, and without which there could not be one body. Realization of this interdependence leads to an ethic of care and compassion. The truth of our interdependence, she says, is poetically captured in the Buddhist imagery of Indra's Net, which is a kind of cosmic canopy in which each being is imagined as a jewel at a node in the net that reflects all other nodes, even as all other nodes reflect each other. "That is what we find when we listen to the sounds of the Earth crying within us – that the tears that arise are not ours alone; they are the tears of an Iraqi mother looking for her children in the rubble; they are the tears of a Navajo uranium miner learning that he is dying of lung cancer. We find we are interwoven threads in the intricate tapestry of life, its deep ecology" (1991a: 33).

Joanna Macy sees history as passing through three turning points. (1) In the primal origins of the human race, tribal peoples experienced the world around them as a living presence through a kind of "participation mystique." There was no sharp separation between self and world but continuity and oneness. (2) Then, self-consciousness emerged, creating a kind of distance between self and world – a distance that is necessary in order to observe regularities, make judgments, and choose. (In this text we have called this the process of doubling produced by urbanization.) With this stage the lonely heroic journey of the ego begins (as exemplified in *The Epic of Gilgamesh,* for instance). While the emergence of ego separated humans from each other and from nature, she argues, it made possible such gifts as scientific observation, trial by jury, and the Bill of Rights. (3) In the third movement, having achieved the rich benefits of separation, "we are ready to return. . . . Having gained distance and sophistication of perception, we can turn and recognize who we have been all along. Now it can dawn on us: we are our world knowing itself. We can relinquish our separateness. We can come home again – and participate in our world in a richer, more responsible and poignantly beautiful way than before, in our infancy" (1991a: 13–14).

In Joanna Macy's spiritual vision, there have been three turnings of the Wheel of Dharma – each meant to undo the illusion of separate self or "own-being" (svabhava). The first, carried out by Theravada Buddhism, was the message of dependent co-arising proclaimed by Siddhartha Gautama to undo the egoism of the self that came with expulsion from the participation mystique. The second was the emergence of Mahayana Buddhism to correct the scholastic individualism that later emerged in Theravada by teaching the "Perfection of Wisdom" (Prajnaparamita). Mahayana recovered the wisdom of emptiness and interdependence in its Bodhisattva ideal of selfless compassion. This Perfection of Wisdom is called the "Mother of All Buddhas." She embodies the deep feminine wisdom of relationality or interdependence. She is especially embodied in the female Bodhisattvas of Kuan-Yin and Tara. "Her gestures will recall this active, compassionate aspect; for the right arm is outstretched to help, and the right leg, no longer tucked up in the aloof serenity of the lotus posture, extends downward, in readiness to step into the world" (1991a: 113).

The Mother of All Buddhas, argues Macy, must not be confused with images of the goddess found in patriarchal cultures. Even Hinduism reflects the dualism of the male sky god and the feminine earth goddess, a dualism mirrored in eternal self and transient matter. In this model, consciousness, as the male principle, finds its self trapped in the female principle of nature or materiality. And it can only find liberation (moksha) in release from this material realm of samsara – whether the goddess assumes the form of Devi, Durga, or Kali:

> Whether adorned with peacock feathers or garlanded with skulls, she is the ceaselessly active one, *prakrti*, *maya*, *shakti*. She is the restlessness of primal matter, the fecund and cruel mother. As the creative power of the male gods, from whom she issues, she complements their pure, passive intelligence. The goddess is both indulgent [mother] and terrible [seductress]. . . . As a sexual partner, the woman tends to be seen as a dangerous and enfeebling seductress, a semen-stealer; but as a mother – the mother of a son, that is – she is revered and accorded prerogatives denied her as a person (1991a: 114).

These dual roles lead to the ambivalent masculine image of the goddess as "terrible mother" both revered for her nurturing qualities and feared for her lover's wrath – or else revered for the pleasure she offers and feared as the clinging mother who will not let go.

The spirituality of the terrible mother tends to result in either the way of hedonism or the way of asceticism. But the Mother of Perfect Wisdom offers the middle way, for mind and matter are not seen as opposites but as empty, which is to say "dependently co-arising," and therefore the goal is not to escape matter and the wheel of samsara but to embrace it in selfless compassion – a care for all beings.

The third turning of the Wheel of Dharma, according to Joanna Macy, is occurring in our own time. The categories in which people understand reality are changing radically and making us more ready for a non-dualistic spirituality such as that offered by the message of the Buddha. We are witnessing the dissolution of individualism and its replacement by an ecological way of understanding reality. The "self," Joanna Macy reminds us, is a "metaphoric construct" that until recently was equated with the boundaries of one's skin and focused on self-preservation and self-interest. That metaphoric understanding is now being replaced by "the ecological self or the eco-self, co-extensive with other beings and the life of our planet. It is what I will call 'the greening of the self'" (1991a: 183).

People are coming to the awareness that no individual can exist except in interdependence with the wider environment or web of life. The sun, the forests of trees that cover the earth, and my bodily self all co-exist in an interdependent web. I cannot be who I am apart from that interdependent web. My self and the rainforest, for instance, are one interdependent reality. Therefore, I am not an individual seeking to protect the rainforest, " 'I am part of the rainforest protecting itself. I am that part of the rainforest recently emerged into human thinking' [quoting a friend, John Seed]. This is what I mean by the greening of the self. It involves a combining of the mystical with the practical and the pragmatic, transcending separateness, alienation, and fragmentation. It is . . . 'a spiritual change,' generating a sense of profound interconnectedness with all life" (1991a: 184).

Mindfulness and interdependence

The threat of nuclear annihilation that has dominated the post-World War II era has awakened in human beings a deep grief and anger over the possible loss of our future as a species and as a planet. This grief unites us in a common plight across religions and cultures, and across the boundary between humans and nature. We shall all die together or all survive together. We are one in our interdependence. Indeed, from a scientific point of view, all reality is a web of interdependent, self-organizing systems. "Matter, energy and information . . . move through us and sustain us" (1991a: 188) – there is no clear boundary between self and world. This deeper sense of ecological self, Joanna Macy argues, can become the basis for a spirituality that can empower effective action. The spiritual insight of Buddhism converges with this new awareness to create the "third turning of the Wheel of Dharma." Even our anxiety, depression and anger over the fate of the world can serve to awaken in us the universal compassion of the Bodhisattva. Our pain for the world is a measure of that compassion. Our sense of interdependence with all the suffering of the world can serve to awaken in us the need for "social engagement" to alleviate that suffering. This spirituality carries us beyond all narrow self-interest. "It would not occur to me to plead with you, 'Oh, don't saw off your leg. That would be an act of violence.' It wouldn't occur to me because your leg is part of your body. Well, so are the trees in the Amazon rain basin. They are our external lungs. And we are beginning to realize that the world is our body" (1991a: 192).

The simple practice of mindfulness in following our breath can remind us of this truth. For the average breath contains "ten sextillion atoms" and with every breath each of us is exchanging atoms with all other beings so that we eventually breathe the same atoms breathed by every person who ever existed. " 'Your next breath will include a million odd atoms of oxygen and nitrogen once breathed by Pythagoras, Socrates, Confucius, Moses, Columbus, Einstein, or anyone you can think of . . . [including] the mighty blowings of the whale that swallowed Jonah, from the snorts of Mohammed's white mare, from the restive raven that Noah sent forth from the ark' " (1991a: 230, quoting scientist Guy Murchie). The truth of the web of life is that we breathe each other.

And we need to rediscover our interdependence not only through the practice of mindfulness but through story. We are in trouble, says Joanna Macy, "because we do not have a good story" (1991a: 214) – one that expands our sense of self not only in space but in time. We need to "reinhabit time and own our story as a species" – the story of Gaia, our living mother earth as the womb and web of all life. "We were present . . . in the primordial seas. We remember that in our mother's womb, where we wear vestigial gills and tail and fins for hands. We remember that" (1991a: 192). When we expand our story we begin to realize our ecological self and foster a spirituality of "deep ecology." And just as we must learn to expand our story into our evolutionary past, so must we also embrace our future. It is here that Joanna Macy's spirituality leads her to imagine our nuclear waste sites as the locations of the monasteries of the future. For if our willingness to create nuclear waste is rooted in an illusory sense of self as unrelated to the future of distant millennia, our willingness to commit to monitoring our nuclear legacy for coming generations will permit us to reclaim the future as part of our story – the story of who we are. Our self neither begins with our birth nor ends with our death. Our true self is past, present, and future in interdependence.

This consciousness is especially valuable for the social activist, we are told, because activists feel acutely how fast time is running out. But "when I began to focus on nuclear waste, when the longevity of its terrible toxicity dawned on me, when I glimpsed what this challenge would mean in terms of sustained human attention, the demands of time reversed themselves. The quest of how fast one could get something done was replaced with the question of how long . . . a period one could do it in. Will we actually be able to remember the danger of these wastes and protect ourselves for a hundred years, a thousand, a hundred thousand? . . . The horror of the waste was helping me inhabit time" (1991a: 217).

To spiritually inhabit time is to realize that "all the children for centuries to come are my children" (1991a: 222). So Joanna Macy imagines that citizen encampments around nuclear waste and nuclear weapons sites could herald the beginning of a new monastic movement. Just as the monasteries of the Middle Ages once kept learning and spiritual wisdom alive, so can these new monastic communities. They would form "Guardian Sites" that not only monitor the levels of radiation, decade after decade, century after century, but also serve humanity as a perpetual reminder to see all the children of the future as one's own. Such communities would exercise both a spiritual and moral guardianship of the future of humanity in its ecological reality.

> When you return to your communities to organize, saying no to the machinery of death and yes to life, remember your true identity. Remember your story, our story . . . You speak not only as yourself or for yourself. You were not born yesterday. You have been through many dyings and know in your heartbeat and bones the precarious, exquisite balance of life. Out of that knowledge you can speak and act. You will speak and act with the courage and endurance that has been yours through the long, beautiful aeons of your life story as Gaia. (1991a: 229)

Life Story: Rosemary Ruether and Christian Ecofeminism

Life story

Rosemary Ruether was born into a moderately prosperous family in 1936. Her father was an Anglican and a Republican. He had little influence on her development, nor did most of her relatives, who were "politically conservative, 'genteelly' chauvinist and racist!" (Snyder 1988: 3, Ruether 1981: 47). On the other hand, her mother, Rebecca, was Catholic, broad-minded, progressive, ecumenical in religious outlook, and very much a feminist. Her father was often away during her youth and his death, when she was 12, left Rosemary's upbringing solely to her mother. Rebecca raised her daughter as a Catholic and instilled in her a self-confidence and respect for her abilities as a person worthy of professional aspirations. Recounting a game they played, called "what you are going to do when you grow up," Ruether recalls that her mother "'would mention all kinds of fantastic possibilities, such as doctor, lawyer, merchant, or chief,' but I never remember once her mentioning wife or mother" (Ruether 1982: 111). She also taught Rosemary to reject "chauvinism and racism"(Snyder 1988: 5), embrace ecumenism, and to do both in the context of a feminism shared by Rebecca and her Protestant friends. Her uncle, David Sandow, who was Jewish, showed her that men can be nurturing and supportive of women as persons and "predisposed her to be sensitive to Jews and to question the prevailing assumptions Christians and Christianity had about them" (Snyder 1988: 7). A high-school teacher had a profound impact on Rosemary Ruether's understanding of racism, teaching her about the racism endemic to American society. All these experiences of Ruether's early life contradicted prevailing cultural norms. They had created in her a willingness to question what passed as truth and an openness to answers beyond the narrow framework of inherited dogmas of class and religion.

By the time she entered Scripps College, Ruether was well prepared to deal with the "several kinds of contradictions that challenged her heretofore 'elitist and secure' Catholic sensibilities" (Snyder 1988: 87, Ruether 1975: 38). As early as her freshman year she revealed her activist sensibilities, "organizing a protest . . . against an authoritarian way of teaching," which led to a warning from her French teacher: " 'Watch out, you will become a feminist!' " It was at Scripps that she experienced her first " 'negativity experience' of social contradiction" (Snyder 1988: 8). Its source was not the authoritarian teaching, but rather her discovery that the church had both endorsed slavery and was one of the last institutions to abandon serfdom. As she wrote later: "This certainly set my mind working about the credibility of the church as a moral teacher," but she was equally outraged by "a kind of implicit triumphalism in [her] Protestant professors" (Ruether 1982: 36). Her interest in religion and its contradictions led her to " 'set out to find the deeper and more intellectually challenging heritage of Catholicism'; one that would firmly contradict the unjust social positions that it held" (Snyder 1988: 9, Ruether 1982: 37). It also led her to graduate studies at Claremont and eventually her recognition as one of the leading theologians of the twentieth century.

In her junior year of college she met a graduate student in political science, Herman Ruether. They were soon married. Herman's professional activities as a political scientist led Rosemary to "read the newspapers more than she previously had" (Snyder 1988: 10). The newspapers, as well as the social disruptions of the 1960s, reawakened the progressive attitudes that had been instilled in Ruether by her mother. Moreover, the Second Vatican Council inspired her to become affiliated with ecumenical Catholics who were seeking to meld their monastic tradition with Zen Buddhism. She would come to be friends with another Catholic who sought to bring these two together – Thomas Merton. In 1965 she worked in the civil rights movement in Mississippi, which was "a watershed experience" for her, where she "learned to see [her] base in the black community and to look with fear on carloads of whites or white policemen"(Ruether 1982: 76). The following year she was given a position at predominantly black Howard University, where she taught theology for ten years. She later moved from Washington, DC to Garrett-Evangelical Theological Seminary in Evanston, Illinois. She was also active in the peace movement, supporting the Berrigan brothers and establishing close ties with the Community for Creative Non-Violence, "which combined peace activism with traditional Catholic worker activities like soup kitchens and medical and legal defense for the poor, . . . the right combination of persistence and good humor to save it from the sectarian styles of self-righteousness" (Ruether 1982: 41). During this time, Ruether published several books and numerous articles, establishing herself as a major theorist in liberation theology, feminist theology,

Christian antisemitism, and what would come to be called ecofeminism. Three of her most well-known books were fruits of this productive decade – *Liberation Theology: Human Hope Confronts Christian History and American Power*; *Faith and Fratricide: The Theological Roots of Anti-Semitism* (both 1974); and *New Woman, New Earth: Sexist Ideologies and Human Liberation* (1975). The titles of these important texts suggest something of the range of Ruether's scholarship as well as the interrelatedness of the problems with which she wrestles.

In these three texts, and throughout her work, Ruether exposes the deep-structural linkage of oppressive institutions and their common foundation in patriarchy. She explains her understanding of the situation and its development quite nicely in her preface to the twentieth anniversary edition of *New Woman, New Earth*: "My study of the Church Fathers . . . made me aware of the peculiar parallel in their thought, in which women as 'sinful body' and Jews as 'sinful materiality' seemed to express a similar projection of mind–body dualism. I began to speculate about the patterns of binary dualism in Christian thought in which women, Jews, Blacks, Indians, lower class people, and the earth itself were all located as variants of 'bad body,' over against a controlling white male Christian ruling class center" (Ruether 1995: xv–xvi). Although the initial catalyst to her recognition of the interrelatedness of oppressive systems seems to have been her study of Christian antisemitism, in recent years Ruether's work has focused more closely on issues directly related to feminist theology and ecofeminism. This has led to a further development of ethical themes first articulated in her 1975 book, *New Woman, New Earth*. Specifically, she has intensified her emphasis on the ecumenical dimensions of feminist theology and expanded her use of pagan concepts and motifs long neglected (if not in fact demonized) in Western religious thought.

Regarding feminism, she writes: "Feminists across religious, ethnic, racial, and class lines need to be clear that what unites us in a common struggle and social vision is far more important than the differences that distinguish us" (1995: xix). Regarding the use of pagan concepts and motifs in her work, she comments: "we must affirm the need for a new rapprochement between the historical and eschatological rituals of the Jewish and Christian traditions and the religions that have remained close to nature and sought to fit humanity into the rhythms and disciplines of nature . . . To deny these rhythms is to deny the concrete foundations of our continuing life. To teach contempt for these interconnections is to create a culture and technology that has brought us perilously close to destroying the very earth, air, and waters that sustain our being" (1986: 104–5). Here, as elsewhere, in her constructive deployment of pagan elements, she affirms that a genuine ethics of interdependence cannot ignore our intimate relationship with nature and our enduring kinship with all of life.

Rosemary Ruether has always been more than a critic. She has also been an articulate visionary of reform, renewal, redemption, and re-creation. And although she noted in 1995 that the problems she first diagnosed two decades earlier "seem no closer to being decisively ameliorated," she also charged all concerned with justice "to recommit ourselves to expressions of prophetic faith that inspire our work for justice, rather than a piety that sacralizes hatred and contempt for the victims" (1995: xvii, xviii–xix).

Spirituality and ethics

The question that Ruether raises as a woman and as a Christian in her book *Gaia and God: An Ecofeminist Theology of Earth Healing* is whether or not the God of monotheistic religions and Gaia, "the living and sacred earth, . . . [are] on speaking terms with each other?" Ecofeminism brings together ecology and feminism in order to critique the patriarchal structures of societies that have dominated and exploited both women and nature, for ecofeminism argues that the two are interlinked. While acknowledging that such patterns are global, being found in both Eastern and Western cultures, Ruether has assumed the specific task of an ecofeminist critique of Christianity and Western culture, because of the major impact this civilization has had on the rest of the world through its science and technology, as well as its political and economic outreach.

The task of such a critique, she says, is "earth healing, a healed relationship between men and women, between classes and nations, and between humans and the earth" (Ruether 1992: 1). This critique is an exercise in what she calls "deep ecology" that analyses the destructive "symbolic, psychological and ethical patterns" of relations between humans and nature, showing how "male domination of women and domination of nature are interconnected, both in cultural ideology and in social structures" (1992: 2). Once we understand this, she argues, we will realize that our relationship to the earth can only be healed by transforming our relationships between the sexes, races and nations. Eco-justice demands that we realize that the domination of the earth is deeply embedded in patterns of social domination. The one cannot be addressed without addressing the other.

The Greek, Latin and Hebrew cultural roots of Western civilization, she argues, coalesced between 500 BCE and 800 CE to form a patriarchal civilization that sacralized relations of domination over women and nature with the view that these expressed "the will of God." And yet these same traditions also contain elements of justice and love that can promote eco-justice, if they can be extricated from the systems of domination in which they are embedded. What is required is a critique that can give birth to a new cultural consciousness and a new spirituality capable of healing our relationship to nature and to each other. "We must see the work of eco-justice and the work of spirituality as interrelated, the inner and outer aspects of one process of conversion and transformation" (1992: 4).

Four cosmic stories

The human understanding of nature and of our relationship to nature, she reminds us, is socially constructed. In Western civilization three ancient mythic stories have had a major impact on our understanding, shaping our classical worldview concerning the spiritual and the physical, men and women, humans and nature, humans and the divine. A fourth, modern scientific narrative, she believes, offers a profound corrective.

The first of these was the Babylonian creation story, the Enuma Elish, in which the male deity, Marduk, slays the female dragon goddess, Tiamat, and creates the earth out of her dead body. The political background for this myth is the ascendancy of Babylonia over other city-states and their gods. The conquest of Marduk represents the rising of a new generation of rulers who overthrow the more ancient order that is reflected mythologically as a political struggle among the gods. In the earlier myths, "Apsu, the primordial begetter of all things, commingles in a single body with Tiamat, who bears all things." Creation is parthenogenic. Then the generation of Marduk comes along and introduces a new mode of creation through military violence. "Marduk extinguishes the life from Tiamat's body, reducing it to dead 'stuff' from which he then fashions the cosmos" (1992: 18). Those who were once gestated from the body of "the mother" now take possession of it as dead matter, creating a hierarchical social order with religious and political aristocracies at the top, followed by serfs and slaves – and women subservient at every level. Those at the top live well by exploiting those beneath them.

The second creation story to shape Western civilization is that of the people of Israel. There are two creation stories in the first three chapters of Genesis. In the first biblical story, God is masculine and "the Mother has been already reduced to formless but also malleable 'stuff' that responds instantly to the Creator's command" (1992: 19). Over seven days God creates the world, starting with light and darkness, heaven and earth, plants and animals, and finally he creates humans "male and female" equally in his own image and then rests on the seventh day. "In this story God is modeled after the intellectual power of the priestly class, who call all things into being through ritual naming" (1992: 20). Yet, unlike the Babylonian myth, leisure is not just for the upper classes, when God rests on the seventh day, so must all creatures (animal and human), and on every seventh day thereafter.

However, the second story of creation in Genesis 2 seems to undermine this story of equality. In it God creates Adam first and Eve out of a rib of Adam, specifically mandating the patriarchal structure of society. And yet, at the same time the story suggests that humans are not the owners of the earth but its stewards. They are given "dominion," not "domination," of the earth as their charge. They must care for the earth and answer to God for their actions.

The third creation story to shape Western civilization came from the Greeks – the philosophical myth created by Plato in the *Timaeus*. For Plato, the invisible eternal spiritual realm of mind gives birth to the visible temporal, physical realm through the mediation of the Demiurgos – a kind of cosmic artisan or creator who shapes things from dead "stuff." The cosmos is made, not begotten. The creator creates a geocentric and hierarchical cosmos. The earth is at the center of seven planetary spheres. Everything below the moon is physical and temporal, everything above it, spiritual and eternal. The creator then infuses the created world with a world-soul. Human souls come from the spiritual realm above and are infused into physical male bodies. If the originally male soul succeeds in controlling its bodily passions, it will return to the spiritual realm among the stars at death. If it fails, it will be reincarnated as a woman. Her task will be to succeed at controlling the passions and reincarnating as man who can then, at death, enter the spiritual realm. In the Platonic myth the mind is higher than the body even as male is higher than female, and the human is higher than the animal realm and nature. In the *Republic*, Plato elaborates further that society's hierarchy should be one in which philosophers are at the top, followed by warriors and then manual laborers.

When Christianity emerged it inherited elements from all three mythic worldviews in an ambiguous and paradoxical synthesis. In this synthesis, male is equated with spirit, reason, and the eternal (beyond nature), while female is equated with matter, emotion, and the temporal decay and death that belong to the natural order. Woman and nature represent the seductiveness of bodily pleasure that lures man away from the spiritual and eternal. "Female subordination is explained as both 'natural,' reflecting the inferiority of the female body and personality, and also as punishment for causing original sin" (i.e., Eve seducing Adam into eating from the forbidden tree of knowledge of Good and Evil in the Garden of Eden, resulting in all human beings having to suffer and die).

Nevertheless, these equations are ambivalent and ambiguous. For "women are also equal before God in regard to redemption" (1992: 29). This is further complicated by the body–soul dualism that stands in conflict with the Hebraic notion of resurrected body and redeemed earth. However, "operative Christian eschatology for the most part is one of an immortal soul that escapes from and is not limited by the mortal fate of earth's creatures" (1992: 30). Finally, Christianity introduced the concept that matter was created out of nothing. The created world is viewed as not divine, yet having no existence apart from the divine. Ruether concludes that the Christian synthesis of earlier worldviews left an ambiguous message: on the one hand, humans (Eve and therefore women first of all) are responsible for the fallen nature of creation as subject to decay and death (original sin), and yet humans are seen as spiritual beings who escape the fate of nature (through resurrection or eternal life), and therefore do not share a common destiny with the rest of nature.

The Western worldview was radically altered with the emergence of modernity, for science offered a new and competing one. In the early stages Newtonian science saw the world as dead "stuff" organized into a great machine. More recently, however, a biological, evolutionary, and organic cosmology has re-placed that view. The evolutionary worldview undermines the anthropocentrism of the earlier cosmologies and sees human life as the most recent development in an evolutionary process that is billions of years old. Humans have been around for only one-tenth of 1 percent of evolutionary history. We now understand ourselves as a part of the growing edge of the web of life, where nature has become conscious of itself. In the 4.5 billion years of evolution on earth, the elements that make up our bodies have circulated through other beings. "Like the great nature mystic, Francis of Assisi, we may learn to greet as our brothers and sisters, the wolf and the lamb, trees and grasses, fire and water, and even 'holy death,' the means by which all living things are returned to earth to be regenerated as new organisms" (48–9).

We have a new appreciation of the complex interdependence that makes life possible. "Through photosynthesis plants capture solar energy and transform it into organic molecules. Animals in turn sustain their life and growth by con-suming the carbohydrates . . . and proteins of plants," and so on (50). The web of life is endlessly interconnected and diversity is essential. The more variety there is in an ecosystem, the more "sustainable the interdependency," while the more simplified an ecosystem becomes, the more it is in danger of dying (54). The earth, it turns out, is not made up of dead "stuff" but is Gaia, a living organism composed of exquisite interdependencies.

Healing the earth

Ruether raises the question of whether, given its ancient suspicion of matter and the physical world, Christianity can play an important role in healing the earth. What is needed is an ecological spirituality that can sustain an ethic of earth healing. She sees important themes in two aspects of the Christian tradi-tion that she believes can be reclaimed for such an ethic: the covenantal and the sacramental.

The covenantal tradition of Mount Sinai, which lies at the heart of biblical religion, finds its most powerful ecological expression, for Ruether, in the tradi-tion of Jubilee. This tradition saw all creation as belonging to God and human beings as stewards. Human beings do not own the earth's resources nor other human beings, and there are limits placed on their relationship to both. Hence, just as every seventh day all of creation is to rest (males and females, owners and slaves, animals and fields, and so on), so every seventh year (the sabbatical year) the earth is to lie fallow and regenerate, and likewise all of its creatures – so that all may be renewed. Finally, after seven cycles of seven years, in the fiftieth year, a Jubilee year is declared. In the Jubilee year, all debt was to be forgiven, all property lost was to be restored, all slaves were to be set free, the land was to lie fallow, and all life was to be renewed. The Jubilee, Ruether argues, provides a model of redemptive eco-justice.

However, while this model is carried through from the Old Testament to the

New, its focus is diminished. In Luke's Gospel, Jesus announces in his very first public sermon (Luke 4) that he has come to proclaim "the year of the Lord's favor, in which the lame will walk, the blind will see and the captive will be set free." But animals and the land are not mentioned. The focus has been narrowed from eco-justice to human social justice. Nevertheless, the rudiments are there to build on for recovering the Jubilee tradition. "We need," says Ruether, "to learn to envision humans and nonhumans in biotic communities, in which a plurality of values needs to be balanced in relation to each other" (226). For "the covenantal vision recognizes that humans and other life forms are part of one family, sisters and brothers in one community of interdependence" (227).

The way to recover the full ecological integrity of the covenantal tradition in Christianity is to link it to the sacramental tradition that sees the physical world as expressing the grace of God through the cosmic body of Christ. The sacramental tradition (which emphasizes the importance of physical reality, e.g., bread, wine, water) has its roots in the New Testament understanding of the body of Christ as a cosmic reality embracing the whole of creation. The tradition was central to the medieval world, but largely neglected since the Protestant Reformation. Its recovery, Ruether argues, could represent an important resource for an ecofeminist ethic. The medieval Catholic vision synthesized elements of Platonic, Stoic, and Aristotelian philosophy with elements of the Hebraic view of God's creative activity as expressing his divine wisdom, which is feminine. We reviewed this strand of the tradition in discussing Paul's cosmic vision of Christ as the cosmic reality in which all things are created, held together and brought to fulfillment as one body (Colossians 1: 15–20) in chapter 7. In this tradition, a strong emphasis is placed in the "incarnation" of God in flesh, in the world, so that Christ comes to redeem the whole of creation, not just individual souls. Nature is not dead matter but alive with the presence of Christ. Nature too is the body of Christ. "The bodily becomes the sacramental bearer of the divine, and the divine deifies the bodily" (235).

Ruether argues that a new ecofeminist vision must be bold in synthesizing modern cosmological understandings into Christianity, much the way the medieval tradition incorporated pagan philosophy. She finds promising resources in the evolutionary theology of Teilhard de Chardin and the process philosophy of Alfred North Whitehead. Both are open to the insights of modern evolutionary biology and cosmology. In both, human beings are seen as organic parts of an interdependent universe in a process of continuous change and transformation. The human body is viewed as that place where nature gives birth to self-consciousness and both see the divine as manifested in the inner telos of nature to give birth to self-consciousness.

An ecological spirituality, Ruether argues, will need to be "built on three premises: the transience of selves, the living interdependency of all things, and the value of the personal in communion" (251). Ruether's position here brings her into close affinity with the Buddhist ecofeminism of Joanna Macy, for Ruether too rejects any notion of an eternal or immortal self and affirms uniqueness within interdependency. At the same time this position puts her in some tension with a central tenet of Christianity, namely, that every person is of infinite value and so not destroyed by death. Ruether argues that not only is the view of the survival of the self beyond death incommensurate with modern understandings of reality but it is the source of much "destructive behavior toward the earth and other humans" fostered by creating the illusion that human destiny need not take the body, and therefore the welfare of the earth, seriously. What we need instead, she argues, are "psalms and meditations" that affirm our interdependence with all the elements of the universe and fill us with compassion for all living things by "breaking down the illusion of otherness" (252).

These two traditions – of covenant and sacrament – speak with two different voices:

> One speaks from the mountaintops in the thunderous masculine tones of "thou shalt" and "thou shalt not." It is the voice of power and law, but speaking (at its most authentic) on behalf of the weak, as a mandate to protect the powerless and to restrain the power of the mighty. There is another voice, one that speaks from the intimate heart of matter. It has long been silenced by the masculine voice, but today is finding again her own voice. This is the voice of Gaia. Her voice does not translate into laws or intellectual knowledge, but beckons us into communion. (254)

In a manner that echoes Carol Gilligan, Ruether argues that these are complementary voices. We need the first voice to remind us of the requirements of justice and the second to remind us of the requirements of compassion.

For most of history humans have defined good and evil in a way that leads to projecting evil on the other so that reality is divided into "us" vs. "them." We need an ethic that is not predicated on a "dualistic negation of the 'other'" (256). We need to understand, says Ruether, that the evil lies not in the other but in wrong relationships with the other. We need relationships that are in ecological balance "so that the whole remains in life-sustaining harmony" (256). Every civilization fosters both cultures of deceit and domination and their opposite – cultures of compassion with the audacity to unmask deceit. The ecofeminist task is to discourage the first and encourage the second.

An ecofeminist ethic does not require the integration of women into a masculine world but the transformation of relationships between men and women, which will in turn lead to a transformation of the human relationship to nature (and vice versa). What is required is not autonomous women and dependent men but rather, "both men and women as individuated persons in mutual interdependency with each other and with the earth" (266). What is required is equity between men and women, between human communities around the globe, between humans and the biotic community, and finally, equity between the generations. Such a social transformation will require local "base communities of celebration and resistance" (269) engaged in a three-pronged task: (1) shaping personal and corporate spiritualities and rituals that foster "biophilic consciousness"; (2) the transformation of our local community institutions into "pilot projects of ecological living"; (3) the building of organizational structures with an international outreach to transform global power structures. "Our revolution," says Ruether, "is not just for us, but for our children, for the generations of living beings to come. What we can do is to plant a seed, nurture a seed-bearing plant here and there, and hope for a harvest that goes beyond the limits of our powers and the span of our lives" (273–4).

Conclusion

With our review of the feminist challenge to masculine spirituality and ethics in this chapter we are nearing the end of our journey, our pilgrimage along the way of all the earth. Consequently, we are deferring our comparative reflections on the relation of ecofeminism to the traditions of Gandhian spirituality to the final chapter. For we see in ecofeminism a possible bridge between East and West, one that integrates both with an evolutionary worldview and the web of all life.

Questions for Discussion

1   Compare the story of the two women who come to Solomon with the story of Abraham's near-sacrifice of Isaac. In what ways does Gilligan see in these two stories the difference between female and male approaches to ethics? Are her interpretations of these stories plausible, or do you find them problematic?

2   What parallels do you find between the chutzpah of Abraham Joshua Heschel and the feminist audacity of Catherine Keller?

3   Why does Keller think that Christian kenosis and Buddhist emptiness are ethically problematic?

4   Carol Gilligan argues that an ethic of care and an ethic of justice can be reconciled. What are the characteristics of these two ethics, and how does she propose to reconcile them? Would Keller, Macy, and Ruether all agree with her proposal?

5   Gilligan suggests that the developmental psychology of Kohlberg and others has been dominated by masculine myths of the heroic journey. What examples of this myth can you find in the stories we have studied in previous chapters? Why is the heroic myth problematic for women's experience?

6   Gilligan says that narrative is a better vehicle for women's ethical sensibility

than is abstract logic. Why is this so, in her view? Finally, how does this thesis relate to that of the authors of this book?

7   Explain the similarities and differences of the ecofeminist ethical visions and spiritualities of Joanna Macy and Rosemary Ruether.

8   Both Ruether and Macy seek to overcome the anthropocentric bias of Western religious ethics by developing an understanding of self more attuned to Eastern understandings of the place of humans in nature. In doing so they both develop a similar narrative strategy. Describe this strategy and assess its strengths and weaknesses. Also, what spiritual strategies do each offer to bring about the needed ethical revolution?

9   As we pointed out in chapter 1, Eastern religious stories emphasize human continuity with, and responsibility to, nature, whereas Western religious stories seem to emphasize human justice. As ecofeminists, Ruether and Macy seem to offer a vision of eco-justice that could possibly serve as a bridge between Eastern and Western religious ethics, as well as a bridge between masculine and feminine ethical sensibilities. Explain how their views could serve as such a bridge and outline any problems you see with their being successful.

10 In what sense do Ruether and Macy meet the ethical challenges of Auschwitz and Hiroshima as outlined in chapter 2?

11 Are Ruether and Macy good models for "the way of all the earth"? Explain.

References

Abe, Masao. 1990. "Kenotic God and Dynamic Sunyata," and "A Rejoinder." In John B. Cobb, Jr. and Christopher Ives (eds.), *The Emptying God: A Buddhist–Jewish–Christian Conversation*. Maryknoll, NY: Orbis Books, 3–68, 157–202.

Gilligan, Carol. 1982. *In a Different Voice*. Cambridge, MA: Harvard University Press.

Ingram, Catherine. 1990. *In the Footsteps of Gandhi*. Berkeley: Parallax Press.

Keller, Catherine. 1990. "Scoop Up the Water and the Moon Is in Your Hands: On Feminist Theology and Dynamic Self-Emptying." In John B. Cobb, Jr. and Christopher Ives (eds), *The Emptying God: A Buddhist–Jewish–Christian Conversation*. Maryknoll, NY: Orbis Books, 102–15.

Macy, Joanna. 1983a. *Dharma and Development*. West Hartford, CT: Kumarian Press.

——. 1983b. *Despair and Personal Power in the Nuclear Age*. Philadelphia: New Society Publishers.

——. 1991a. *World as Lover, World as Self*. Berkeley: Parallax Press.

——. 1991b. *Mutual Causality in Buddhism and General Systems Theory*. Albany: State University of New York Press.

Ruether, Rosemary Radford. 1975. "Beginnings: An Intellectual Autobiography." In Gregory Baum (editor), *Journeys: The Impact of Personal Experience on Religious Thought*. New York: Paulist Press.

——. 1981. "Social Sin," *Commonweal* 108, January 30: 46–8.

——. 1982. *Disputed Questions: On Being A Christian.* Journeys in Faith Series, ed. Robert A. Raines. Nashville: Abingdon.

——. 1986. *Women–Church: Theology and Practice of Feminist Liturgical Communities.*

——. 1992. *Gaia and God: An Ecofeminist Theology of Earth Healing.* San Francisco: HarperSanFrancisco.

——. 1995. "Preface to Twentieth Anniversary Edition." Preface in *New Woman/New Earth: Sexist Ideologies and Human Liberation.* 20th anniversary edition. Boston: Beacon Press.

Snyder, Mary Hembrow. 1988. *The Christology of Rosemary Radford Ruether.* Mystic, CT: Twenty-third Publications.

10

THE WAY OF ALL THE EARTH

We begin with the story of Babel found in the biblical writings, and suggest that it is a story that invites us to abandon the quest for the unity of identity implied in sacred order, and discover what we seek through hospitality to the stranger in a pluralistic world of interdependence. Then we turn to the Christian and Buddhist ecofeminism of Rosemary Ruether and Joanna Macy to discover in their work an integration of audacity and interdependence which creates a bridge not only between masculine and feminine but also between humanity and nature, and religious ethics East and West. We then offer our own model for understanding the ethical life based on the bridge of ecofeminism – a model we call "the social ecology of conscience." Finally, we conclude by revisiting and reevaluating Masao Abe's models for religion and ethics, and end with an invitation to continue our individual journeys along a path called "the way of all the earth."

The Story of Babel: From Ethnocentrism to Interdependence

Now the whole earth had one language and the same words. And as they migrated from the east, they came upon a plain in the land of Shinar and settled there. And they said to one another, "Come, let us make bricks, and burn them thoroughly." And they had brick for stone, and bitumen for mortar. Then they said, "Come, let us build ourselves a city, and a tower with its top in the heavens, and let us make a name for ourselves; otherwise we shall be scattered abroad upon the face of the whole earth." The LORD came down to see the city and the tower, which mortals had built. And the LORD said, "Look, they are one people, and they have all one language; and this is only the beginning of what they will do; nothing that they propose to do will now be impossible for them. Come, let us go down, and confuse their language there, so that they will not understand one another's speech." So the LORD scattered them abroad from there over the face of all the earth, and they left off building the city. Therefore it was called Babel, because there the LORD confused the language of all the earth; and from there the LORD scattered them abroad over the face of all the earth. (Genesis 11: 1–9)

The story of Babel is a story uniquely suited to illuminating the ethical challenge of a post/modern world of global diversity. For it is a story about the very human tendency of all societies to seek greatness through a uniformity that sets them apart from all strangers. For the citizens of Babel, uniformity was their answer to the problem of death. Mortality could be transcended by "making a name" for themselves through the technical and social power that they could achieve by creating a society in which everyone was the same – unified in language, meaning, and values. By sharing a common story, they seemed to believe, they could storm the heavens. They could be like God and take control of human destiny. But God, seeing what the citizens of Babel had in mind, confused their tongues so that they no longer were able to understand each other. They became strangers to each other and so had to abandon the dream of transcendence through societal uniformity and technological superiority.

There is a great deal of Babel's spiritual pathology present in our own technological civilization. Ethnocentrism is a pervasive characteristic of all cultures and the link between it and techno-bureaucratic rationality has proven hazardous to life, both human and non-human. This was true of Nazi Germany, of Meiji Japan, and of Western colonialism, to name three examples. This is the link that produced Auschwitz and Hiroshima. Ethnocentrism is only one of many "centrisms" we have examined in this text that violate life. For not only does every sacred society set itself apart from all others (us vs. them) who are less than human, but each also makes similar internal differentiations. For, internal to the sacred order of every *ethne* or community, there is a hierarchy that reserves greater privileges for those "most fully human" who stand at the center of the sacred circle. These hierarchies result in racism, sexism, religious prejudice, and violation of the natural world.

Human beings find comfort in uniformity. There is still much in us as human beings that longs to return to the imagined days before Babel's disintegration, when everyone in the public square had a sense of belonging to the same sacred society, speaking the same language, and sharing the same "values" that were expressed from its sacred center. However, after Auschwitz and Hiroshima we must recognize the MADness (Mutually Assured Destruction) of such fantasies which threaten to engulf the whole world in total conflagration. This is the same madness that is repeated on a smaller scale in every act of racism, sexism, religious prejudice, and disregard for the environment.

The usual exegesis of the story of Babel suggests that God punished the citizens of Babel for their hubris in trying to reach the realm of the divine through uniformity. This was done by confusing their tongues so that each spoke a different language, and therefore they could not cooperate with each other in finishing their technological project. However, we suggest that this is a misreading of the significance of the story. Given the overwhelming emphasis on hospitality to the stranger in the Torah (a command repeated more often than any other), we must understand this story differently. Accordingly, as we read the story, God saw that human efforts to reach the holy were misguided and so reoriented human efforts by creating a world of strangers where the holy is to be encountered in the midst of diversity – through the encounter with the stranger. Stories of hospitality have unique ethical power, for they recognize the humanity of the one who does not share one's own story and cannot be defined by it – the one who remains a stranger. Through such stories the sacred center is desacralized and the holy is encountered outside one's ethnocentric community – in the coming of the stranger. Stories of hospitality de-center our ethnocentrisms and foster an awareness of our interdependence – our unity in diversity.

Stories such as those of Gilgamesh, Socrates, Arjuna, Siddhartha, Jacob, Jesus, and Muhammad suggest that religious ethics is about wrestling with the stranger, and oneself, as with God (or the gods) in order to find wisdom and justice in the face of mortality. Thus religious ethics is intimately involved in spirituality as a way of wrestling meaning from existence – whether through Gandhi's asceticism, Thich Nhat Hanh's practice of mindfulness, Heschel's audacity (chutzpah), King's way of the cross, or Malcolm X's way of pilgrimage. In each such wrestling, a realization of the interdependence of all beings occurs. "Injustice anywhere is a threat to justice everywhere," King argued: "we are caught in an inescapable network of mutuality, tied in a single garment of destiny. Whatever affects one directly affects all indirectly." To this, Heschel added: "We are all involved with one another. Spiritual betrayal on the part of one of us affects the faith of all of us . . . whenever one man is hurt, we are all injured. The human is a disclosure of the divine, and all men are one in God's care for man."

However, in the lives of these men the emphasis has been on the interdependence among all *men*. It is feminist voices, such as those of Rosemary Ruether and Joanna Macy, that have most dramatically corrected this vision to include not only women but all of nature. It is women who have had to find a voice not only for themselves but also for the whole of creation.

In a sacred society human beings see the "ultimate reality" as created in their own image (the image of those at the sacred center of society). The sacred becomes a projection of the identity of whatever group has the power and status to define reality. So, for example, the Nazis defined "God," and even Jesus, as Aryan. In a holy community, however, ultimate reality (God, Sunyata, Tao, etc.) is not understood as created in the image of human beings but rather, human beings are thought to be created in the image of an ultimate reality without image. The difference is profound. If God or the holy is created in "our image," then those who are like us (the privileged group who is doing the defining – for example, white males) are human, and all who are different are less than human. However, if we are created in the image of a God/holy without image, then it is not possible that some human image (ideal or stereotype) more closely approximates the image of God/holy than others. On the contrary, the holy is mirrored in our diversity. All are equal by virtue of being created in the image of an ultimate reality that cannot be imaged.

In our pluralistic world many long for the common morality of a sacred society and lament our fragmented ethical diversity and the confusion it seems to bring. Many wish for everything to be once more clear and unambiguous. From such a perspective the actions of a God who would deliberately make a sacred community into a society of strangers seems at best perverse – a perverse judgment on human effort. But for a God who is a stranger (whose ways are not our ways) such an act might seem to be a blessing rather than a curse. For it is through the stranger that the infinite enters the finite and closed world of a sacred society, calling it into question and opening it up to its utopian possibilities. For those who have the ears to hear and the eyes to see, Babel may not be so much a curse as a blessing – offering the utopian promise of a new world of diversity and interdependence.

However, if we are to realize the promise of Babel, we must abandon the dreams of domination, the dreams of colonialist, racist, sexist, and religious domination. We must abandon the dreams of conformity through power and coercion that seeks ritual purification by "killing in order to heal" so as to "remove" all who are "not worthy" to share in our life. We must do so in order to make a place for human dignity and human rights – especially those of the stranger. The "saints" (those whose lives are models of the way of holiness) of our post/modern era whom we have become acquainted with in this book – Gandhi, King, Heschel, Nhat Hanh, and Malcolm X (after his pilgrimage to Mecca) – all have stood firmly against sacral uniformity and saw the promise of Babel's diversity. They were committed to audacity on behalf of the dignity of the stranger through non-violent resistance. The partial exception is Malcolm X, who argues for the just use of violence. And, to the degree their spiritual visions failed to be fully inclusive of women and the environment, they stand corrected by a feminist vision manifested in the lives of still other "saints," women like Rosemary Ruether and Joanna Macy. Out of the vision of Gandhi, his heirs, and his feminist critics, comes an interreligious and international ethic of human dignity, human rights, and liberation for all the earth. It is an ethic not of uniformity but of interdependence or unity-in-diversity.

Ecofeminism and the Ecology of Conscience

The dispute over ethical consciousness

In our journey of passing over from one life story to another, we uncovered what seems to be a tension between justice and compassion, one that suggests a disagreement about the nature of ethical consciousness. Thich Nhat Hanh's poem, *Call Me By My True Names*, suggested that ethical consciousness requires omnipartiality. One must "become the other" – not only the other of the victim but also of the victimizer. In so doing one transcends the dualism of ethical judgments (good and evil) and comes to have equal compassion for all.

Abraham Joshua Heschel also speaks of becoming the other, but Heschel seems to mean by this what we found exemplified in the Jewish story of David and Nathan. That is, becoming the other means identifying with the victim in order to demand justice from the victimizer. This same understanding of ethical consciousness is found in contemporary Latin American liberation theology, which argues that justice requires a preferential option for the poor and the oppressed. This, we also argued, was the lesson of John Rawls's theory of the "veil of ignorance." As applied to the story of David and Nathan, we argued that the veil of ignorance created by the story functions, at first, to make David omnipartial. But once it did so, it then moved him to emotionally identify with the stranger and take the side of the victim – demanding justice. Yet Thich Nhat Hanh, we noted, explicitly rejects any "preferential option" for the poor and the oppressed. For him, such an option expresses a dualistic consciousness that is typical of ethics. And so he, like Masao Abe, insists that ethics must be transcended and left behind by a non-dualistic spirituality leading to religious enlightenment.

We think the feminist authors we have studied offer a perspective that balances these seemingly opposed requirements. The dispute that seems to exist between Thich Nhat Hanh and Abraham Joshua Heschel could be seen as a version of what Carol Gilligan identifies as the dispute between a masculine ethic of justice and a feminine ethic of care. From Gilligan's perspective, these two ethics are complementary. Care and justice are dialectically related and mutually limiting. The ethics of care sacrifices self for the good of others (the way of "kenosis," or "emptiness"). The ethics of justice places a limit on this sacrifice by recognizing that even one's self is an "other" in need of care. Hence a feminist ethic, as Catherine Keller points out, is deeply suspicious of any ethic whose spirituality requires a total death of the self. Historically, such an ethic of selflessness has been used to promote not mutuality but patriarchalism. Such an ethic, in both Christianity and Buddhism, she points out, has led to the unjust oppression of women. Keller's feminist ethic, like Heschel's Jewish ethic, insists on the importance of audacity – the need to challenge all authority, no matter how sacred, in the name of justice and dignity.

This call to audacity, however, is not a reversion to a masculine desire for autonomy, but rather occurs within the context of a feminist awareness of interdependence – the web of life. In this context, audacity is not an expression of individualistic assertion but a call to achieve an ecological balance. The goal is equity, a balanced mutuality that nurtures all relationships. For a relationship that operates in only one direction is not a relationship at all. It is just one more form of illusion that causes suffering. The self, says Keller, is relational and ethics is about establishing an ecology of mutual responsibility able to sustain all selves in their interdependence. Without justice, interdependence is impossible and vice versa. For Keller, interdependence is not an oceanic feeling which dissolves all differences. On the contrary, interdependence requires "otherness" (others to be interdependent with) and justice establishes balanced relationships which allow each life to flourish in interdependence with all others. Keller's observations are strikingly in tune with those of both Ruether and Macy.

What is striking in the ecofeminism of both Ruether and Macy is that not only the chasm between justice and care is bridged, but also the chasm between humans and the environment. In so doing their Christian and Buddhist ecofeminism builds a bridge between Eastern and Western ethics. While concern for the environment is not entirely absent, the overwhelming emphasis in Western religious ethics (as we saw in Heschel, King, and Malcolm X) is on social justice. In some ways, Gandhi's Hinduism bridges East and West, living simply in harmony with nature yet clearly focused on social justice. However, Thich Nhat Hanh stands unambiguously in the Eastern tradition, emphasizing the continuity or interdependence of humanity and nature, while mistrustful of Western notions of justice, which he fears are dualistic. What Macy and Ruether show is that social injustice and environmental injustice are closely linked and one cannot be corrected without addressing the other. Interdependence requires us to recognize the need for "eco-justice" – justice for the whole ecology, human and non-human.

Both Ruether and Macy insist that an important element in the development of eco-justice is finding the right stories to capture the relational nature of the self within the web of life. Here they echo a theme of Gilligan's, namely, that feminist ethics, in contrast to masculine ethics, prefers narrative to the language of abstract rationality because narrative is better able to express relationality. This is, of course, an argument congenial to a fundamental thesis of this book about the importance of narrative for ethics. It also complements another thesis of ours, namely, that narrative is also the natural mode of expression for religious insight. Interestingly, both Ruether and Macy use the same narrative strategy, drawing on evolutionary theory to provide a narrative of the interdependence of all things. For Macy, evolutionary narratives function in a way analogous to narratives of reincarnation, to communicate a Buddhist sense of interdependence. For Ruether, they reintegrate history into nature and evoke the mystical-sacramental understanding of the interdependence of all things in the cosmic body of Christ.

Finally, Gilligan and Macy both suggest that the feminist sense of the web of life leads to a commitment to non-violence. And this is an important point of convergence between the children of Gandhi and their feminist critics. For all, the realization of the interdependence of all life leads to the realization that one cannot do violence to the other without doing violence to oneself. Only Malcolm X stands apart on this issue, arguing for the just use of violence. Our argument (discussed at the end of chapter 8) is that self-defense is not immoral, but it is also not redemptive. Self-defense denies our interdependence and reinforces a sacral dualism of "us" vs. "them." In so doing, it also tends to encourage a continuing cycle of violence. "An eye for an eye," says Martin Luther King, Jr., makes everyone blind. Non-violence offers the possibility of breaking that cycle. After Auschwitz and Hiroshima, as King reminds us, the choice before us is not violence or non-violence, but rather non-violence or non-existence.

The ecology of conscience

What the children of Gandhi share with the ecofeminists is a relational view of ethics rooted in a spiritual realization of the interdependence of all things. This ethical insight offers a possible way to transcend the dualism of all sacred societies and the propensity for demonic doubling that provided the logic for mass violence in the twentieth century. We would therefore like to propose a model for the formation of ethical consciousness based on the ecological metaphor suggested by ecofeminism.

Every social/institutional context in which we live, we argue, has an implicit set of expectations built into it, which constitute the morality of that social context. Each such morality is deeply shaped by storytelling. For instance, when I go to work I enter a social environment that already has a morality attached to it. When I show up the first day on the job, how do I learn that morality? Perhaps there is a personnel lecture that explains company policies, but that does not really tell me about the actual operating morality of the company. That I learn over coffee breaks, when my new peers sit me down and start telling me stories about the company and its various characters. Through these stories I learn what to do and what not to do. I learn how to be a good employee. I learn the story of the company and come to understand my role in the story. In this way I absorb the morality of the company – the patterns of expectation that structure my role – the person (i.e., double) I become in that situation. Our understanding of good and evil, or right and wrong, is determined in these situations by the kind of story we think we are in and the role we see ourselves playing in that story.

The moral complexity of our modern lives has to do precisely with the fact that we are all "multiple personalities." I am a different person with my family than I am with my boss, and different still with my friends, and so on. Each of the social environments we enter – work, family, friendship, voluntary associations, political movements, religious communities, etc. – requires us to be a different person. And every one of the social roles we embrace in constructing our social identities has a story or complex of stories attached to it, which we consciously or unconsciously absorb. Our spouse implicitly conveys to us a story about what it means to be a good marriage partner and parent. Our boss implicitly conveys to us a story about what it means to be a good employee. Our friends obligate us to yet other stories. Even our pets (e.g., the family dog or cat) make an ethical claim upon us: they too have expectations we try to meet. And so it goes: with every social role that we embrace we add a new narrative (or collection of narratives) to our repertoire.

The challenge of the ethical life in our time has to do with the complexity of the narrative expectations that are placed upon us in each of the institutional contexts of our lives. The problem is that the narratives that structure our role in each institutional context seem to demand all of our time, talents, and our very being. The narratives that structure the workplace seem to make being a good worker an absolute obligation. The narratives that structure our marriage and family life seem to make another set of obligations absolute and primary, and likewise with our friends. Nobody wants just a piece of us, everybody wants our whole being.

Maintaining multiple identities is made possible by our capacity to "double." As we noted in chapter 2, doubling is the process of developing a self adequate to a new social/institutional context. In chapter 3 we called this capacity "secondary doubling" and argued that it presupposes a "primary doubling," which is our capacity for alienation which enables us to see our actions as if we were strangers to our selves. Without this capacity ethical reflection is impossible. The doubling of the Nazi doctors was demonic, because instead of doubling to engage in reflection on their actions, they used psychological rationalizations to disown responsibility for the actions of their "other" self, surrendering themselves in unquestioning obedience to a "higher authority." This is an inherent temptation in all techno-bureaucratic organizations where ends are chosen by those at the top of the hierarchy which "experts" lower down in the hierarchy, having the required means or skills, are expected to carry out. In our personal lives we choose both the ends and the means of our actions. We feel the connection between the goals we choose and the way we realize them and so feel some sense of personal responsibility. But in a bureaucracy, those in authority higher up are thought to be the only ones with the knowledge to see the big picture and choose the ends, while experts are expected to use their skills to achieve these ends (which they have not chosen) with unquestioning obedience. Hence they do not feel personally responsible for their actions. They conclude instead that "it is not I, but some higher authority that is acting through me." This is what makes doubling demonic – the surrender to a higher authority that alienates us from our own actions, so that we feel no responsibility for them.

The ethical task is to accept responsibility for the actions of all of our diverse selves. Indeed, a genuine ethical life is not possible without doubling, tripling and quadrupling. Despite the conflicting claims they create, having multiple personalities rooted in multiple social/institutional contexts, each of which embraces a unique morality, can actually enhance rather than diminish our ability to be ethical if we know how to respond to this complexity appropriately. In fact, having multiple moral identities is only an ethical problem in so far as we allow one or another of these moralities to become absolute and exclude all

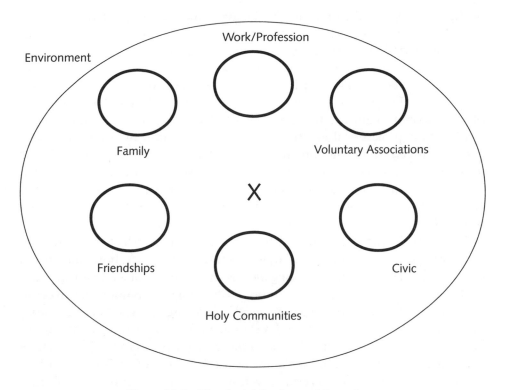

Figure 10.1   The Social Ecology of Conscience

others – especially if it involves a surrender of self that exonerates us from responsibility for our actions.

Our ethical life exists within a complex social ecology (see figure 10.1, The
Social Ecology of Conscience). The more complex a natural environment is,
the more stable and life-sustaining it is. By contrast, the more species that are
removed from an environment, the more it is destabilized until it is in danger of
collapsing and is no longer life-sustaining. By analogy, we would argue that the
ethical life also depends on a complex ecology – a social one, embedded in a
larger natural ecology. The more complexity there is in our social life (i.e., the
more roles we must play in various social/institutional contexts), the more sensitive and life-sustaining our conscience will be. And conversely, the less complex and more simplified our social ecology becomes, the less sensitive and
life-sustaining our conscience will be.

For example, suppose that I am a pharmaceutical executive and my company
has been developing a new drug. We have spent a lot of money not only developing it but also testing it to be sure it is safe. Now suppose that the results are
in and everything looks pretty good, but some of our test results are ambiguous, and to be safe we should really do some additional testing before putting it

on the market. On the other hand, this drug has cost us a lot of money to develop, and if we don't get it on the market soon it is really going to hurt our economic performance. We need to start recovering our costs.

Now, if my only identity is that of a corporate executive, I will only be thinking about the bottom line and I will decide to put the product on the market immediately. However, if I am also married and a parent, and my spouse or one of my children might use this drug, or if I have a friend that might use it, suddenly my professional identity is called into question by my identity as a parent or friend, and I will think twice about this decision and probably decide to run further tests before releasing it. Moreover, suppose the process by which it is created causes serious environmental hazards for both animal and human life. If my family and my pets could be harmed by these hazards I will also think twice. Here social justice and eco-justice converge.

The point is that every one of the social contexts in which I live my life confronts me with genuine ethical obligations towards others, both human and non-human. The awareness of obligation is an awareness of a relationship and its demands. This awareness, while it occurs "within me," is not subjective. On the contrary, the feeling of obligation invades my consciousness. I become aware of my relationship to the other and feel obliged to do something. This awareness is not of my own making. It is something that happens to me just as surely as the blast of cold air that hits me in the face as I step out of my house on a cold winter morning. While I can certainly refuse to honor it, I neither manufacture it by wishing or eliminate an awareness of it by wishing it away. These feelings of obligation are the prerational basis of the ethical life. I feel a sense of obligation to help a friend in distress, for instance, even though we have never talked about what makes a good friend, and even though I may never have actually sat down and thought about it. And the tug and pull of these obligations sensitizes my conscience as I am drawn into the life stories of my friends and acquaintances, and yes, even strangers, and see my own actions through their eyes. My ability to assume more than one identity and see the world through more than one story functions much the way Nathan's story did for David, it allows me to identify with those who will be affected by my actions, and to see my actions through their eyes. It enables me to assume an ethical point of view. It enables me to become the other. It builds empathy on the basis of the genuine feelings of affection and obligation that I experience in the various contexts of my life.

This way of looking at our situation allows us to develop a relational–ecological model of justice. In reference to figure 10.1, the "X" at the center represents the self in its capacity to choose, including its capacity to choose its social roles (represented by the various circles surrounding the X). The presence of the "X" at the center might suggest that there is such a thing as a "naked self" – that is, a self apart from its social roles. This is an "optical illusion." The self is really always in some social role or other, but because it can move from one to another it gives us the illusion of being in the center. An ecologically balanced self would have ties to all of these circles. But as this self cuts its ties to all but one of these circles this complex ecology is simplified and collapses, and the self becomes a prisoner of a singular identity with no means of stepping outside itself and seeing its actions from another's perspective. The ethical life and justice are fostered by nurturing the complexity of our social ecology. The more complexity there is, the more strangers enter into our life and the broader and more inclusive our ethical consciousness becomes. The ethical life requires more than just taking care of one's friends; it demands hospitality to the stranger (both human and non-human).

Injustice occurs when we are willing to sacrifice most of our obligations in the various circles of our life in order to excel in just one sphere. Today, it is most often work and professional life that tempts many to sacrifice everything and everyone else to it, because the recognition and rewards are so great. As we focus on our work and simplify the social ecology of our life, we cut the ties of empathy and obligation that enable us to identify with the joy and pain of others and our conscience is desensitized. It ceases to be life-sustaining. So we may neglect and violate the dignity of the many – family, friends and strangers, even our pets – who need and depend upon us in the various other spheres of our life. Indeed, our pets are our ethical link with the rest of the universe. Through our emotional ties to them we feel the joy and pain of the universe.

In a world where we have to juggle multiple identities, most institutions compete with each other for our absolute loyalty. Only a few – religious communities, universities, eco-justice organizations, human rights organizations (if they are doing their job properly) – nurture narratives that ask us not to give our ultimate loyalties to it as one more institution, but rather, to weigh our loyalties against each other in light of a commitment to eco-justice and human dignity for all, especially the stranger. Their function, properly understood, is the function of every holy community – to ask us to put our whole life into perspective, weighing and balancing the obligations placed upon us by the diverse narrative contexts of our lives. Justice occurs when we achieve an ecological balance between these diverse narrative contexts, accepting the ethical claims that others (human and non-human) make upon us when our consciousness is sensitized by empathy (becoming the other), and so becomes our conscience.

Neither individuals nor societies can be considered good if they sacrifice human dignity and the environment to either personal autonomy and ambition (individualistic libertarianism) or to established rules and principles ("law and order") viewed as sacred and unquestionable (collective authoritarianism). Some laws are made to be broken, as both Gandhi and Martin Luther King, Jr. knew, but only for the sake of protecting human dignity and ecological integrity. No person, law or society that violates either can be considered good. Indeed, without ecological integrity there can be no human dignity. For if we grasp the interdependence of all things we will understand, as Joanna Macy suggests, that the world is our body without which there can be no dignity.

The stranger is the one whose identity escapes the defining categories of one's society, and so illuminates the myths of one's own identity. The only way we know to define "human dignity" is to not define it, using what mystics call "the way of negation" (*via negativa*). The violation of human dignity almost always begins by defining others (especially strangers) so as to show how they are not as human as we are (ethnocentrism, racism, sexism, etc.). The claim of human dignity is that we all share a common humanity despite our definable differences – that therefore what makes us human lies beyond all definition, and every effort to define it is a violation of it. We are equal, regardless of race, social class, gender, ethnicity or religion. It is no accident that hospitality to the stranger and audacity on behalf of the stranger play important roles in Jewish, Christian, Muslim, and Buddhist ethics – as well as in Gandhi's Hinduism – for important strands in each affirm, in differing ways, that what we all have in common is a self that cannot be defined, and therefore, all selves are equal.

It is this dignity that the UN Universal Declaration of Human Rights seeks to protect through an interreligious and international ethic. The movement for human rights arose in response to the atrocities of World War II symbolized by Auschwitz and Hiroshima, and culminated in the formation of the United Nations (UN) in 1946. The Declaration of Rights followed in 1948, the same year as the UN backed the founding of the State of Israel. The Preamble to the Declaration recalls the "barbarous acts which have outraged the conscience of mankind," and prepares the way for a strong affirmation of the unity of humanity in the main body of the declaration. Consequently, this document stands against all sacred stories that would divide humanity, racially or otherwise, into superior and inferior groups in order to claim the world and its resources for the superior ones, as both the German and Japanese mythologies of the World War II period sought to do. The unity and sanctity of the human community, it declares, may not be violated by any political order. Human dignity transcends all social and political orders. It is the true measure of a just society – the limit which no political authority may transgress.

The power of the ethical vision of human rights expressed in the UN document lies in the fact that it too is rooted in a visceral response, one which cuts across cultures and creeds. Unlike the language of most academic reflection on ethics, which remains technical and esoteric, human rights language has spontaneously taken root in cross-cultural public discourse. The language of human rights has become embedded in the language of politics and international relations. Even if in many cases the political use of this language is hypocritical, still that is the compliment that vice pays to virtue, which means that this standard has taken root in public life and can be used as the criterion for social and political criticism.

The origins of human rights thought are controversial. We do not think it is either possible or desirable to trace a human rights ethic to a single source. Human rights emerged as a distinct theme of modern ethical consciousness as the result of the influences of a variety of sources, both ancient and modern, both secular and religious. We can identify at least four. The *first* is the awareness of our humanity as in the image of the holy, that which cannot be named or imaged, and the formation of holy communities hospitable to strangers on the basis of such experiences. The Buddhist experiences of emptiness and the sangha, and the Jewish experiences of being created in the image of a God without image and the synagogue, provide two examples. *Second*, the Socratic experience of doubt which opens the self to the infinite unseen measure. Like the Athenian state, every state fears the power to doubt and to question. In every totalitarian society the drive toward genocide is rooted in this fear. If the doubter could be separated from his or her doubt and totally conformed to the demands of society, violent coercion would be unnecessary. But there is no way to prevent doubts from occurring, so to eliminate the doubts one must eliminate the doubter. All violence and coercion is rooted in fear of the holy – fear of our openness to the infinite that, through doubt, prevents us from being confined to the finite (i.e., the way things are). *Third*, the experience of indignation as the root of rebellion against sacred order. Such experiences are an expression of a visceral awareness of our openness to the infinite; for instance, when Rosa Parks refused to be defined as a "Negro" and relegated to the back of the bus. Or when Gandhi refused to be defined as "colored" and relegated to the baggage car. Each refused to be defined by, and confined to, a system of segregation. Their indignation was an instinctive reaction rooted in their openness to the infinite. Each knew they were and could be more than the sacred order of society allowed them to be, and out of indignation they refused to conform to "the way things are." *Fourth*, and finally, the recognition that is fundamental to the social sciences, that no society has ever succeeded in completely socializing any of its members. Our dignity is inalienable. No culture (composed of a finite set of roles and expectations) has ever succeeded in estranging us from it. No matter how well indoctrinated we are in our culture, there always remains a part of us that refuses to be defined, that cannot be defined, and so remains deviant and a stranger. Our openness to the infinite places an inviolable limit on all cultures and societies and the sacred roles they would impose on us. Hence human dignity manifests itself in every culture as a limit which no culture can successfully transgress.

Human rights is the name for a new covenant with the whole human race that has emerged through a wrestling with the stranger who comes from other cultures, other religions, other races. A human rights ethic is an ethic of audacity on behalf of the stranger. Its purpose is to protect the human dignity of strangers no matter what race, religion or culture they come from. We must wrestle with the stranger as if with God or the holy – the God/holy who remains hidden, who refuses to reveal a name, who remains transcendent yet immanent, the God who blesses us and offers us a new name and a new identity. This covenant is a response to the hiddenness of the holy beneath the countenance of the stranger. This new identity and new covenant can only be embraced by embracing the stranger, by welcoming the stranger, and by the audacity to champion the dignity of the stranger against all the dark social, political, and religious forces of dehumanization. And as ecofeminists would remind us, it is a covenant that can be honored only by respecting our interdependence with the earth as our body, without which our common humanity is not possible.

The Way of All the Earth

We began the second part of this book by laying out Masao Abe's comparative models of religious ethics for Judaism, Christianity, and Buddhism. To review this one more time: Abe argued there is a two-way path between religion and ethics in Judaism. This, we said, enables Jews to engage in chutzpah, the audacity to call even God into question in the name of justice and human dignity. Christianity, according to Abe, creates a path from religion to ethics but no path from ethics to religion. This, we said, is because Christians view human freedom as being in bondage to sin (original sin), so that until the self is transformed by dying and rising with Christ, it is not free to do the good it intends. Finally, Abe argued, that there is no path between ethics and religion in Buddhism in either direction. There is only a relation of mutual negation. This is because, in Abe's view, ethics always involves dualistic judgments of good and evil which create negative karma, while spiritual enlightenment is non-dualistic and therefore transcends ethics altogether. The realization of the "emptiness" of all things, which is enlightenment, requires "the great death" of precisely that self that makes ethical judgments. Therefore, from Abe's point of view, what Buddhism and Christianity have in common that separates them from Judaism is the death of the self as the highest spiritual attainment, and what Judaism and Christianity have in common that separates them from Buddhism is the notion of justice as an expression of the highest spiritual attainment.

Hinduism, Islam, and feminism were not explicitly addressed by Abe's theory. However, we can utilize Abe's model to suggest that Gandhi's Hinduism approximates the Judaic model, for even the sacred Upanishads, insofar as they legitimize caste inequality, can be called into question in the name of human dignity, in Gandhi's view. We would also suggest that the Judaic model works for feminism as well. Catherine Keller's critique of both Buddhism and Christianity calls into question the kenotic/self-emptying model (which emphasizes selflessness and obedience) of both, and affirms the importance of audacity as essential to a relational view of the self, and of justice, within the web of life. However, the Judaic model does not work well for Islam. For as we noted in chapter 8, in Islam no differentiation at all is made between ethics and religion. Islam shares the view of Jews and Christians that the highest spiritual attainment is expressed in a passion for justice. However, it does not see the need for the incarnation of God to overcome original sin as preliminary to ethical action (as Christianity does) any more than it sees the possibility of God being called into question in the name of justice (as Judaism does). Ethics and religion are one and the same thing – submission to the will of God.

The question remains, however, as to just how adequate Abe's models really are. Here we have to say that we find his models useful, but not adequate. They are useful because, as large generalizations, they illuminate important differences of orientation to ethics in diverse religious traditions. And yet, as we have seen, there are important exceptions to his models in some of the traditions he describes. For, as David Keown has shown, important strands of Theravada and Mahayana Buddhism see continuity between religion and ethics (perhaps along the lines of the "Christian" model). In these strands, spiritual enlightenment and ethics both belong to the "farther shore." And while Judaism creates an important place for chutzpah or audacity, it too has its mystical strands that teach the importance of the spiritual death of the self. The mystery is that in Hasidism we find the coexistence of both. At the same time, there are strands of Christianity that do not subscribe to "original sin" or "bondage of the will," but instead emphasize human freedom to choose. So we see that there are important qualifications that have to be placed on Abe's model.

And yet, although we cannot fully subscribe to Abe's theory about the need for spirituality to carry one beyond ethics, we do believe that it contains an important "kernel of truth." There is no reason that "ethics" must be defined by dualism. We have argued that "ethics" transcends not religion but "morality." Religion, we have said, expresses itself in human experience in two modes: the sacred and the holy. Consequently, we have made a distinction between two types of normative religious claims: sacred morality and the ethics of the holy. The sacred, we have argued, tends to divide the world into dualistic categories of good and evil, giving rise to an ethic of violence and hostility toward the stranger unless it is critiqued and transformed by the holy. The holy, by comparison, expresses itself in a way that transcends such dualism, emphasizing interdependence through an ethic of hospitality to the stranger.

The way we have put the issue is that ethics is the questioning of sacred morality in the name of human dignity so as to bring morality into harmony with the demands of holiness. And dignity, we have argued, is precisely that which makes our humanity indefinable. Thus, from this perspective, it is not a matter of transcending ethics through religion but of transcending sacred morality in order to embrace a religious ethic of holiness. Such an ethic transcends dualism precisely by welcoming the stranger and loving one's enemies, and yet is prepared to make ethical judgments about justice and take action on behalf of those treated unjustly – but only by acting non-violently. This is the ethic we see accounted for, in theory and practice, in Gandhi, King, and Heschel, and also found in the practice of Thich Nhat Hanh.

We should also note that Ronald Green's theory of the relations between prudential, moral, and religious reason suggests an insight similar to ours on the relation between religion and ethics, but from a more philosophical perspective. There is continuity between the ethical and the religious as one moves beyond prudential reason (concern for punishment and reward) to moral reason (selfless action), which in turn requires one to go beyond morality to religion in order to find the spiritual strength that the ethical life requires. For Green, the religious stage does transcend the ethical, but only for the purpose of enabling one to persevere in living an ethical life.

Finally, there is also some similarity between Abe's models and Kohlberg's theory of pre-conventional, conventional, and post-conventional ethics in which one has to leave behind conventional (feminine) morality in order to assume the moral autonomy, required by universal principles of a mature (masculine) ethical consciousness. However, Kohlberg's highest ethical stage, as Gilligan has shown, completely fails to understand or appreciate the concrete interdependence within the web of life that is the common core to the ethic that feminism shares with the spiritual children of Gandhi. For both feminists and the children of Gandhi the claim of autonomy is dysfunctional, for it fails to recognize the concrete and complex interdependence that lies at the heart of ethical compassion and the demand for justice. The ethics of interdependence, as modified by ecofeminism, arrives at a post-conventional morality, but it is not based on abstract rational norms. On the contrary, it calls the sacred "conventional" norms of any community into question through an experience of holiness that balances relationality and justice within the web of life.

And so we come to the end of our journey together. Having passed over into the lives of Gandhi, Nhat Hanh, King, Heschel, Malcolm X, Ruether, and Macy, we must each come back to our own religion and culture – and our own lives. We will almost certainly come back different persons, transformed by our journey. And yet the journey does not end, for each of us will have other adventures, meet, wrestle with, and be inspired by other people, and gain yet further insights. And each time we do so, we will build bridges of understanding and compassion between ourselves and the stranger, bridges that enlarge our own understanding of who we ourselves are, to the degree that we find in ourselves what we first discovered in the other. And so we discover ourselves in the lives and stories of others.

The scandal of our age, said Heschel, is that in a world of diplomacy, "only religions are not on speaking terms." But no religion, he argues, is an island, and we all need to realize that "holiness is not the monopoly of any particular religion or tradition." Buddhism, says Thich Nhat Hanh, is made up of non-Buddhist elements, including Jewish and Christian ones. And likewise with every tradition. "We have to allow what is good, beautiful, and meaningful in the other's tradition to transform us," he says. The purpose of dialogue is to allow each to return to his or her own tradition transformed. What is astonishing, he adds, is how we will find kindred spirits in other traditions with whom we share more than we do with many in our own tradition.

What may we hope for from the practice of passing over and coming back? Certainly, our goal should not be to make everyone the same. The global ethic we envision emerging from the way of all the earth need not (indeed must not) aspire to make everyone conform. "All reform has been brought about by the action of minorities in all countries and under all climes," says Gandhi. "Majorities simply follow minorities" (Gandhi 1962: 93). We need only recall our argument at the end of chapter 2. There we noted that approximately 10 percent of the European population participated in the Renaissance, and yet the Renaissance transformed Europe. Creative minorities can be a powerful fermenting influence, bringing about profound cultural transformations in morality. Ten percent of the world's population, engaged in passing over and coming back, working through the presence of diverse holy communities – Buddhist, Jewish, Christian, and other kindred religious and secular communities – can be a saving remnant.

The journey of passing over and coming back is itself a kind of spiritual practice – a pilgrimage involving hospitality to the stranger. On this pilgrimage we wrestle with the stranger, ourselves, and the mystery of the holy. Out of such a pilgrimage could emerge a new way of life for a new millennium. Such is the promise of the way of all the earth opened up for us by Tolstoy, Gandhi and King, Heschel and Nhat Hanh, and broadened by the critiques of Malcolm X and ecofeminists like Rosemary Ruether and Joanna Macy.

Questions for Discussion

1 In what way do the authors find the contrast between the sacred and the holy embodied in the story of Babel?
2 In what way does the story of Babel express the central argument of this book as presented by the authors?
3 What alternative interpretations of the story of Babel can you think of, and what would be the ethical implications of these alternative readings?
4 In what way does the ecofeminism of Rosemary Ruether and Joanna Macy offer a bridge not only between masculine and feminine ethics, but between Eastern and Western ethics?
5 What is the connection between hospitality to the stranger and an ethic of human dignity?
6 Why are stories of hospitality to the stranger the key to ethical cooperation between different religions and cultures, according to the authors of this book?
7 What do the authors mean when they say that the experience of obligation forms the basis for the ethical life?
8 What are the ethical advantages of being "multiple personalities"? What are the disadvantages?
9 Explain "demonic doubling," using the model of the social ecology of conscience.
10 How does the model of the social ecology of conscience offer a solution to demonic doubling?
11 What is the importance of wrestling with the stranger and hospitality to the stranger for the successful functioning of a social ecology of conscience?

12   Why are holy communities essential to the ethical function of a social ecology of conscience?

13   What are the strengths and weaknesses of Abe's models of religion and ethics (figure 3.1) for the traditions we have studied in this book?

14   In light of the alternative views explored in this book, what are the strengths and weaknesses of Abe's view that religion should take one beyond ethics?

15   What are the strengths and weakness of the model of "passing over" and "coming back" advocated by the authors of this book?

REFERENCE

Gandhi, M. K. 1962. *The Essential Gandhi* (ed. Louis Fischer). New York: Vintage Books, Random House.

INDEX OF SUBJECTS

INDEX OF NAMES AND TERMS

DATE DUE